MY HAPPY MARRIAGE

3

ORIGINAL CONCEPT
AKUMI AGITOGI
(Fujimi L Bunko/KADOKAWA)

ART
RITO KOHSAKA

CHARACTER DESIGN
TSUKIHO TSUKIOKA

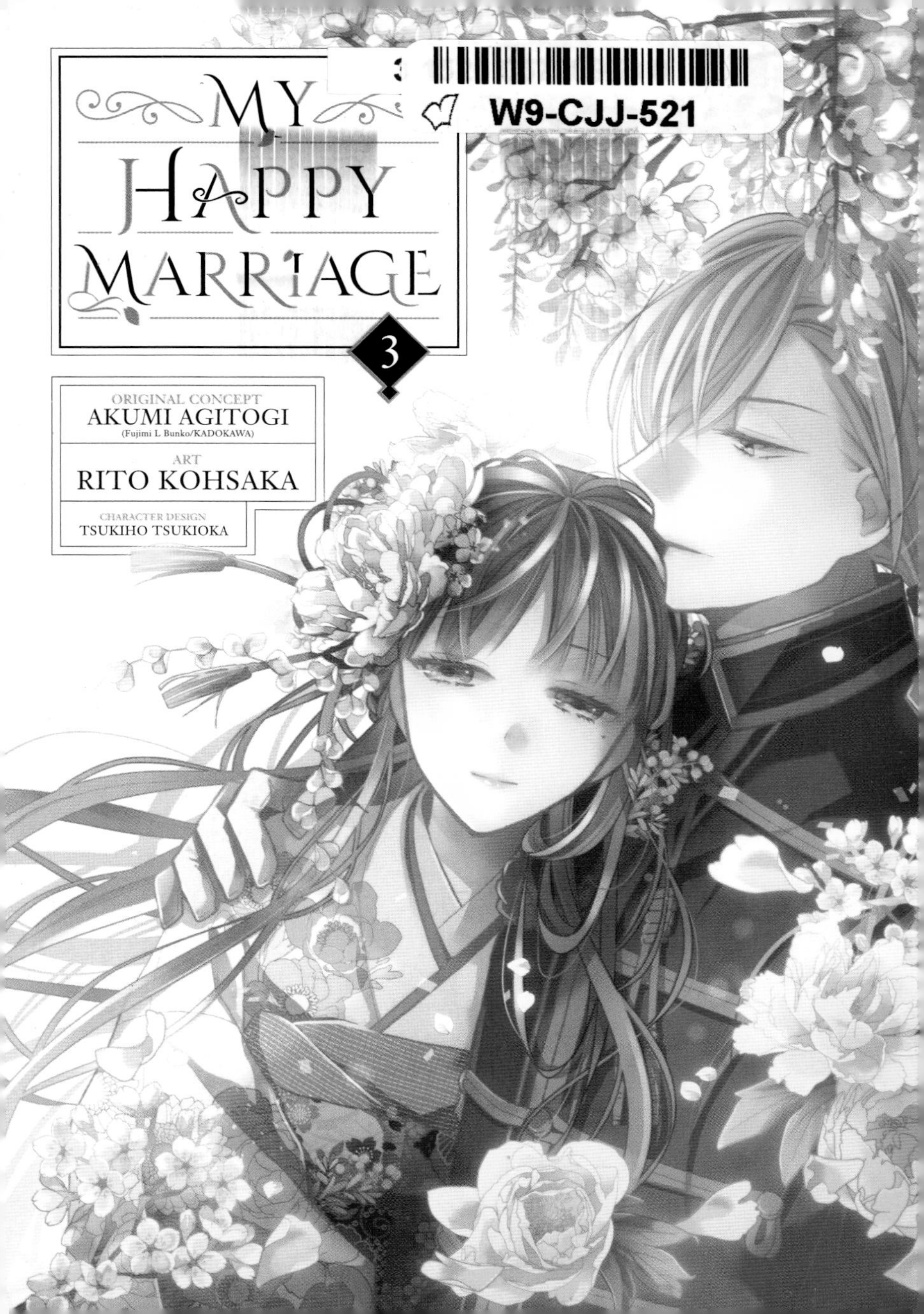

CONTENTS

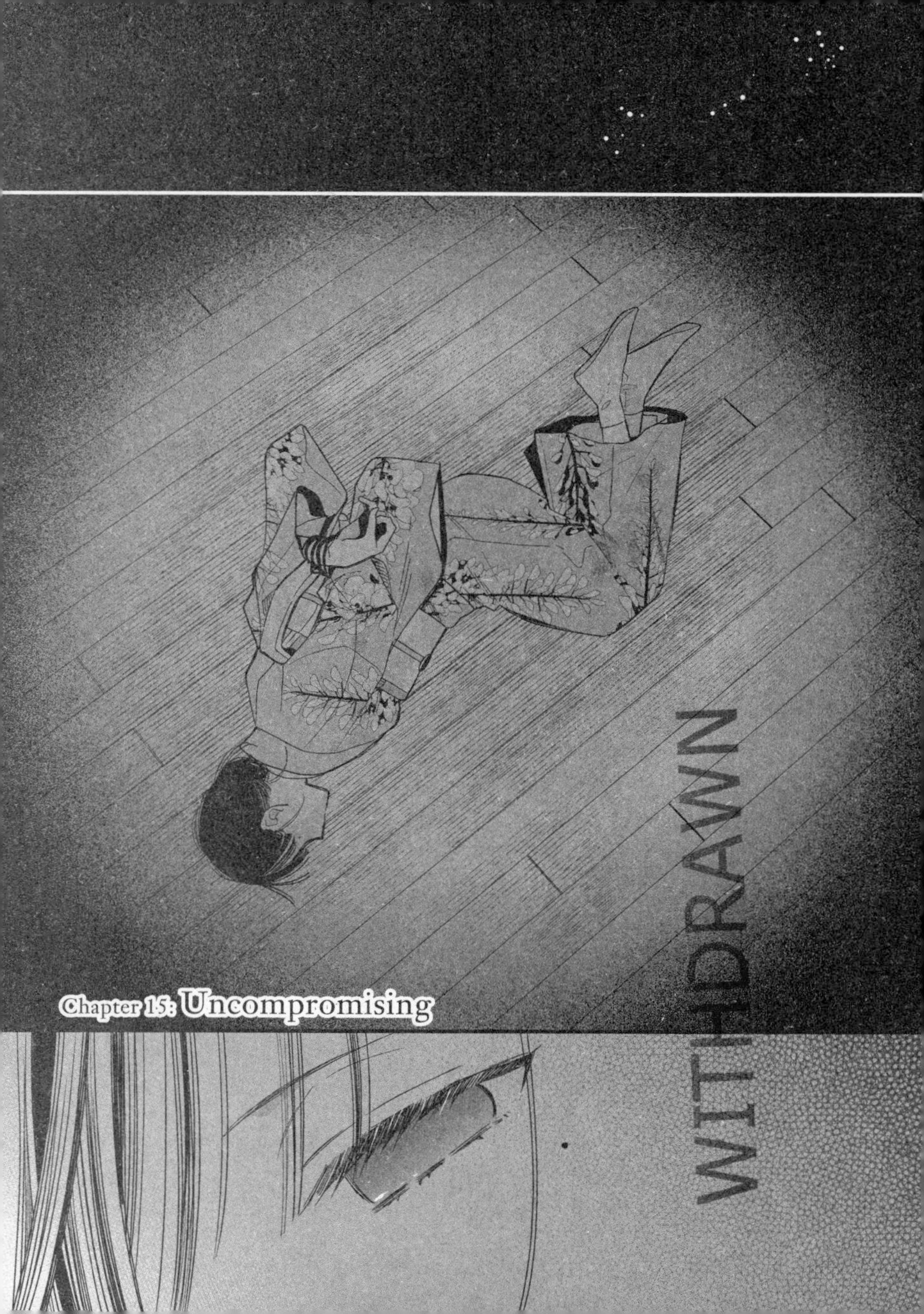
Chapter 15: Uncompromising

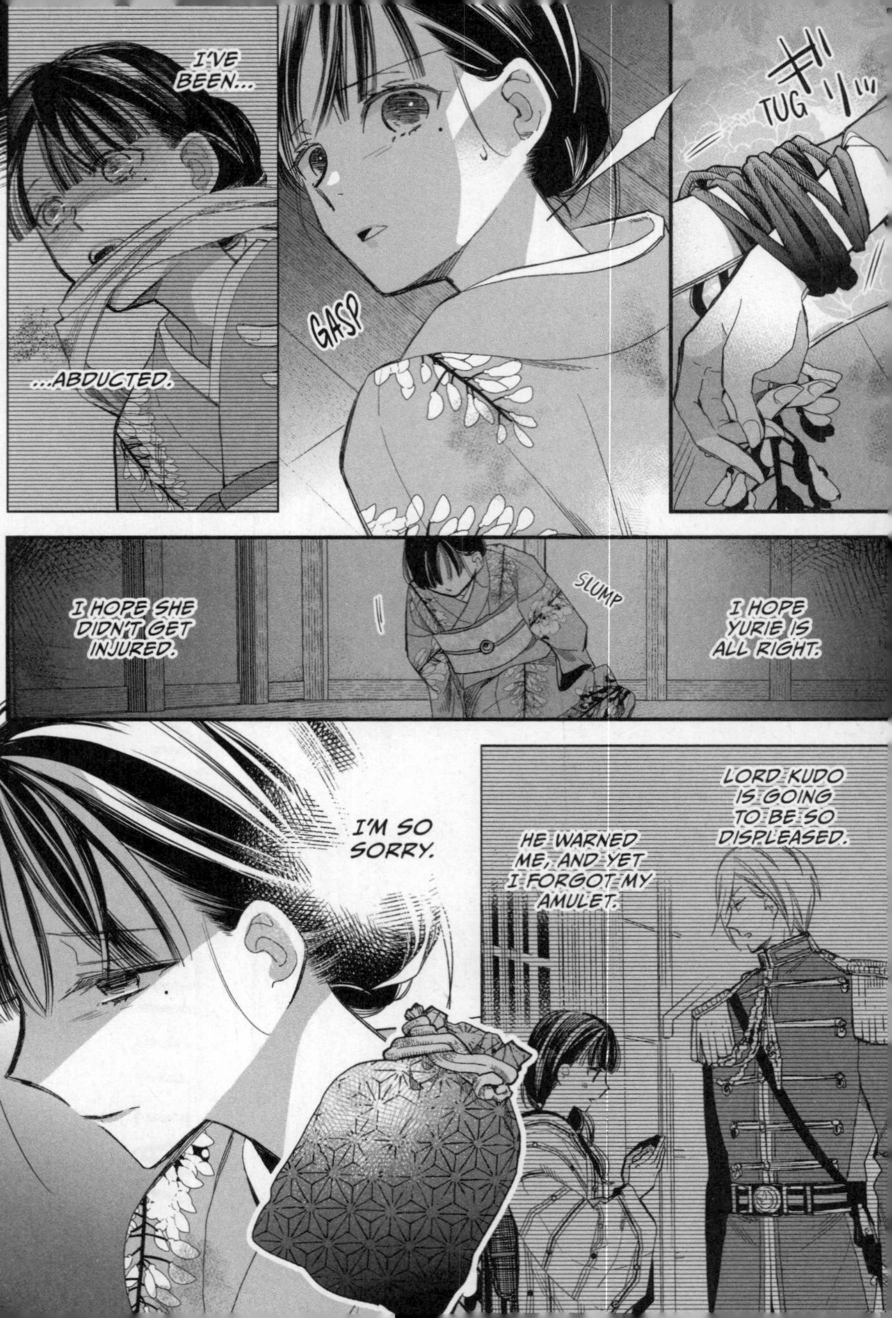
ギリッ
TUG
GASP
I'VE BEEN...
...ABDUCTED.
I HOPE YURIE IS ALL RIGHT.
SLUMP
I HOPE SHE DIDN'T GET INJURED.
LORD KUDO IS GOING TO BE SO DISPLEASED.
HE WARNED ME, AND YET I FORGOT MY AMULET.
I'M SO SORRY.

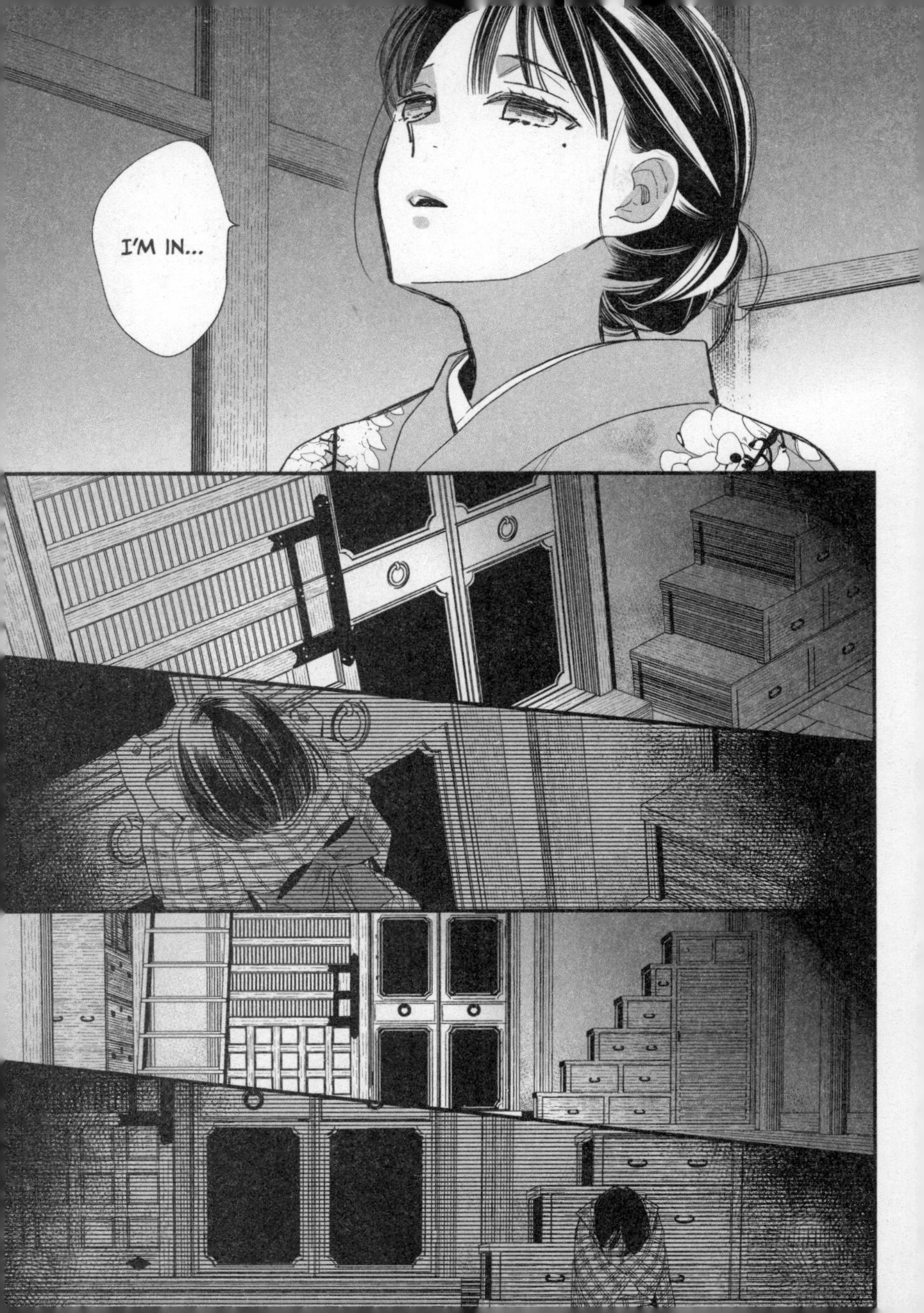
I'M IN...

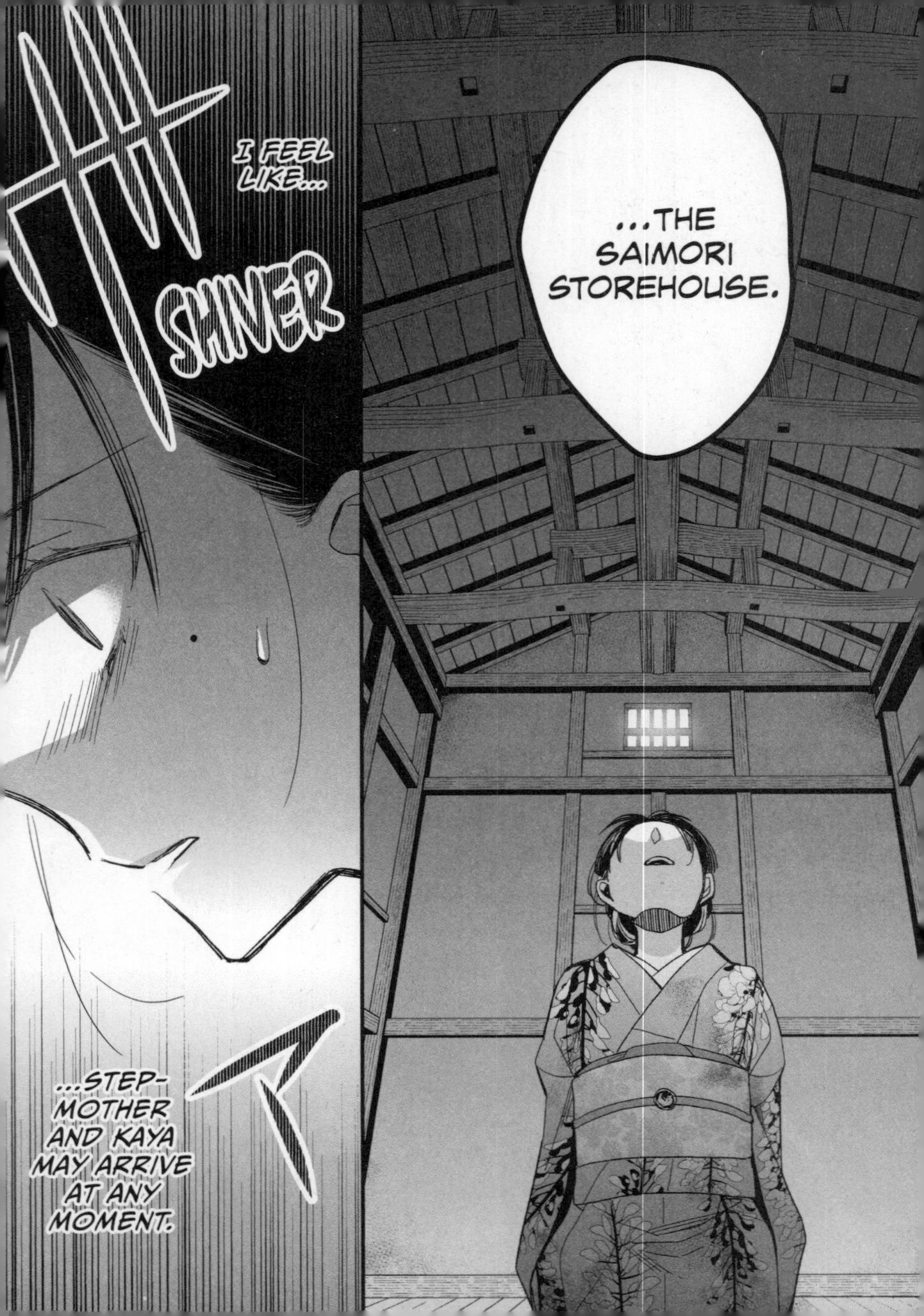
...THE SAIMORI STOREHOUSE.
I FEEL LIKE...
SHIVER
...STEP-MOTHER AND KAYA MAY ARRIVE AT ANY MOMENT.

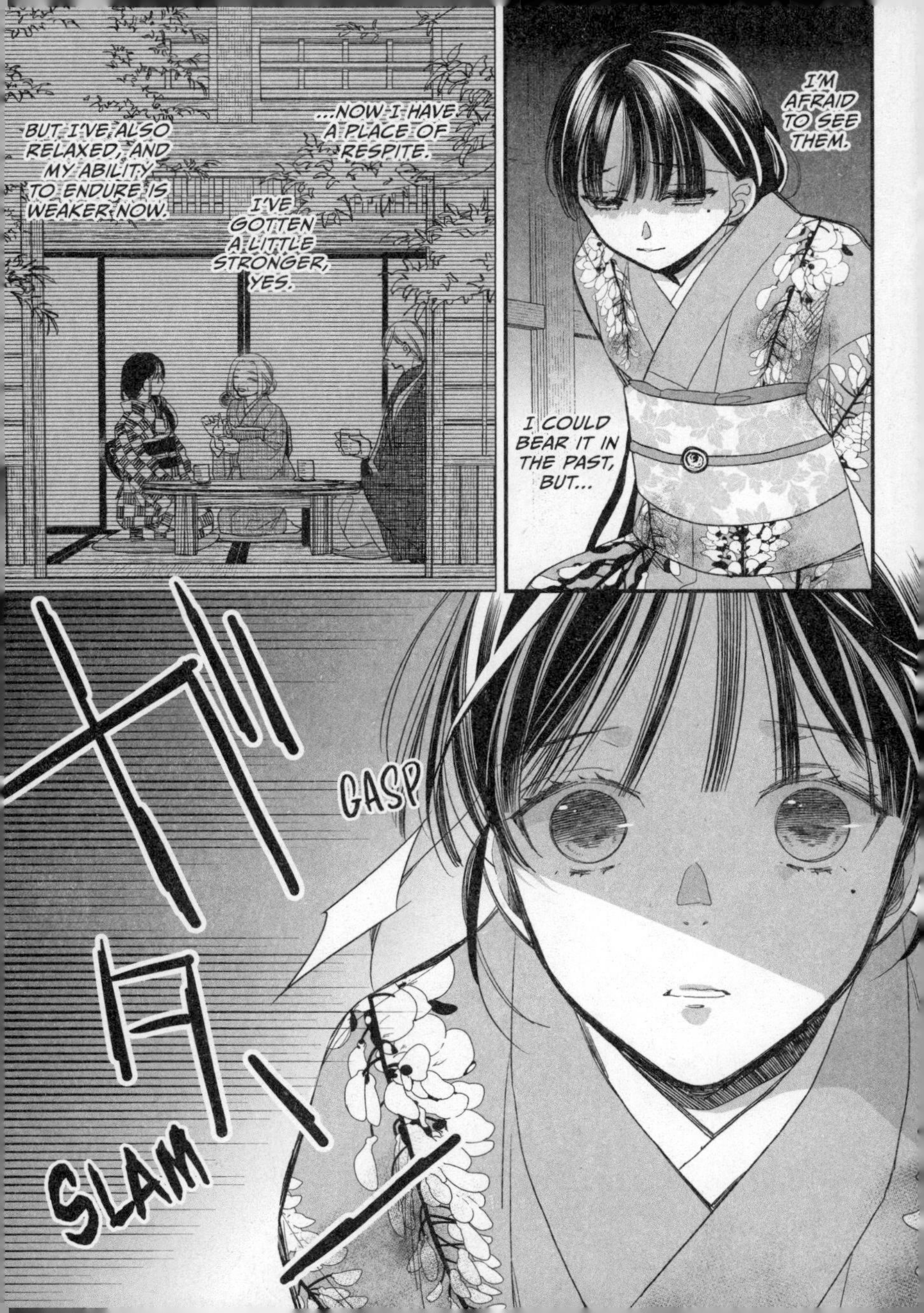
I'M AFRAID TO SEE THEM.
I COULD BEAR IT IN THE PAST, BUT...
I'VE GOTTEN A LITTLE STRONGER, YES.
...NOW I HAVE A PLACE OF RESPITE.
BUT I'VE ALSO RELAXED, AND MY ABILITY TO ENDURE IS WEAKER NOW.
GASP
SLAM

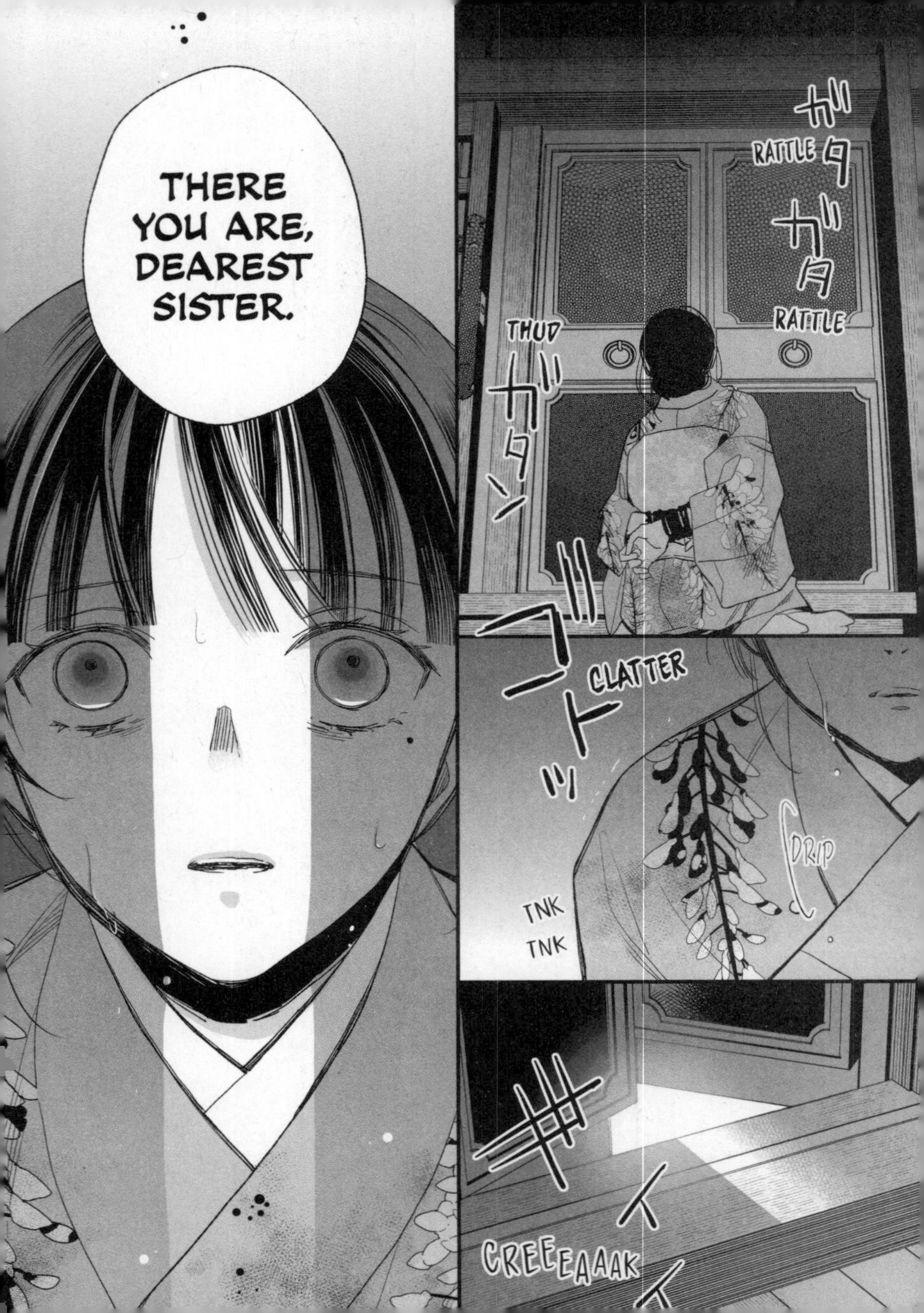
ガタ
RATTLE
ガタ
RATTLE
ガタン
THUD
ゴトッ
CLATTER
DRIP
TNK
TNK
ギイイ
CREEEAAAK
THERE YOU ARE, DEAREST SISTER.

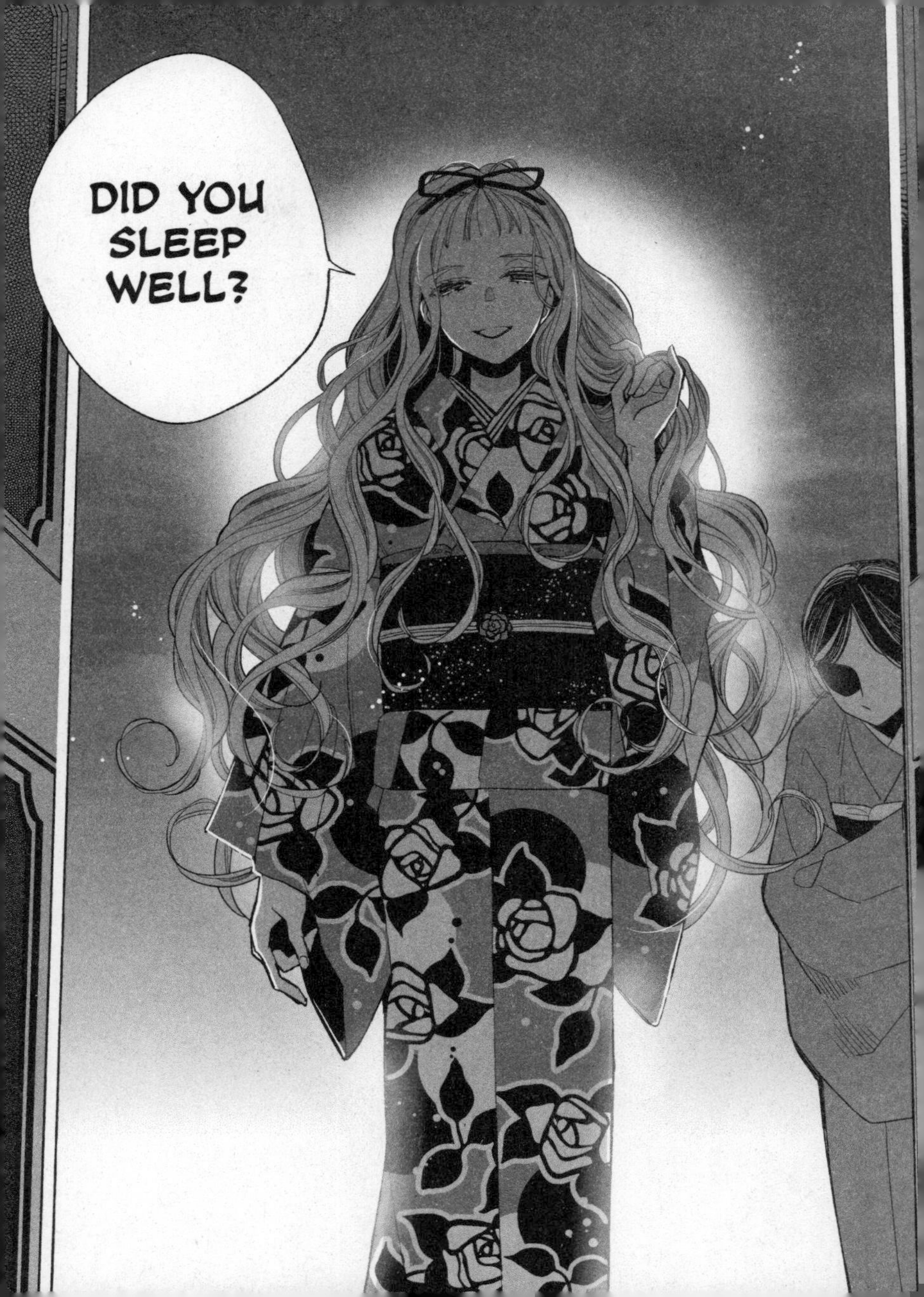
DID YOU SLEEP WELL?

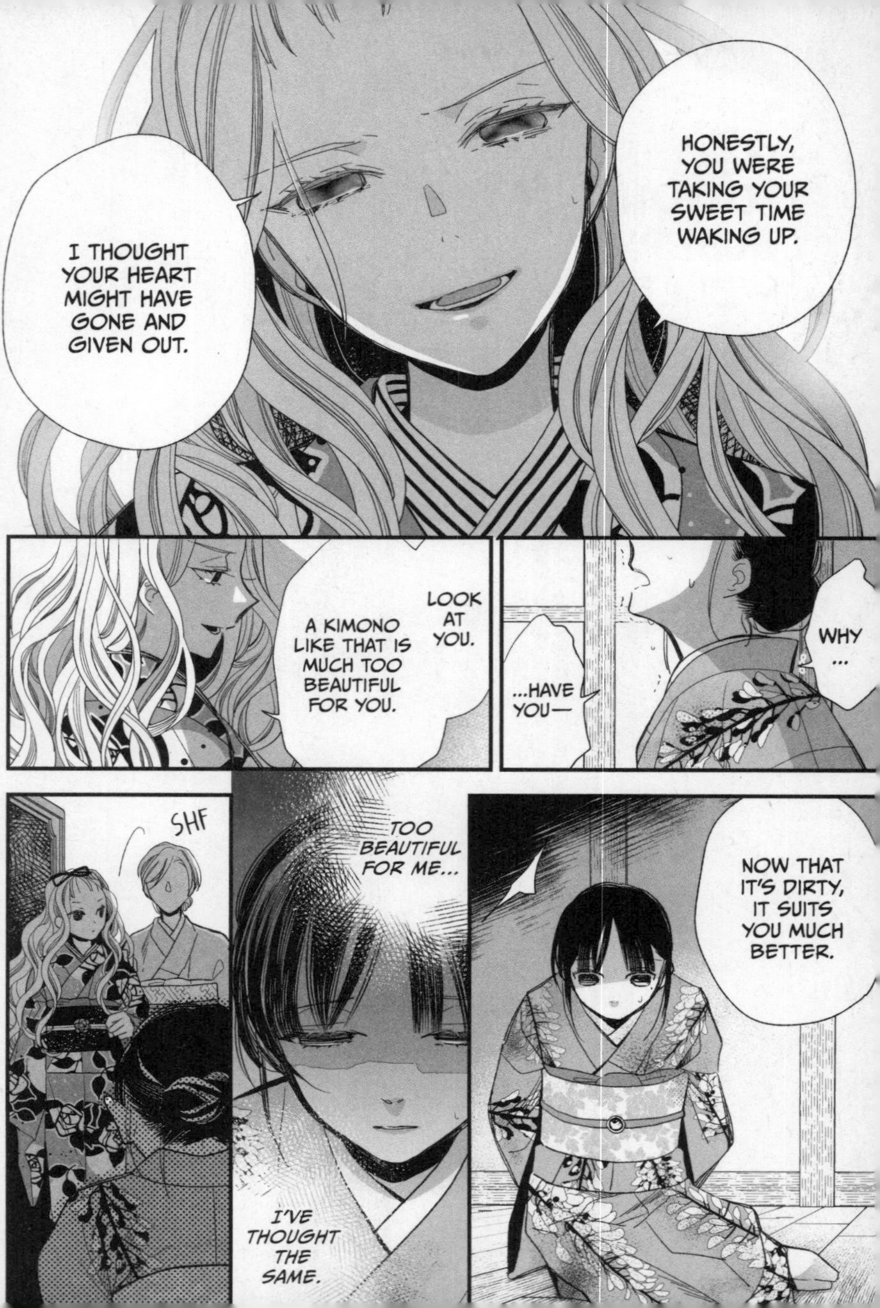
HONESTLY, YOU WERE TAKING YOUR SWEET TIME WAKING UP.
I THOUGHT YOUR HEART MIGHT HAVE GONE AND GIVEN OUT.
WHY ...
...HAVE YOU—
LOOK AT YOU.
A KIMONO LIKE THAT IS MUCH TOO BEAUTIFUL FOR YOU.
NOW THAT IT'S DIRTY, IT SUITS YOU MUCH BETTER.
TOO BEAUTIFUL FOR ME...
I'VE THOUGHT THE SAME.
SHF

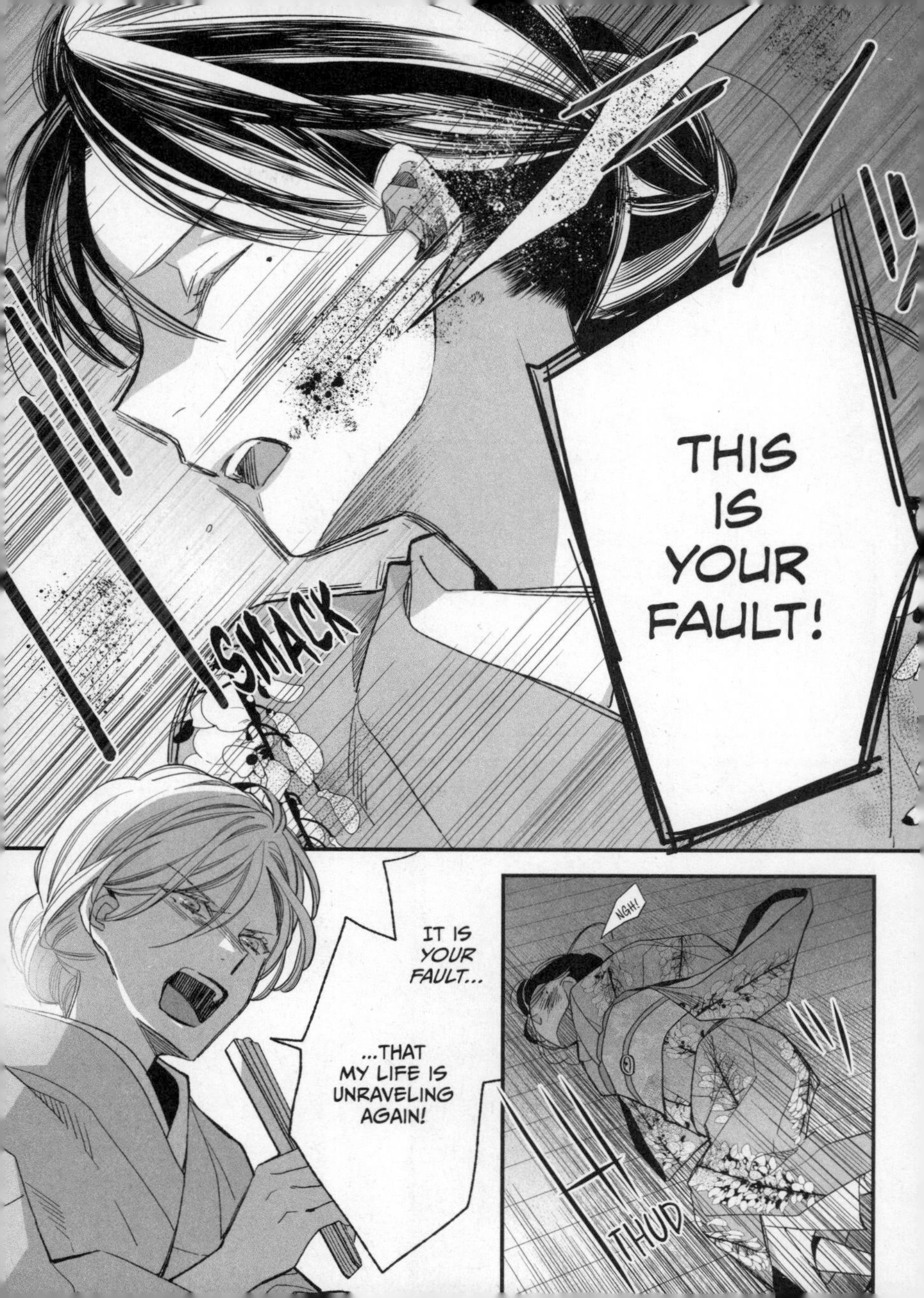
THIS IS YOUR FAULT!
SMACK
NGH!
THUD
IT IS YOUR FAULT...
...THAT MY LIFE IS UNRAVELING AGAIN!

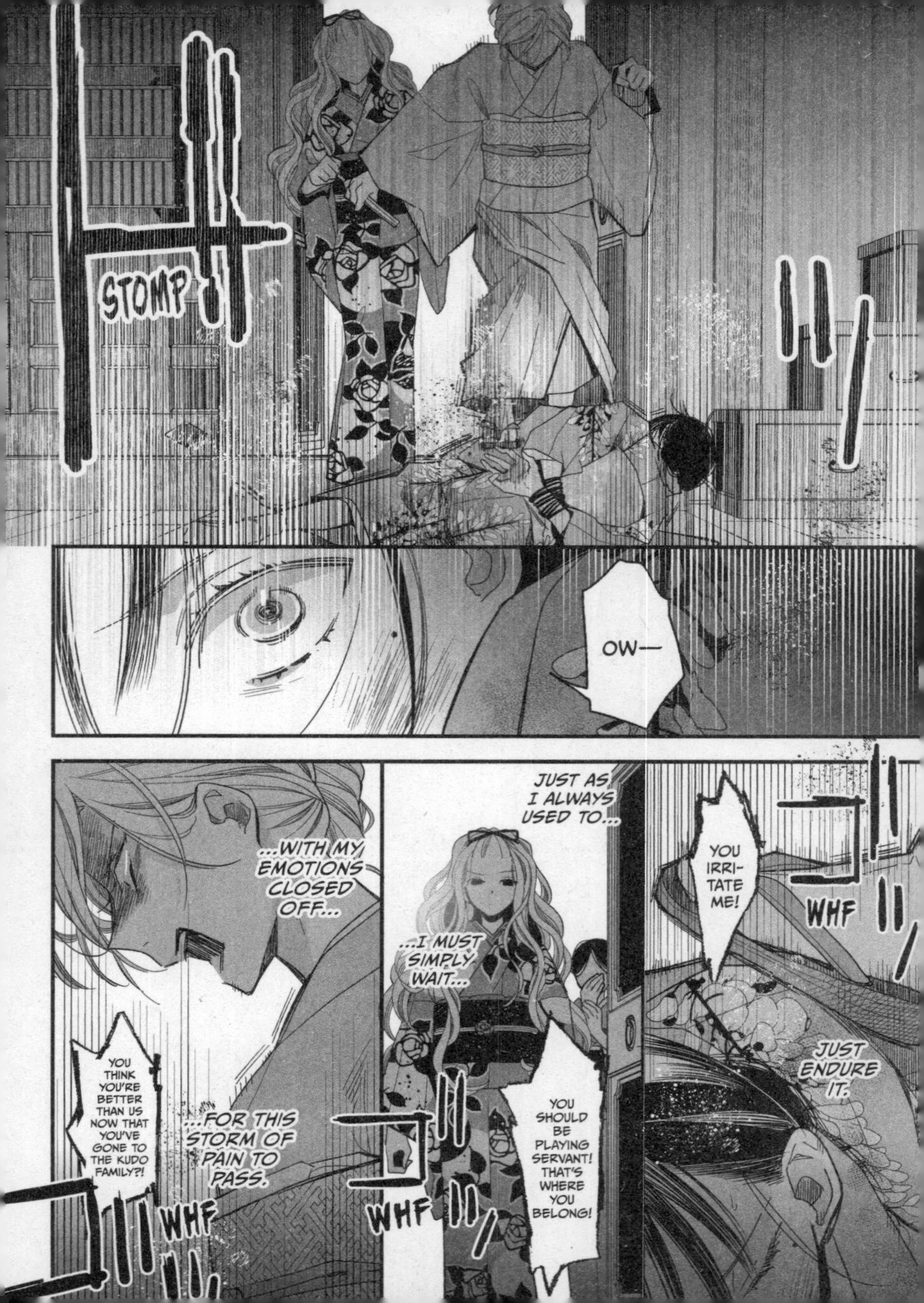
STOMP
OW—
YOU IRRITATE ME!
WHF
JUST ENDURE IT.
JUST AS I ALWAYS USED TO...
...I MUST SIMPLY WAIT...
YOU SHOULD BE PLAYING SERVANT! THAT'S WHERE YOU BELONG!
WHF
...WITH MY EMOTIONS CLOSED OFF...
YOU THINK YOU'RE BETTER THAN US NOW THAT YOU'VE GONE TO THE KUDO FAMILY?!
...FOR THIS STORM OF PAIN TO PASS.
WHF

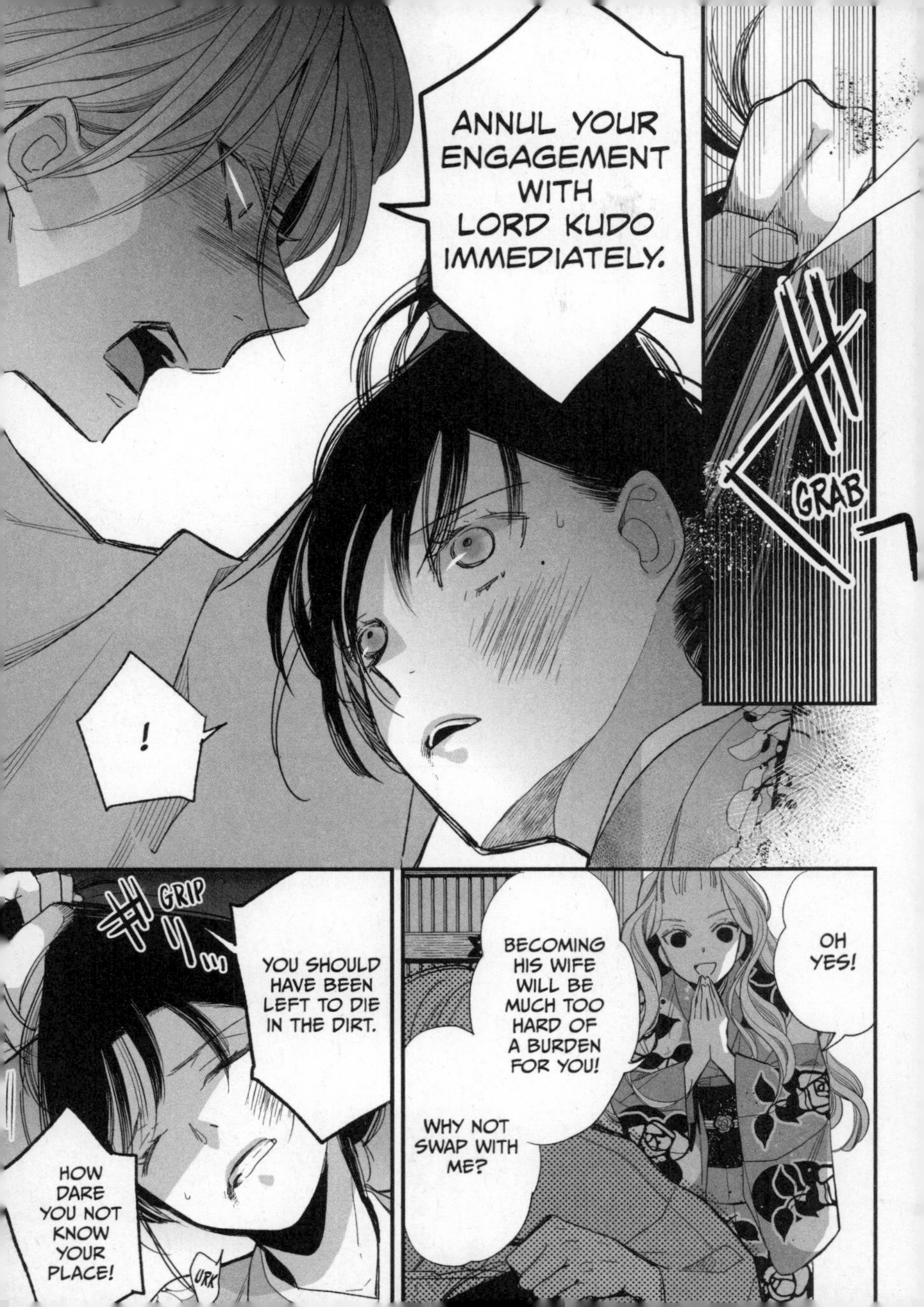
GRAB
ANNUL YOUR ENGAGEMENT WITH LORD KUDO IMMEDIATELY.
!
OH YES!
BECOMING HIS WIFE WILL BE MUCH TOO HARD OF A BURDEN FOR YOU!
WHY NOT SWAP WITH ME?
GRIP
YOU SHOULD HAVE BEEN LEFT TO DIE IN THE DIRT.
HOW DARE YOU NOT KNOW YOUR PLACE!
URK

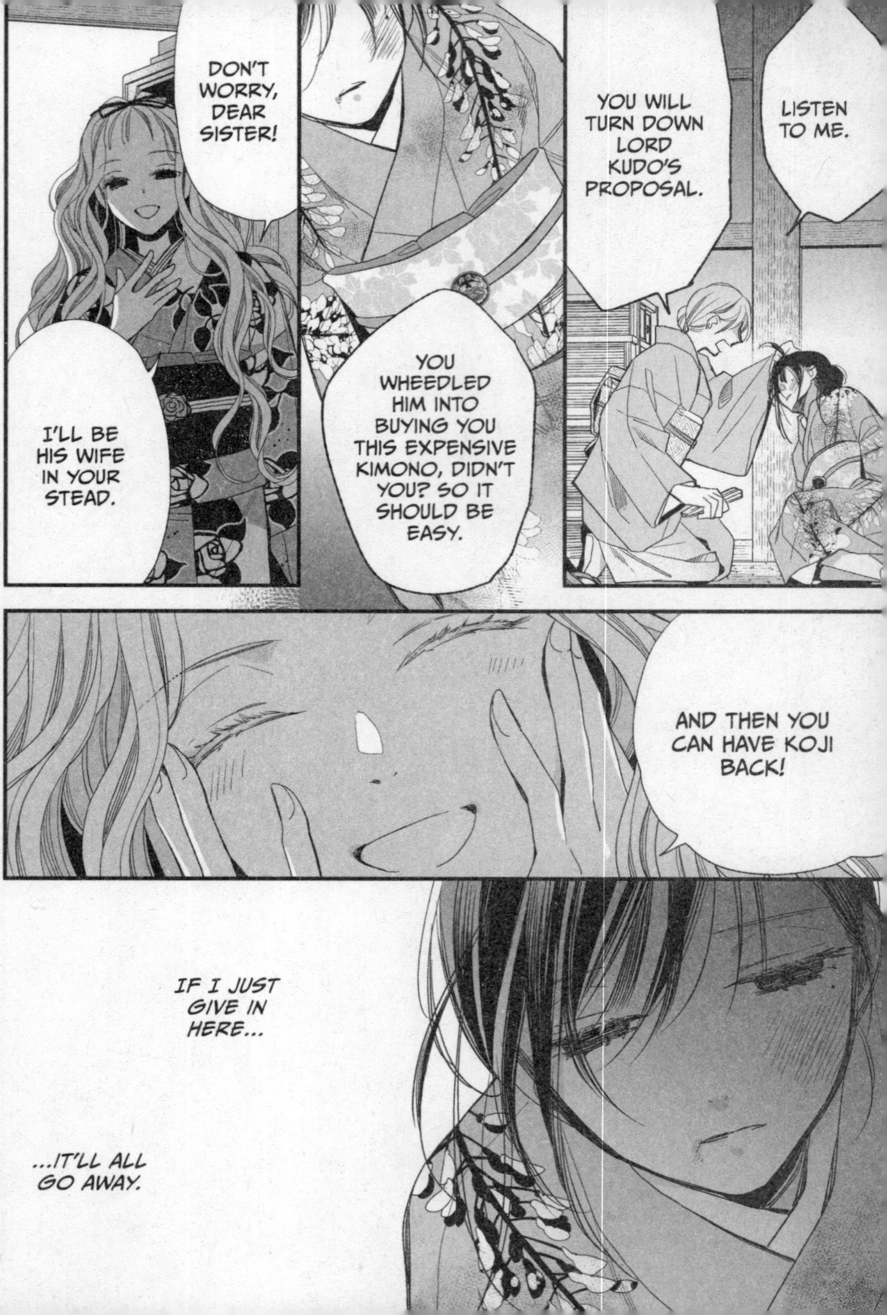
LISTEN TO ME.
YOU WILL TURN DOWN LORD KUDO'S PROPOSAL.
YOU WHEEDLED HIM INTO BUYING YOU THIS EXPENSIVE KIMONO, DIDN'T YOU? SO IT SHOULD BE EASY.
DON'T WORRY, DEAR SISTER!
I'LL BE HIS WIFE IN YOUR STEAD.
AND THEN YOU CAN HAVE KOJI BACK!
IF I JUST GIVE IN HERE...
...IT'LL ALL GO AWAY.

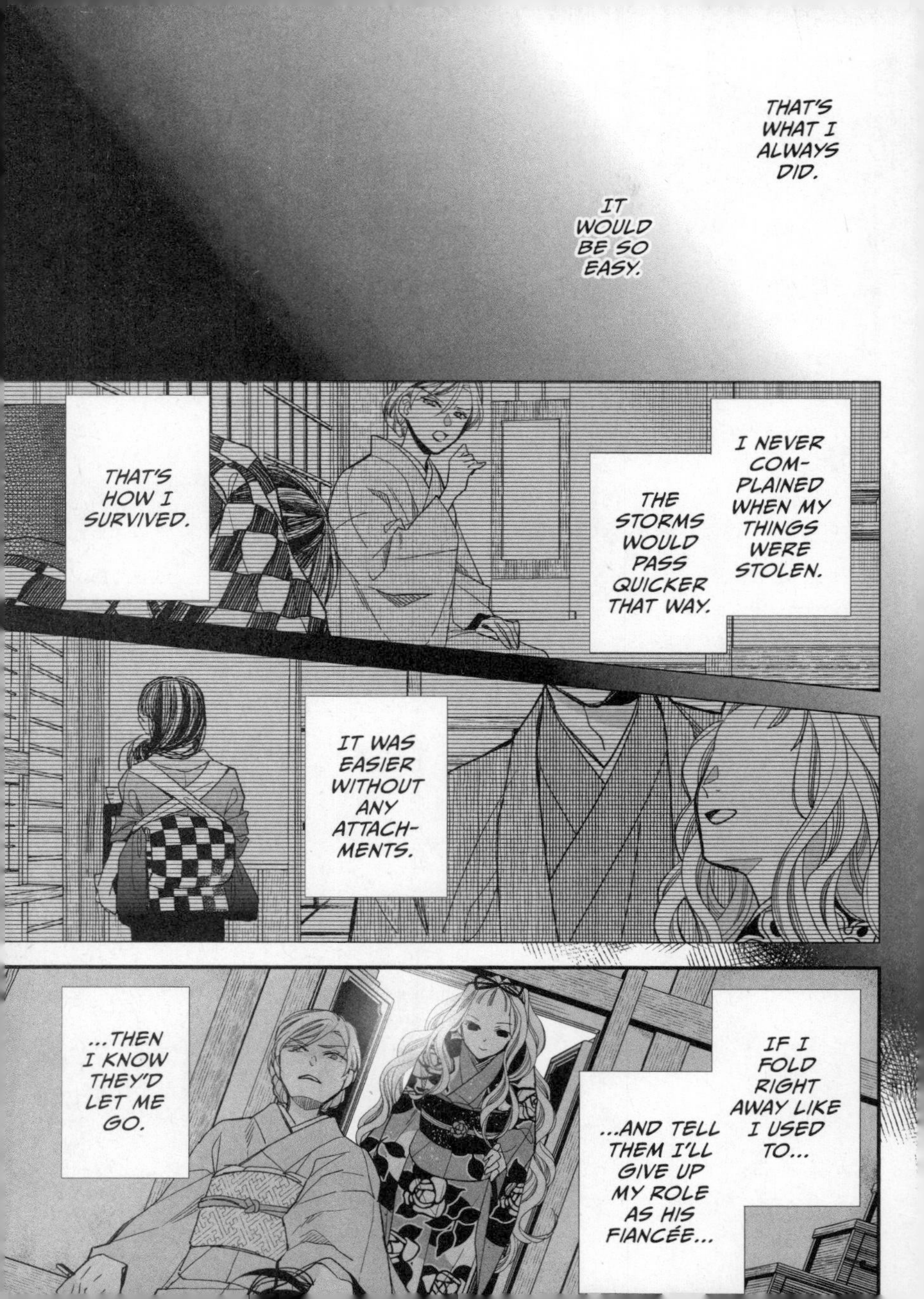
THAT'S WHAT I ALWAYS DID.
IT WOULD BE SO EASY.
I NEVER COMPLAINED WHEN MY THINGS WERE STOLEN.
THE STORMS WOULD PASS QUICKER THAT WAY.
THAT'S HOW I SURVIVED.
IT WAS EASIER WITHOUT ANY ATTACHMENTS.
IF I FOLD RIGHT AWAY LIKE I USED TO...
...AND TELL THEM I'LL GIVE UP MY ROLE AS HIS FIANCÉE...
...THEN I KNOW THEY'D LET ME GO.

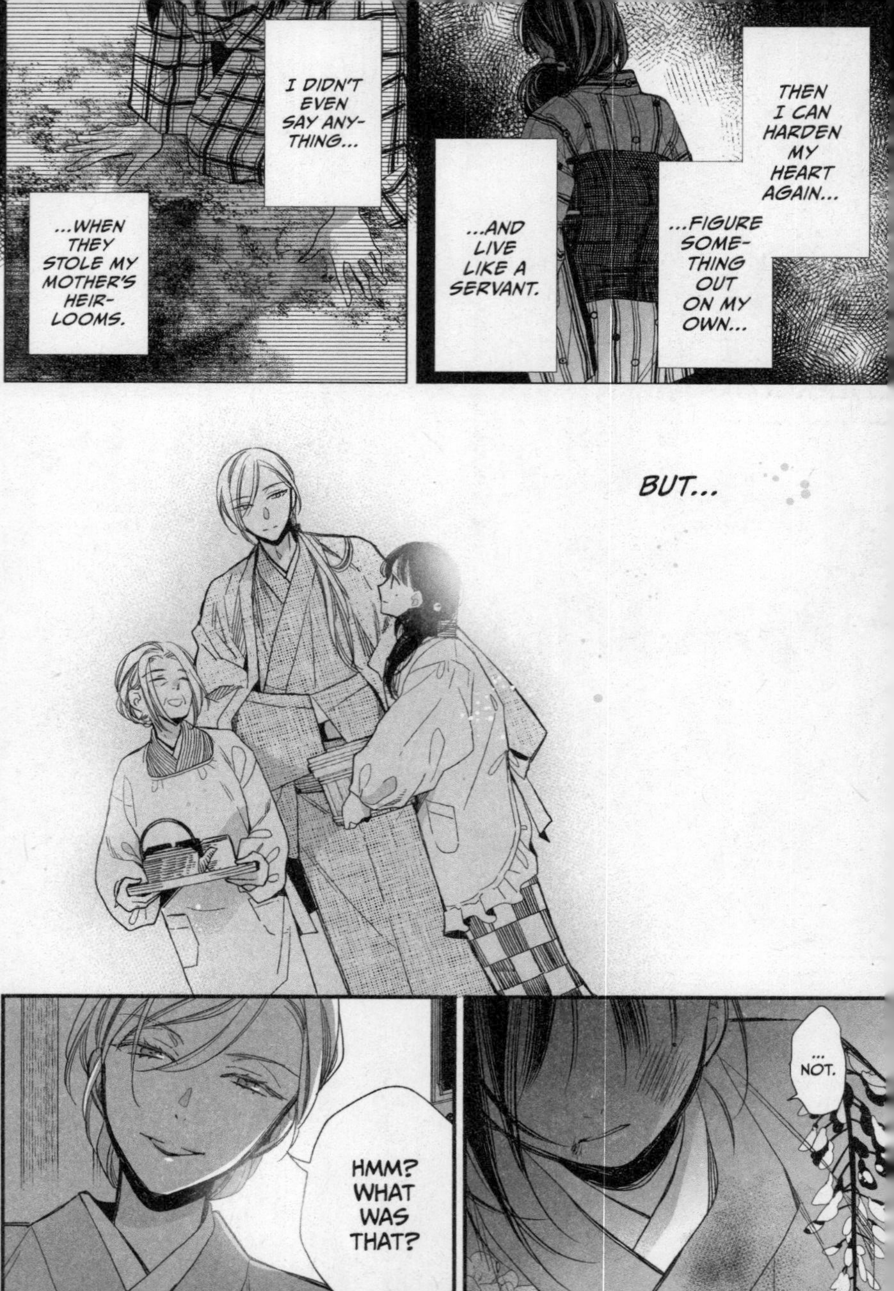
THEN I CAN HARDEN MY HEART AGAIN...
...FIGURE SOMETHING OUT ON MY OWN...
...AND LIVE LIKE A SERVANT.
I DIDN'T EVEN SAY ANY-THING...
...WHEN THEY STOLE MY MOTHER'S HEIR-LOOMS.
BUT...
...NOT.
HMM? WHAT WAS THAT?

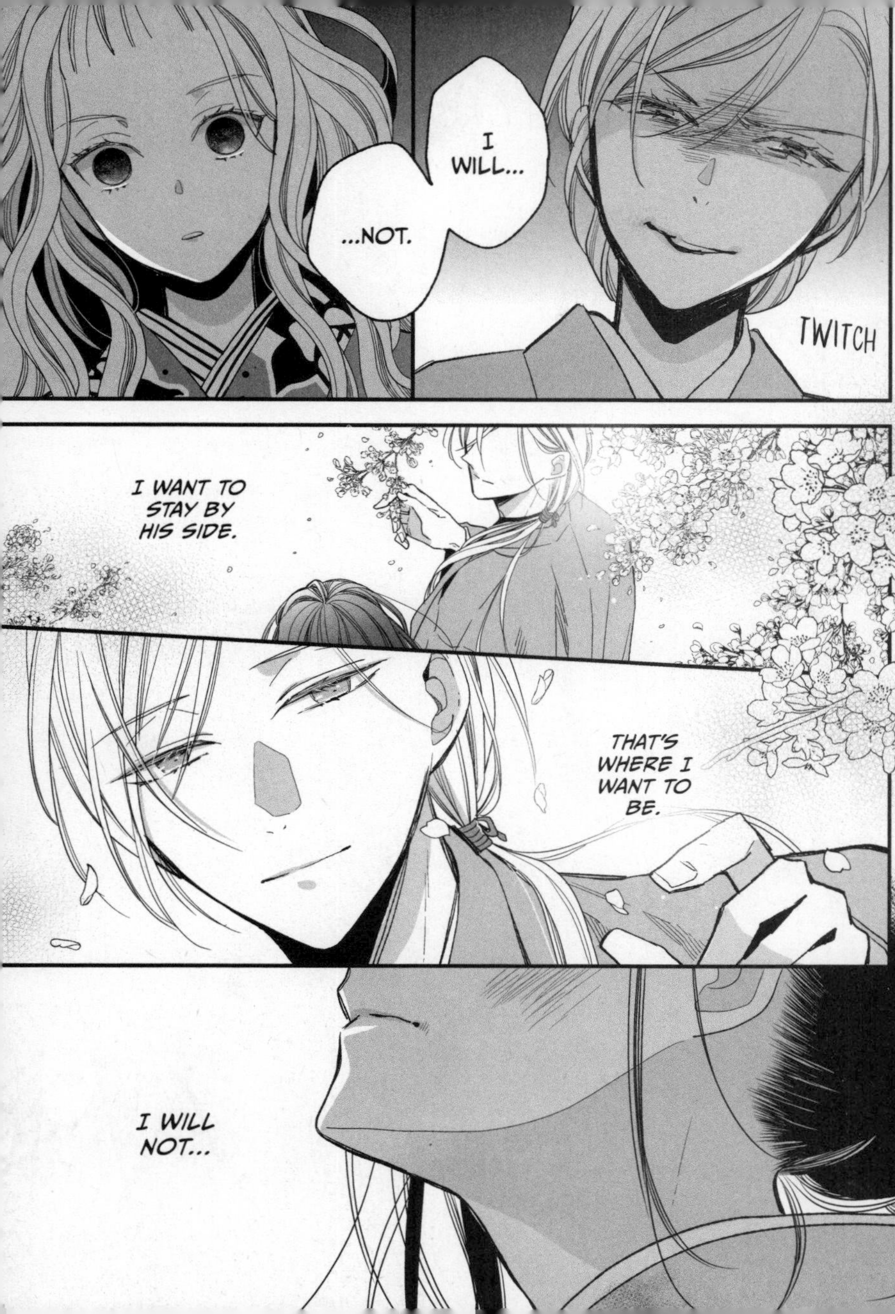
I WILL...
...NOT.
TWITCH
I WANT TO STAY BY HIS SIDE.
THAT'S WHERE I WANT TO BE.
I WILL NOT...

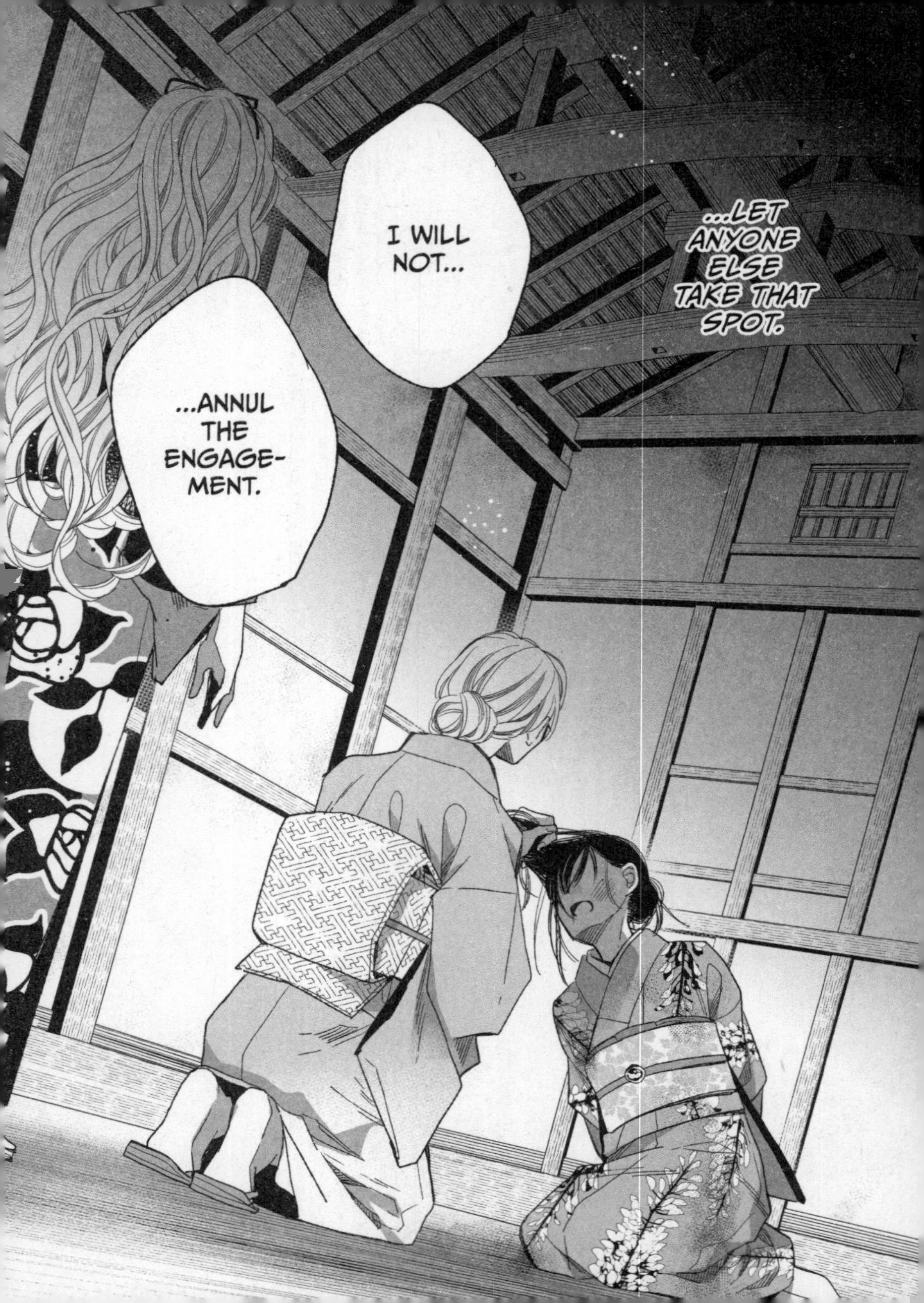
I WILL NOT...
...ANNUL THE ENGAGE-MENT.
...LET ANYONE ELSE TAKE THAT SPOT.

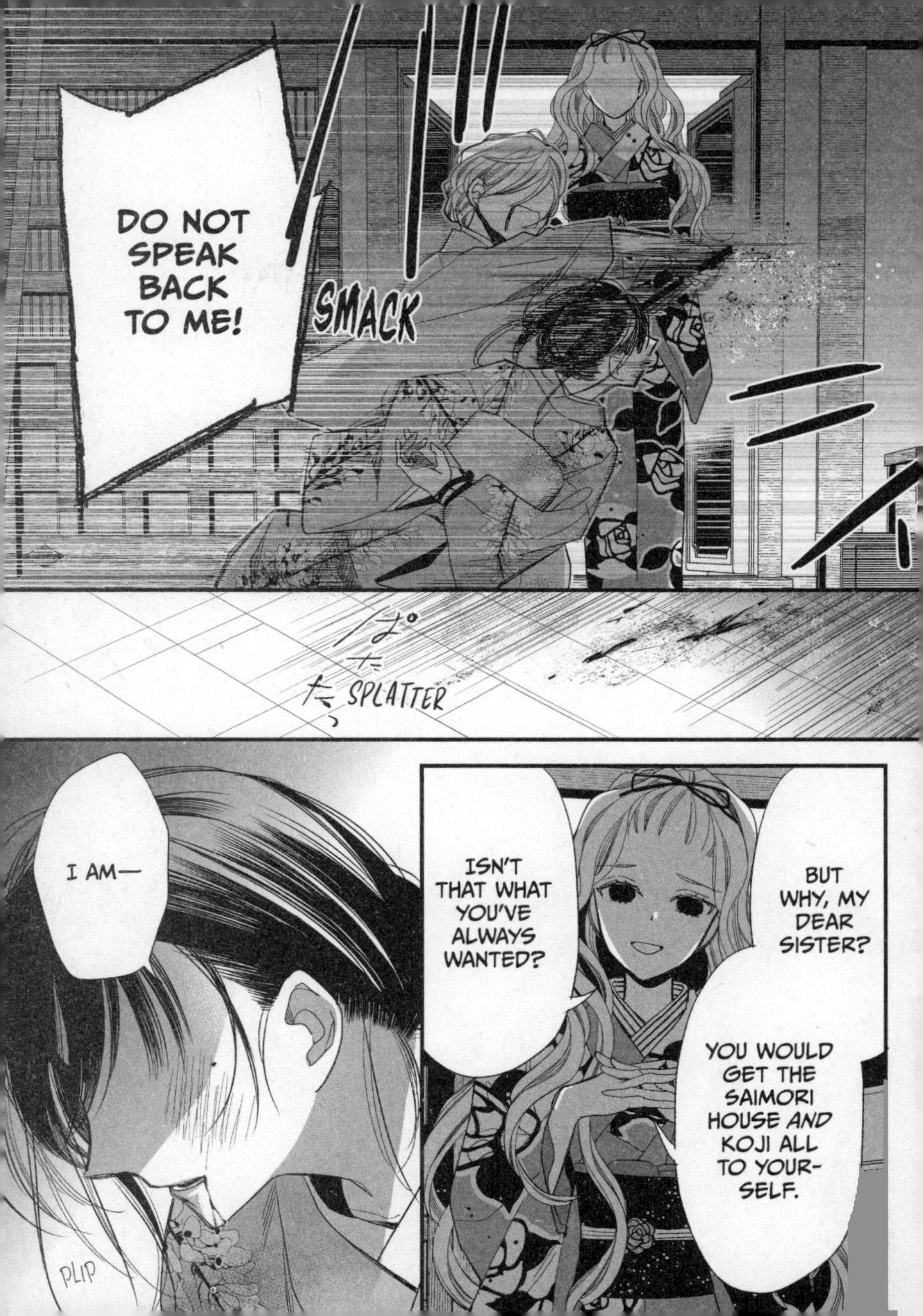
DO NOT SPEAK BACK TO ME!
SMACK
ぱたた
SPLATTER
BUT WHY, MY DEAR SISTER?
ISN'T THAT WHAT YOU'VE ALWAYS WANTED?
YOU WOULD GET THE SAIMORI HOUSE *AND* KOJI ALL TO YOUR-SELF.
I AM—
PLIP

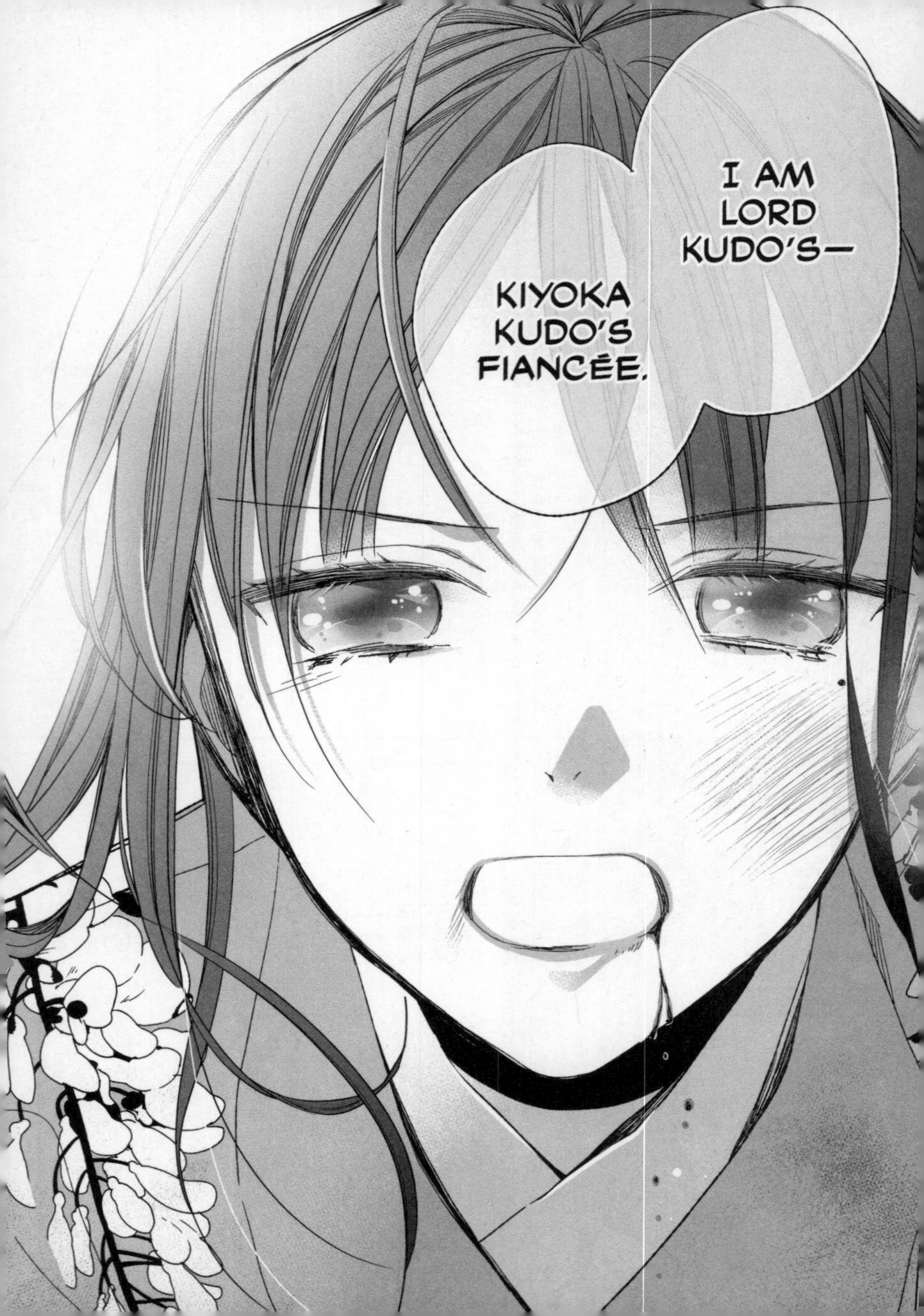
I AM LORD KUDO'S—
KIYOKA KUDO'S FIANCÉE.

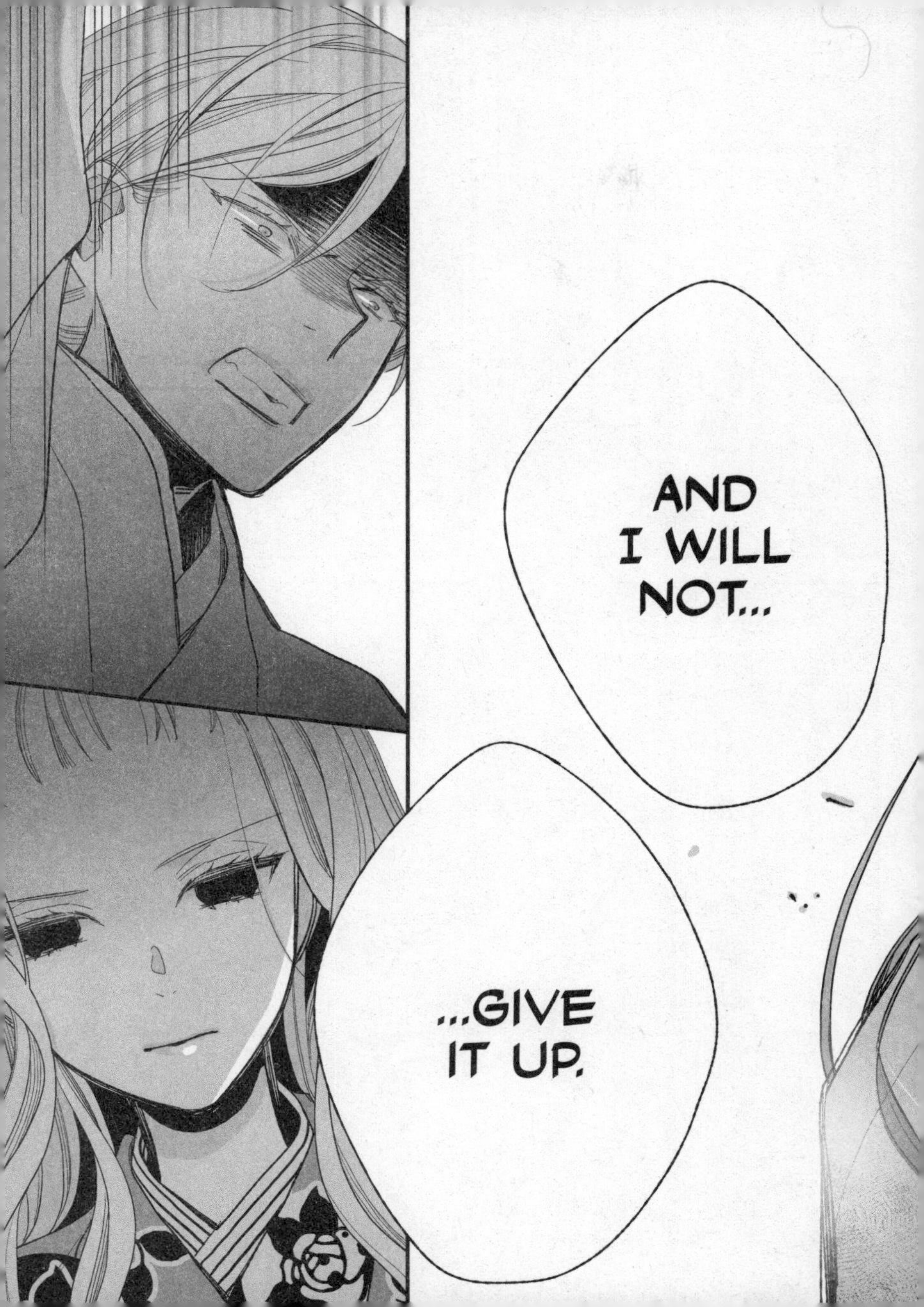
AND I WILL NOT...
...GIVE IT UP.

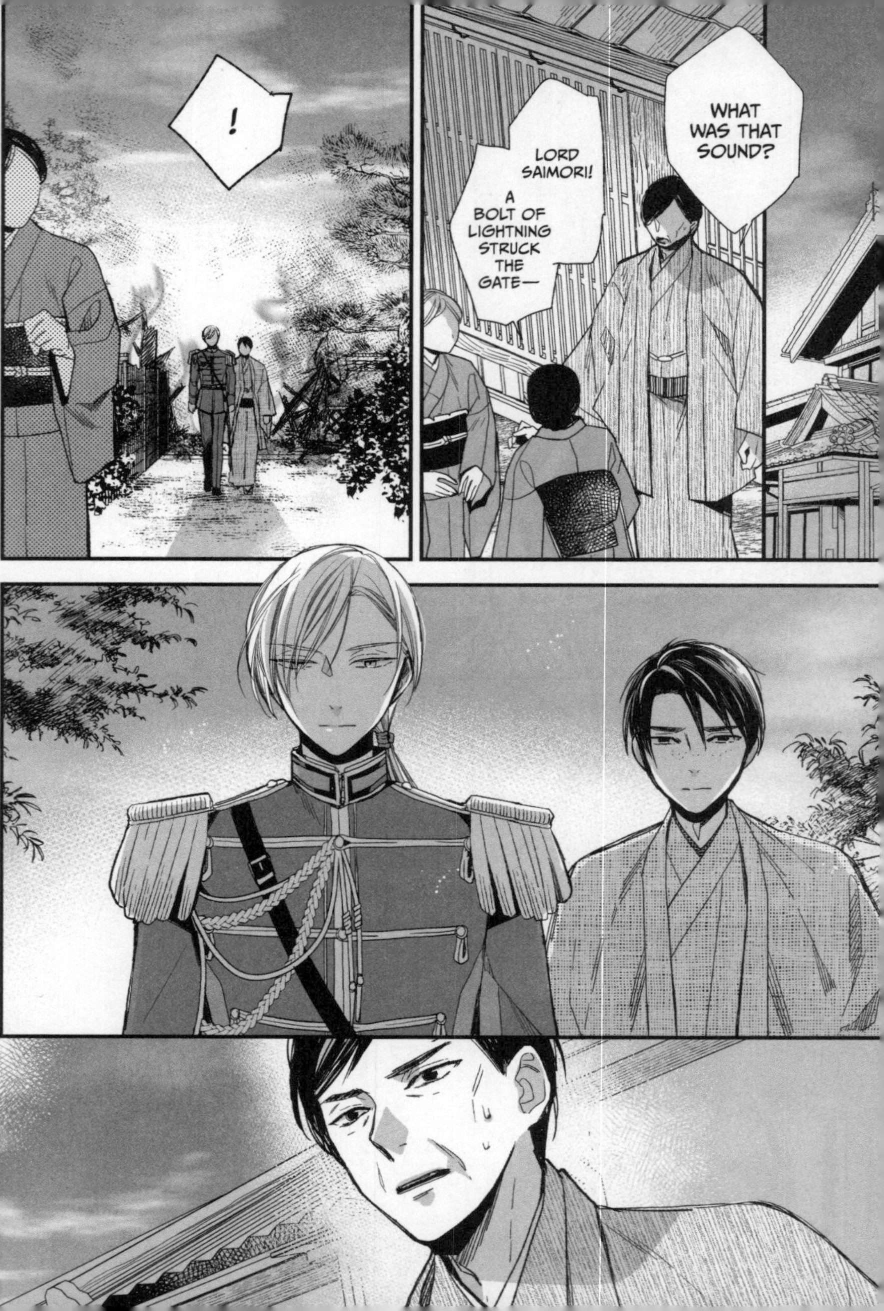
WHAT WAS THAT SOUND?
LORD SAIMORI!
A BOLT OF LIGHTNING STRUCK THE GATE—
!

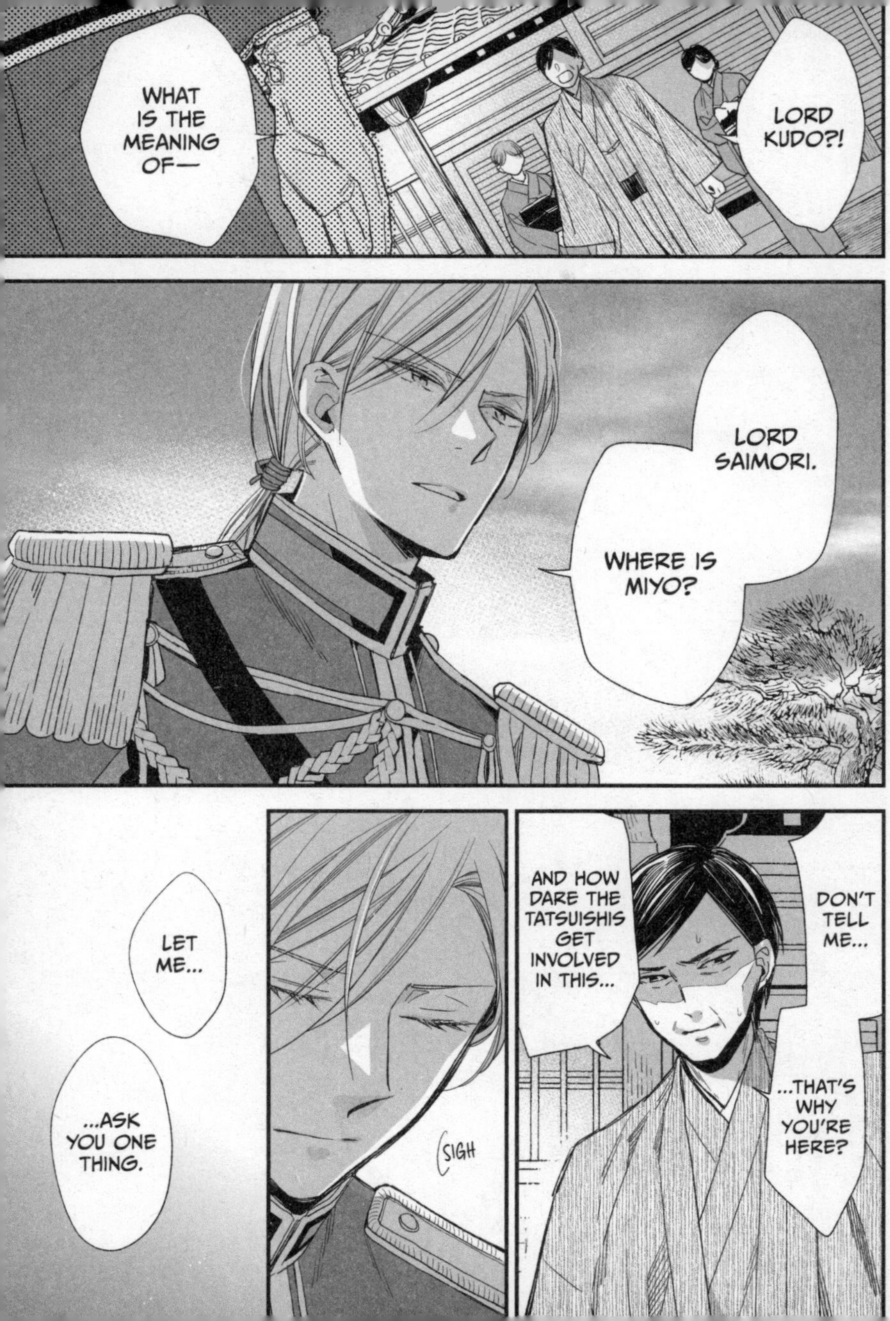
LORD KUDO?!
WHAT IS THE MEANING OF—
LORD SAIMORI.
WHERE IS MIYO?
DON'T TELL ME...
AND HOW DARE THE TATSUISHIS GET INVOLVED IN THIS...
...THAT'S WHY YOU'RE HERE?
LET ME...
SIGH
...ASK YOU ONE THING.

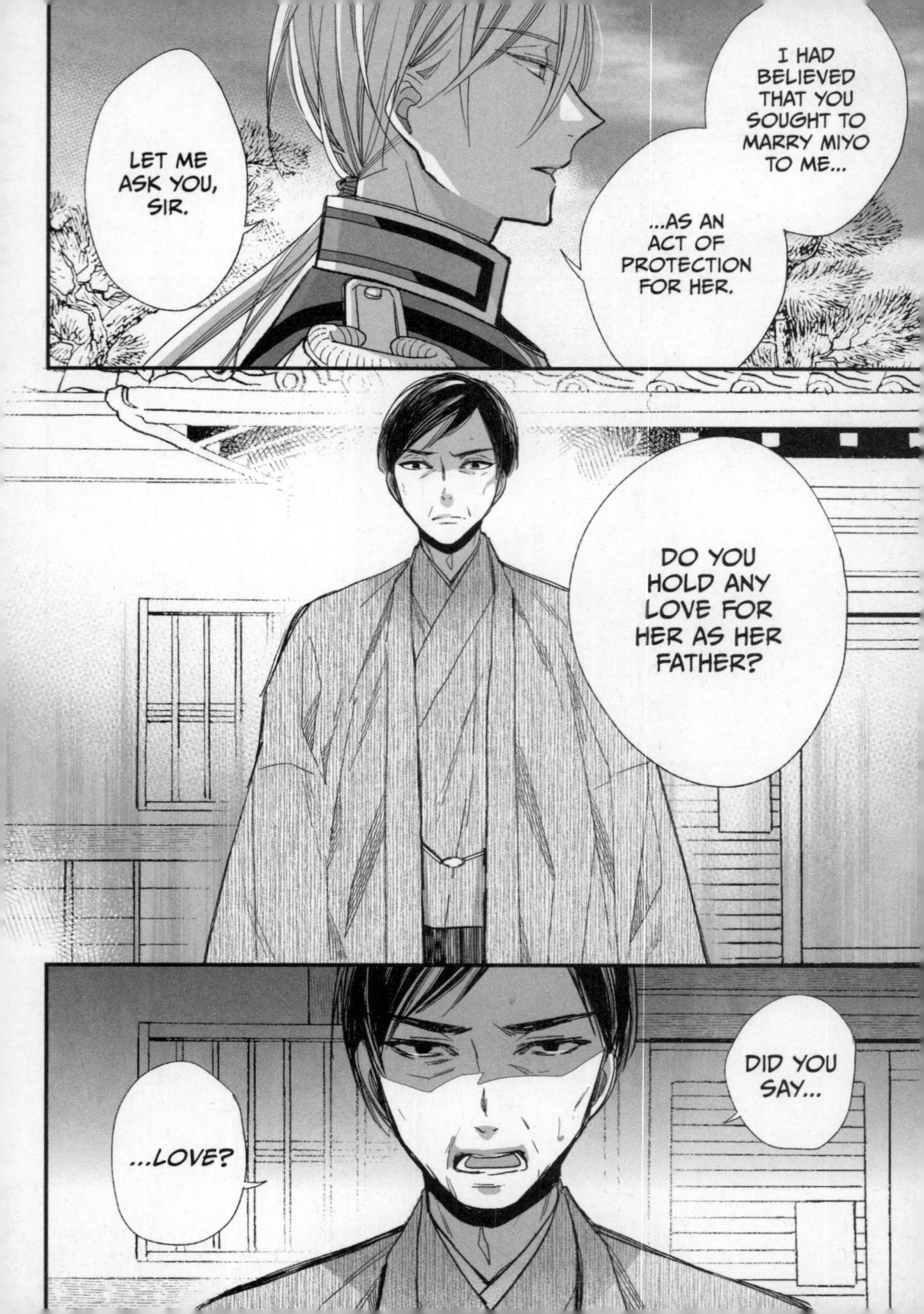
I HAD BELIEVED THAT YOU SOUGHT TO MARRY MIYO TO ME...
...AS AN ACT OF PROTECTION FOR HER.
LET ME ASK YOU, SIR.
DO YOU HOLD ANY LOVE FOR HER AS HER FATHER?
DID YOU SAY...
...LOVE?

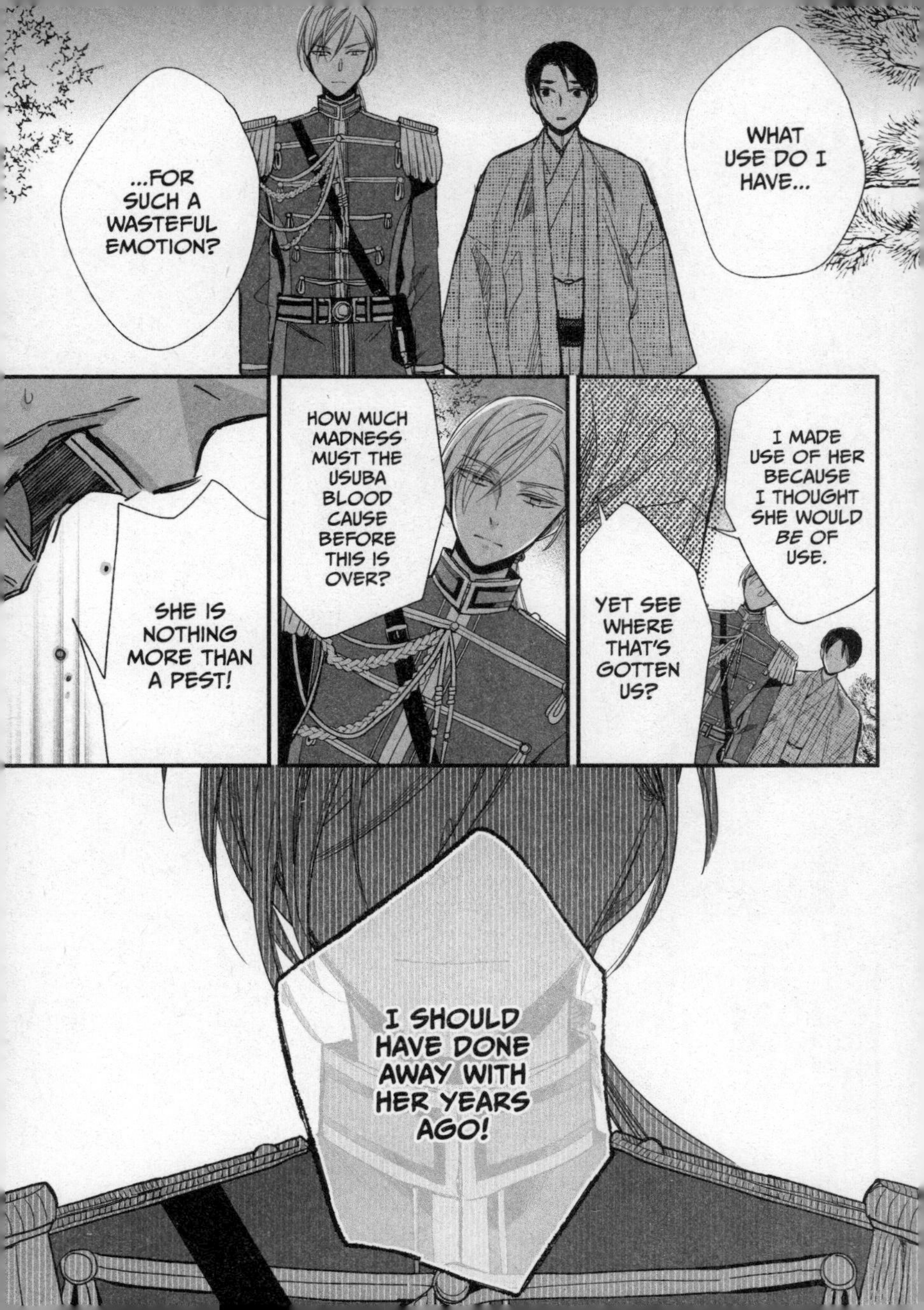
WHAT USE DO I HAVE...
...FOR SUCH A WASTEFUL EMOTION?
I MADE USE OF HER BECAUSE I THOUGHT SHE WOULD BE OF USE.
YET SEE WHERE THAT'S GOTTEN US?
HOW MUCH MADNESS MUST THE USUBA BLOOD CAUSE BEFORE THIS IS OVER?
SHE IS NOTHING MORE THAN A PEST!
I SHOULD HAVE DONE AWAY WITH HER YEARS AGO!

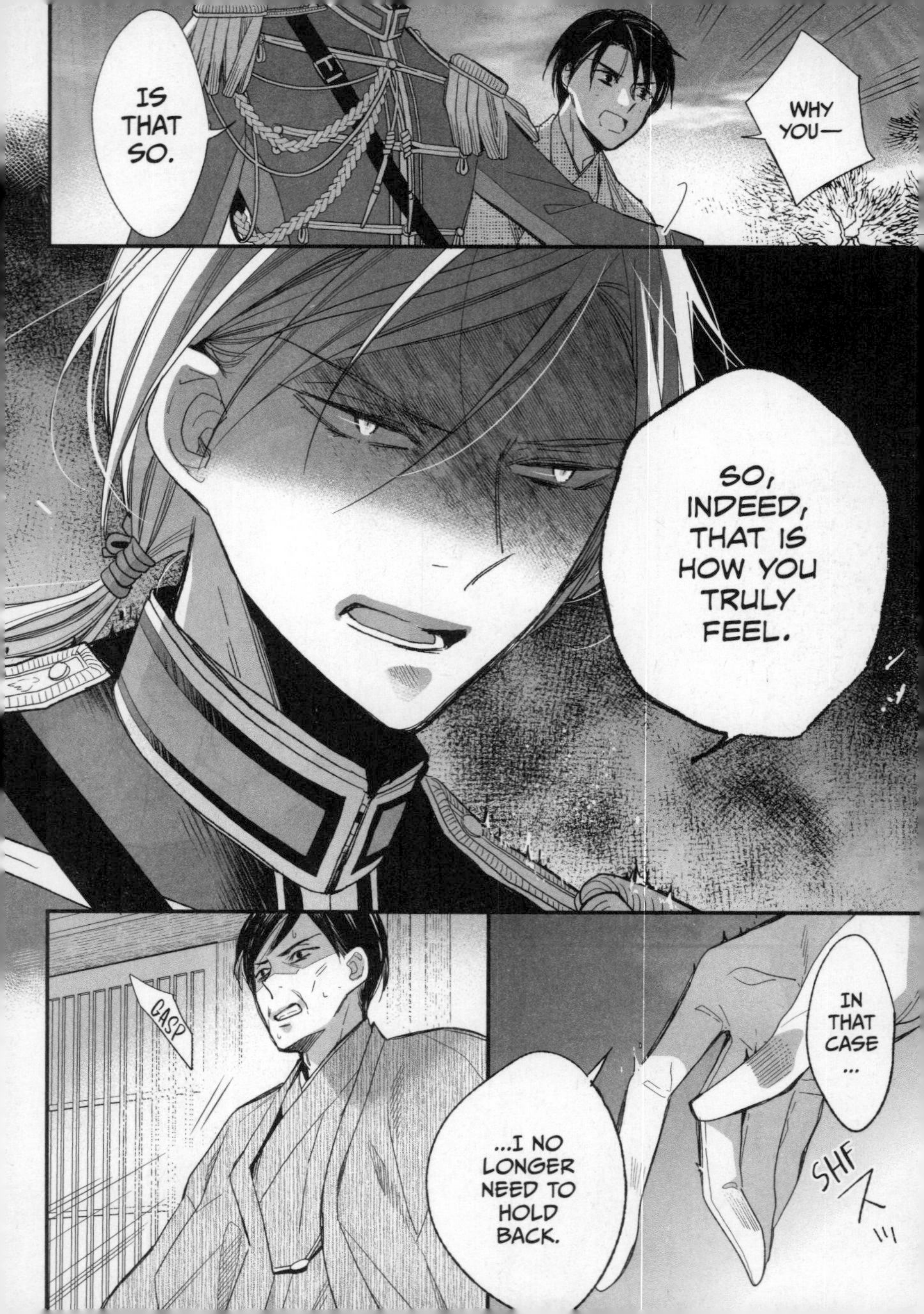
WHY YOU—
IS THAT SO.
SO, INDEED, THAT IS HOW YOU TRULY FEEL.
IN THAT CASE ...
...I NO LONGER NEED TO HOLD BACK.
SHF
GASP

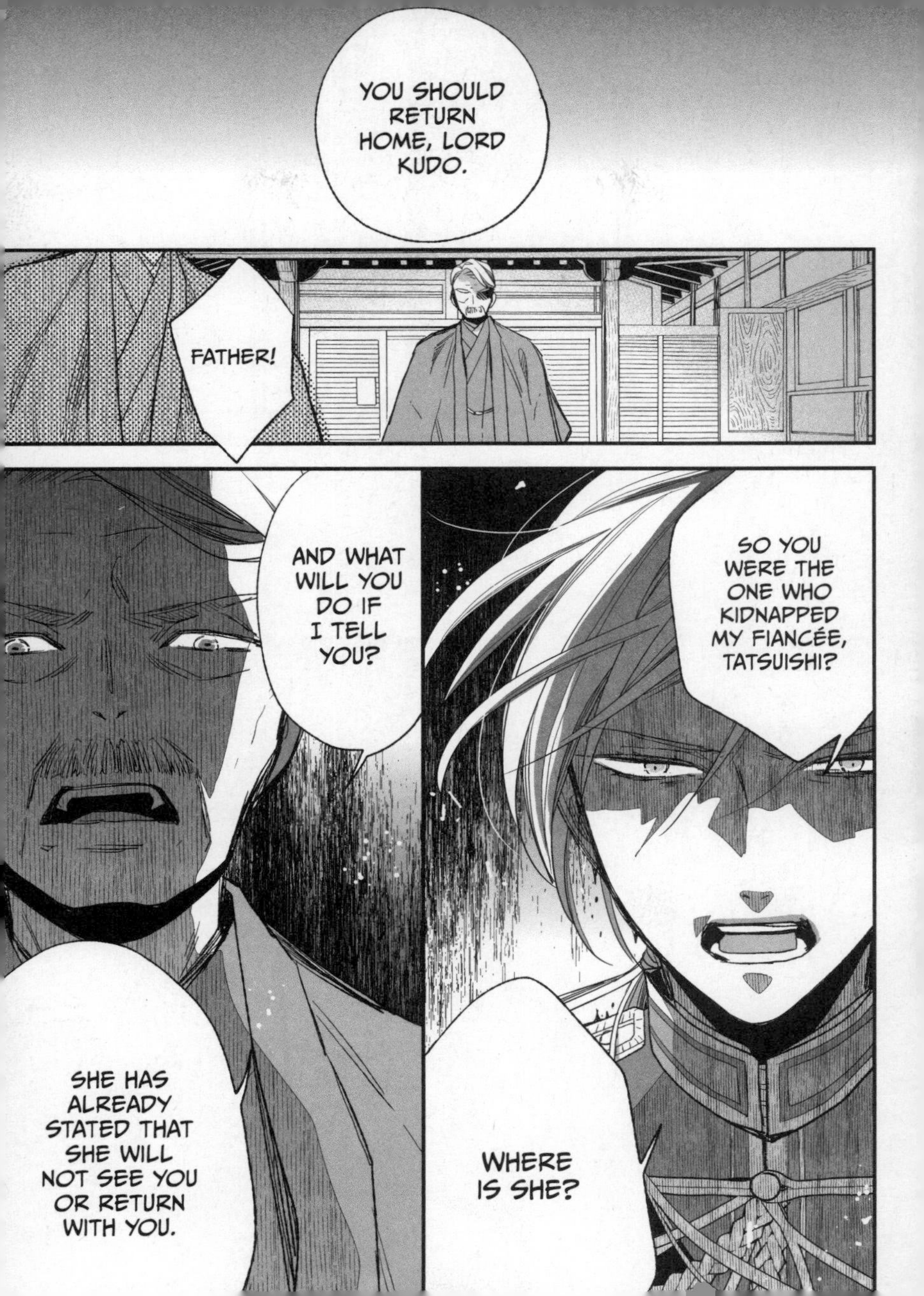
YOU SHOULD RETURN HOME, LORD KUDO.
FATHER!
SO YOU WERE THE ONE WHO KIDNAPPED MY FIANCÉE, TATSUISHI?
WHERE IS SHE?
AND WHAT WILL YOU DO IF I TELL YOU?
SHE HAS ALREADY STATED THAT SHE WILL NOT SEE YOU OR RETURN WITH YOU.

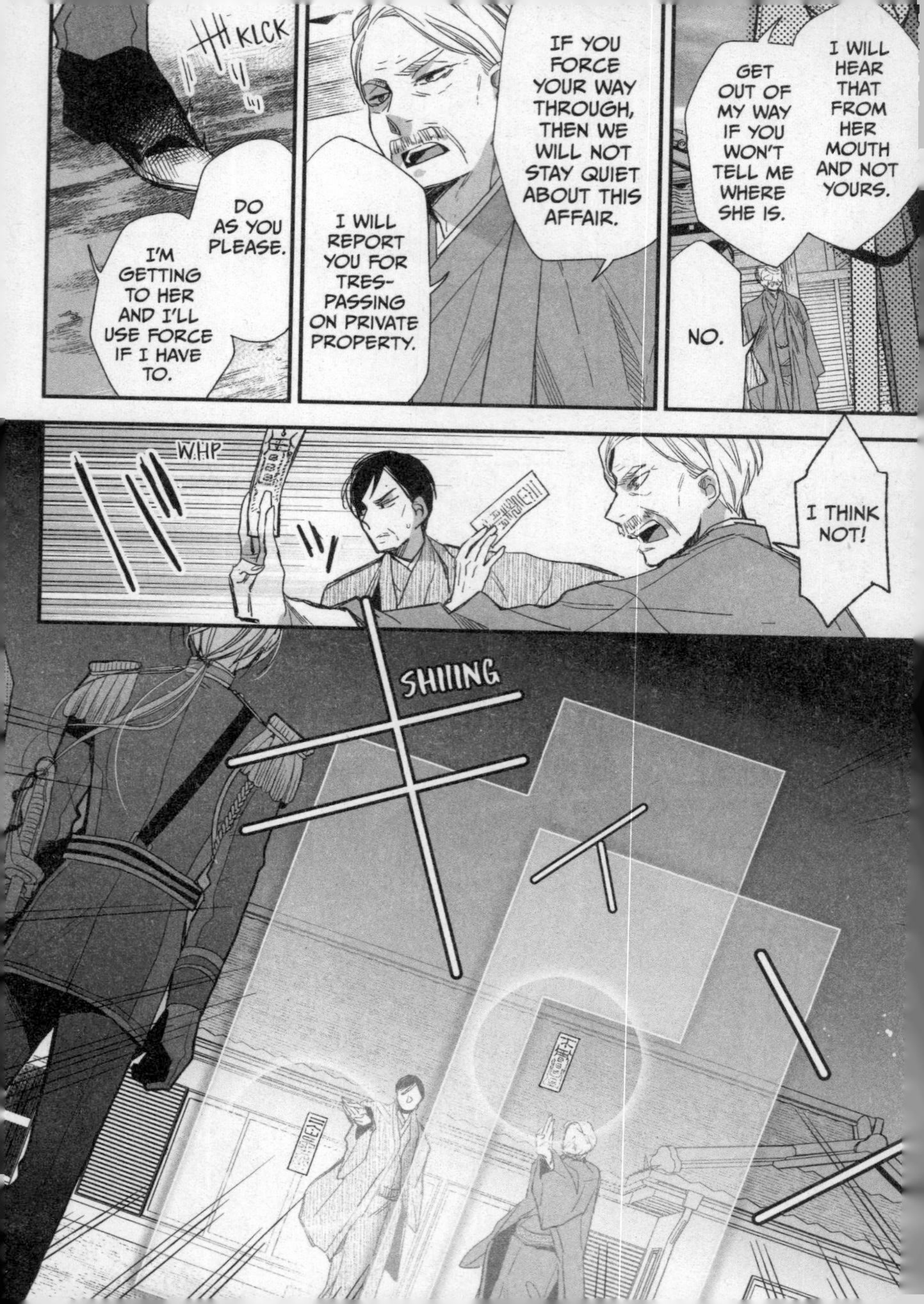
I WILL HEAR THAT FROM HER MOUTH AND NOT YOURS.
GET OUT OF MY WAY IF YOU WON'T TELL ME WHERE SHE IS.
NO.
IF YOU FORCE YOUR WAY THROUGH, THEN WE WILL NOT STAY QUIET ABOUT THIS AFFAIR.
I WILL REPORT YOU FOR TRES-PASSING ON PRIVATE PROPERTY.
KLCK
DO AS YOU PLEASE.
I'M GETTING TO HER AND I'LL USE FORCE IF I HAVE TO.
I THINK NOT!
WHP
SHIIING

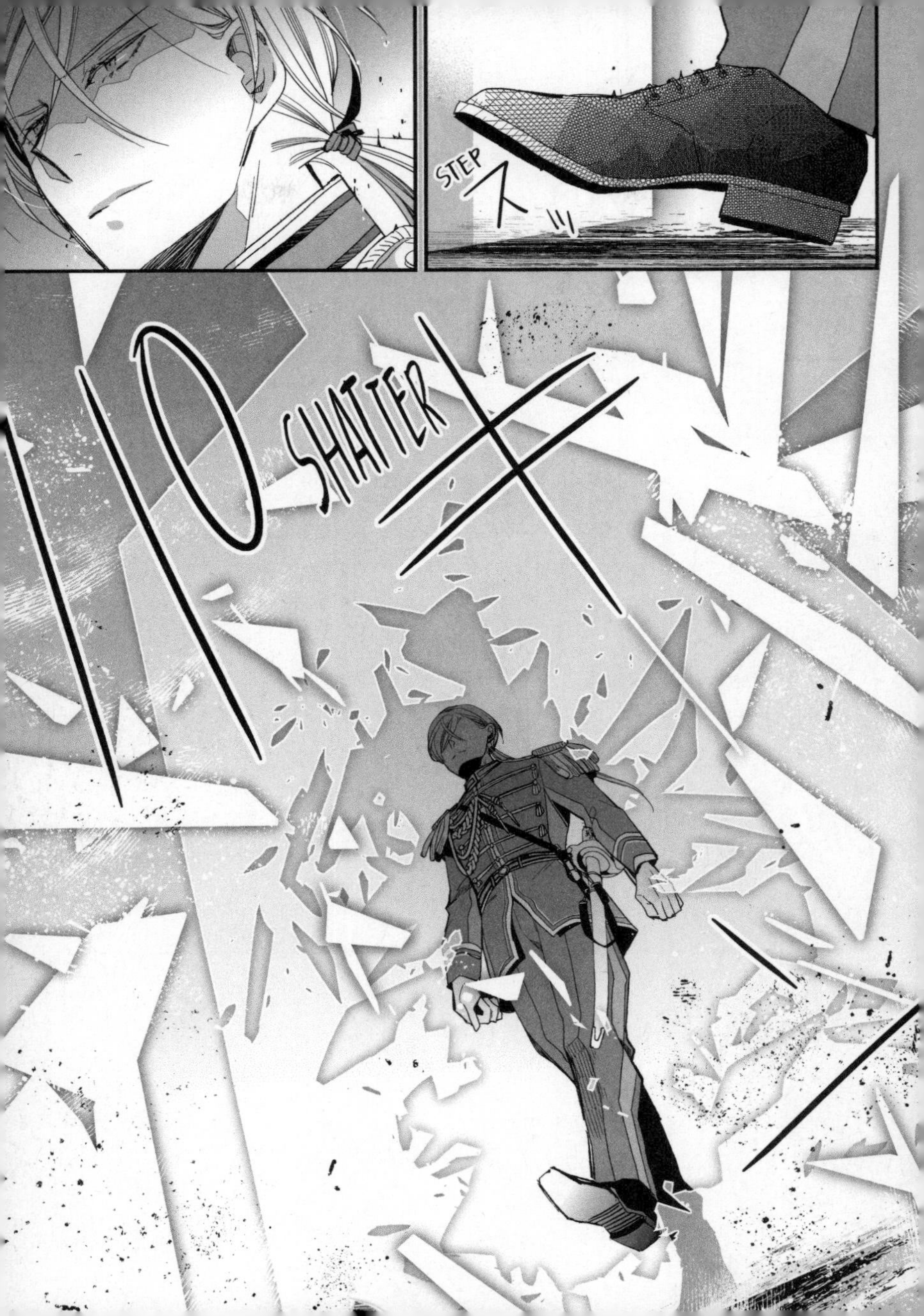
STEP
SHATTER

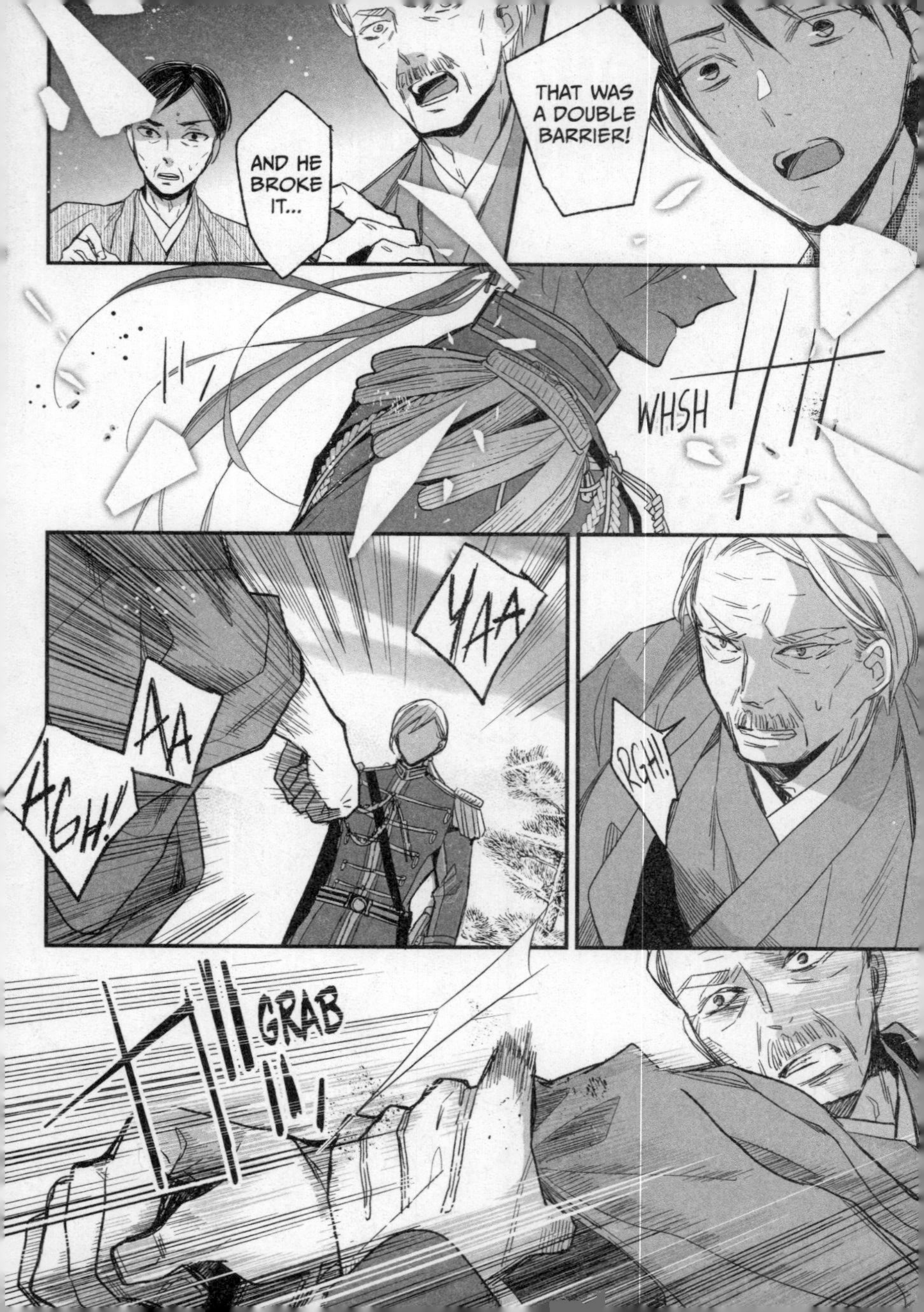
THAT WAS A DOUBLE BARRIER!
AND HE BROKE IT...
WHSH
RGH!
YAA
AA
AGH!
GRAB

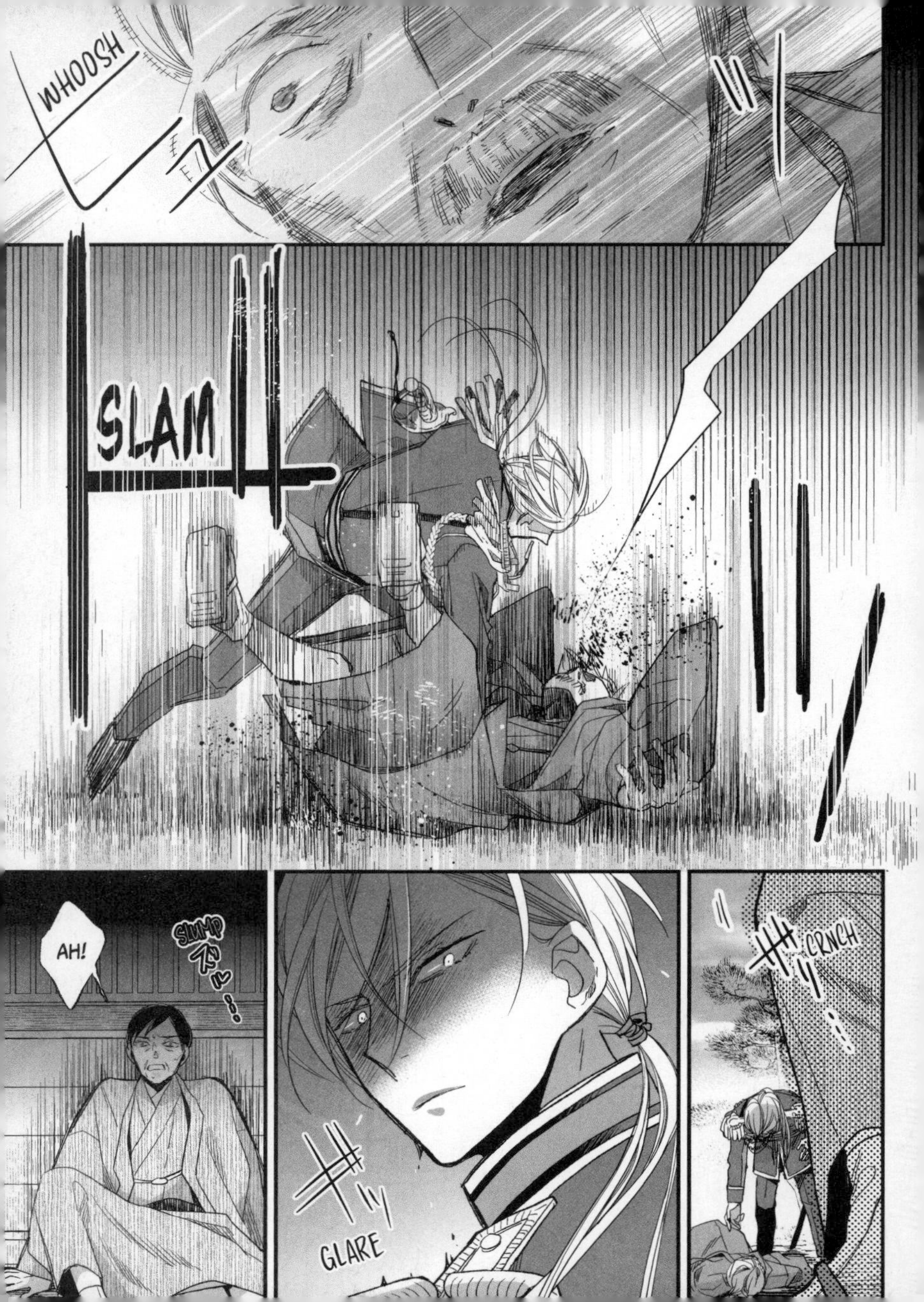
WHOOSH
SLAM
CRNCH
GLARE
AH!
SLUMP

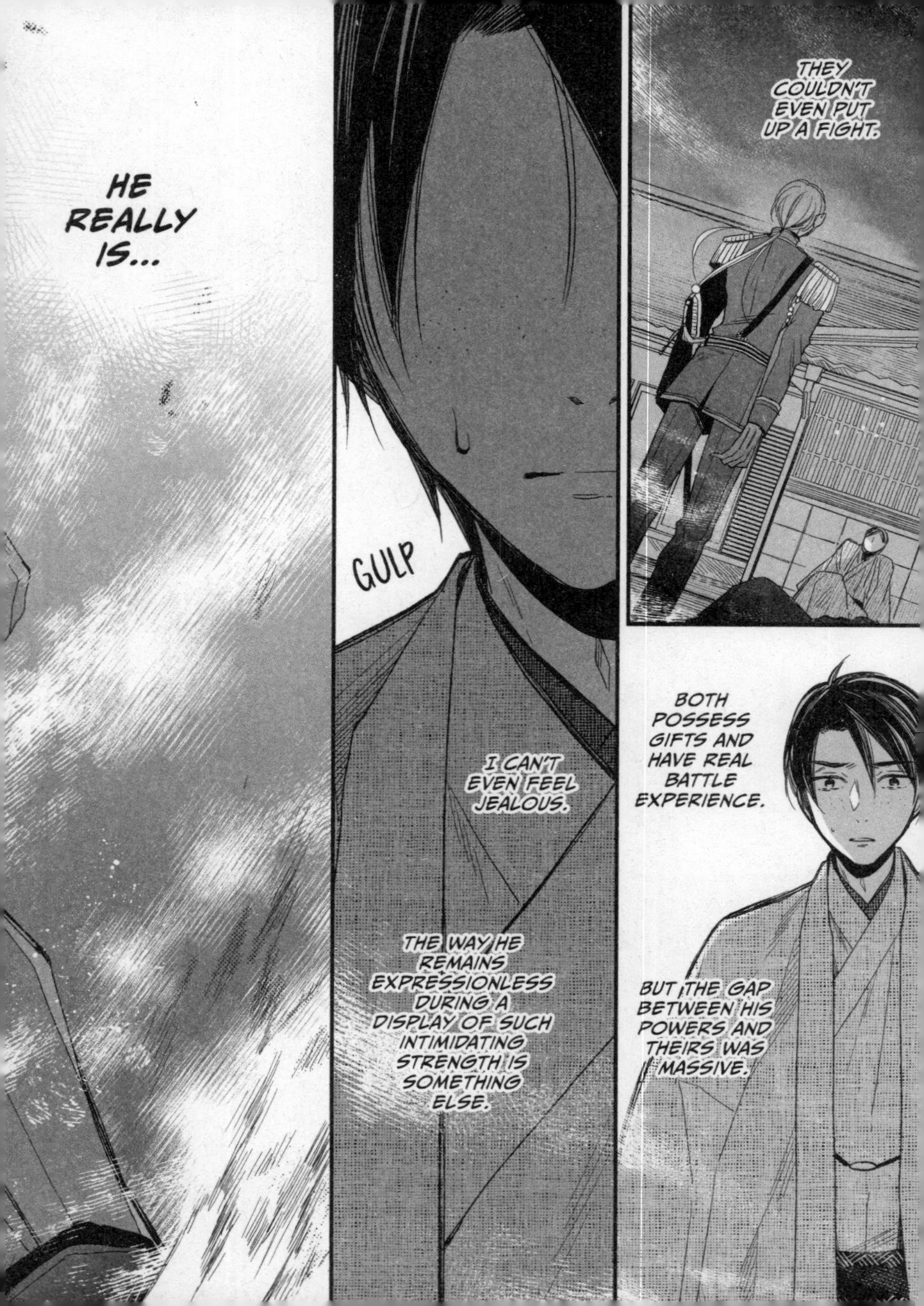
THEY COULDN'T EVEN PUT UP A FIGHT.
BOTH POSSESS GIFTS AND HAVE REAL BATTLE EXPERIENCE.
BUT THE GAP BETWEEN HIS POWERS AND THEIRS WAS MASSIVE.
GULP
I CAN'T EVEN FEEL JEALOUS.
THE WAY HE REMAINS EXPRESSIONLESS DURING A DISPLAY OF SUCH INTIMIDATING STRENGTH IS SOMETHING ELSE.
HE REALLY IS...

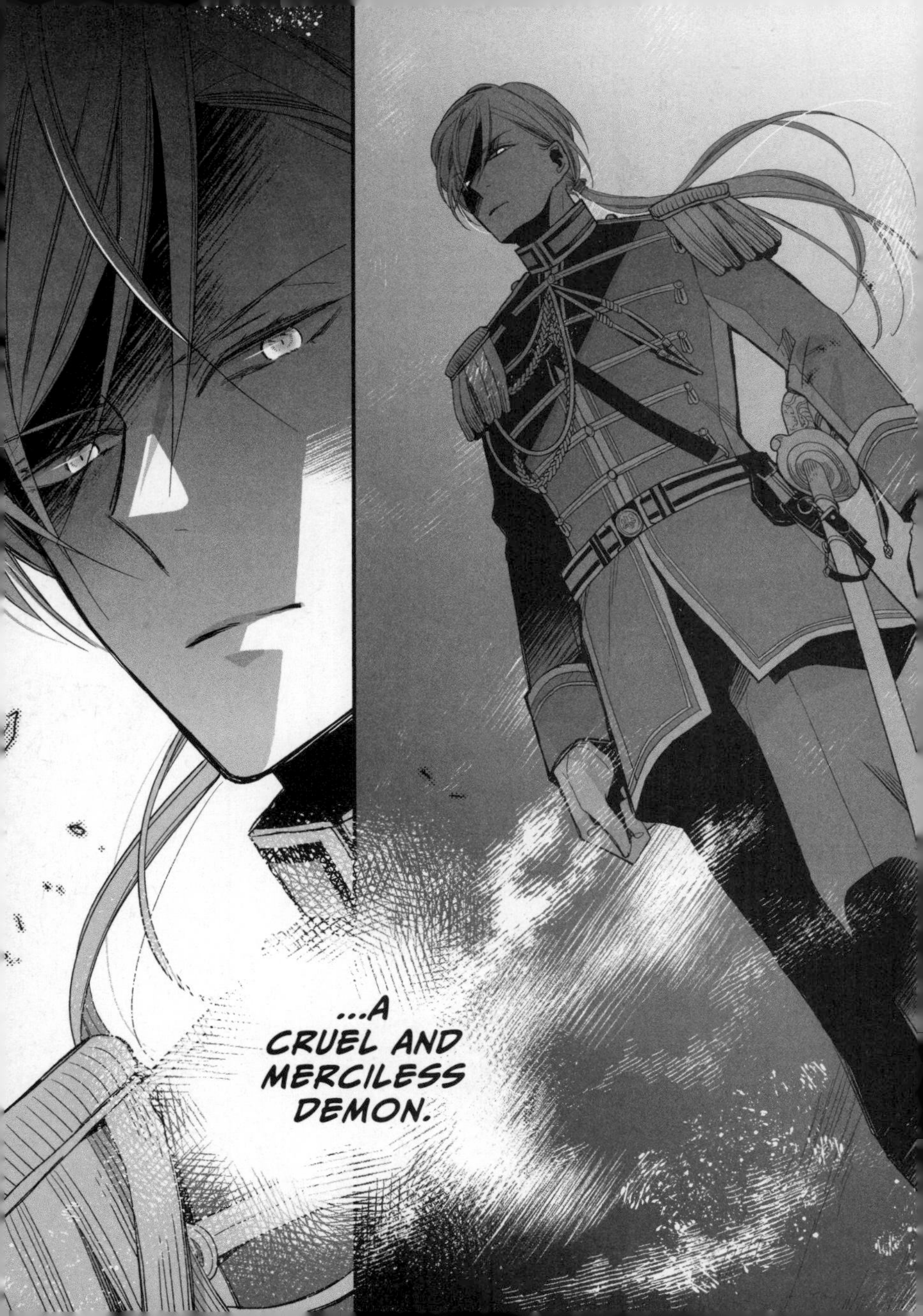
...A CRUEL AND MERCILESS DEMON.

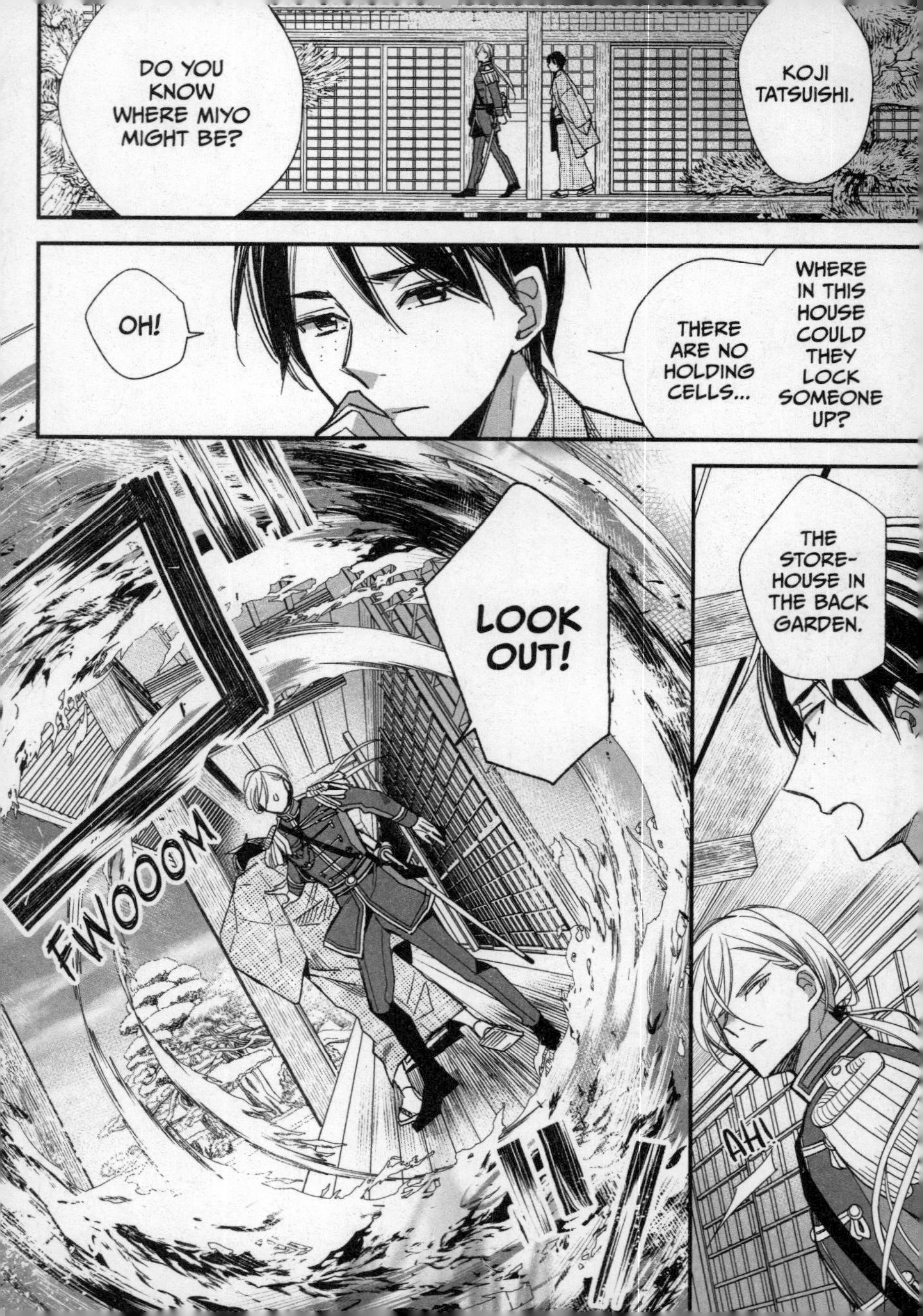
KOJI TATSUISHI.
DO YOU KNOW WHERE MIYO MIGHT BE?
WHERE IN THIS HOUSE COULD THEY LOCK SOMEONE UP?
THERE ARE NO HOLDING CELLS...
OH!
THE STOREHOUSE IN THE BACK GARDEN.
AH!
LOOK OUT!
FWOOOM

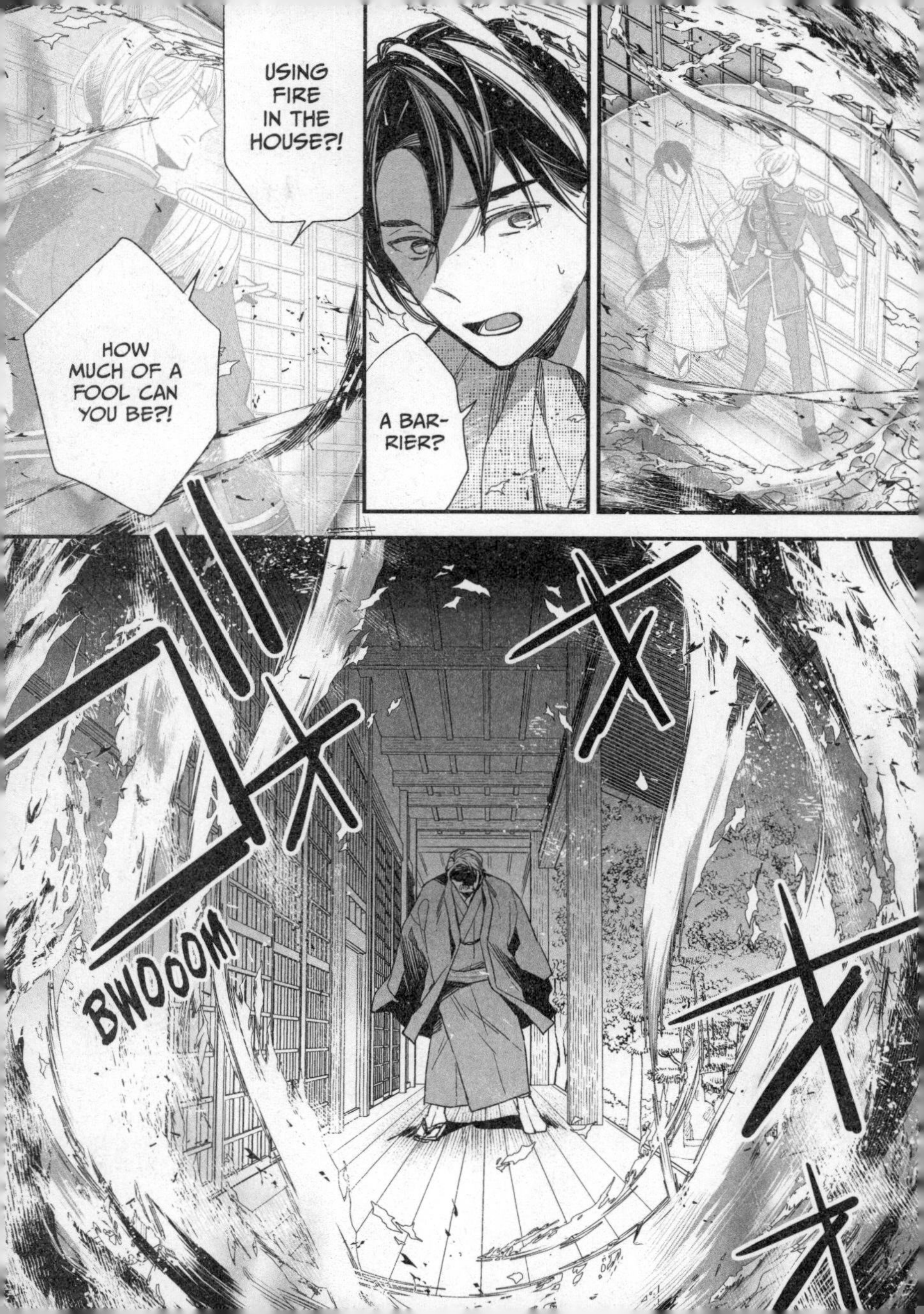
A BARRIER?
USING FIRE IN THE HOUSE?!
HOW MUCH OF A FOOL CAN YOU BE?!
BWOOOM

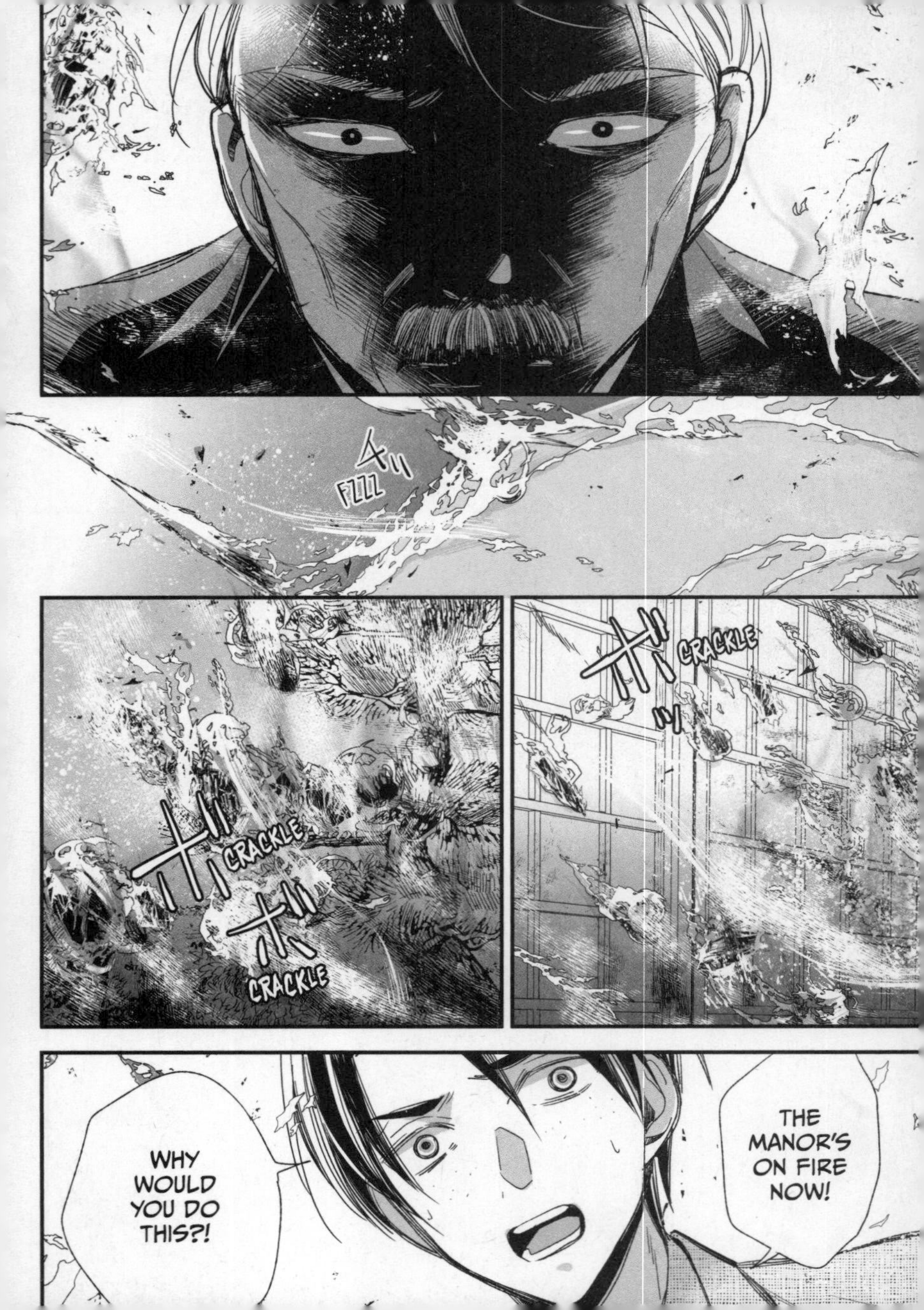
FZZZ
CRACKLE
CRACKLE
CRACKLE
THE MANOR'S ON FIRE NOW!
WHY WOULD YOU DO THIS?!

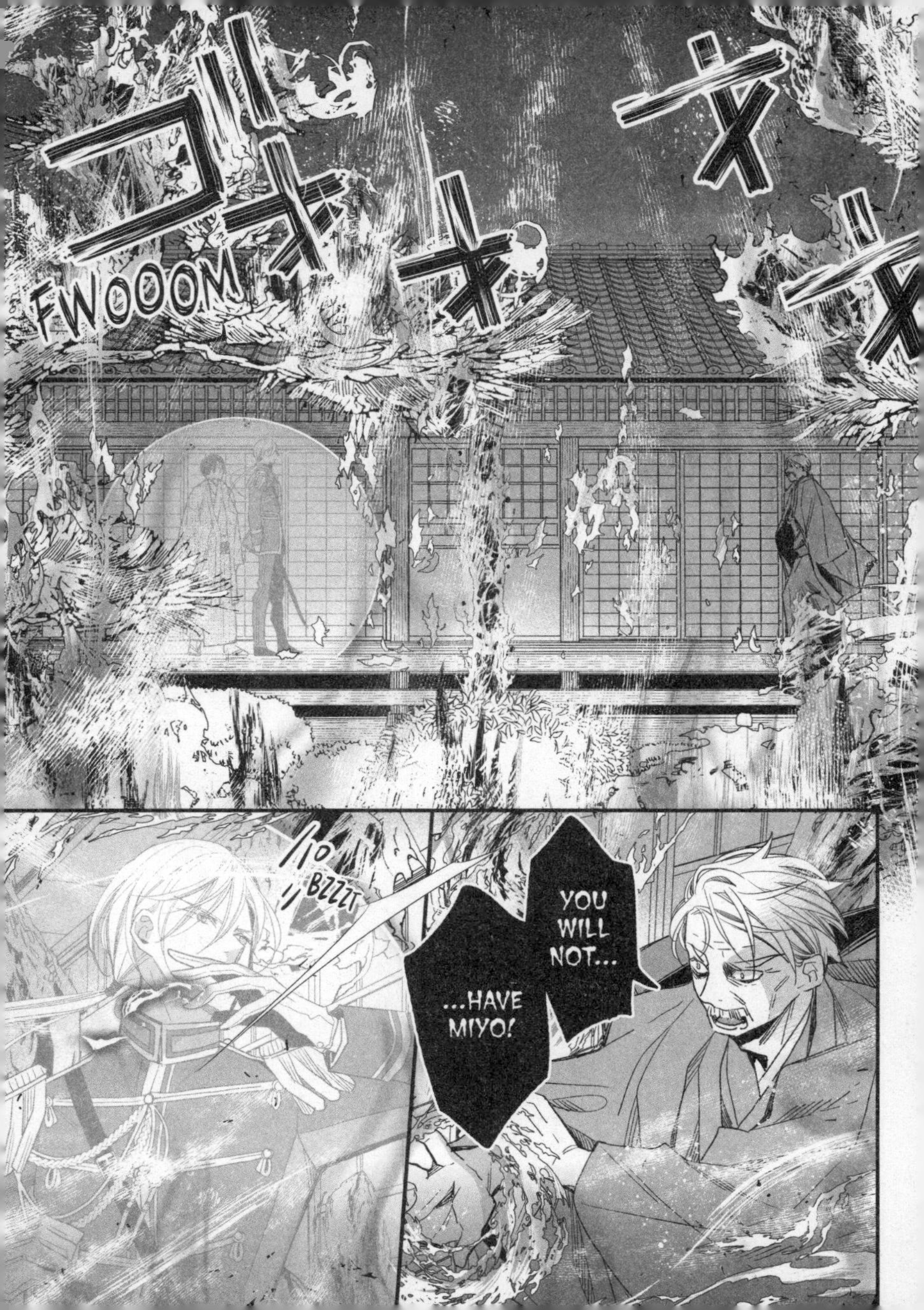
FWOOOM
YOU WILL NOT...
...HAVE MIYO!
BZZZT

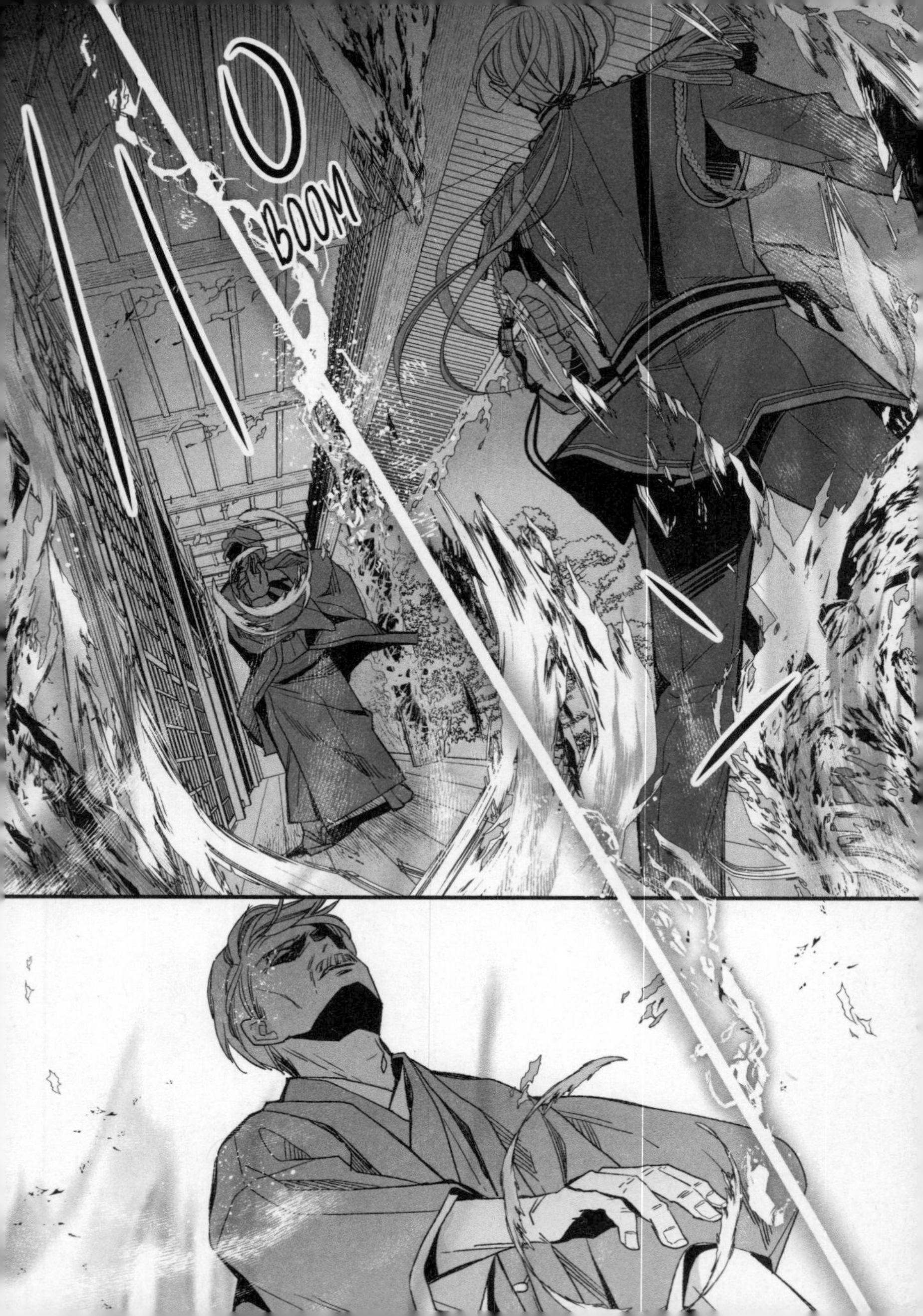
BOOM

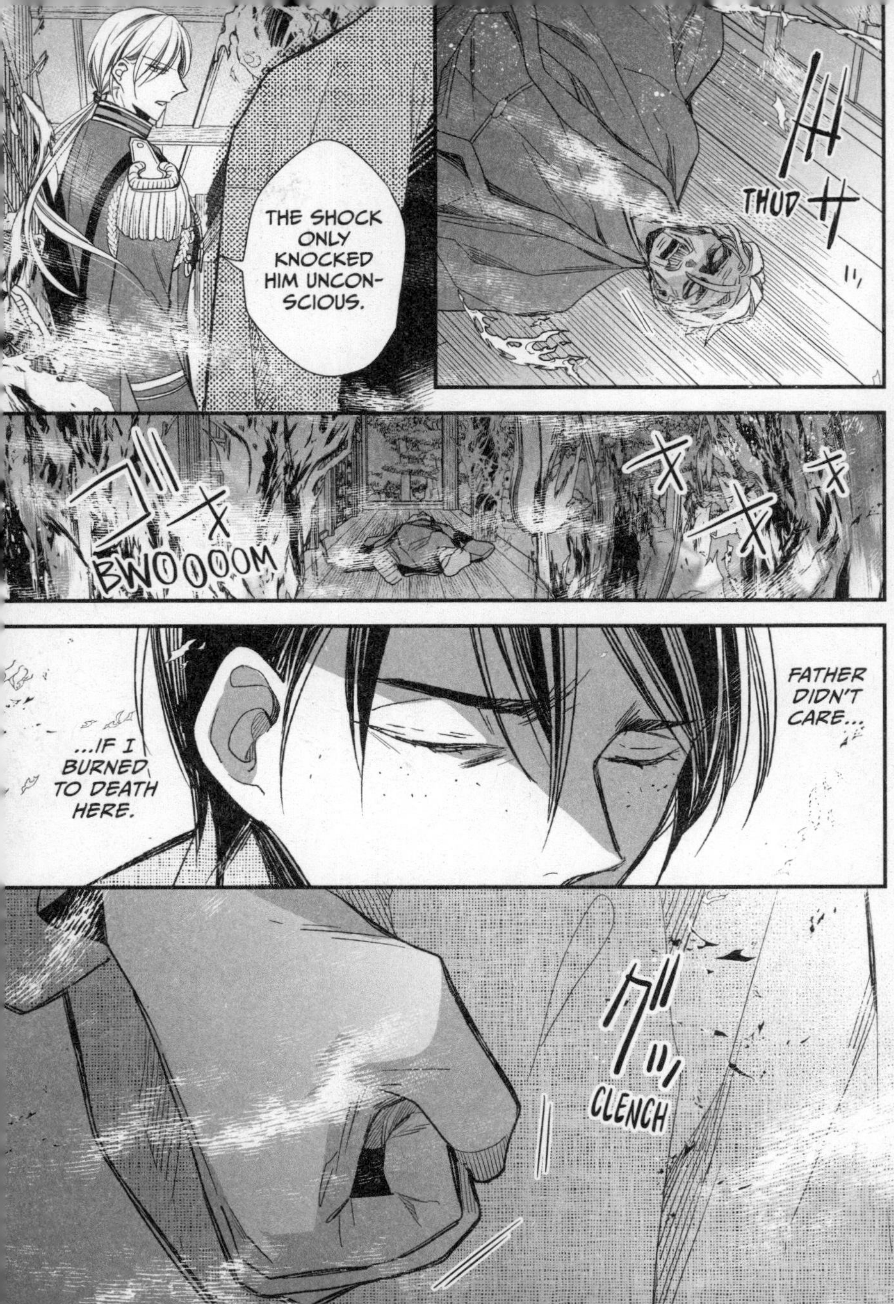
THUD
THE SHOCK ONLY KNOCKED HIM UNCONSCIOUS.
BWOOOOM
FATHER DIDN'T CARE...
...IF I BURNED TO DEATH HERE.
CLENCH

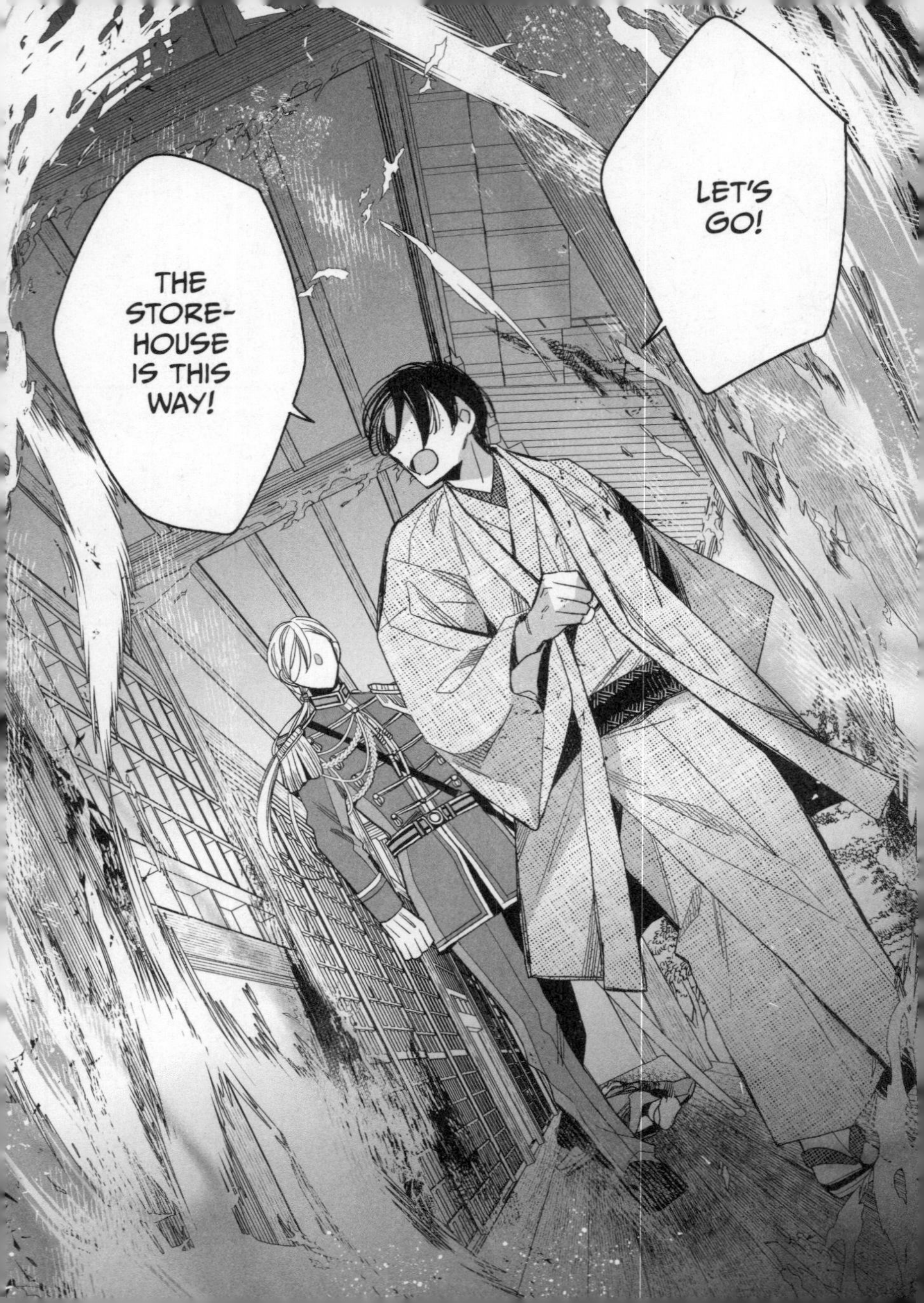
LET'S GO!
THE STORE-HOUSE IS THIS WAY!

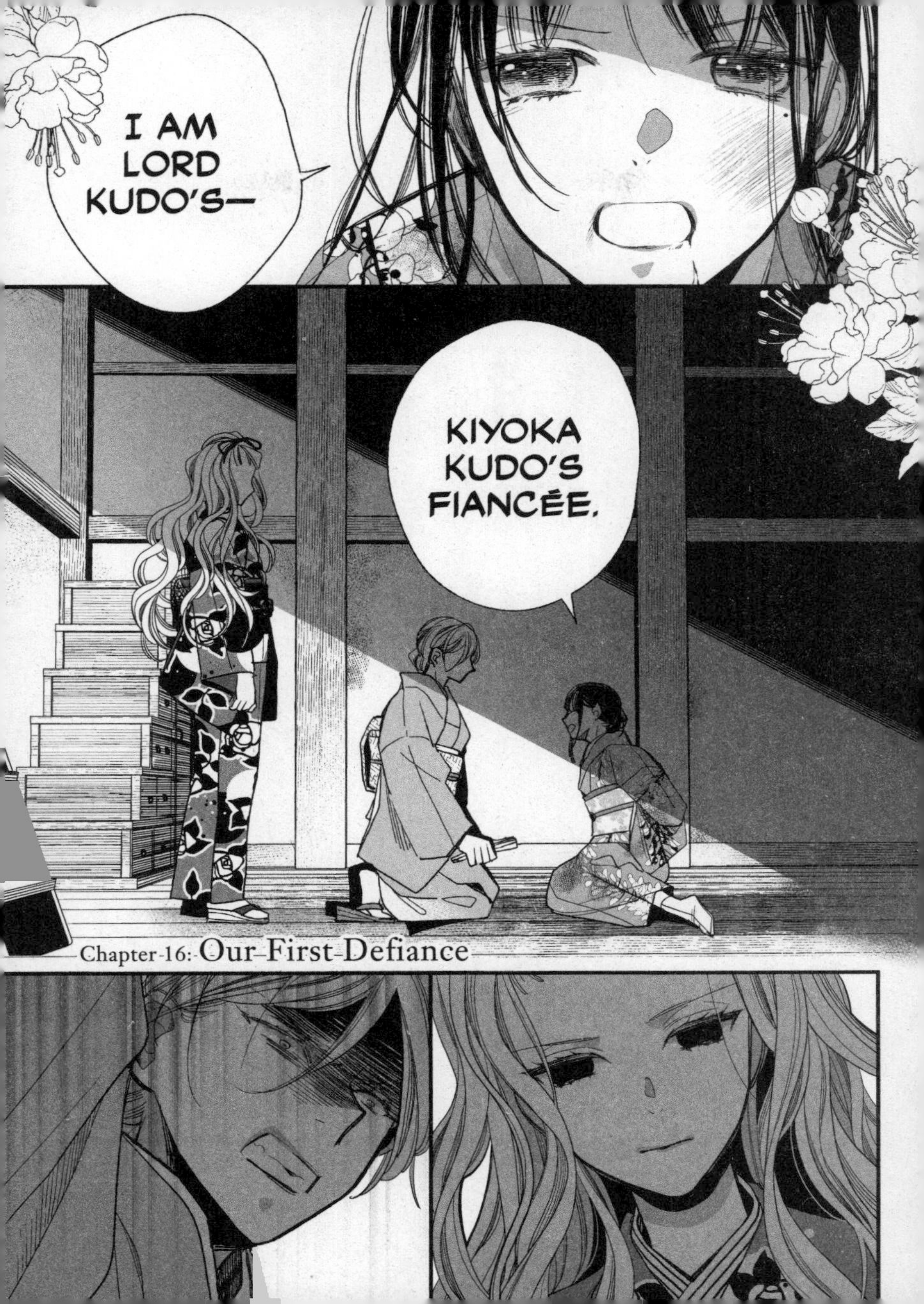
I AM LORD KUDO'S—
KIYOKA KUDO'S FIANCÉE.
Chapter 16: Our First Defiance

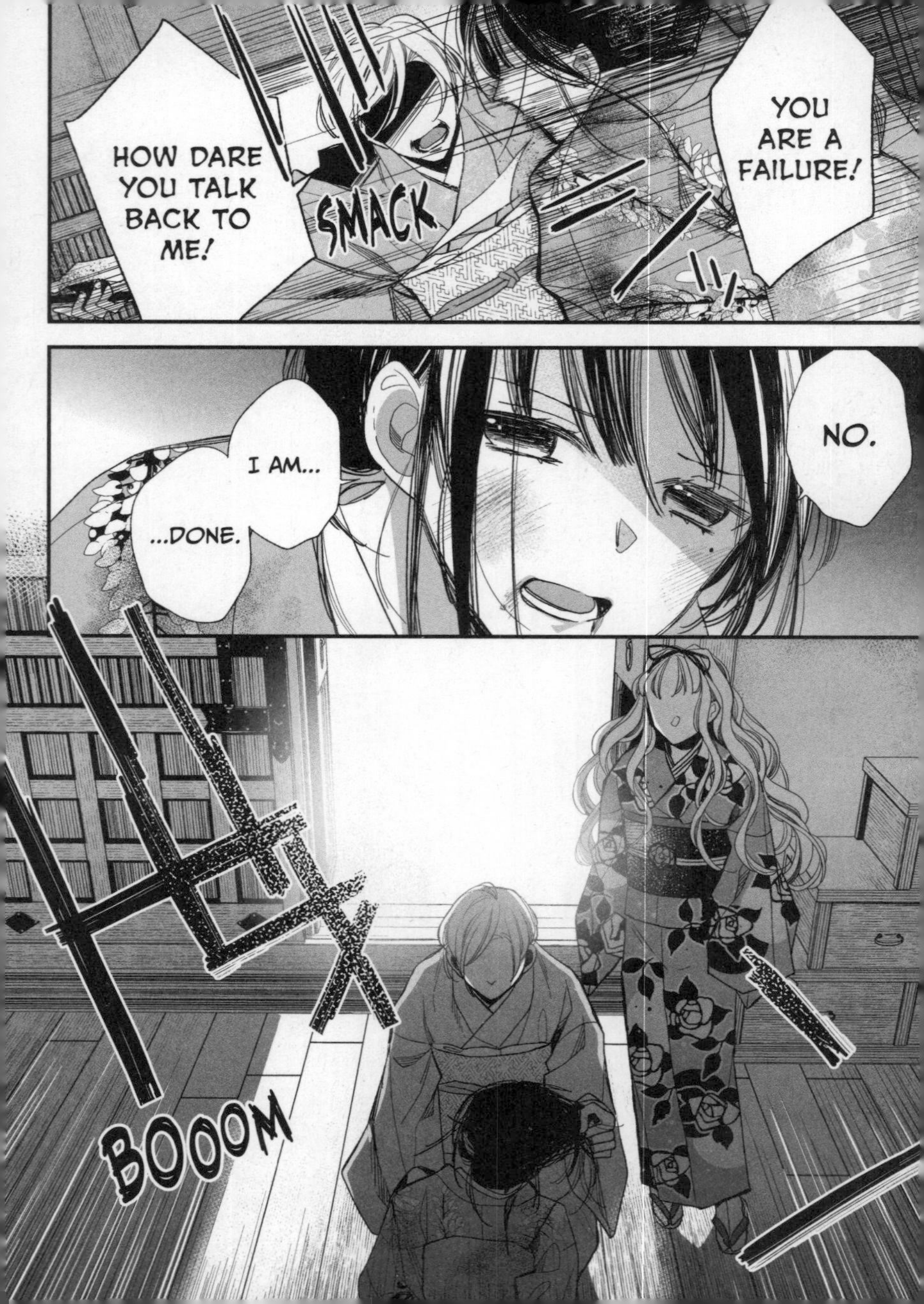
YOU ARE A FAILURE!
SMACK
HOW DARE YOU TALK BACK TO ME!
NO.
I AM...
...DONE.
BOOOM

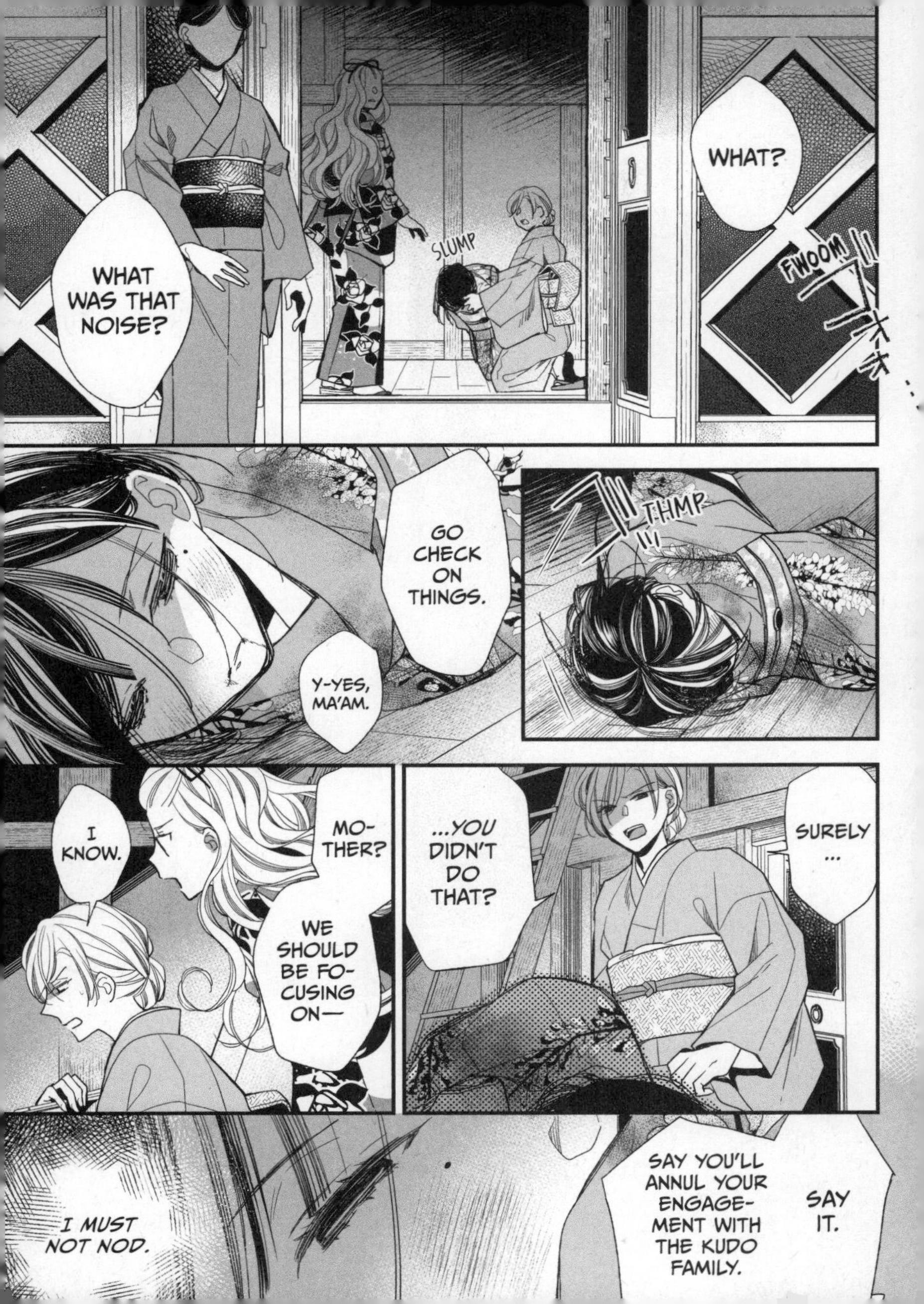
WHAT?
FWOOM
SLUMP
WHAT WAS THAT NOISE?
THMP
GO CHECK ON THINGS.
Y-YES, MA'AM.
SURELY...
...YOU DIDN'T DO THAT?
MO-THER?
WE SHOULD BE FO-CUSING ON—
I KNOW.
SAY IT.
SAY YOU'LL ANNUL YOUR ENGAGE-MENT WITH THE KUDO FAMILY.
I MUST NOT NOD.

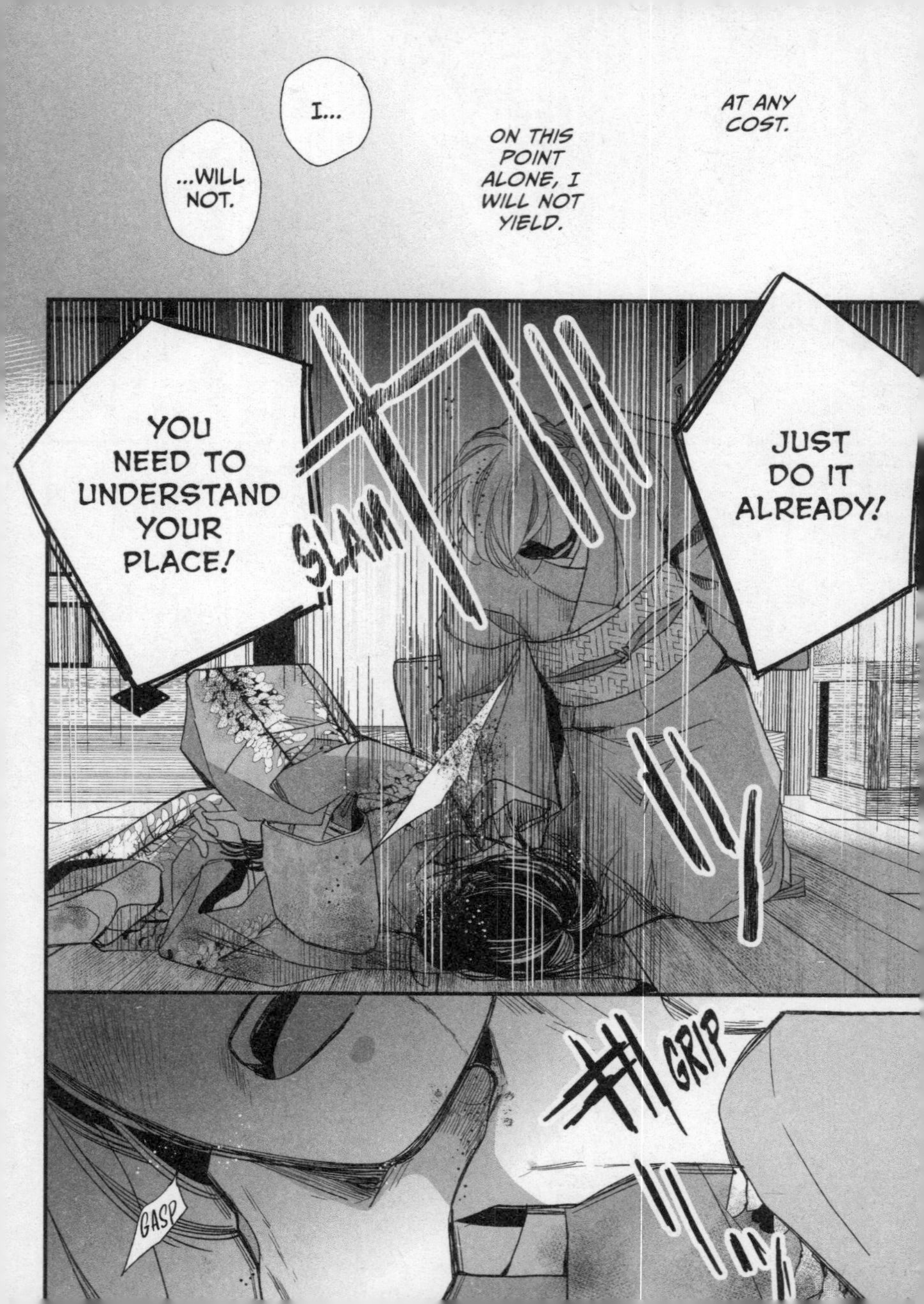
I...
...WILL NOT.
ON THIS POINT ALONE, I WILL NOT YIELD.
AT ANY COST.
JUST DO IT ALREADY!
SLAM
YOU NEED TO UNDERSTAND YOUR PLACE!
GRIP
GASP

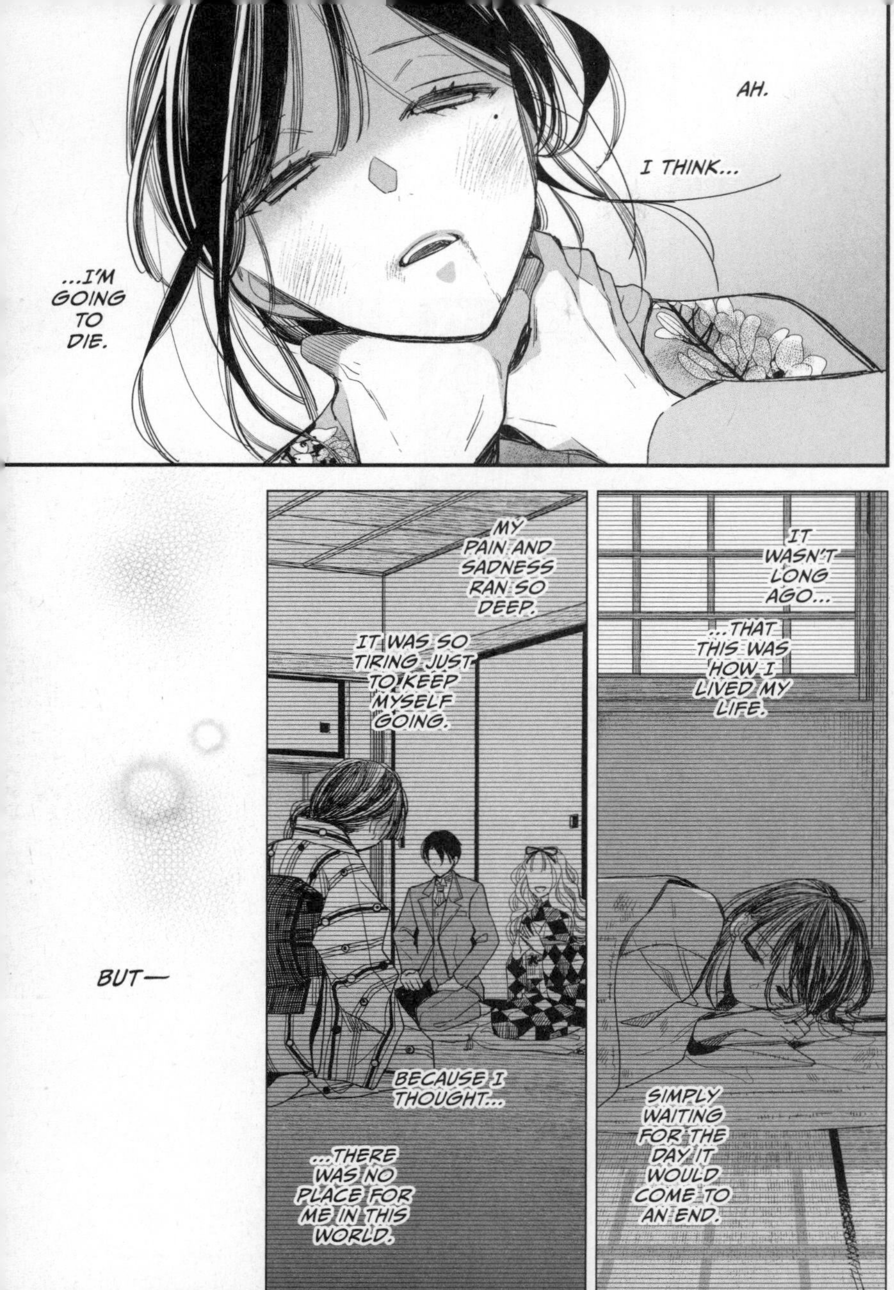
AH.
I THINK...
...I'M GOING TO DIE.
IT WASN'T LONG AGO...
...THAT THIS WAS HOW I LIVED MY LIFE.
SIMPLY WAITING FOR THE DAY IT WOULD COME TO AN END.
MY PAIN AND SADNESS RAN SO DEEP.
IT WAS SO TIRING JUST TO KEEP MYSELF GOING.
BECAUSE I THOUGHT...
...THERE WAS NO PLACE FOR ME IN THIS WORLD.
BUT—

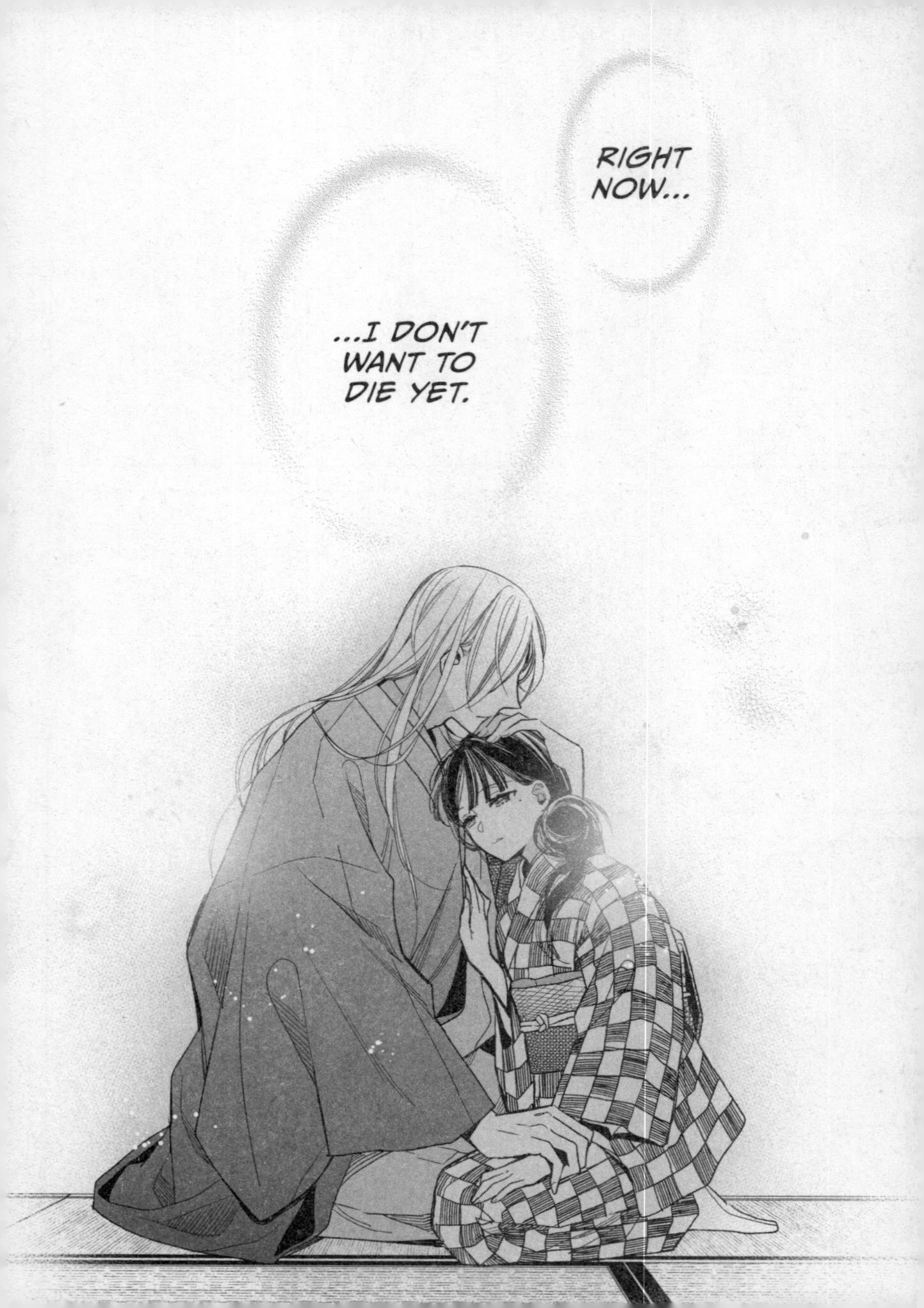
RIGHT NOW...
...I DON'T WANT TO DIE YET.

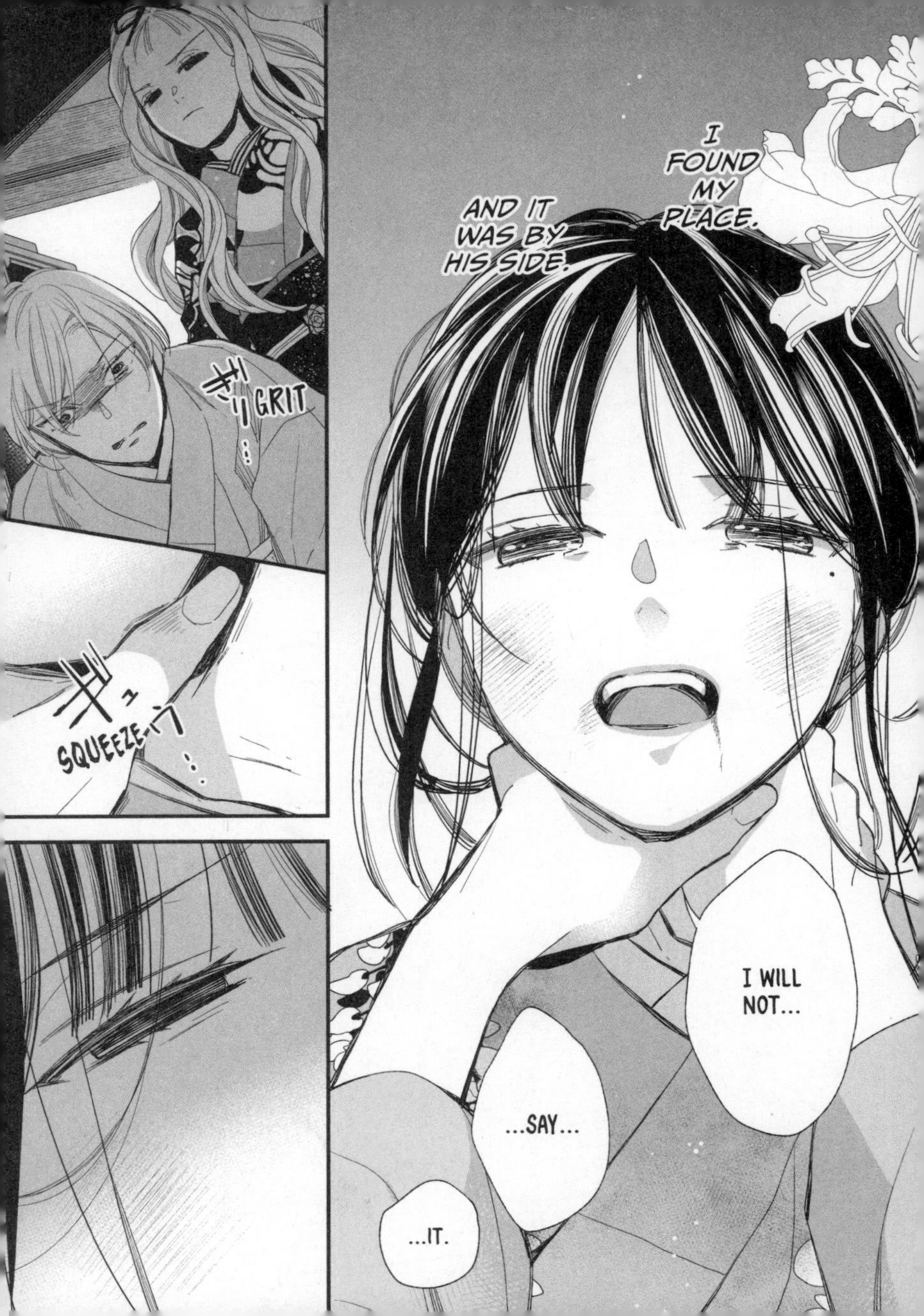
I FOUND MY PLACE.
AND IT WAS BY HIS SIDE.
I WILL NOT...
...SAY...
...IT.
GRIT
SQUEEZE

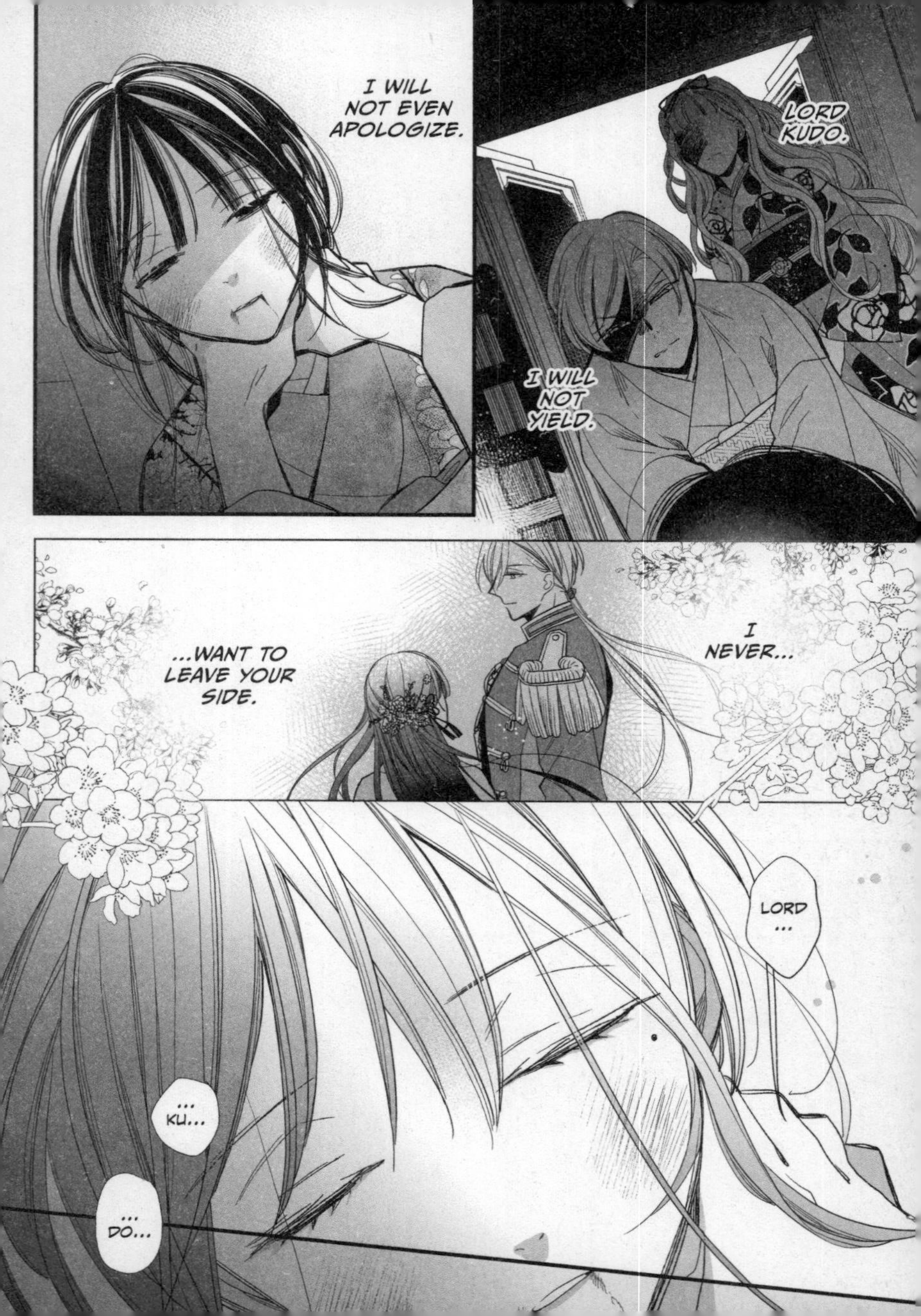
LORD KUDO.
I WILL NOT YIELD.
I WILL NOT EVEN APOLOGIZE.
I NEVER...
...WANT TO LEAVE YOUR SIDE.
LORD ...
... KU...
... DO...

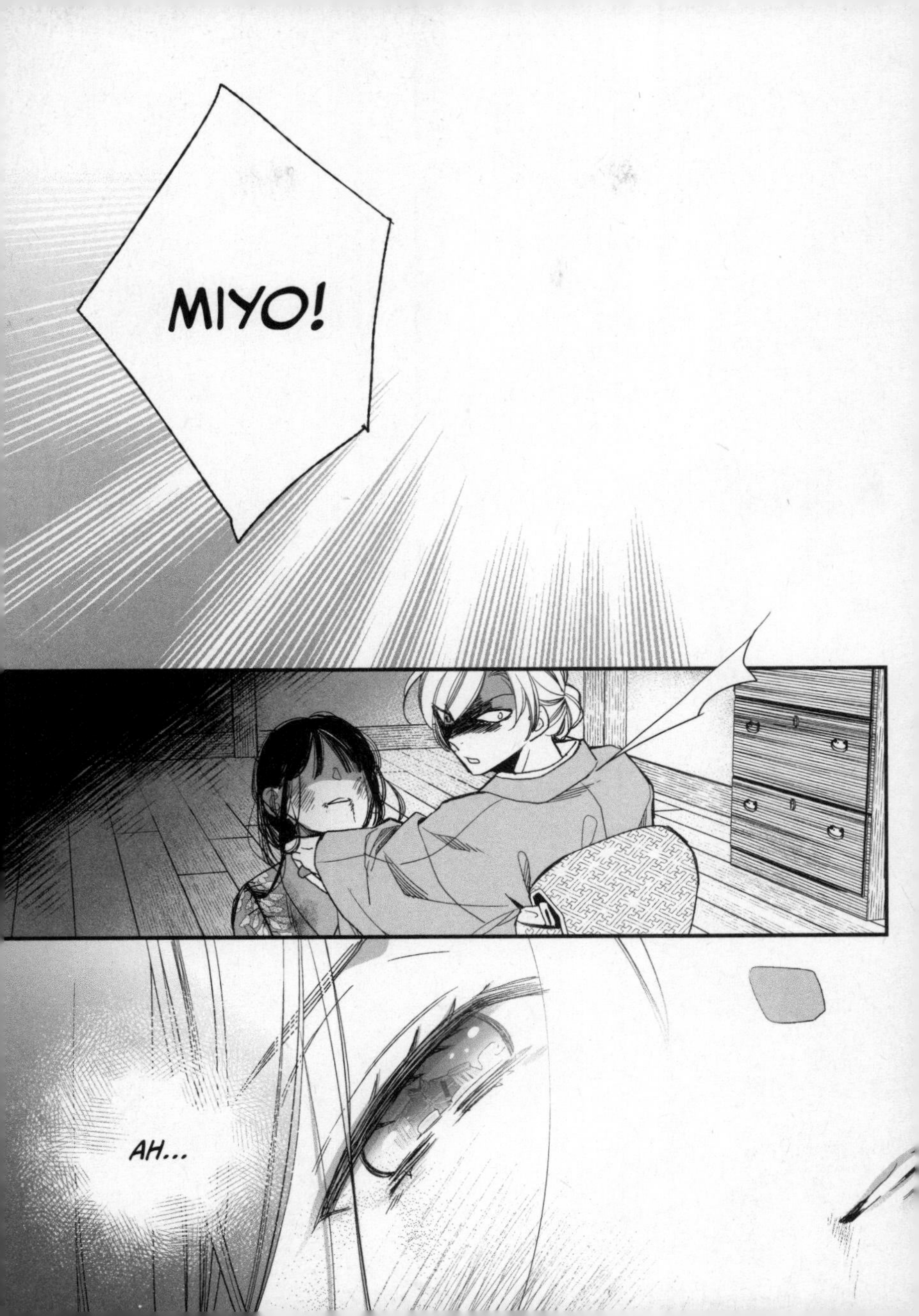
MIYO!
AH...

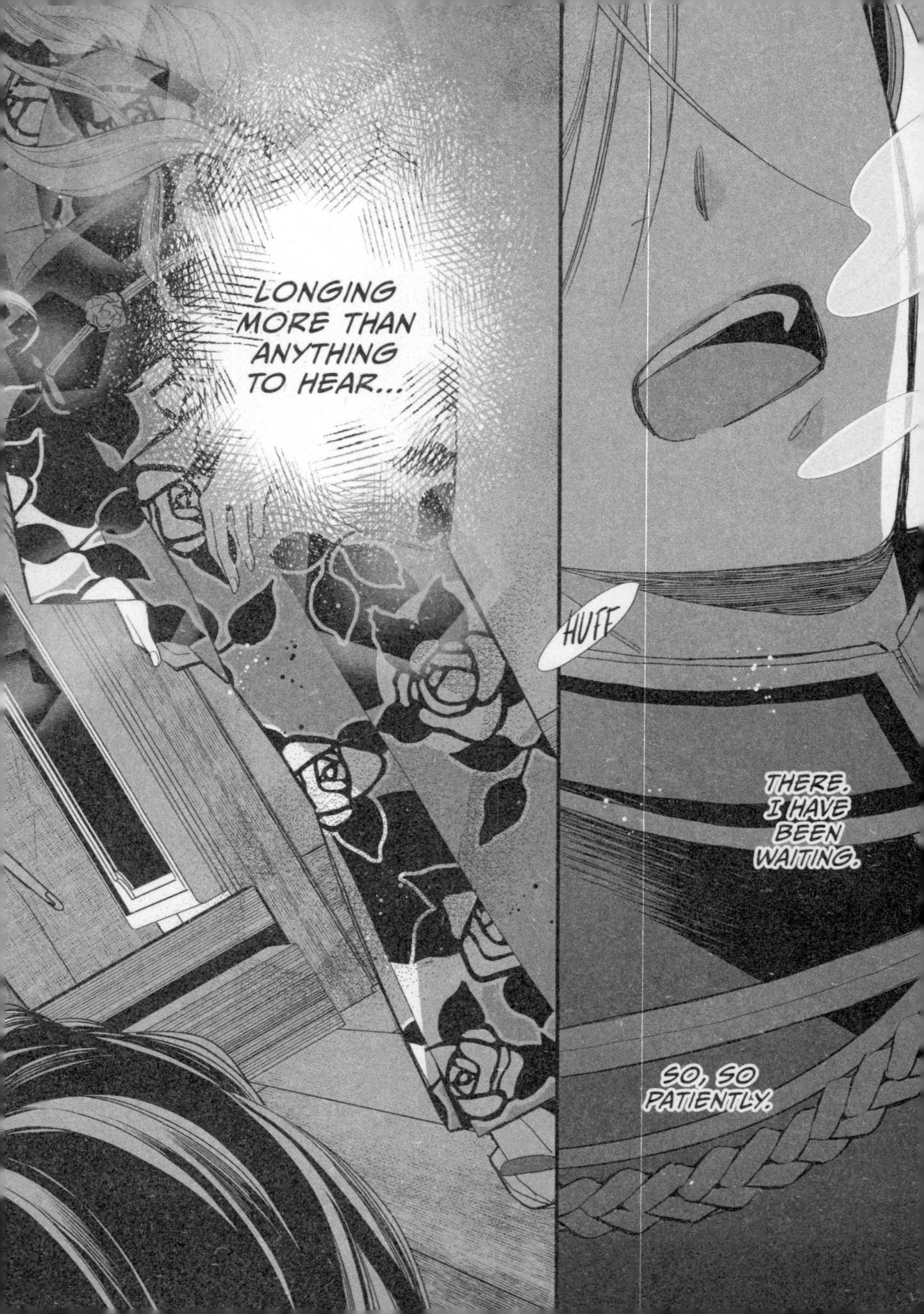
HUFF
THERE. I HAVE BEEN WAITING.
SO, SO PATIENTLY.
LONGING MORE THAN ANYTHING TO HEAR...

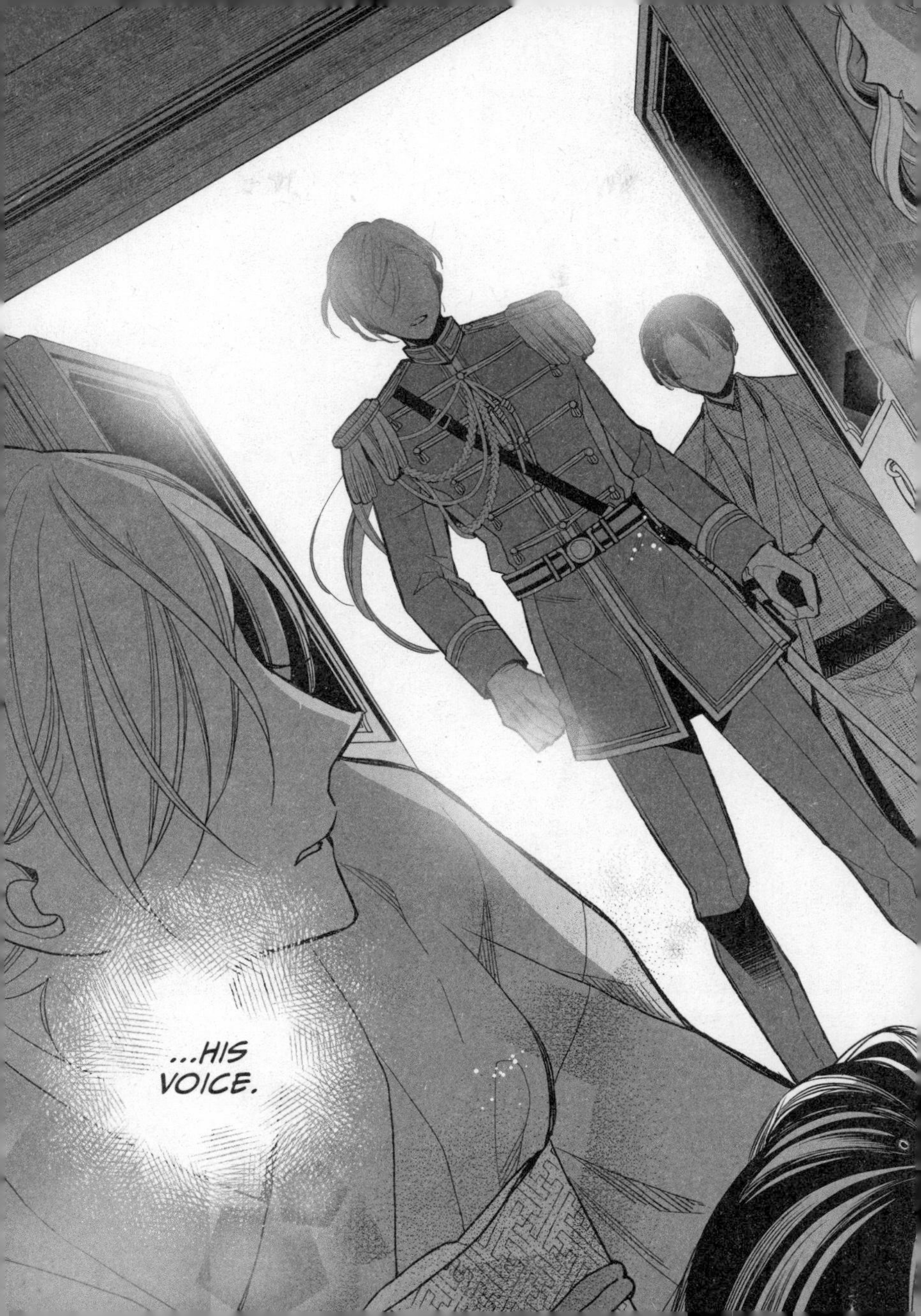
...HIS
VOICE.

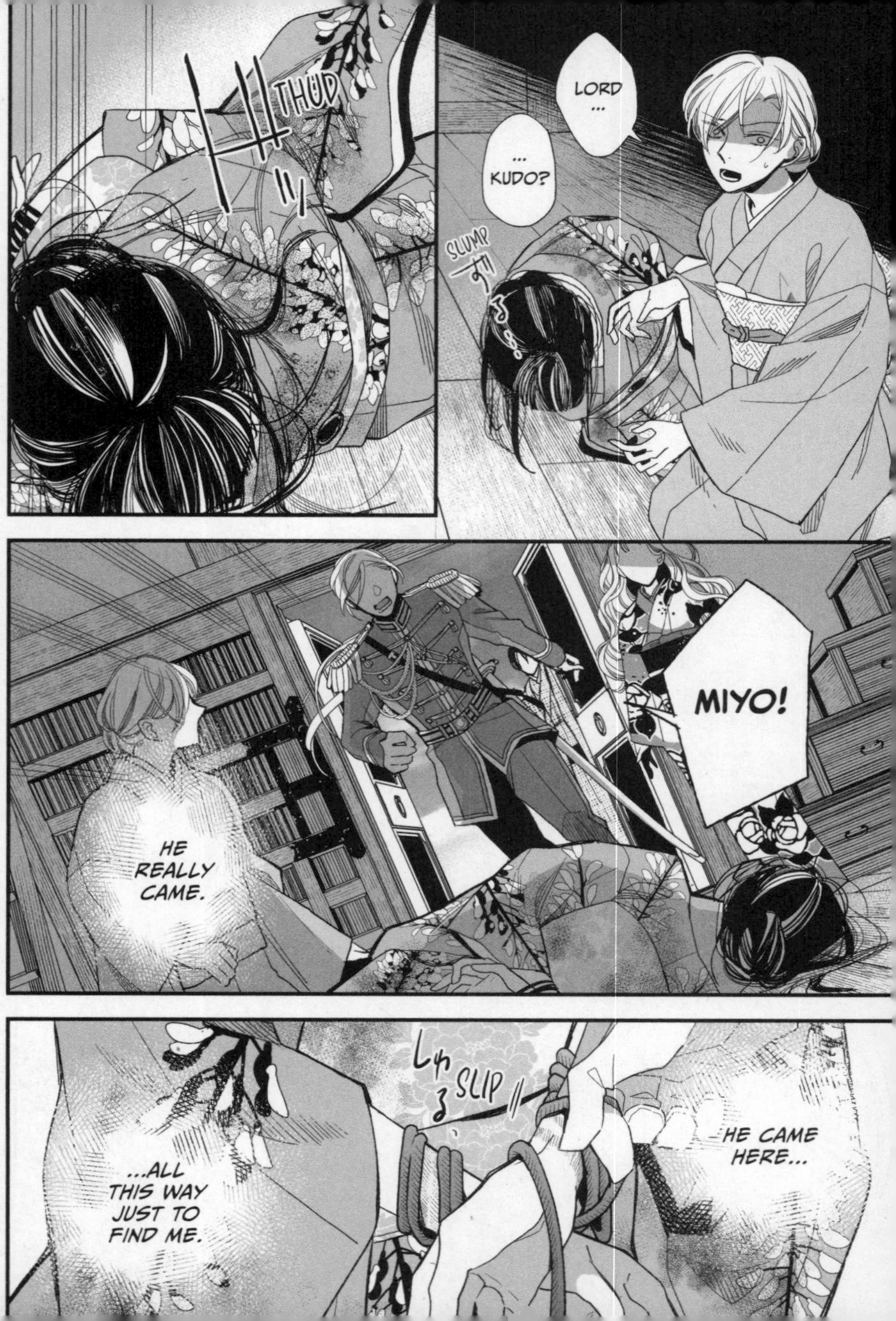
LORD ...
... KUDO?
SLUMP
THUD
MIYO!
HE REALLY CAME.
HE CAME HERE...
SLIP
...ALL THIS WAY JUST TO FIND ME.

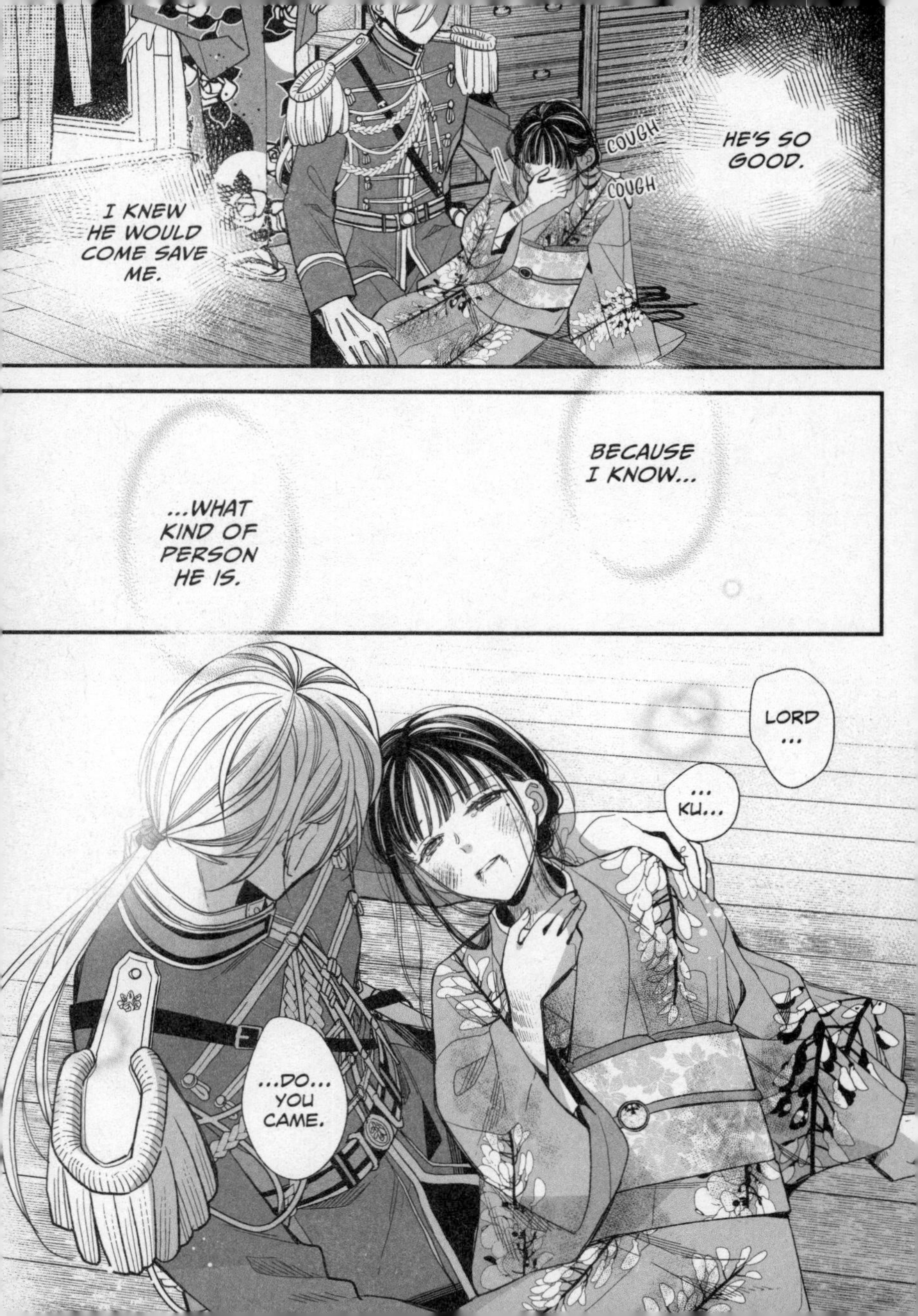
HE'S SO GOOD.
COUGH
COUGH
I KNEW HE WOULD COME SAVE ME.
BECAUSE I KNOW...
...WHAT KIND OF PERSON HE IS.
LORD...
...KU...
...DO... YOU CAME.

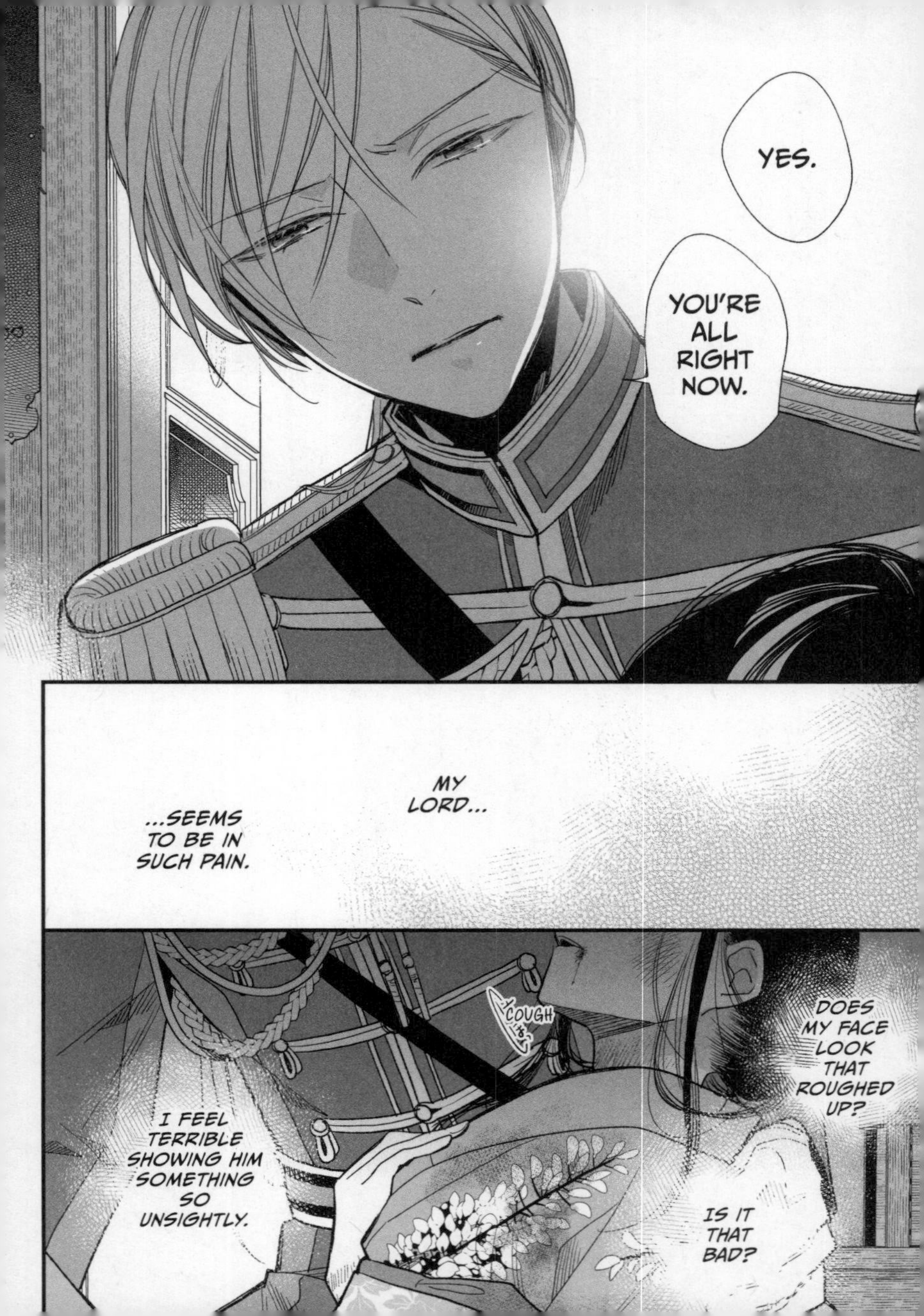
YES.
YOU'RE ALL RIGHT NOW.
MY LORD...
...SEEMS TO BE IN SUCH PAIN.
DOES MY FACE LOOK THAT ROUGHED UP?
COUGH
IS IT THAT BAD?
I FEEL TERRIBLE SHOWING HIM SOMETHING SO UNSIGHTLY.

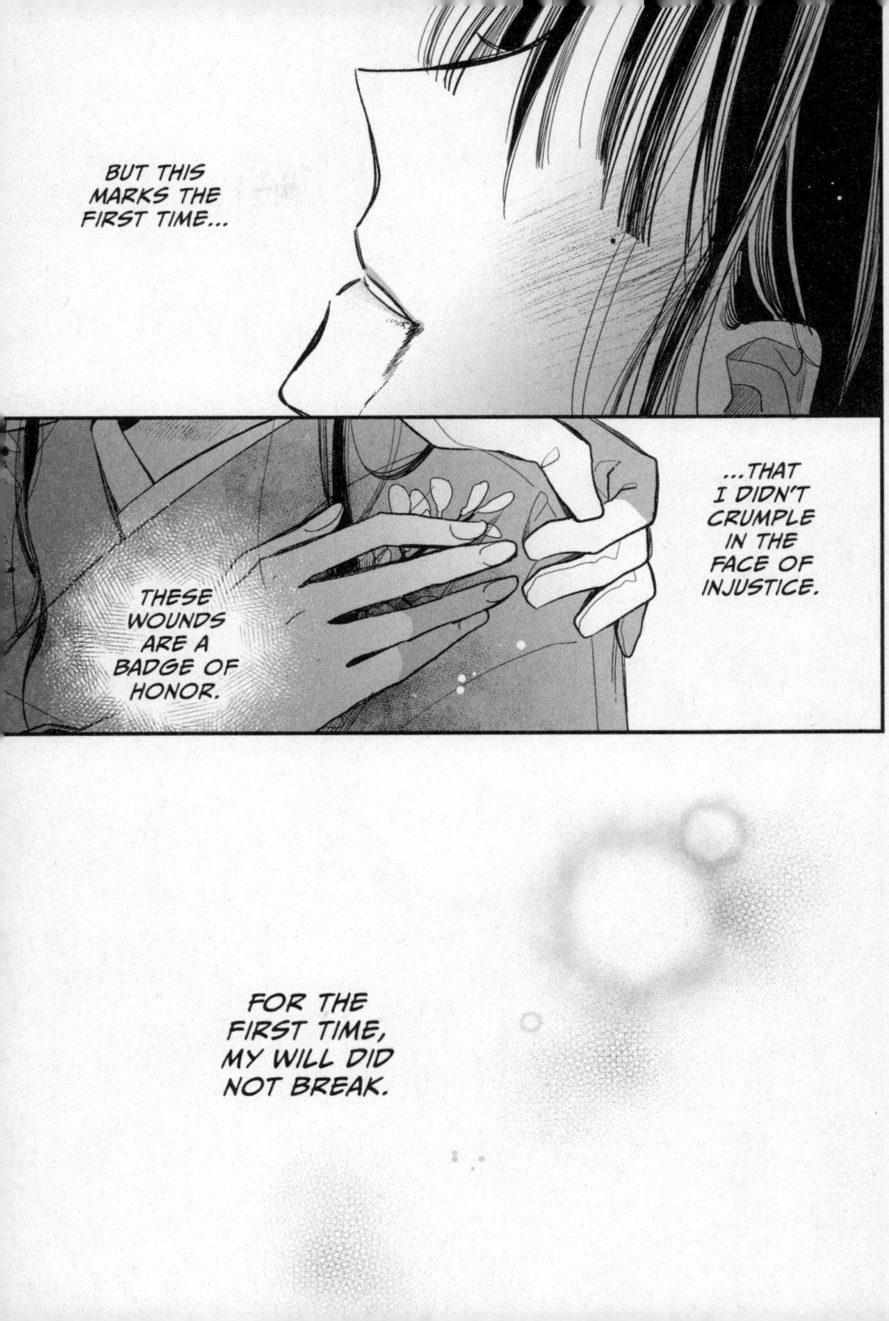
BUT THIS MARKS THE FIRST TIME...
...THAT I DIDN'T CRUMPLE IN THE FACE OF INJUSTICE.
THESE WOUNDS ARE A BADGE OF HONOR.
FOR THE FIRST TIME, MY WILL DID NOT BREAK.

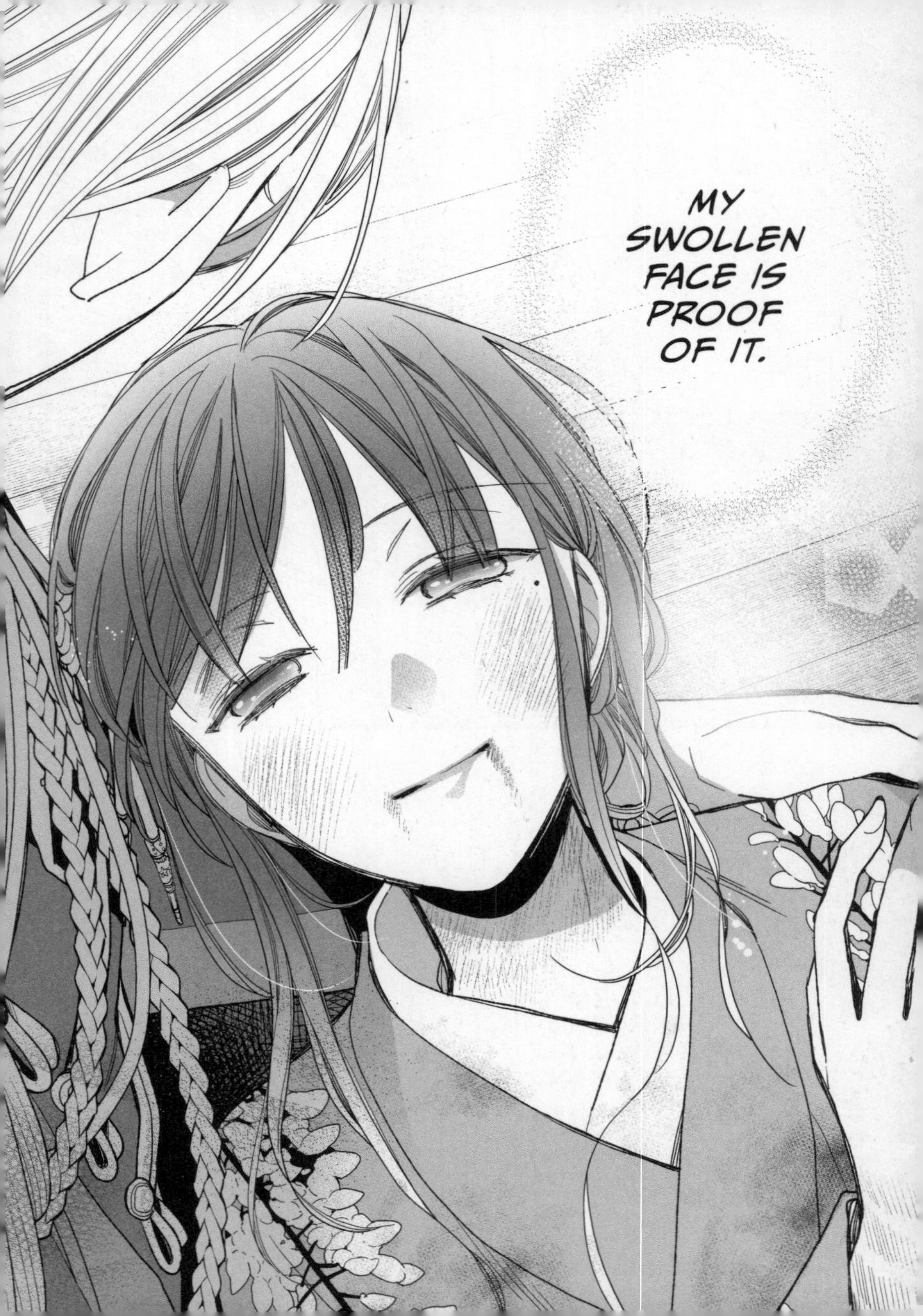
MY SWOLLEN FACE IS PROOF OF IT.

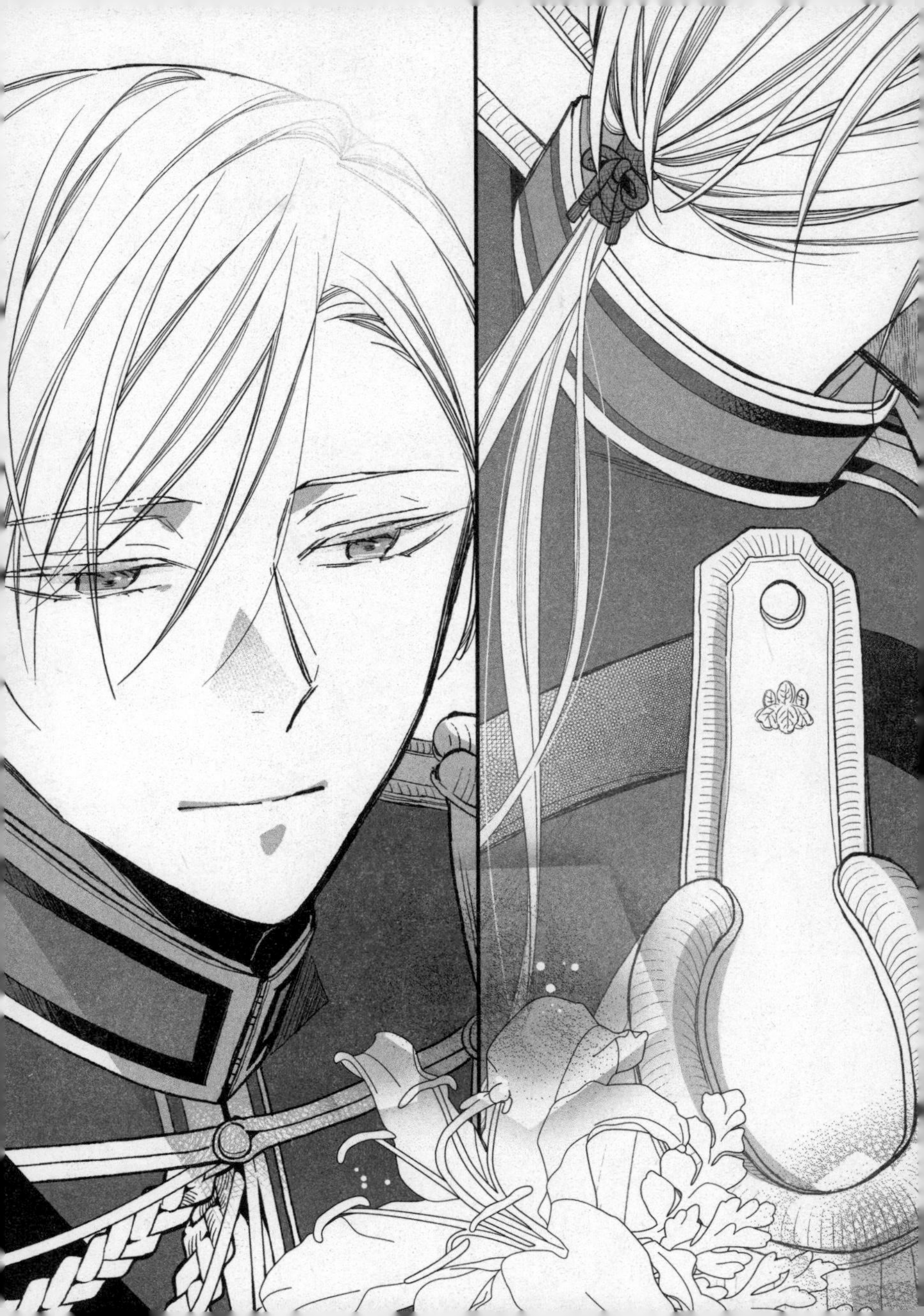

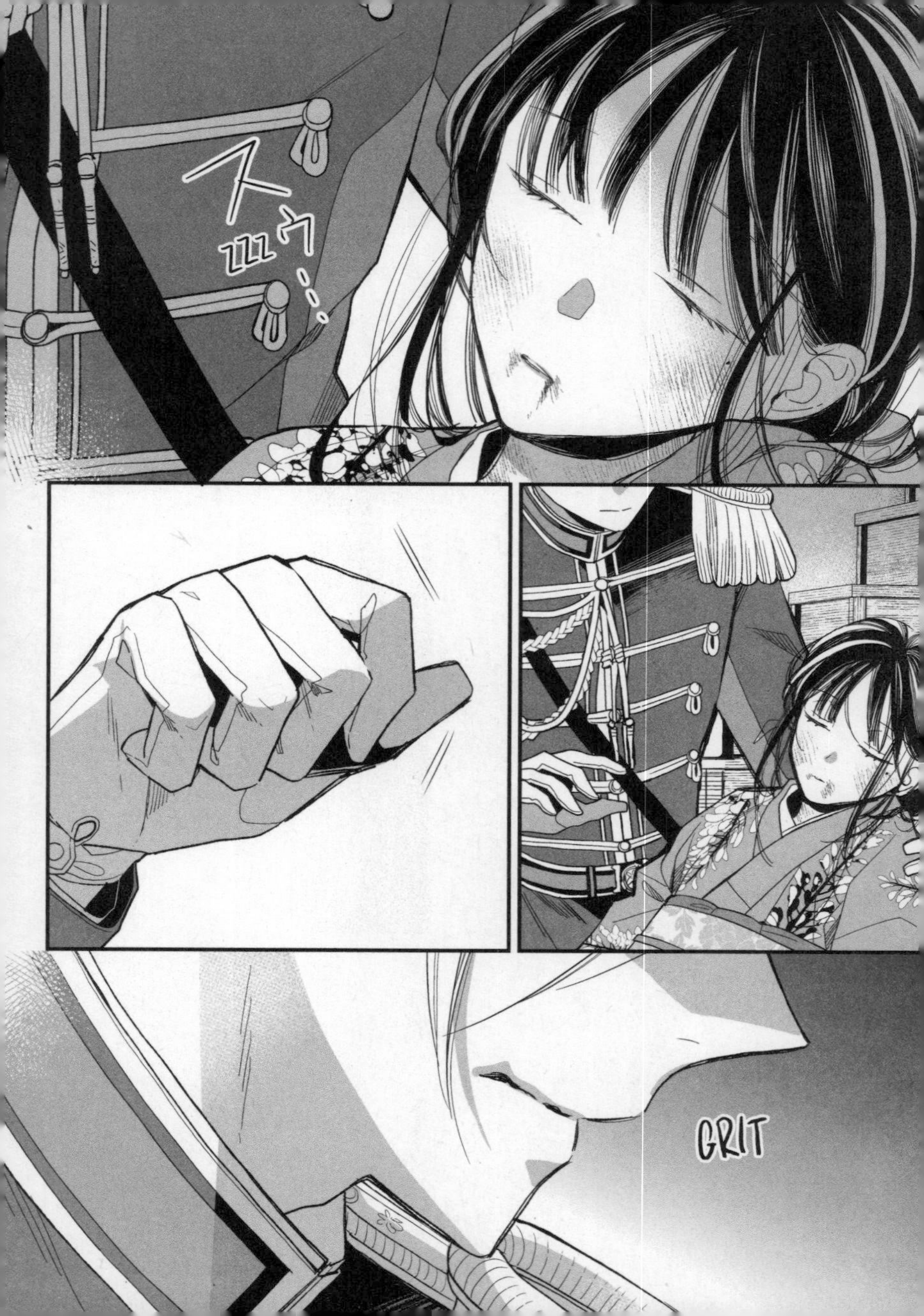
スゥ…
zzz
GRIT

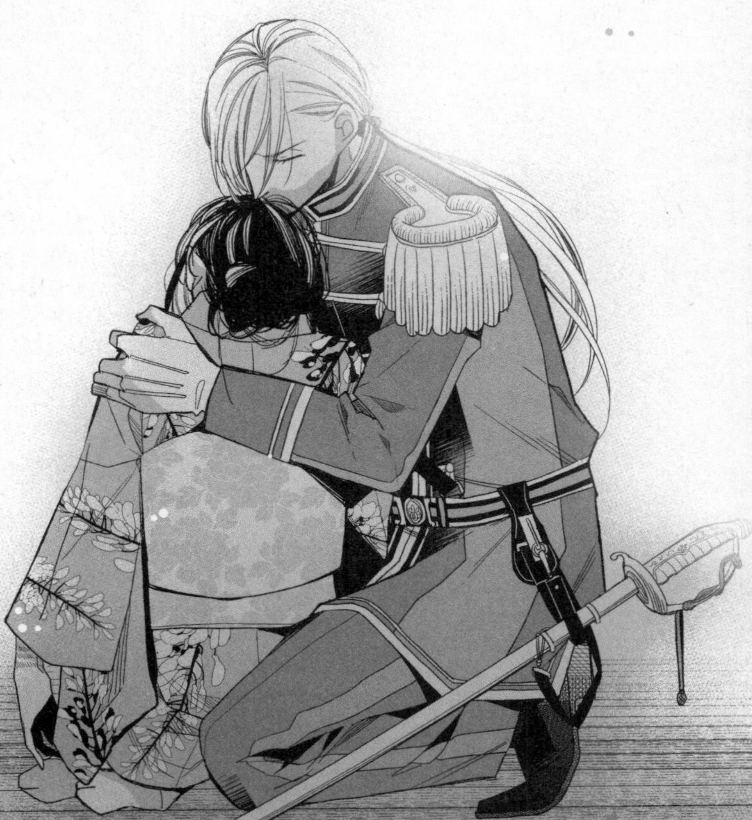

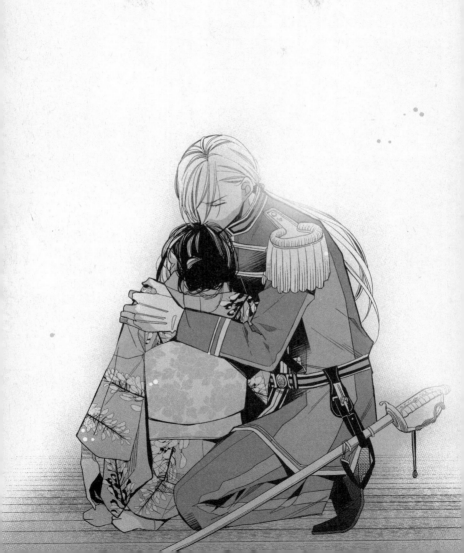

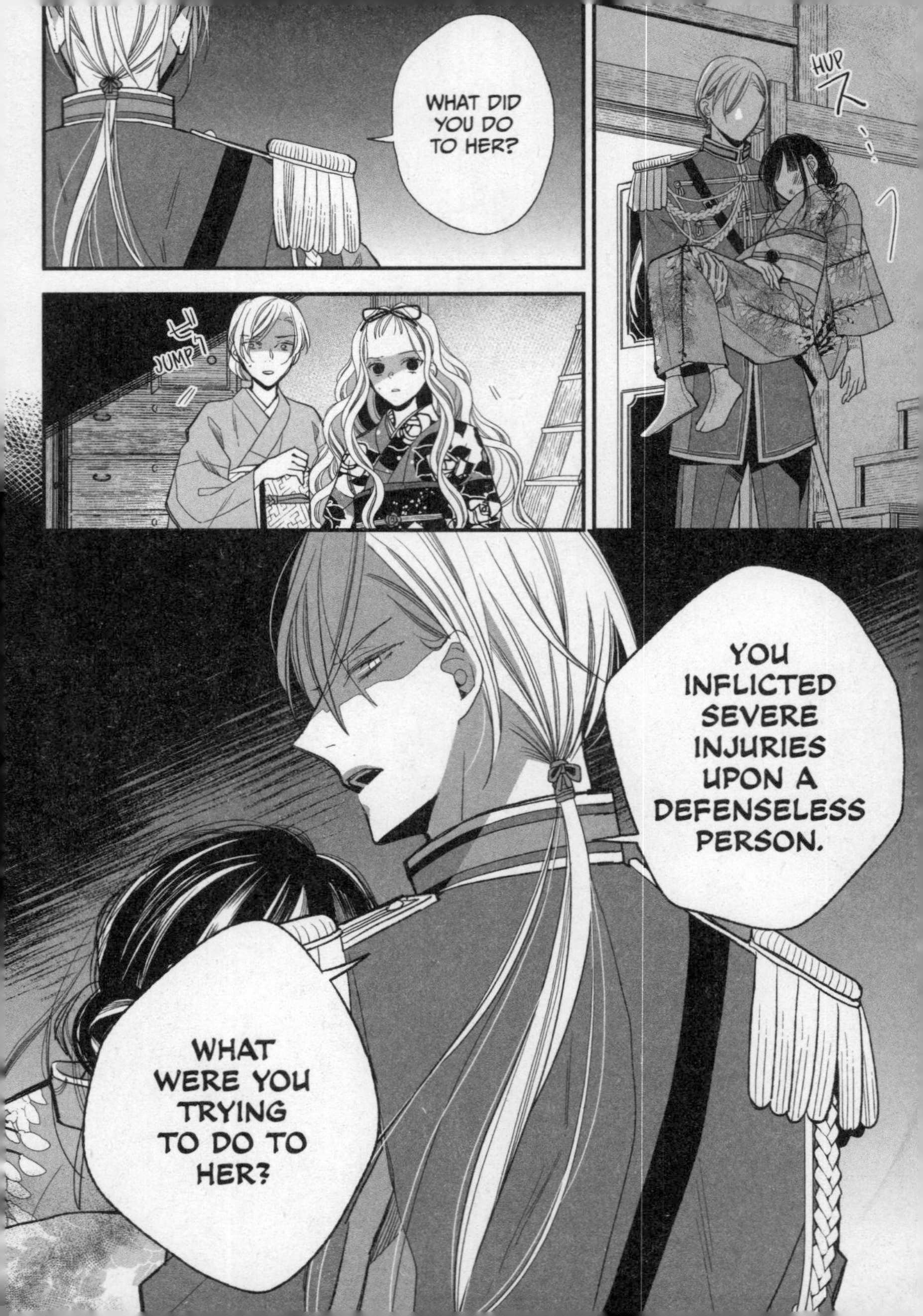
HUP
WHAT DID YOU DO TO HER?
JUMP
YOU INFLICTED SEVERE INJURIES UPON A DEFENSELESS PERSON.
WHAT WERE YOU TRYING TO DO TO HER?

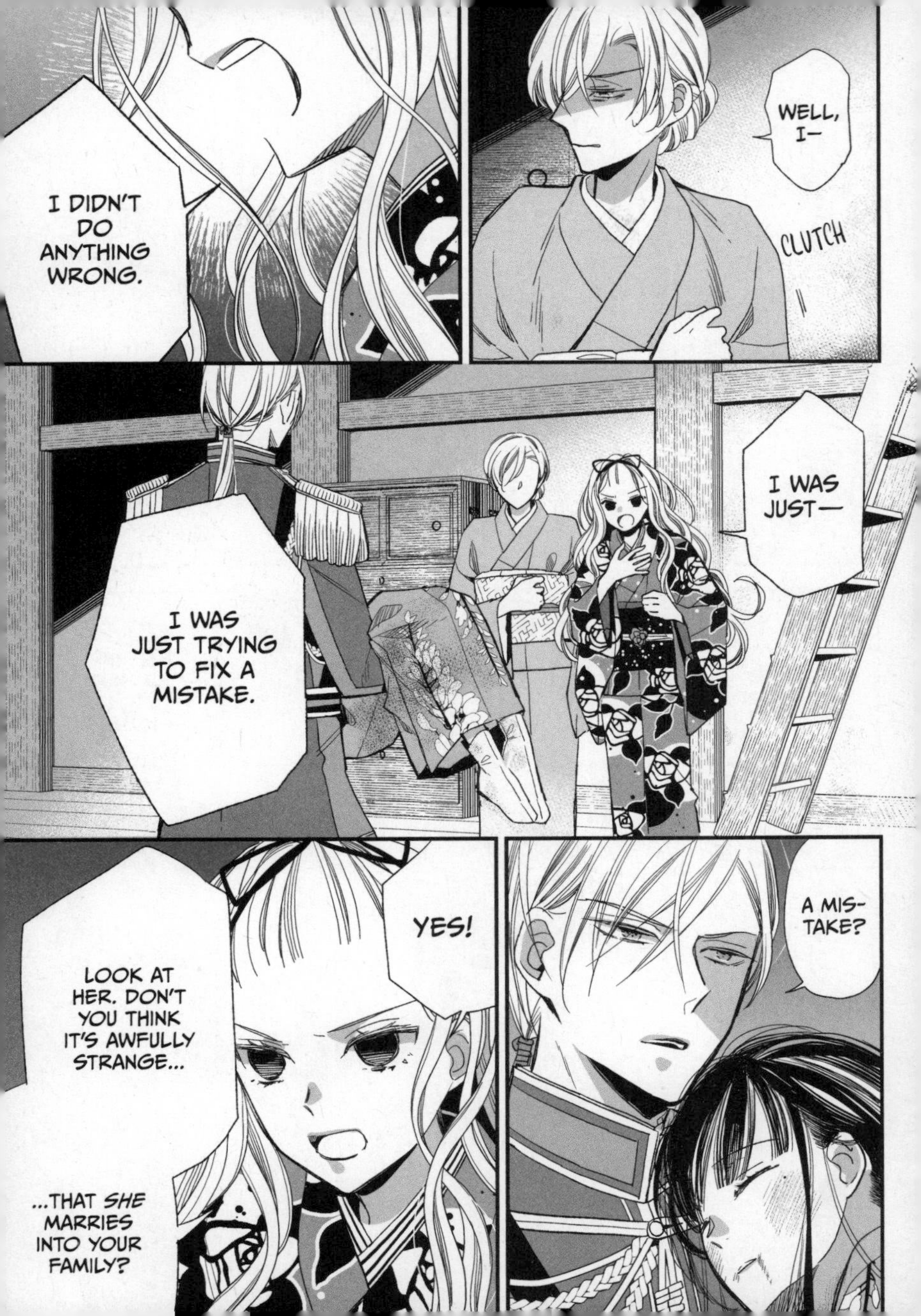
WELL, I—
CLUTCH
I DIDN'T DO ANYTHING WRONG.
I WAS JUST—
I WAS JUST TRYING TO FIX A MISTAKE.
A MIS-TAKE?
YES!
LOOK AT HER. DON'T YOU THINK IT'S AWFULLY STRANGE...
...THAT *SHE* MARRIES INTO YOUR FAMILY?

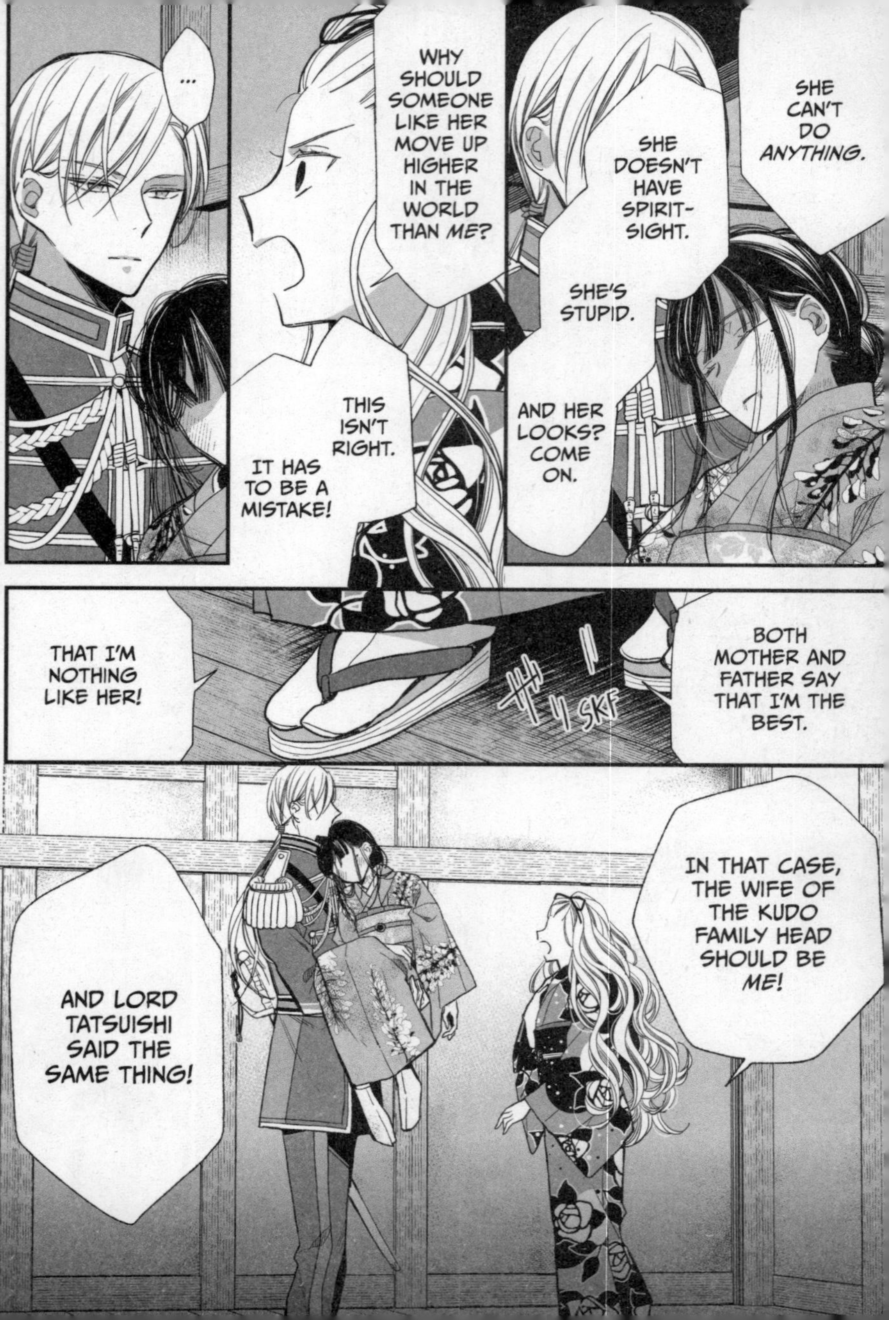
SHE CAN'T DO *ANYTHING*.
SHE DOESN'T HAVE SPIRIT-SIGHT.
SHE'S STUPID.
AND HER LOOKS? COME ON.
WHY SHOULD SOMEONE LIKE HER MOVE UP HIGHER IN THE WORLD THAN *ME*?
THIS ISN'T RIGHT.
IT HAS TO BE A MISTAKE!
...
BOTH MOTHER AND FATHER SAY THAT I'M THE BEST.
SKF
THAT I'M NOTHING LIKE HER!
IN THAT CASE, THE WIFE OF THE KUDO FAMILY HEAD SHOULD BE *ME*!
AND LORD TATSUISHI SAID THE SAME THING!

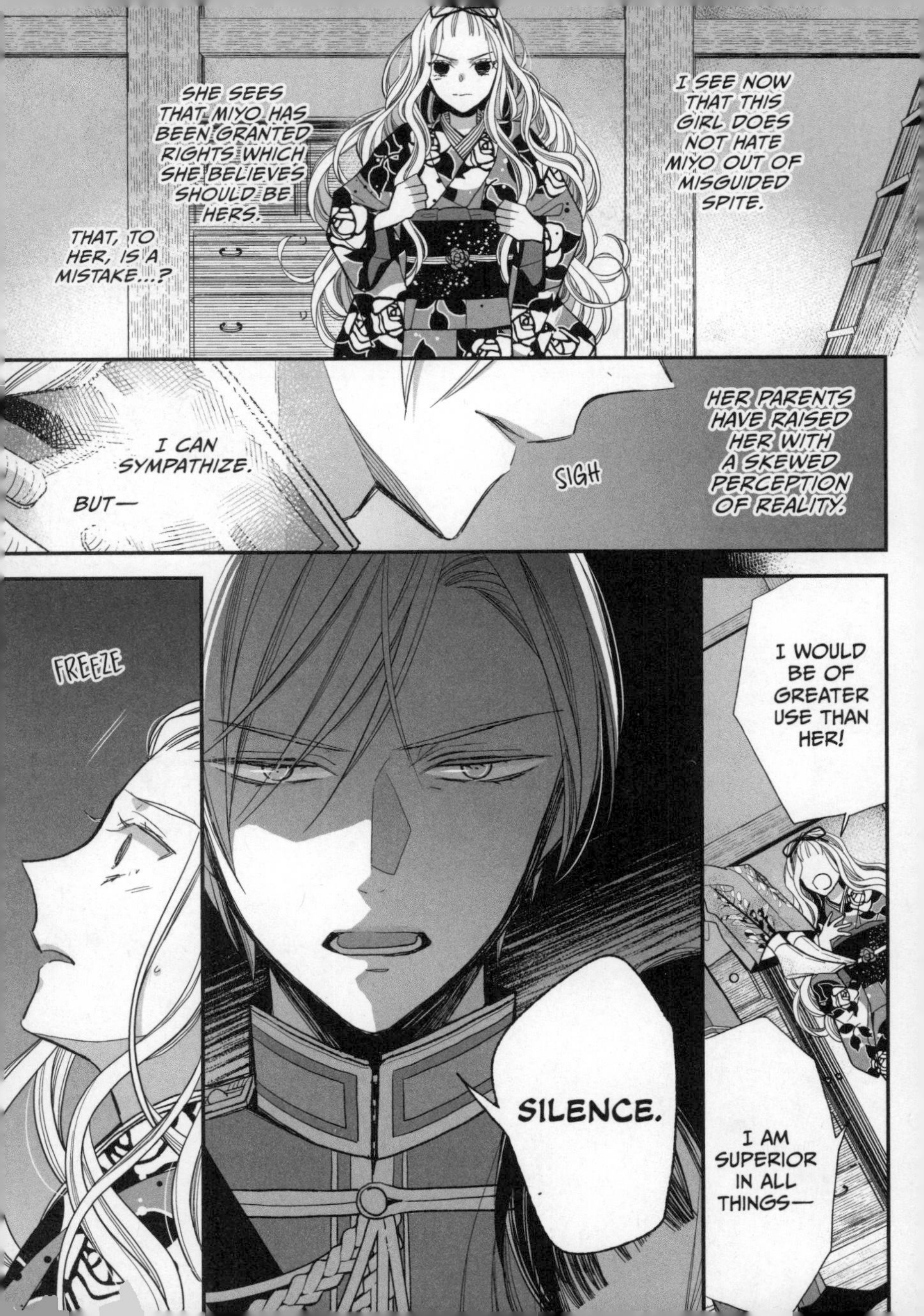
I SEE NOW THAT THIS GIRL DOES NOT HATE MIYO OUT OF MISGUIDED SPITE.
SHE SEES THAT MIYO HAS BEEN GRANTED RIGHTS WHICH SHE BELIEVES SHOULD BE HERS.
THAT, TO HER, IS A MISTAKE...?
HER PARENTS HAVE RAISED HER WITH A SKEWED PERCEPTION OF REALITY.
SIGH
I CAN SYMPATHIZE.
BUT—
I WOULD BE OF GREATER USE THAN HER!
I AM SUPERIOR IN ALL THINGS—
SILENCE.
FREEZE

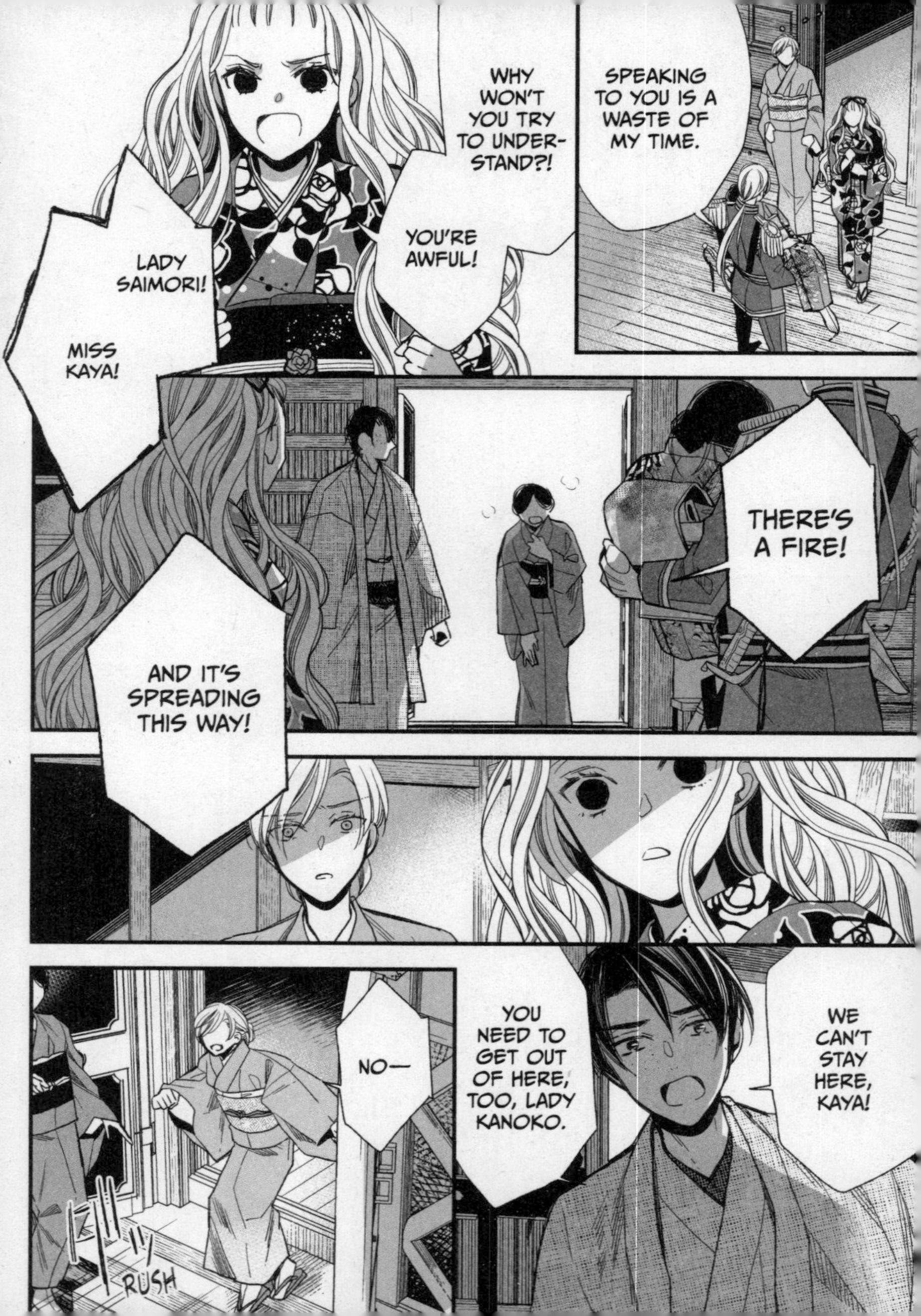
SPEAKING TO YOU IS A WASTE OF MY TIME.
WHY WON'T YOU TRY TO UNDER-STAND?!
YOU'RE AWFUL!
LADY SAIMORI!
MISS KAYA!
THERE'S A FIRE!
AND IT'S SPREADING THIS WAY!
WE CAN'T STAY HERE, KAYA!
YOU NEED TO GET OUT OF HERE, TOO, LADY KANOKO.
NO—
RUSH

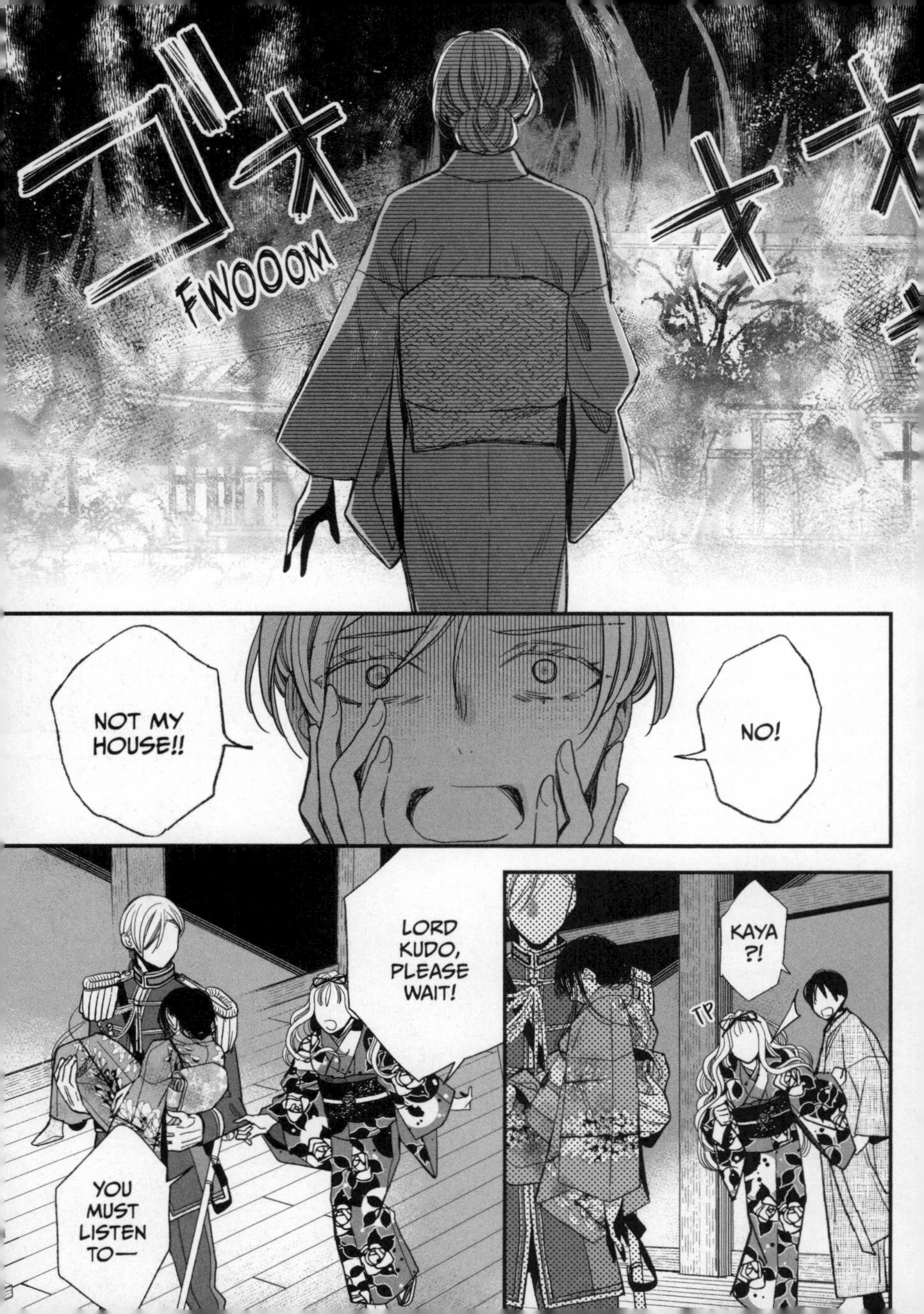
FWOOOM
NO!
NOT MY HOUSE!!
KAYA ?!
TP
LORD KUDO, PLEASE WAIT!
YOU MUST LISTEN TO—

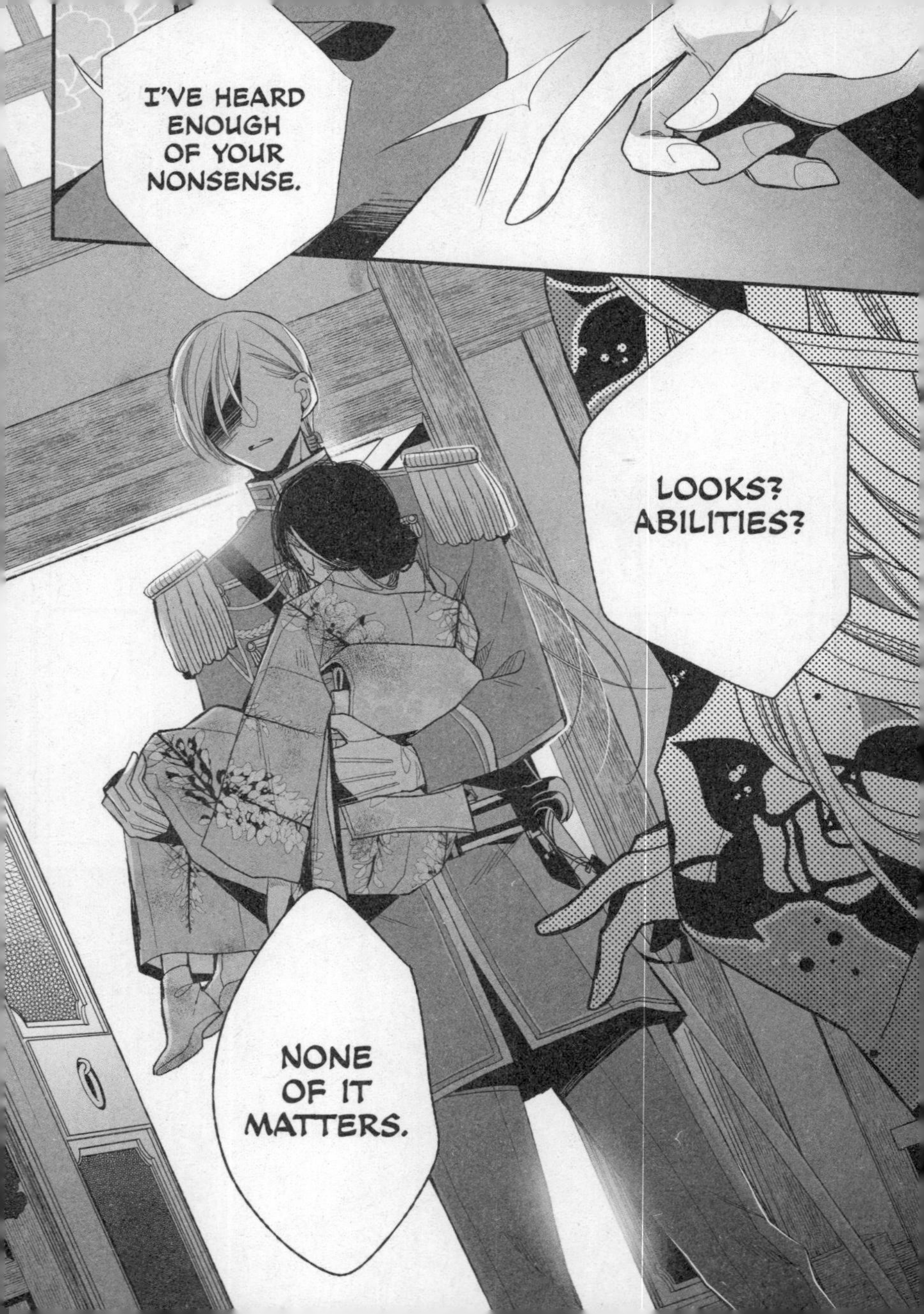
I'VE HEARD ENOUGH OF YOUR NONSENSE.
LOOKS? ABILITIES?
NONE OF IT MATTERS.

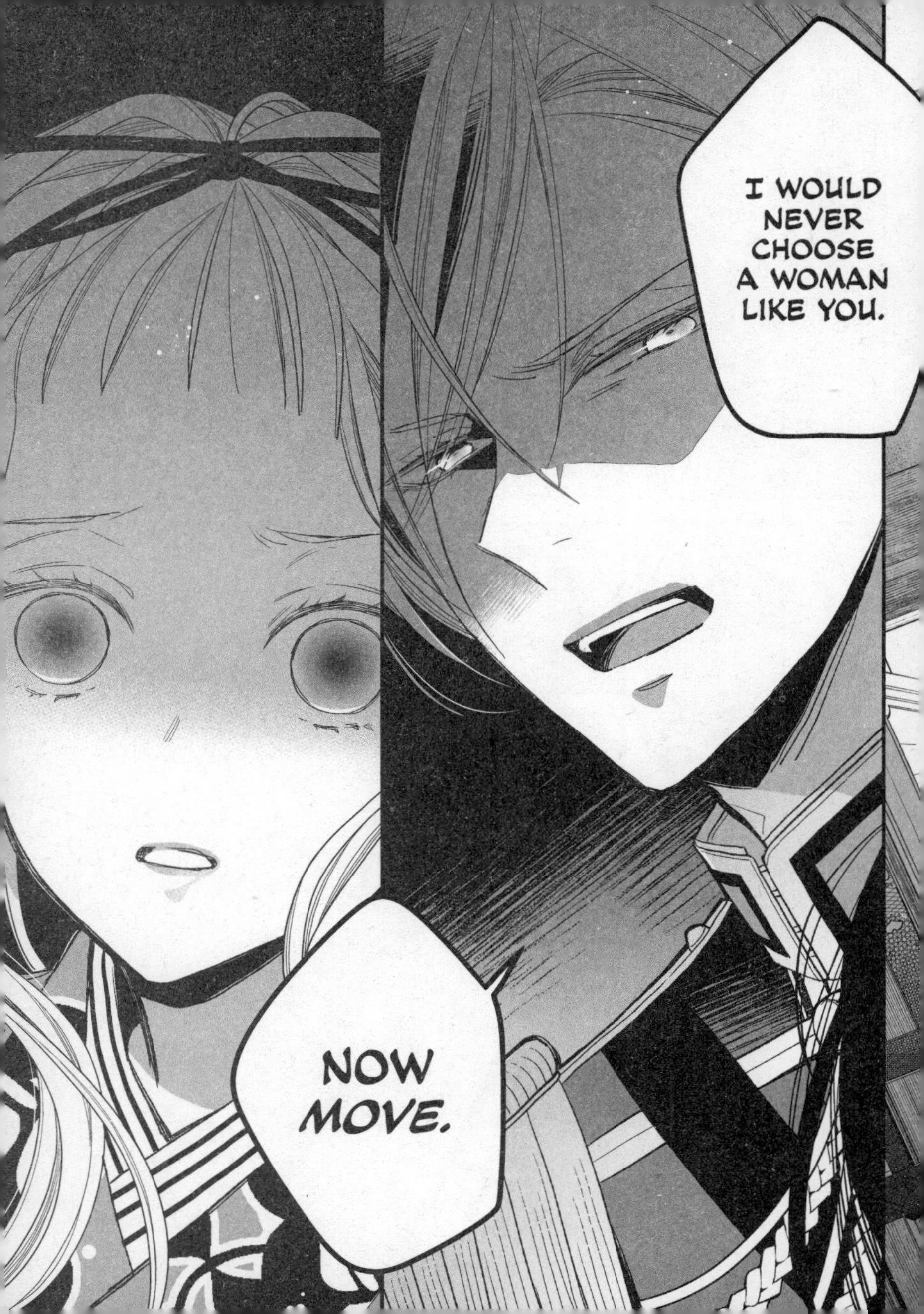
I WOULD NEVER CHOOSE A WOMAN LIKE YOU.
NOW MOVE.

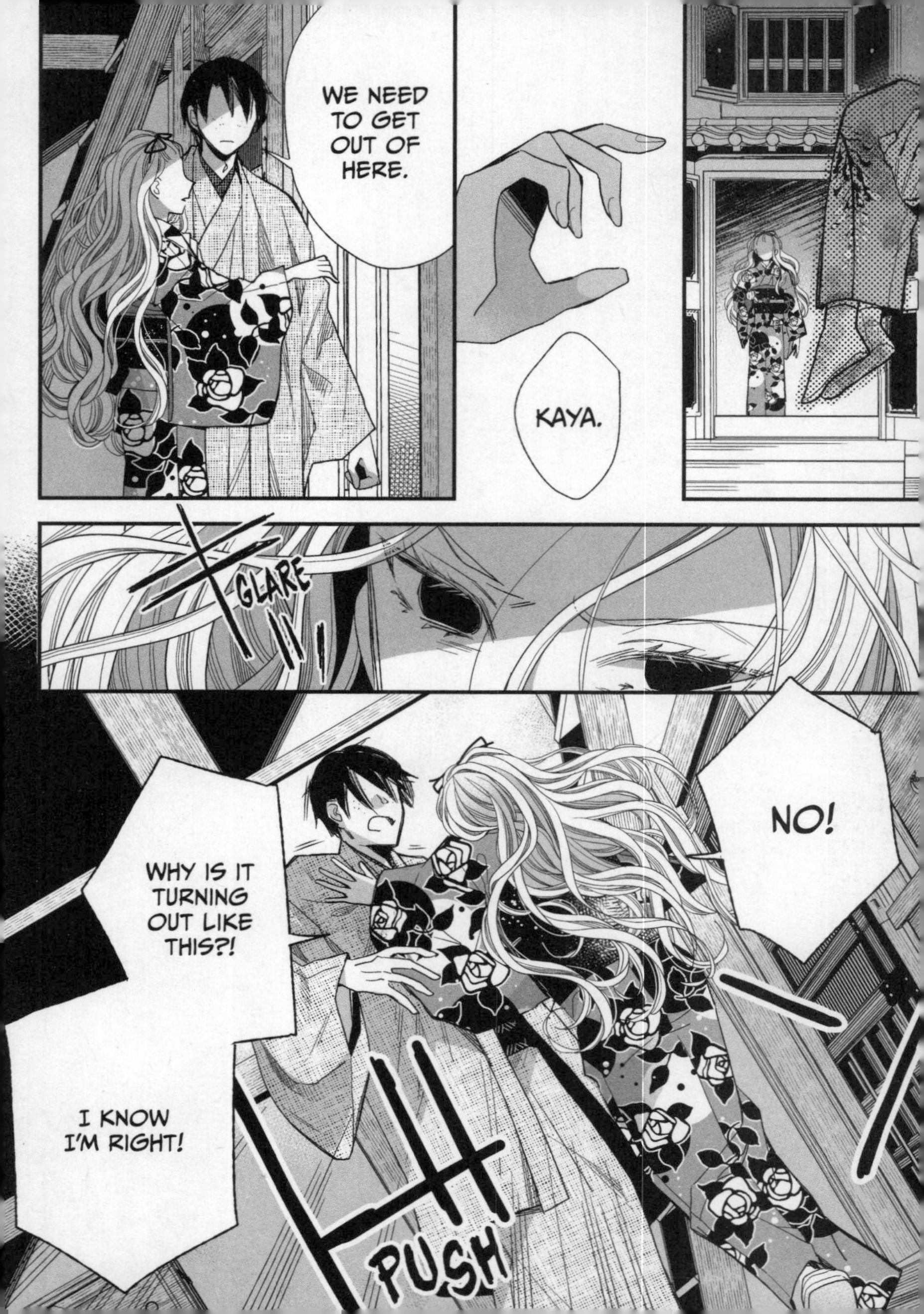
KAYA.
WE NEED TO GET OUT OF HERE.
GLARE
NO!
WHY IS IT TURNING OUT LIKE THIS?!
I KNOW I'M RIGHT!
PUSH

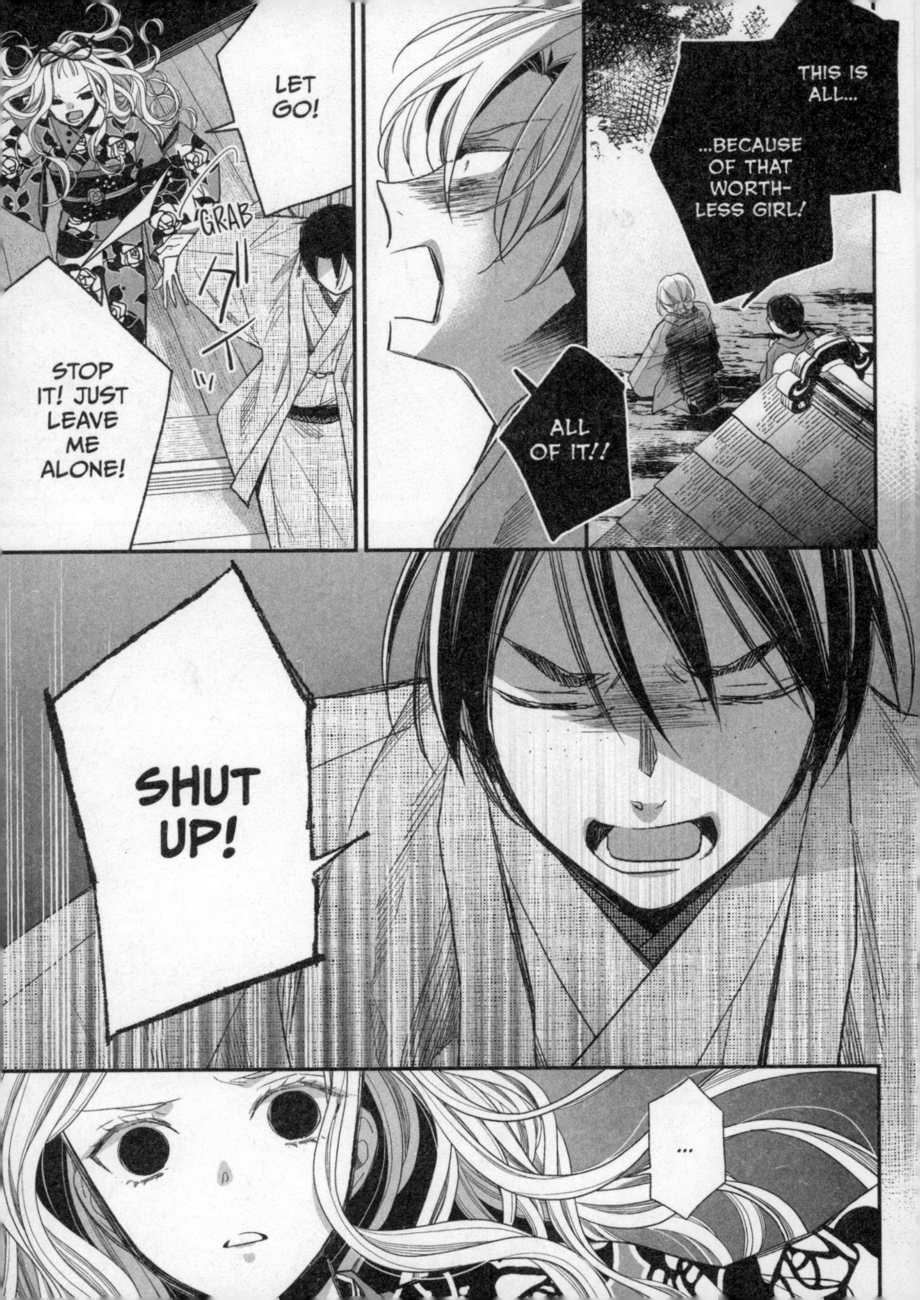
THIS IS ALL...
...BECAUSE OF THAT WORTH-LESS GIRL!
ALL OF IT!!
LET GO!
GRAB
グイッ
STOP IT! JUST LEAVE ME ALONE!
SHUT UP!
...

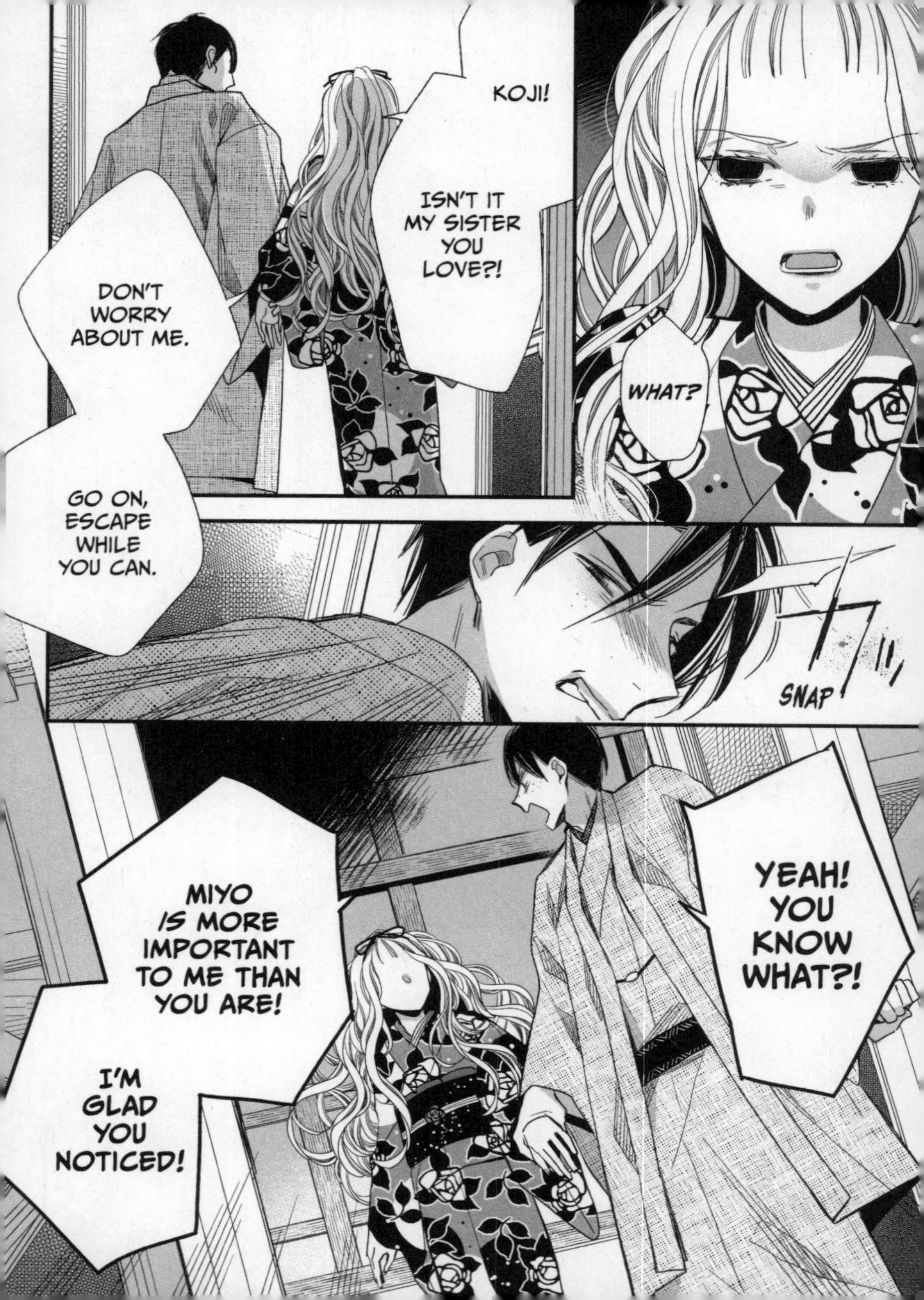
WHAT?
KOJI!
ISN'T IT MY SISTER YOU LOVE?!
DON'T WORRY ABOUT ME.
GO ON, ESCAPE WHILE YOU CAN.
SNAP
YEAH! YOU KNOW WHAT?!
MIYO IS MORE IMPORTANT TO ME THAN YOU ARE!
I'M GLAD YOU NOTICED!

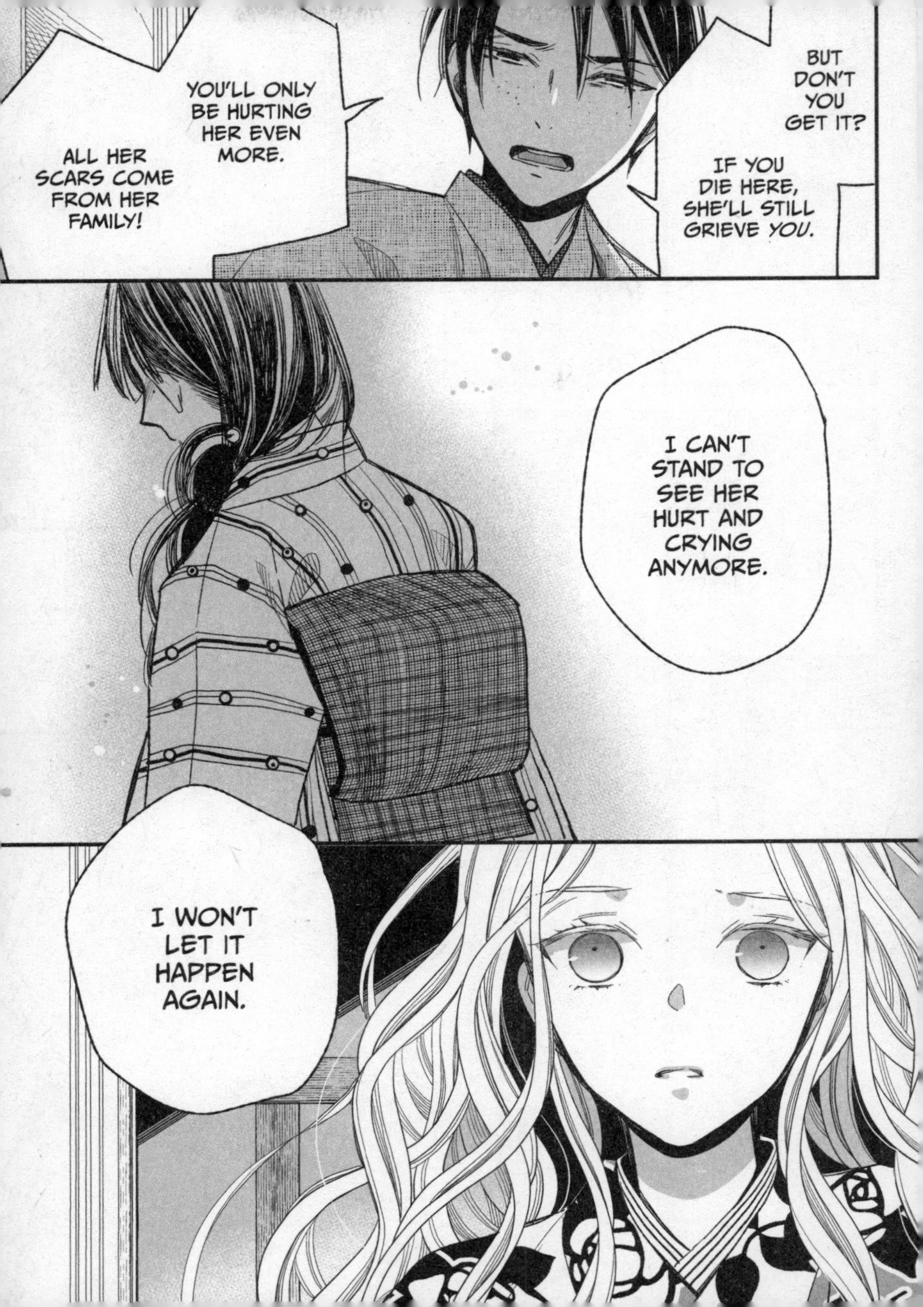
BUT DON'T YOU GET IT?
IF YOU DIE HERE, SHE'LL STILL GRIEVE *YOU*.
YOU'LL ONLY BE HURTING HER EVEN MORE.
ALL HER SCARS COME FROM HER FAMILY!
I CAN'T STAND TO SEE HER HURT AND CRYING ANYMORE.
I WON'T LET IT HAPPEN AGAIN.

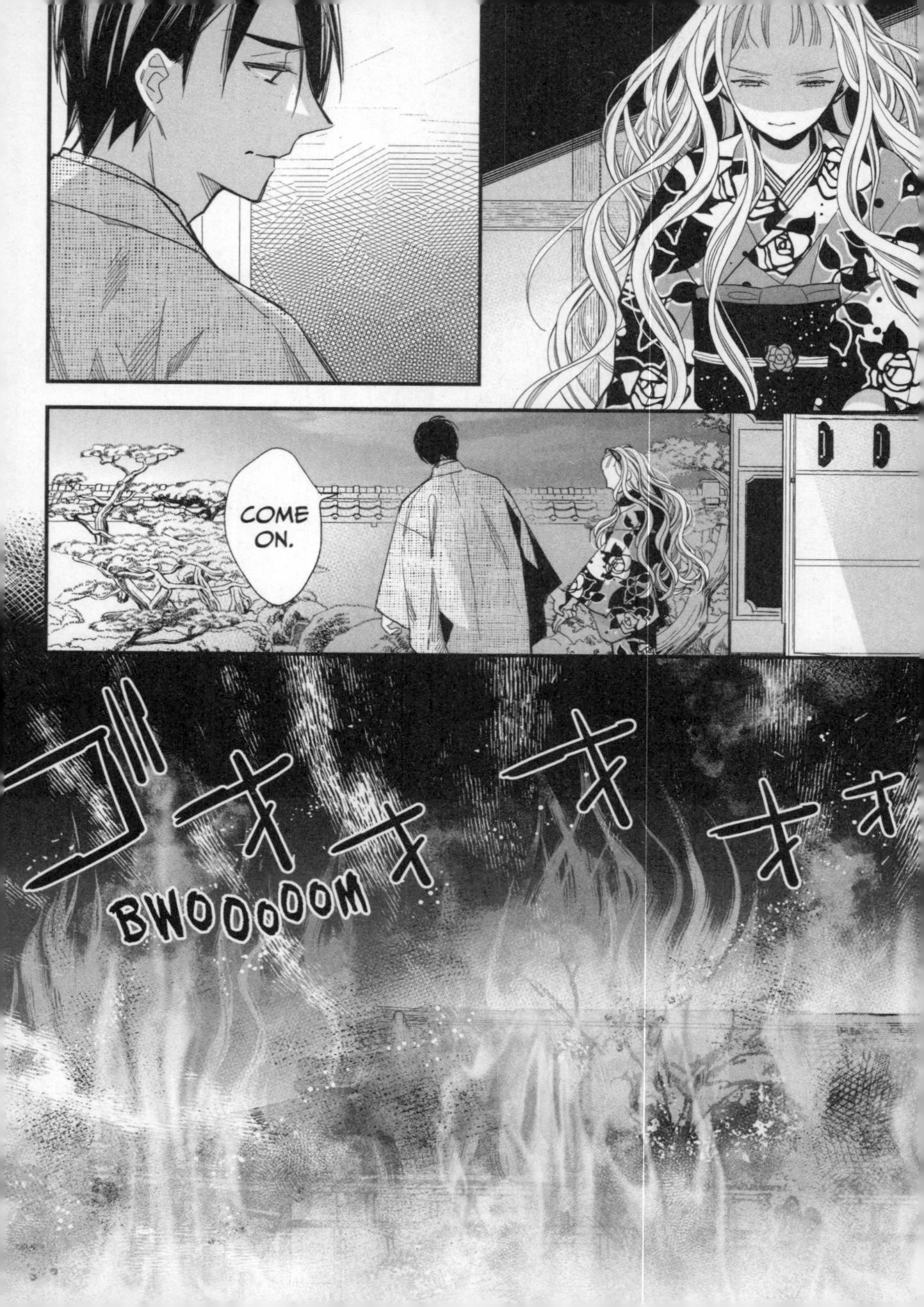
COME ON.
ゴォォォォ
BWOOOOOM

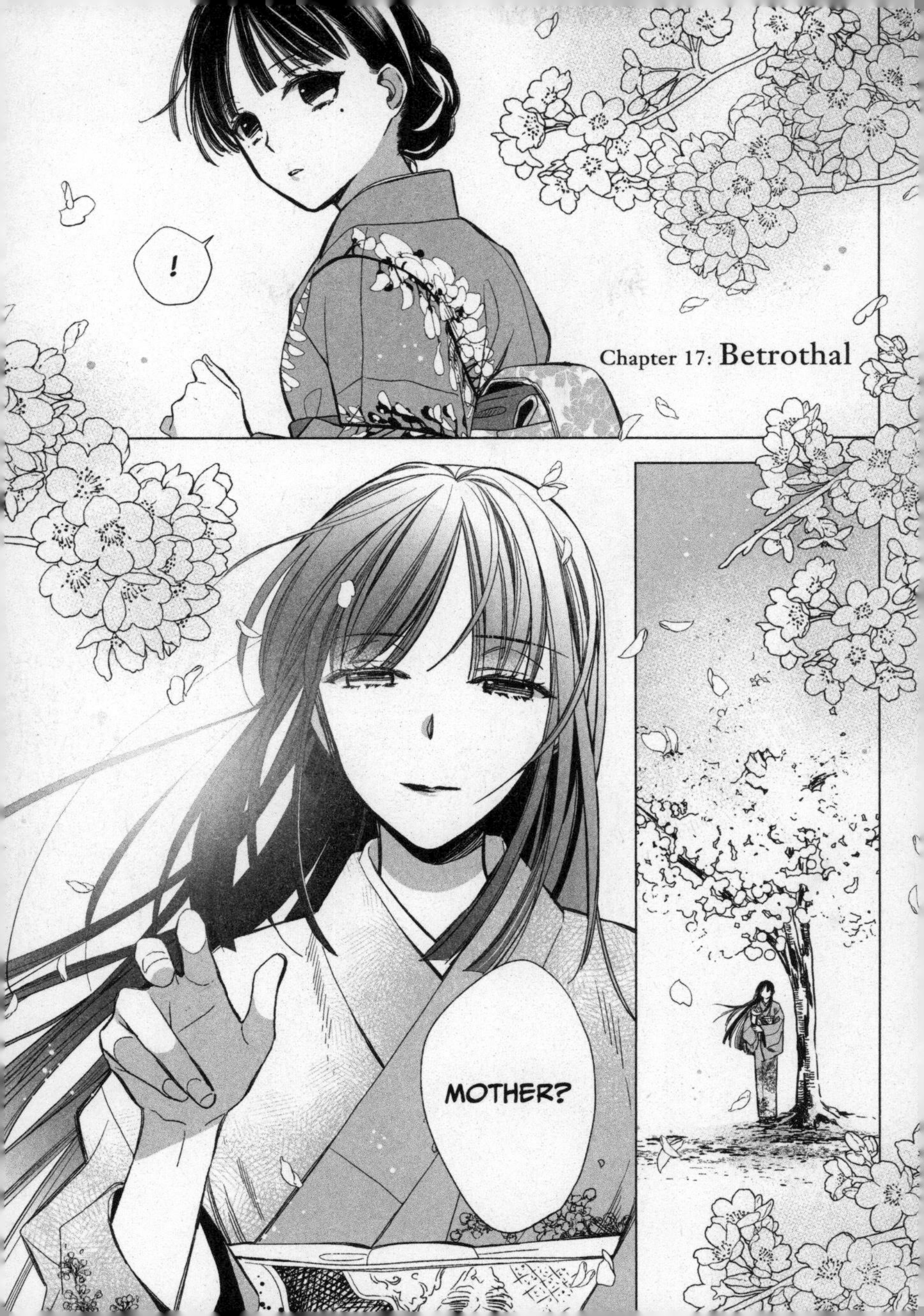
Chapter 17: Betrothal
!
MOTHER?

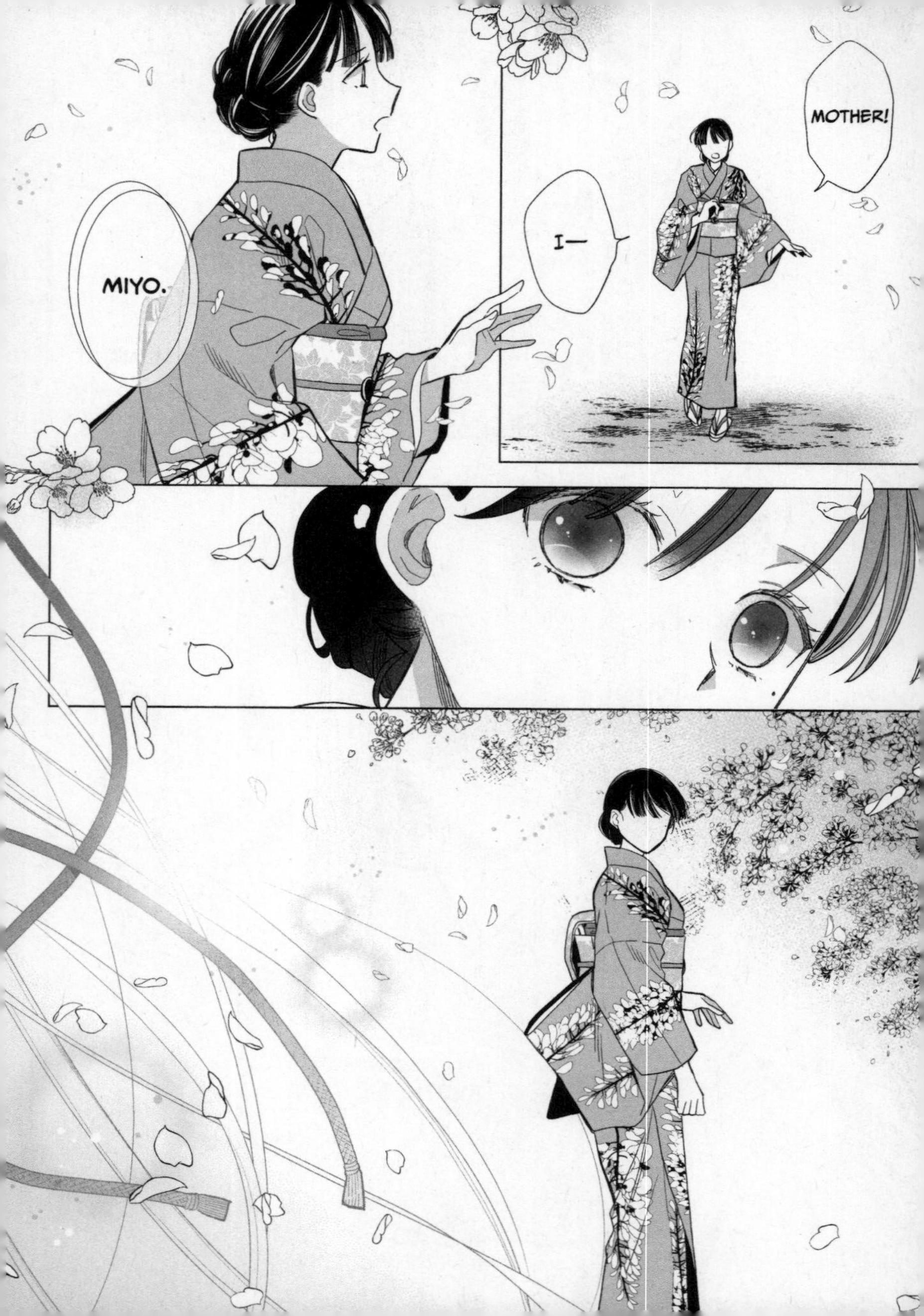
MOTHER!
I—
MIYO.

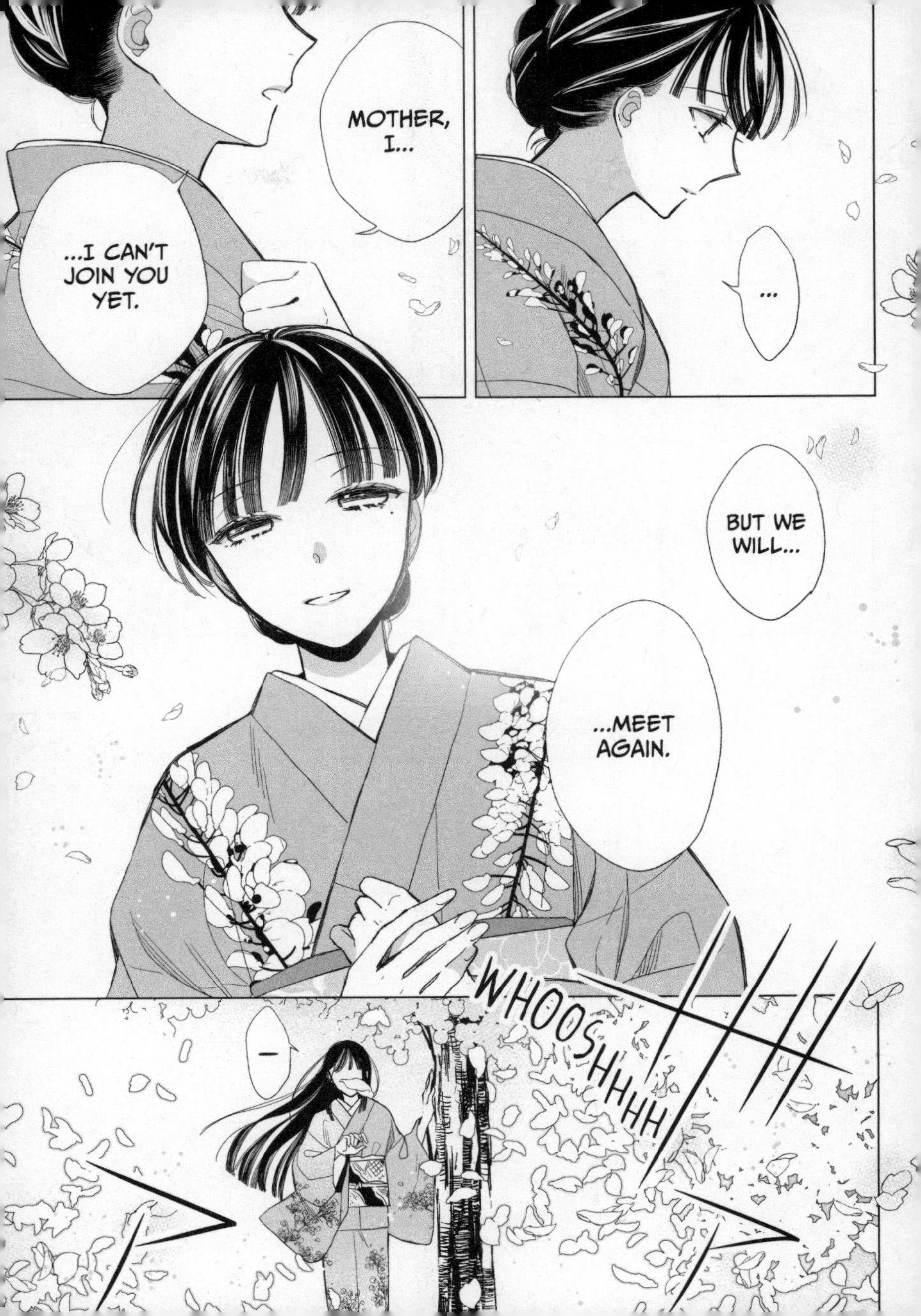
...
MOTHER, I...
...I CAN'T JOIN YOU YET.
BUT WE WILL...
...MEET AGAIN.
WHOOSHHHH
—

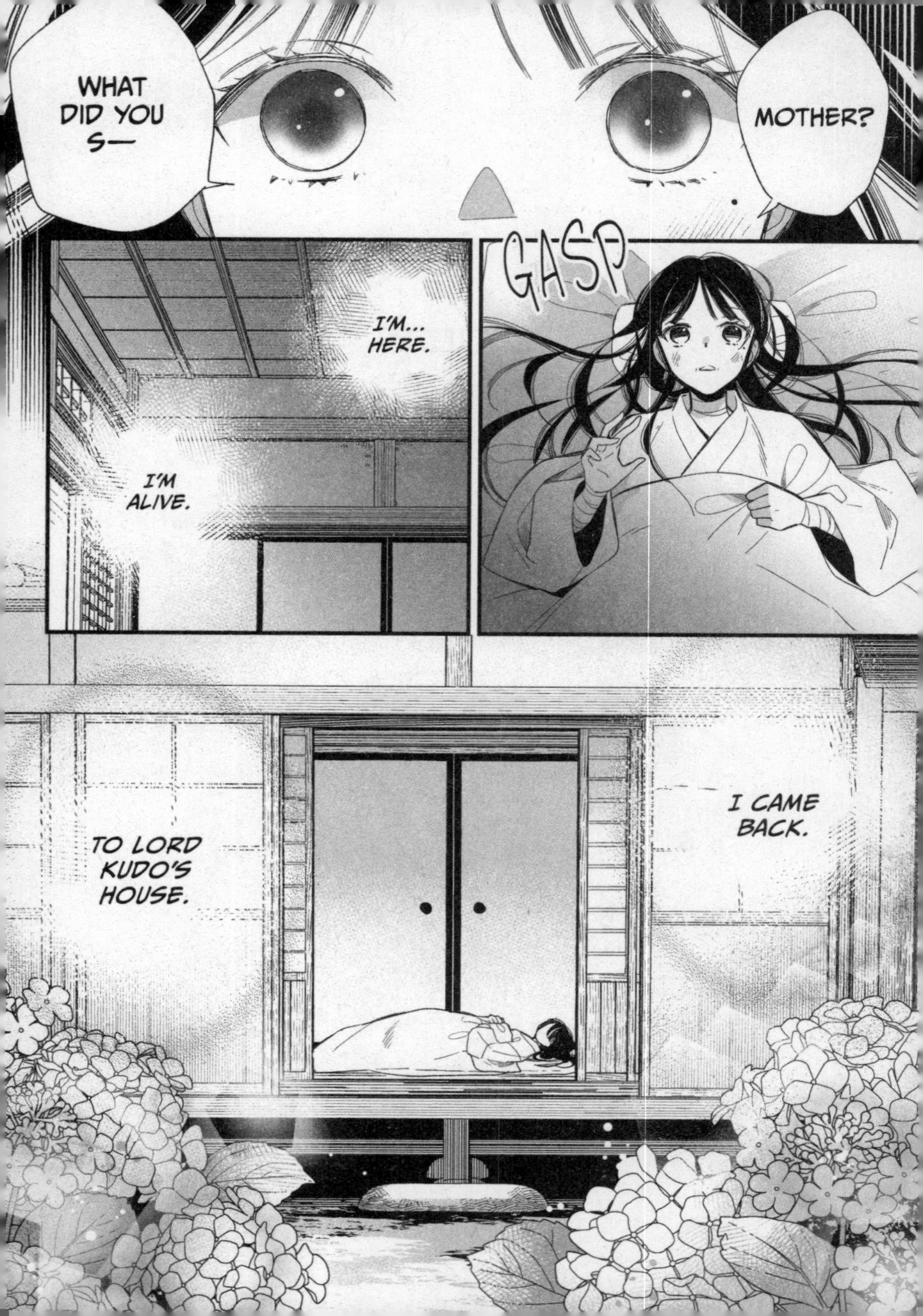
MOTHER?
WHAT DID YOU S—
GASP
I'M... HERE.
I'M ALIVE.
I CAME BACK.
TO LORD KUDO'S HOUSE.

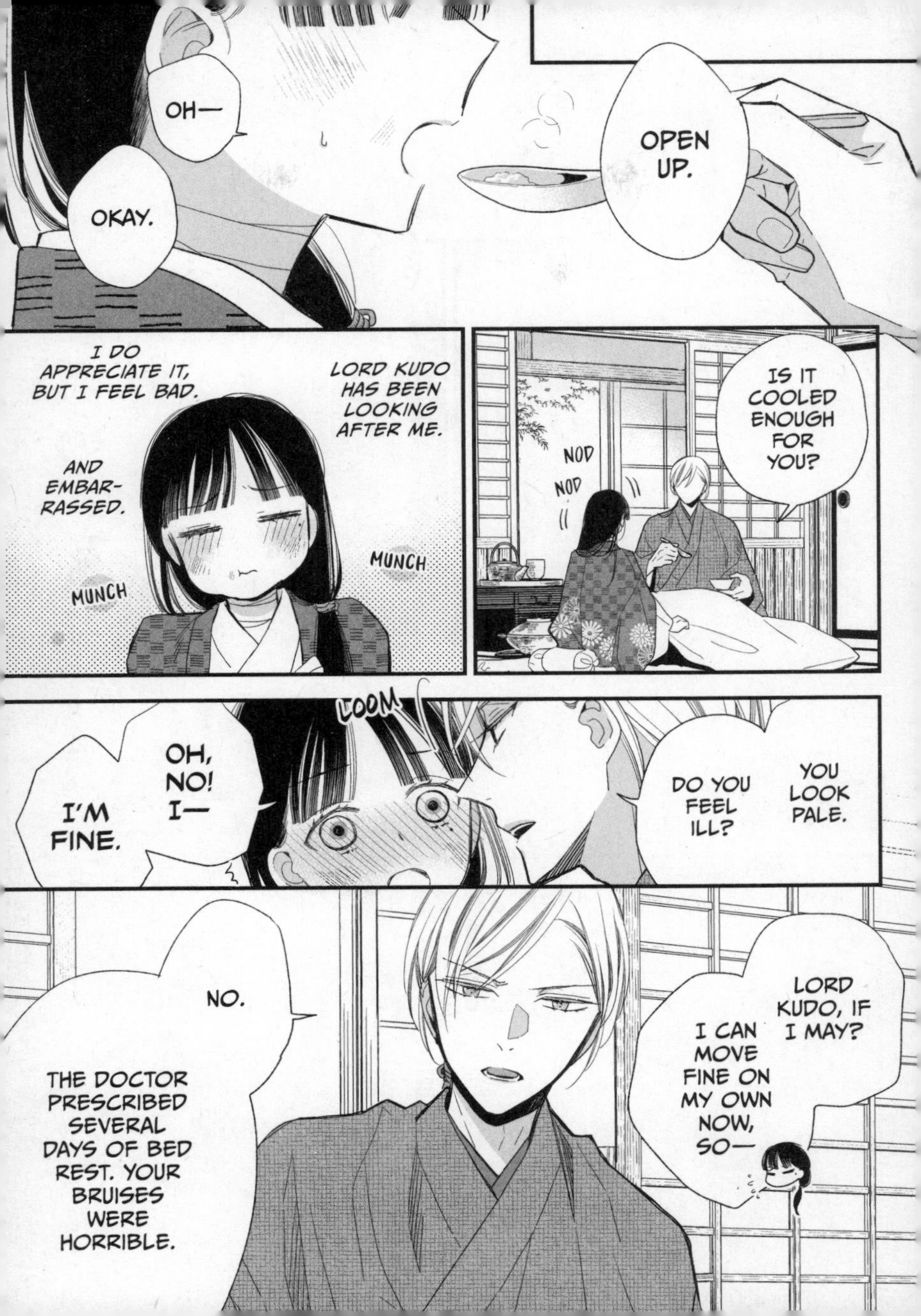
OPEN UP.
OH—
OKAY.
IS IT COOLED ENOUGH FOR YOU?
NOD NOD
LORD KUDO HAS BEEN LOOKING AFTER ME.
I DO APPRECIATE IT, BUT I FEEL BAD.
AND EMBARRASSED.
MUNCH
MUNCH
YOU LOOK PALE.
DO YOU FEEL ILL?
LOOM
OH, NO! I—
I'M FINE.
LORD KUDO, IF I MAY?
I CAN MOVE FINE ON MY OWN NOW, SO—
NO.
THE DOCTOR PRESCRIBED SEVERAL DAYS OF BED REST. YOUR BRUISES WERE HORRIBLE.

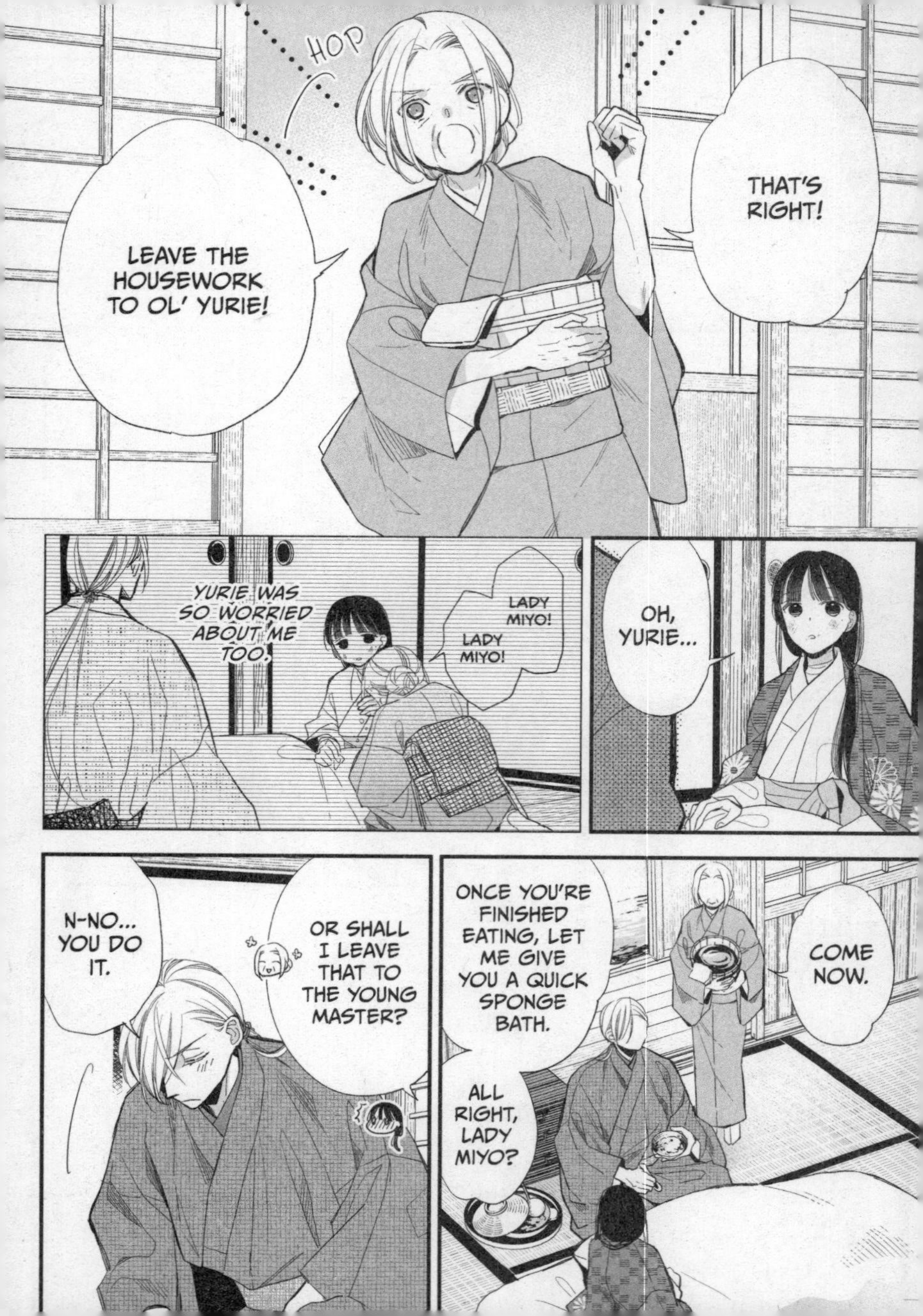
THAT'S RIGHT!
HOP
LEAVE THE HOUSEWORK TO OL' YURIE!
OH, YURIE...
LADY MIYO!
LADY MIYO!
YURIE WAS SO WORRIED ABOUT ME TOO.
COME NOW.
ONCE YOU'RE FINISHED EATING, LET ME GIVE YOU A QUICK SPONGE BATH.
ALL RIGHT, LADY MIYO?
OR SHALL I LEAVE THAT TO THE YOUNG MASTER?
N-NO... YOU DO IT.

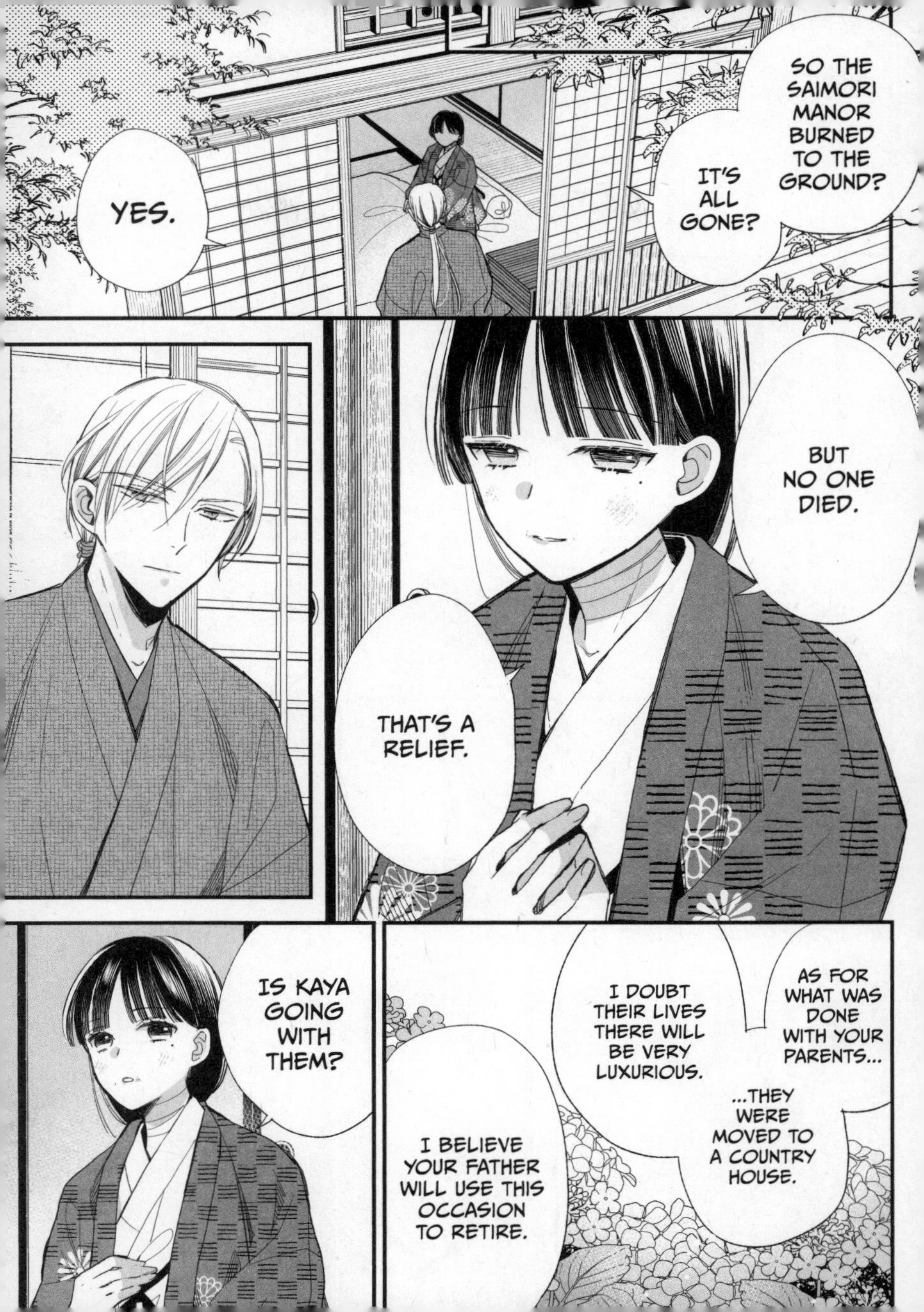
SO THE SAIMORI MANOR BURNED TO THE GROUND?
IT'S ALL GONE?
YES.
BUT NO ONE DIED.
THAT'S A RELIEF.
AS FOR WHAT WAS DONE WITH YOUR PARENTS...
...THEY WERE MOVED TO A COUNTRY HOUSE.
I DOUBT THEIR LIVES THERE WILL BE VERY LUXURIOUS.
I BELIEVE YOUR FATHER WILL USE THIS OCCASION TO RETIRE.
IS KAYA GOING WITH THEM?

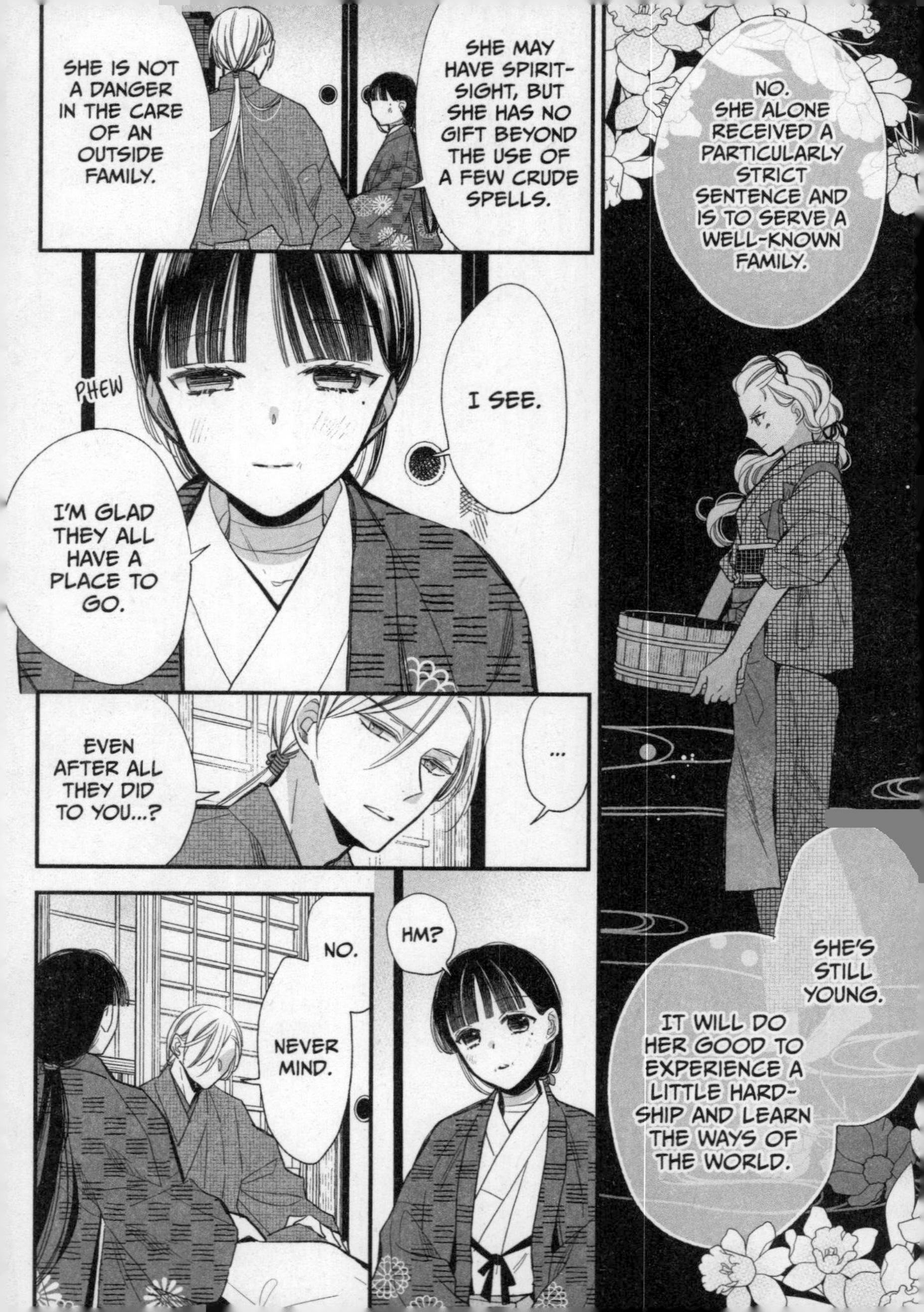
NO. SHE ALONE RECEIVED A PARTICULARLY STRICT SENTENCE AND IS TO SERVE A WELL-KNOWN FAMILY.
SHE'S STILL YOUNG.
IT WILL DO HER GOOD TO EXPERIENCE A LITTLE HARD-SHIP AND LEARN THE WAYS OF THE WORLD.
SHE MAY HAVE SPIRIT-SIGHT, BUT SHE HAS NO GIFT BEYOND THE USE OF A FEW CRUDE SPELLS.
SHE IS NOT A DANGER IN THE CARE OF AN OUTSIDE FAMILY.
I SEE.
PHEW
I'M GLAD THEY ALL HAVE A PLACE TO GO.
...
EVEN AFTER ALL THEY DID TO YOU...?
HM?
NO.
NEVER MIND.

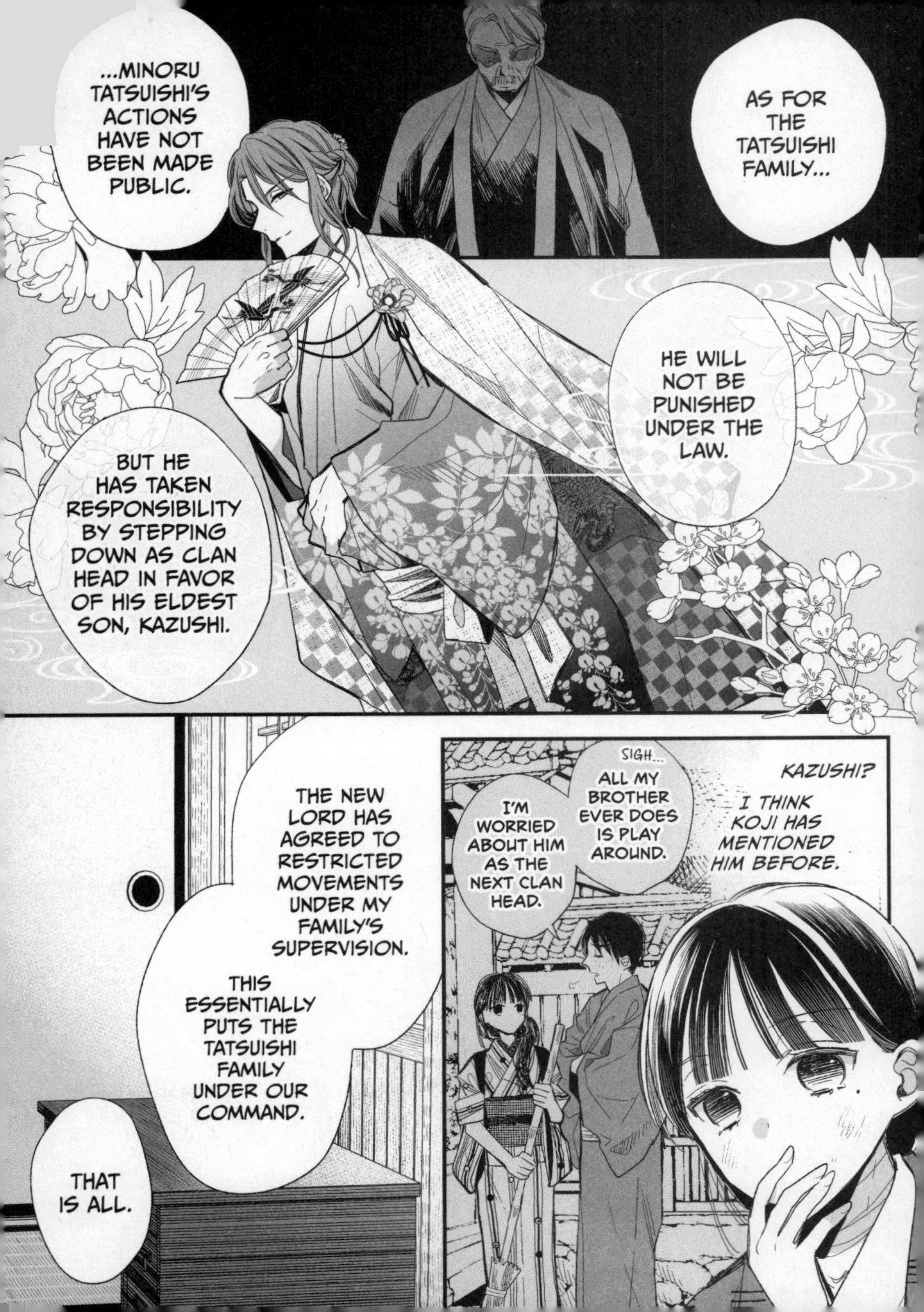
AS FOR THE TATSUISHI FAMILY...
...MINORU TATSUISHI'S ACTIONS HAVE NOT BEEN MADE PUBLIC.
HE WILL NOT BE PUNISHED UNDER THE LAW.
BUT HE HAS TAKEN RESPONSIBILITY BY STEPPING DOWN AS CLAN HEAD IN FAVOR OF HIS ELDEST SON, KAZUSHI.
KAZUSHI?
I THINK KOJI HAS MENTIONED HIM BEFORE.
SIGH...
ALL MY BROTHER EVER DOES IS PLAY AROUND.
I'M WORRIED ABOUT HIM AS THE NEXT CLAN HEAD.
THE NEW LORD HAS AGREED TO RESTRICTED MOVEMENTS UNDER MY FAMILY'S SUPERVISION.
THIS ESSENTIALLY PUTS THE TATSUISHI FAMILY UNDER OUR COMMAND.
THAT IS ALL.

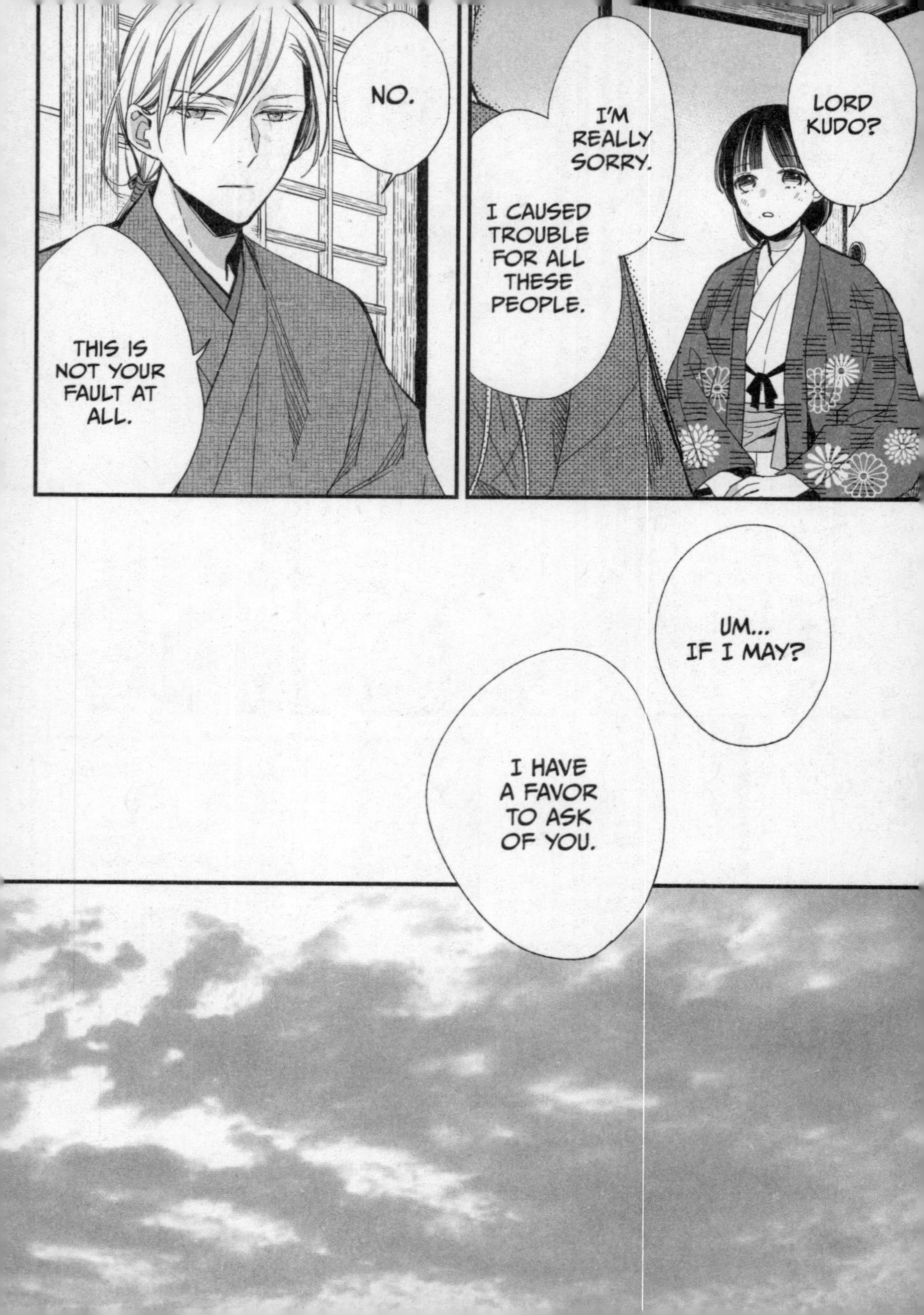
LORD KUDO?
I'M REALLY SORRY.
I CAUSED TROUBLE FOR ALL THESE PEOPLE.
NO.
THIS IS NOT YOUR FAULT AT ALL.
UM... IF I MAY?
I HAVE A FAVOR TO ASK OF YOU.

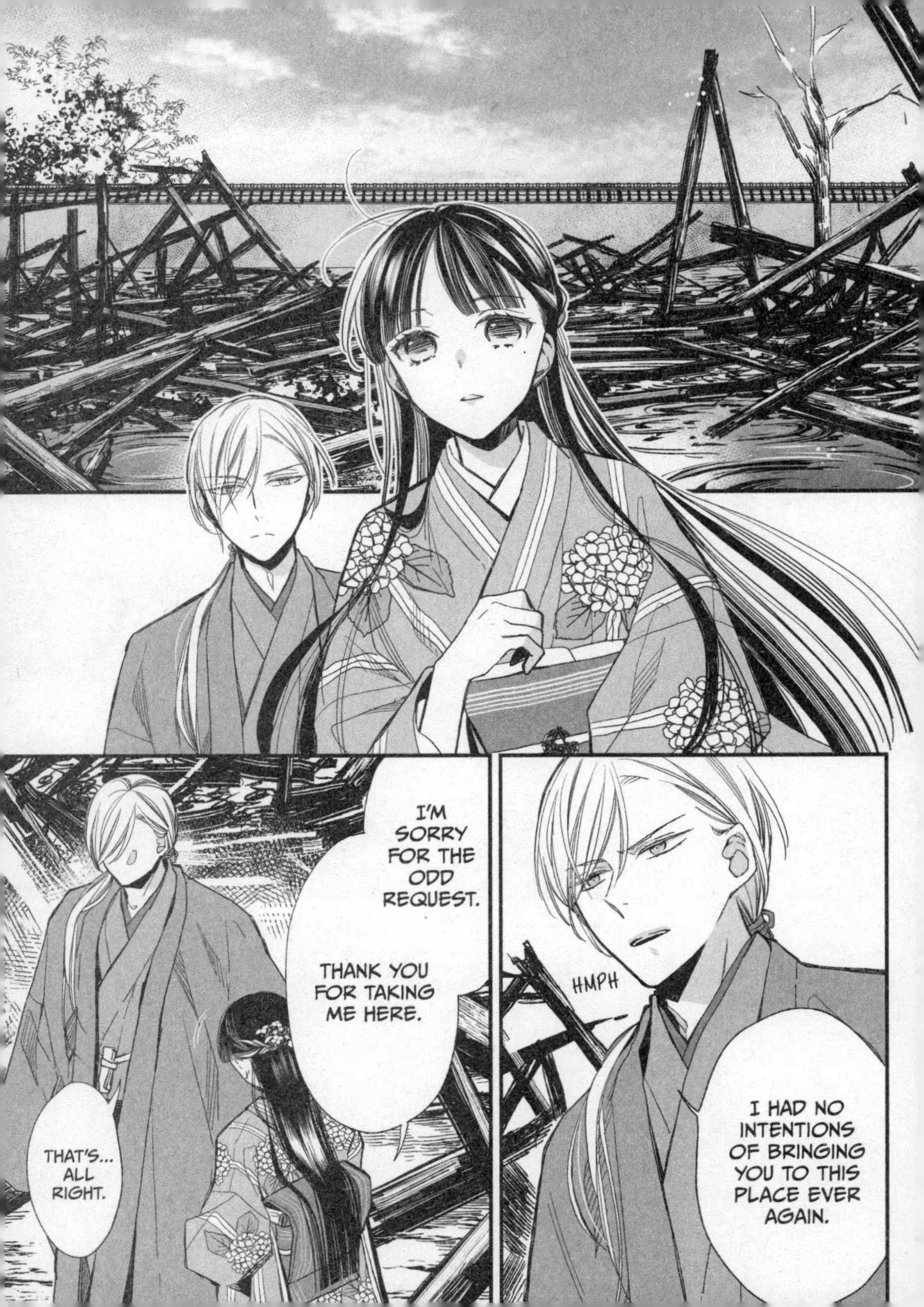
HMPH
I HAD NO INTENTIONS OF BRINGING YOU TO THIS PLACE EVER AGAIN.
I'M SORRY FOR THE ODD REQUEST.
THANK YOU FOR TAKING ME HERE.
THAT'S... ALL RIGHT.

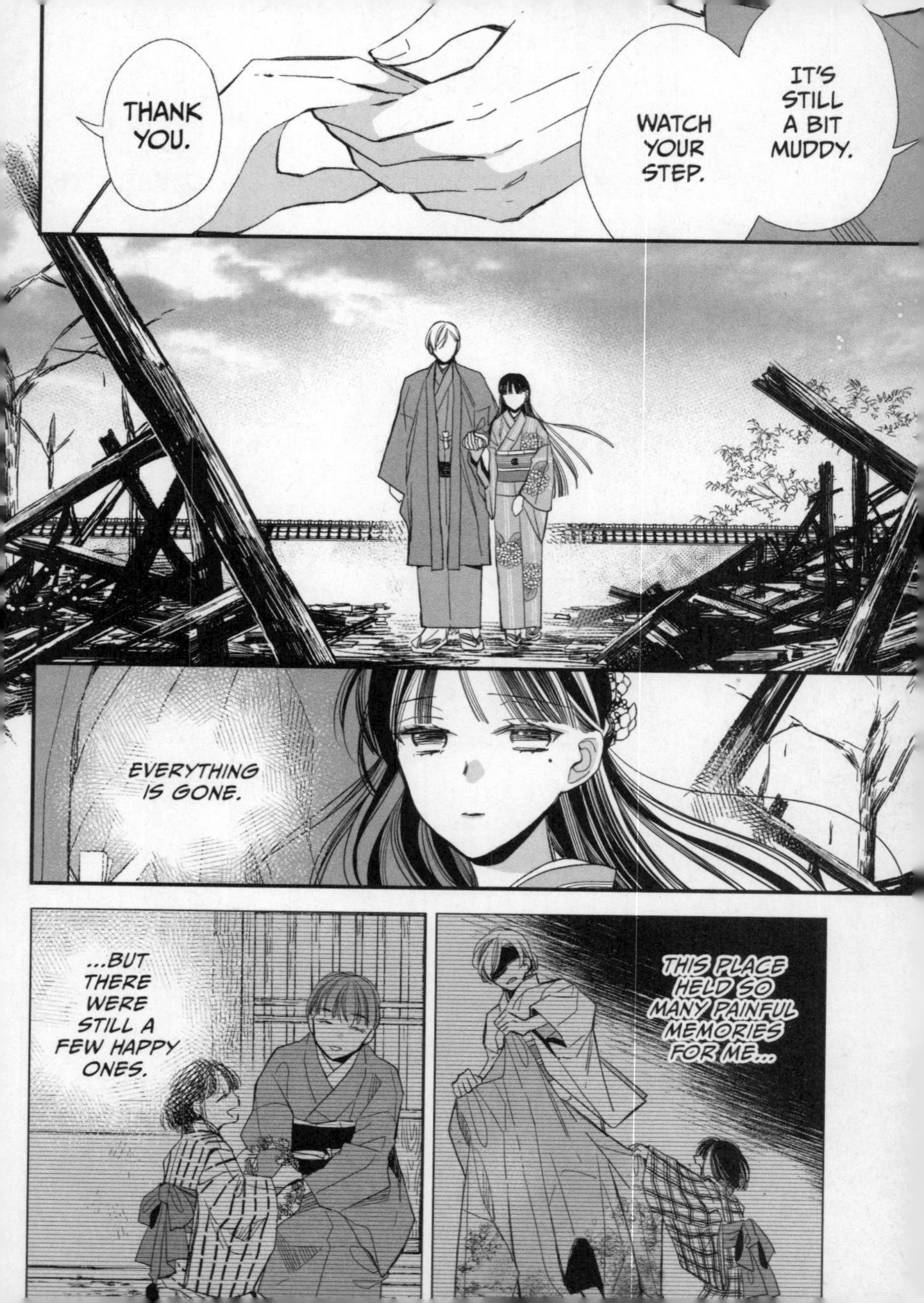
IT'S STILL A BIT MUDDY.
WATCH YOUR STEP.
THANK YOU.
EVERYTHING IS GONE.
THIS PLACE HELD SO MANY PAINFUL MEMORIES FOR ME...
...BUT THERE WERE STILL A FEW HAPPY ONES.

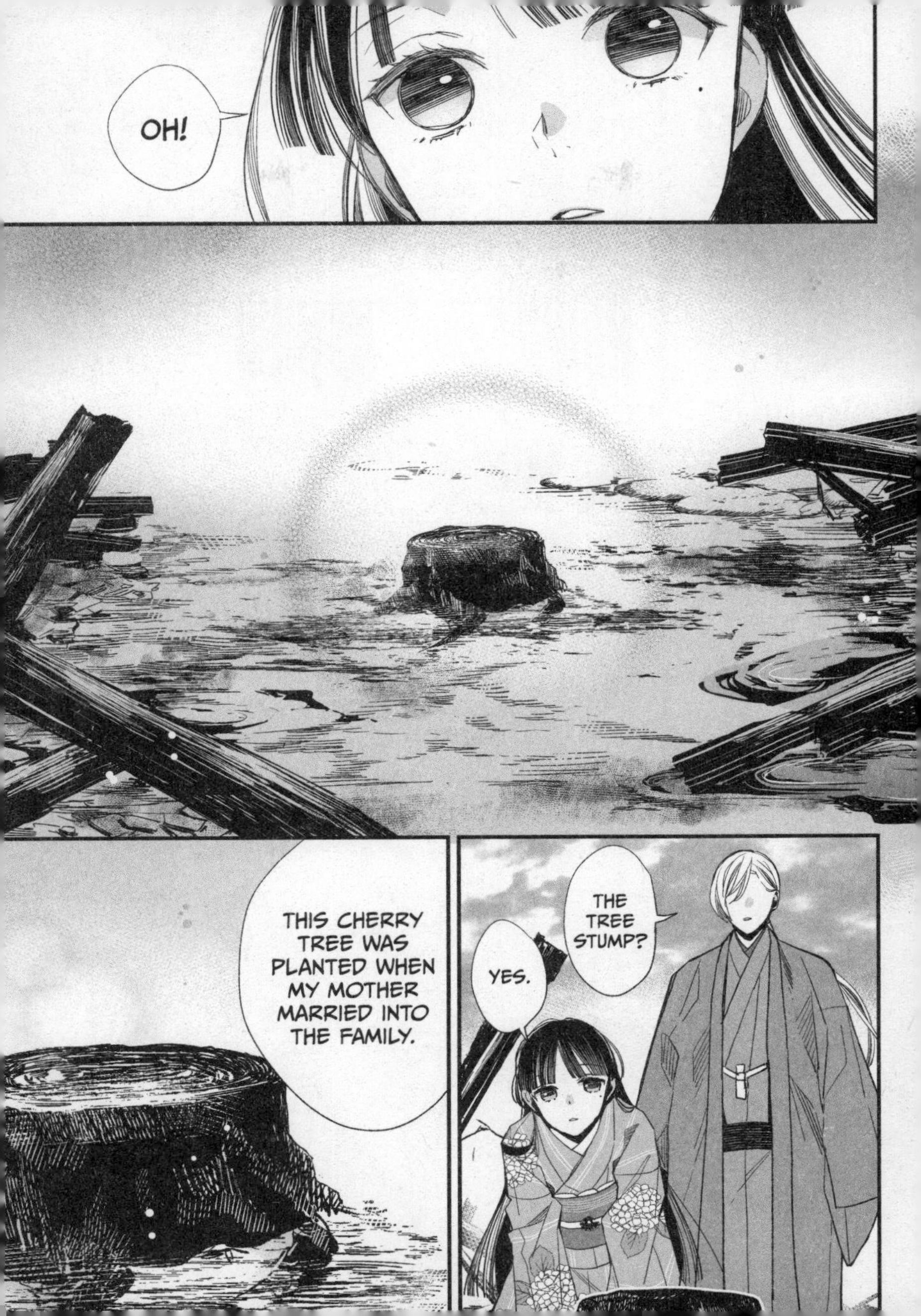
OH!
THE TREE STUMP?
YES.
THIS CHERRY TREE WAS PLANTED WHEN MY MOTHER MARRIED INTO THE FAMILY.

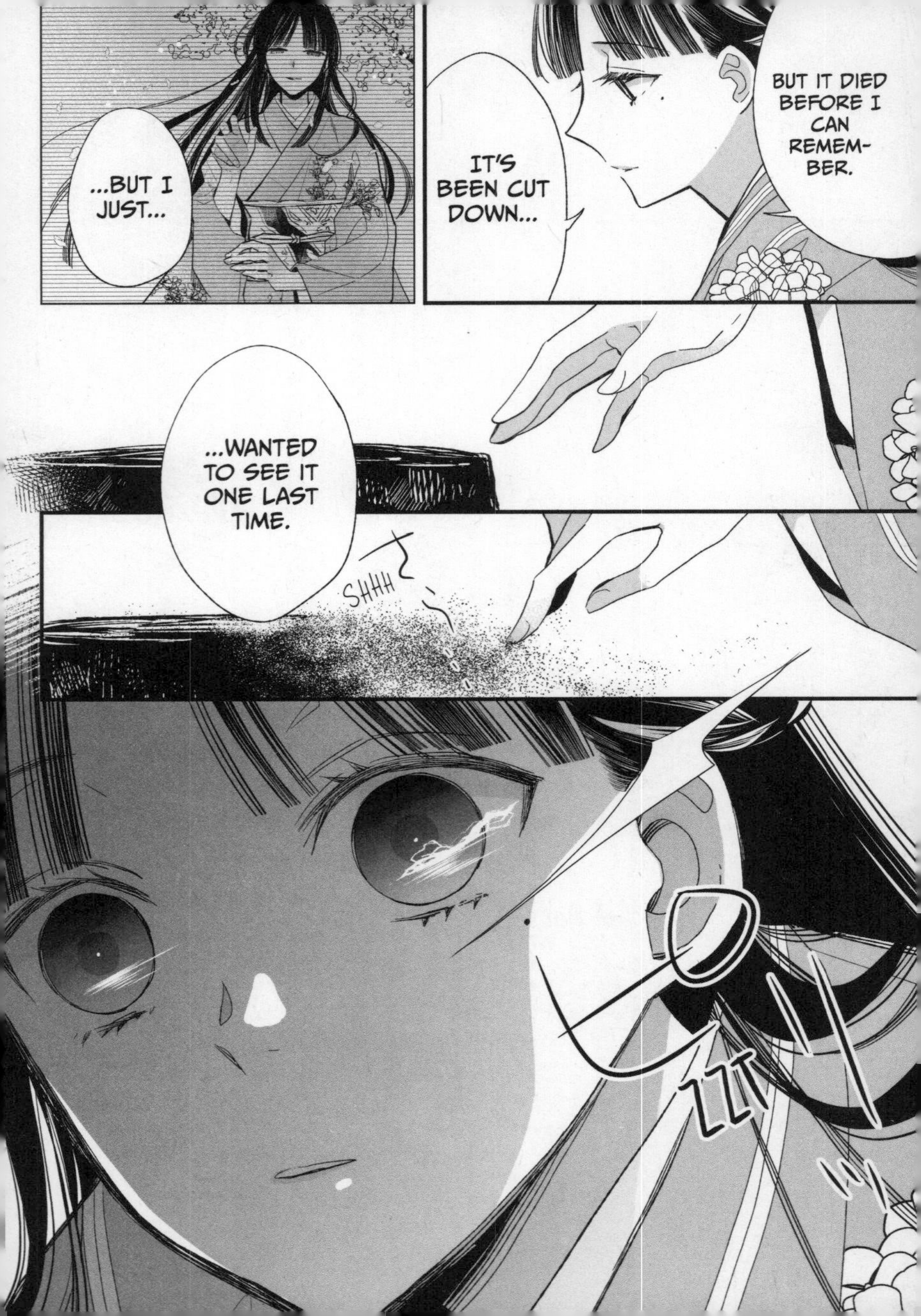
BUT IT DIED BEFORE I CAN REMEM-BER.
IT'S BEEN CUT DOWN...
...BUT I JUST...
...WANTED TO SEE IT ONE LAST TIME.
SHHH
ZZT

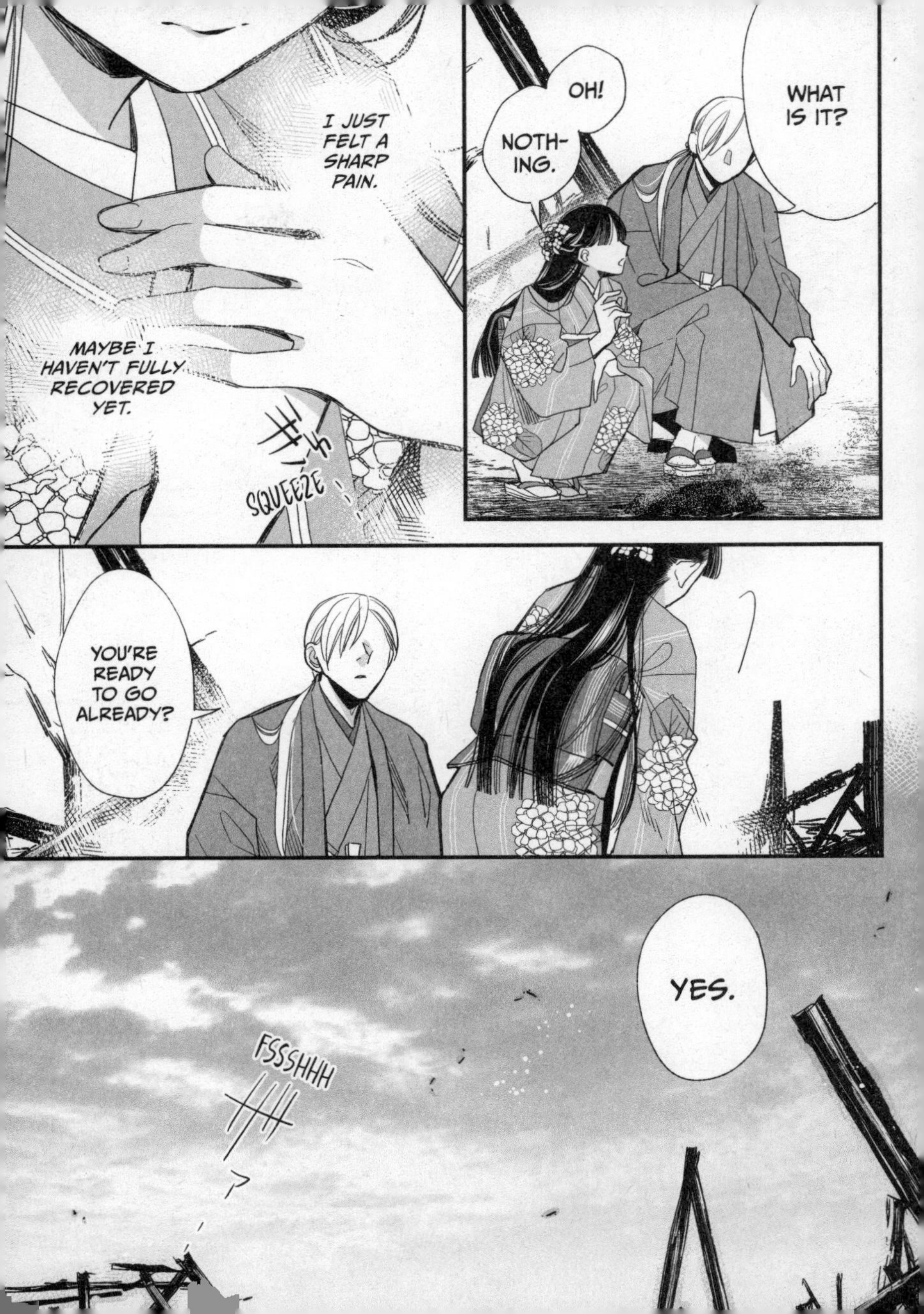
WHAT IS IT?
OH!
NOTH-ING.
I JUST FELT A SHARP PAIN.
MAYBE I HAVEN'T FULLY RECOVERED YET.
SQUEEZE
YOU'RE READY TO GO ALREADY?
YES.
FSSSHHH

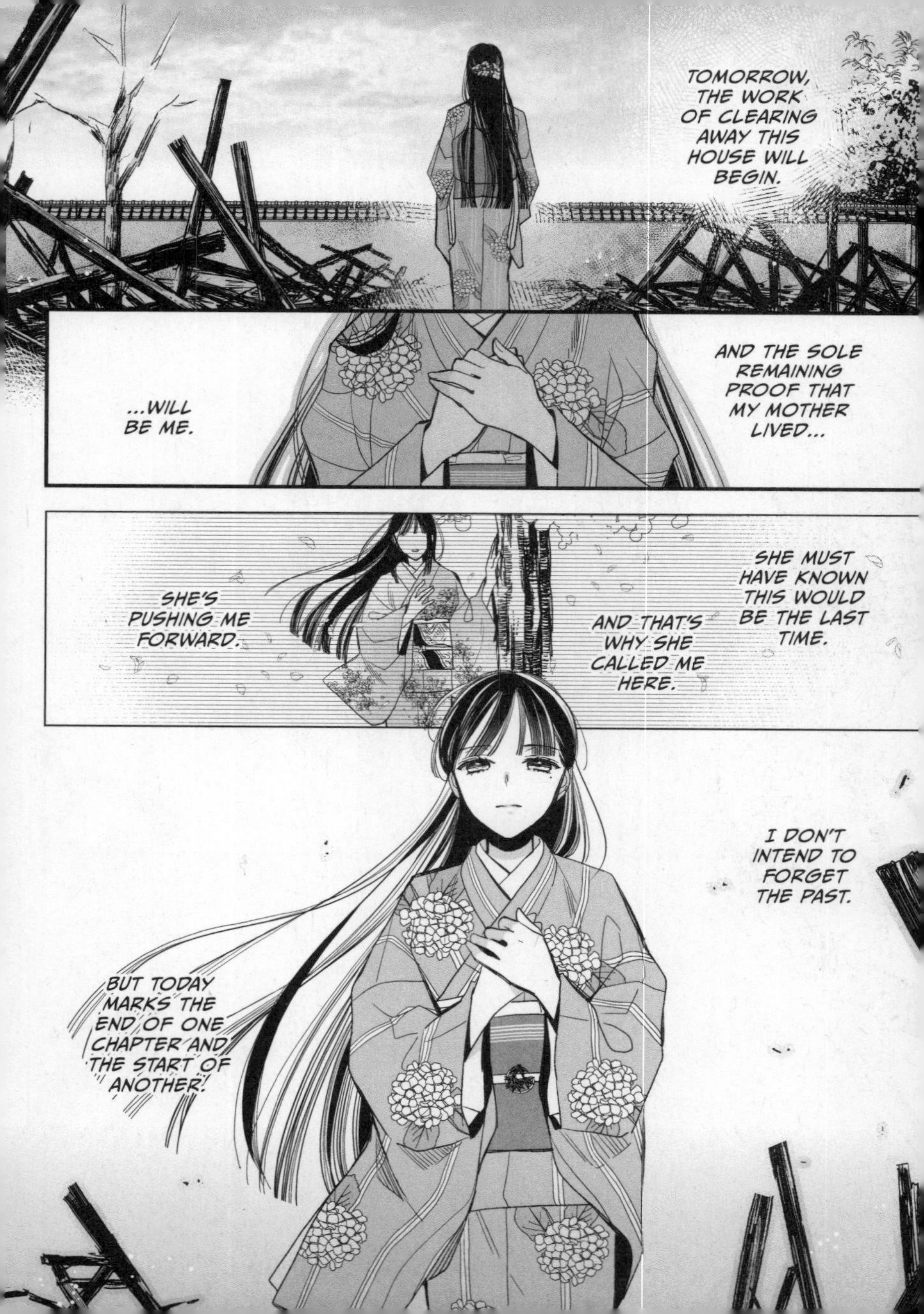
TOMORROW, THE WORK OF CLEARING AWAY THIS HOUSE WILL BEGIN.
AND THE SOLE REMAINING PROOF THAT MY MOTHER LIVED...
...WILL BE ME.
SHE MUST HAVE KNOWN THIS WOULD BE THE LAST TIME.
AND THAT'S WHY SHE CALLED ME HERE.
SHE'S PUSHING ME FORWARD.
I DON'T INTEND TO FORGET THE PAST.
BUT TODAY MARKS THE END OF ONE CHAPTER AND THE START OF ANOTHER.

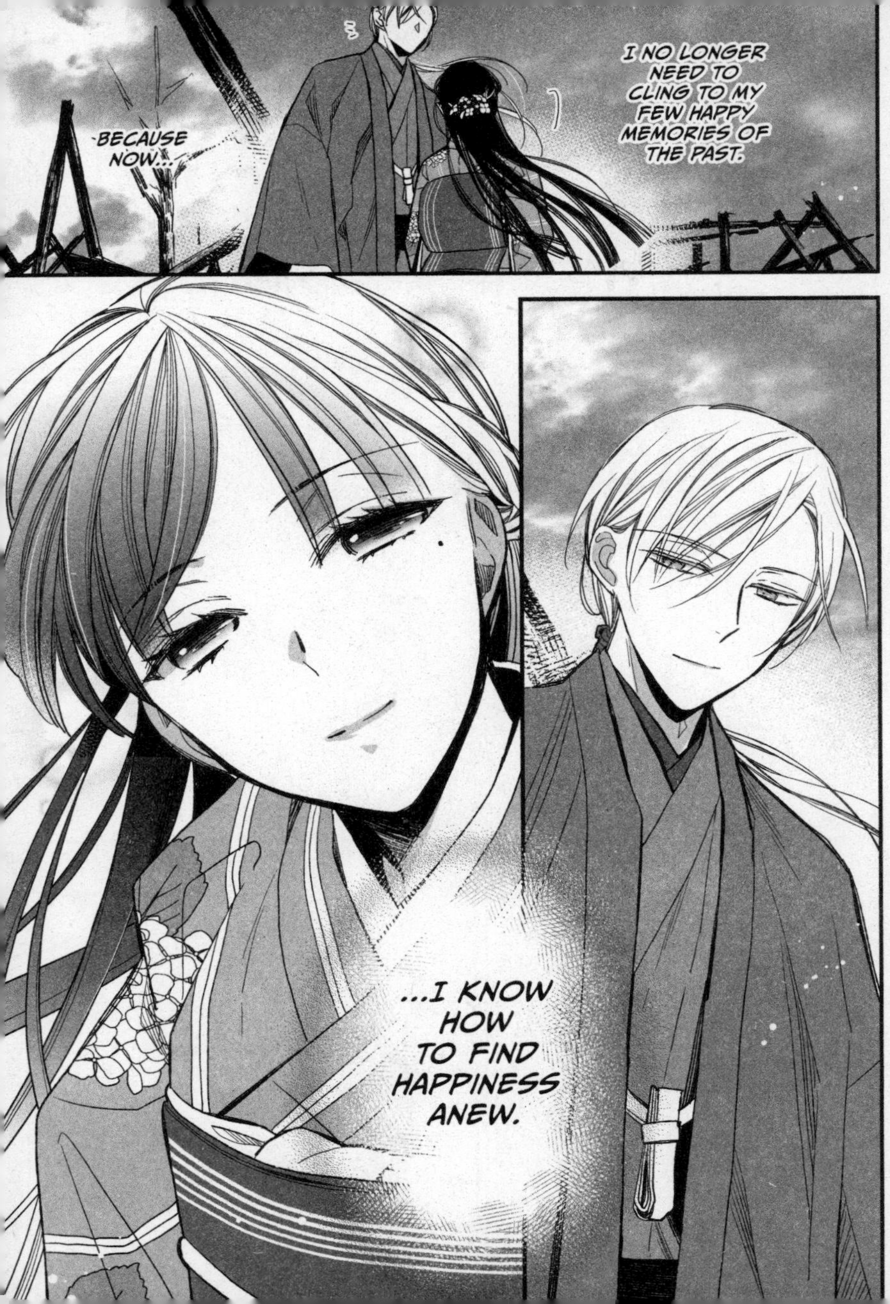
I NO LONGER NEED TO CLING TO MY FEW HAPPY MEMORIES OF THE PAST.
BECAUSE NOW...
...I KNOW HOW TO FIND HAPPINESS ANEW.

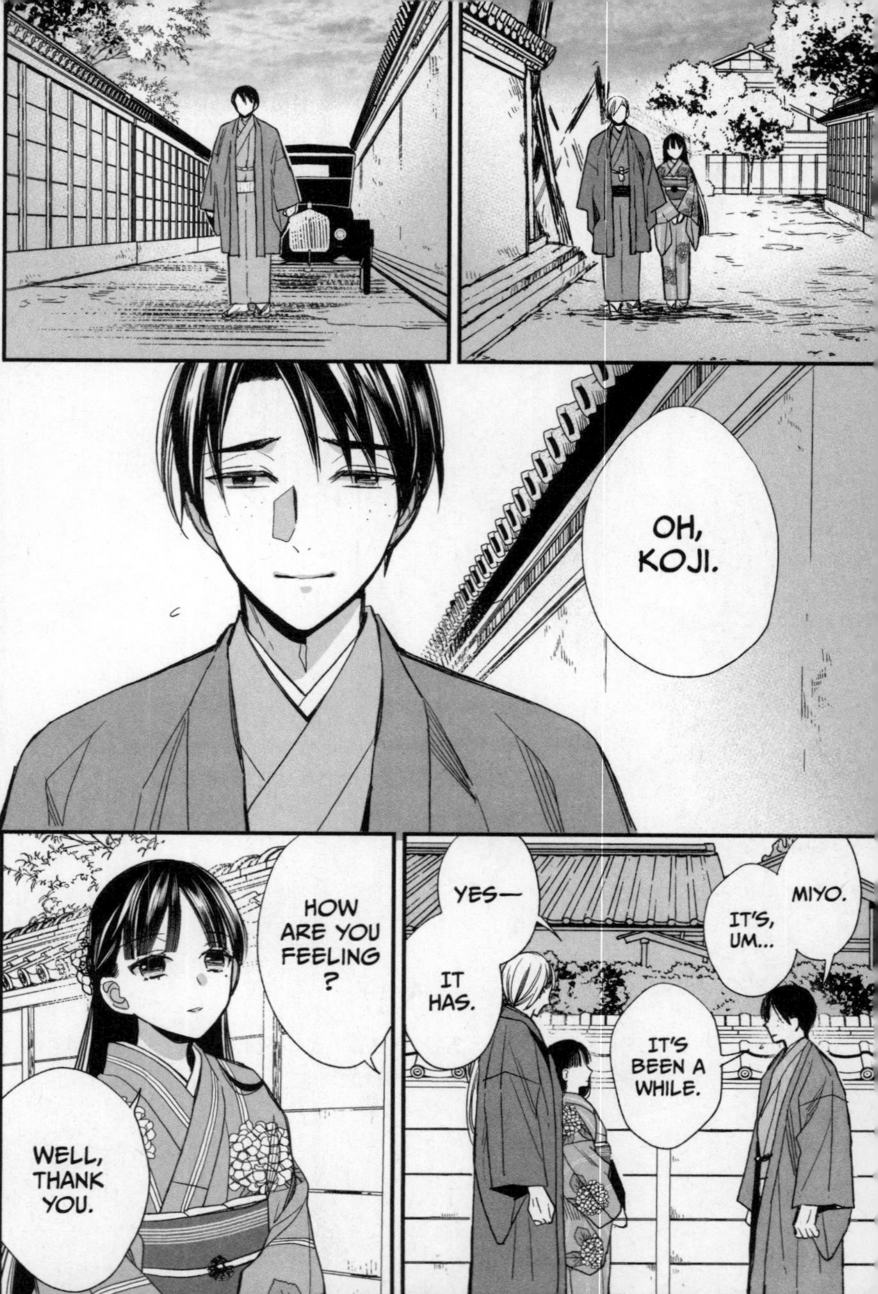
OH, KOJI.
MIYO.
IT'S, UM...
IT'S BEEN A WHILE.
YES—
IT HAS.
HOW ARE YOU FEELING?
WELL, THANK YOU.

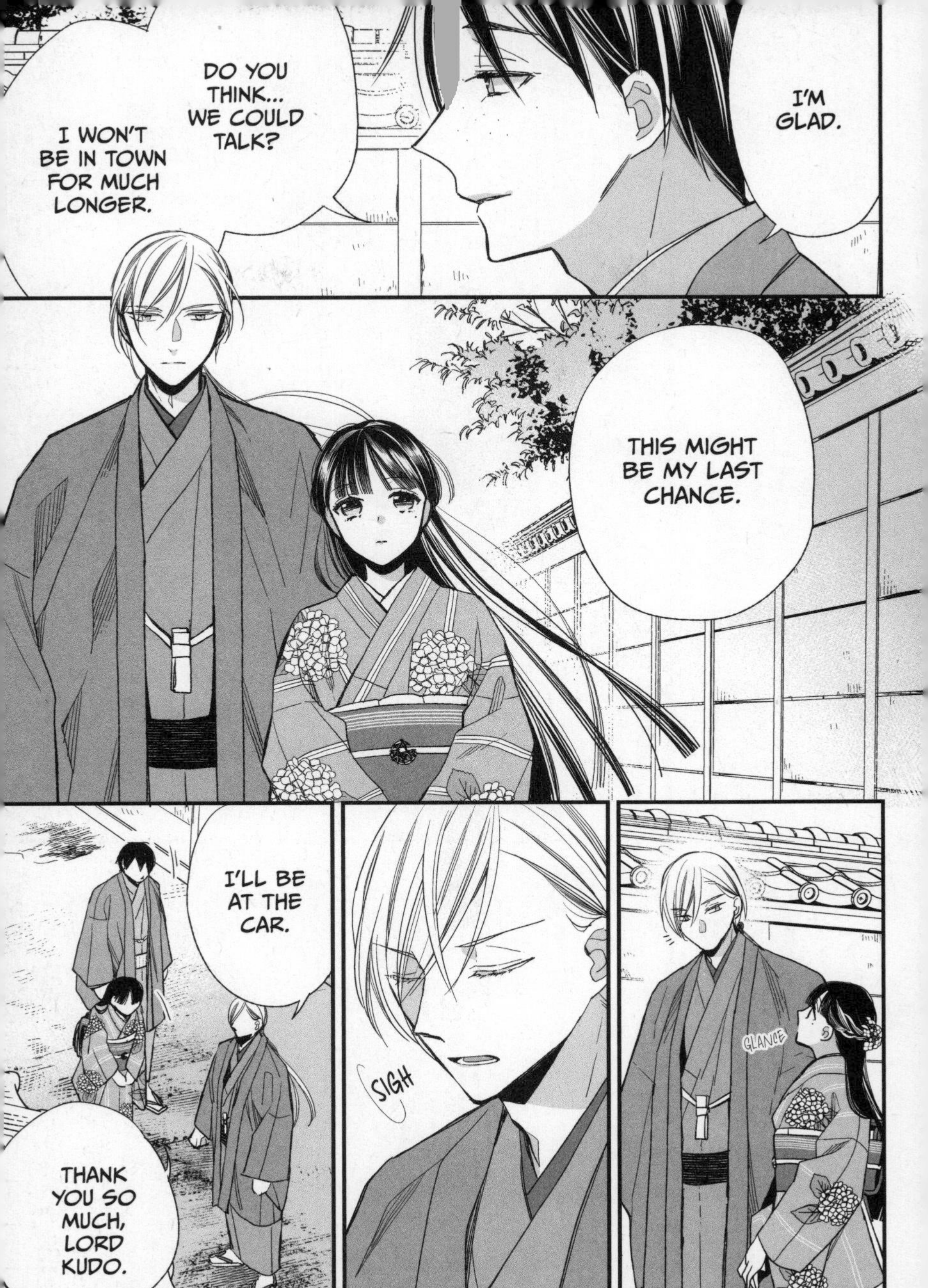
I'M GLAD.
DO YOU THINK... WE COULD TALK?
I WON'T BE IN TOWN FOR MUCH LONGER.
THIS MIGHT BE MY LAST CHANCE.
GLANCE
SIGH
I'LL BE AT THE CAR.
THANK YOU SO MUCH, LORD KUDO.

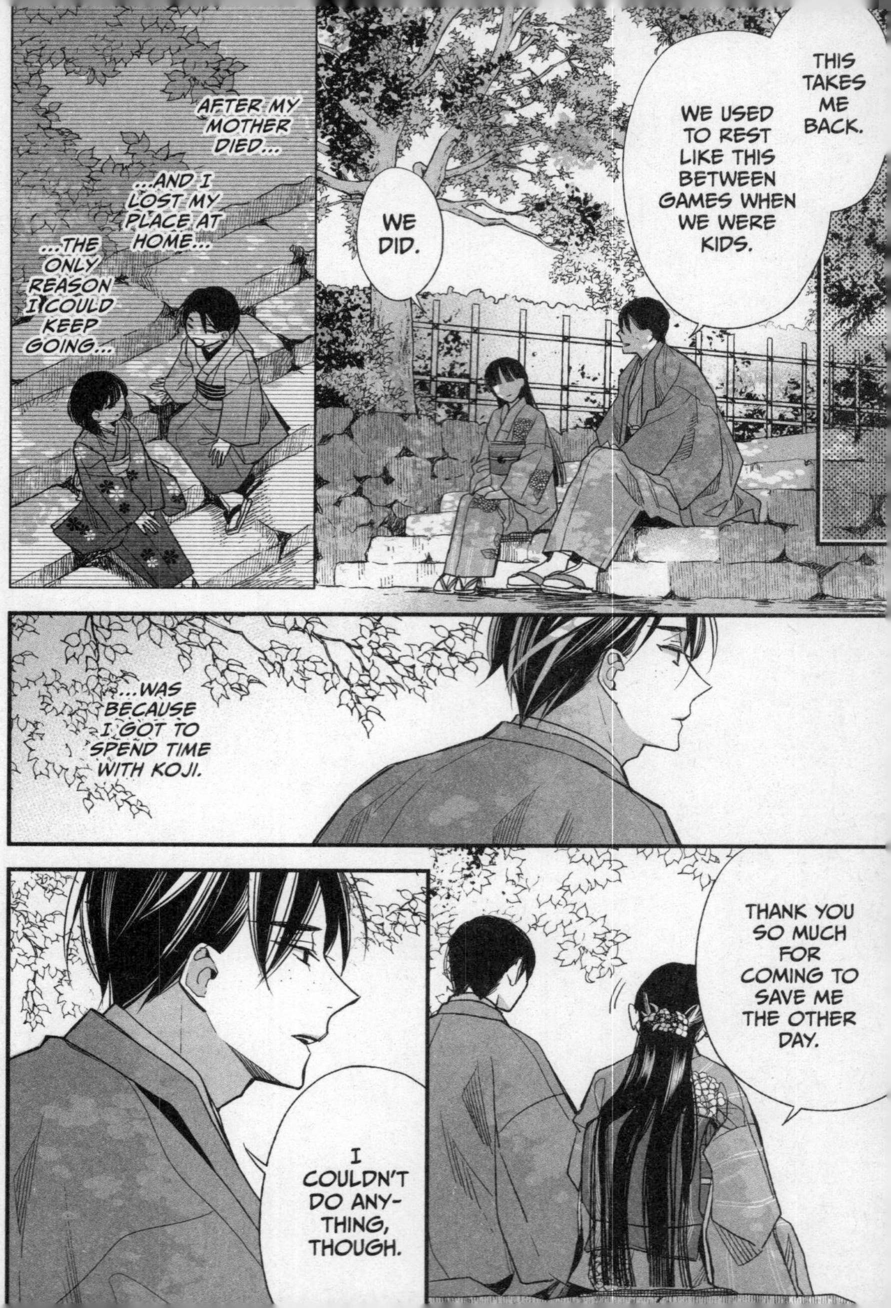
THIS TAKES ME BACK.
WE USED TO REST LIKE THIS BETWEEN GAMES WHEN WE WERE KIDS.
WE DID.
AFTER MY MOTHER DIED...
...AND I LOST MY PLACE AT HOME...
...THE ONLY REASON I COULD KEEP GOING...
...WAS BECAUSE I GOT TO SPEND TIME WITH KOJI.
THANK YOU SO MUCH FOR COMING TO SAVE ME THE OTHER DAY.
I COULDN'T DO ANY-THING, THOUGH.

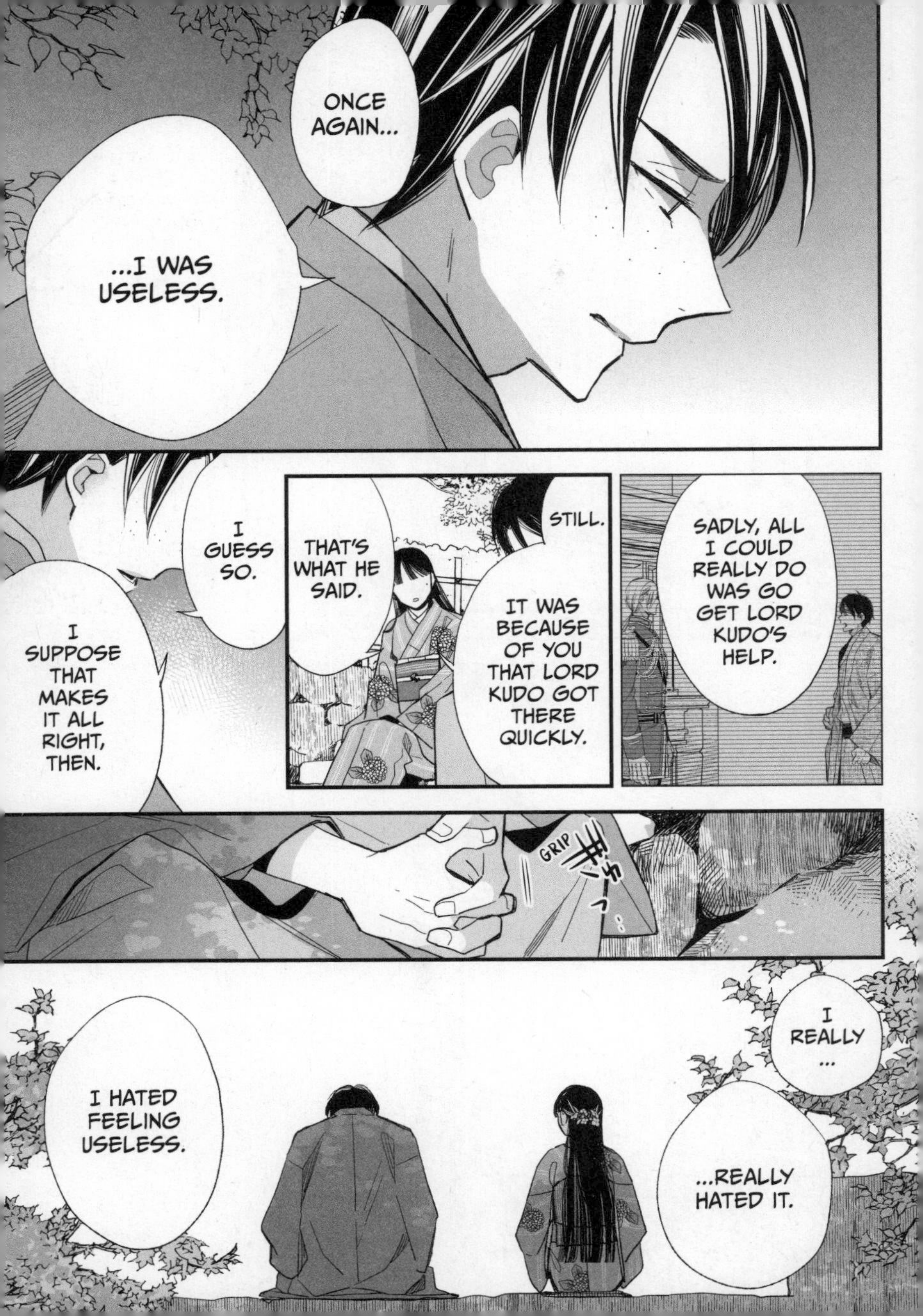
ONCE AGAIN...
...I WAS USELESS.
SADLY, ALL I COULD REALLY DO WAS GO GET LORD KUDO'S HELP.
STILL.
IT WAS BECAUSE OF YOU THAT LORD KUDO GOT THERE QUICKLY.
THAT'S WHAT HE SAID.
I GUESS SO.
I SUPPOSE THAT MAKES IT ALL RIGHT, THEN.
GRIP
I REALLY...
...REALLY HATED IT.
I HATED FEELING USELESS.

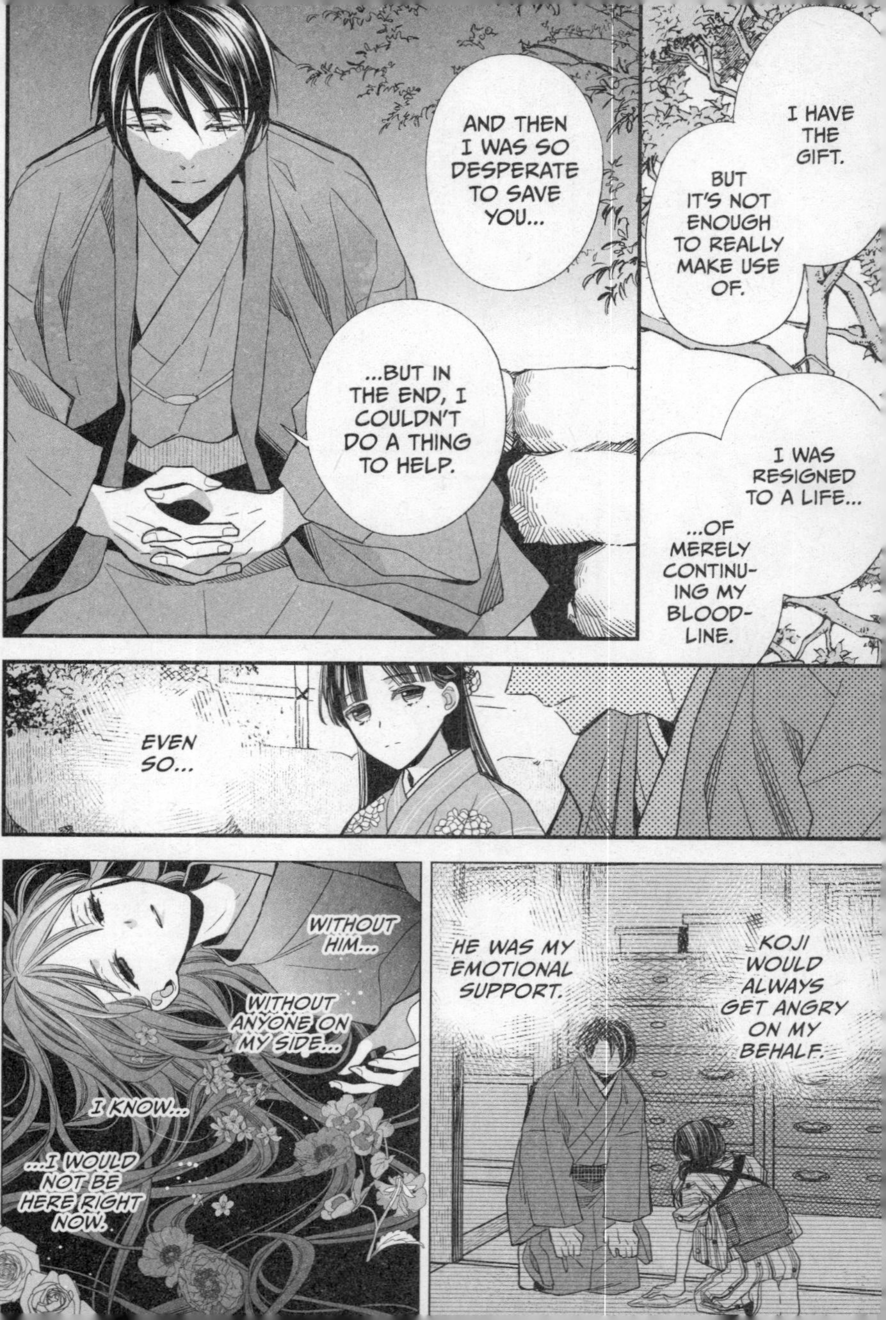
I HAVE THE GIFT.
BUT IT'S NOT ENOUGH TO REALLY MAKE USE OF.
I WAS RESIGNED TO A LIFE...
...OF MERELY CONTINUING MY BLOODLINE.
AND THEN I WAS SO DESPERATE TO SAVE YOU...
...BUT IN THE END, I COULDN'T DO A THING TO HELP.
EVEN SO...
KOJI WOULD ALWAYS GET ANGRY ON MY BEHALF.
HE WAS MY EMOTIONAL SUPPORT.
WITHOUT HIM...
WITHOUT ANYONE ON MY SIDE...
I KNOW...
...I WOULD NOT BE HERE RIGHT NOW.

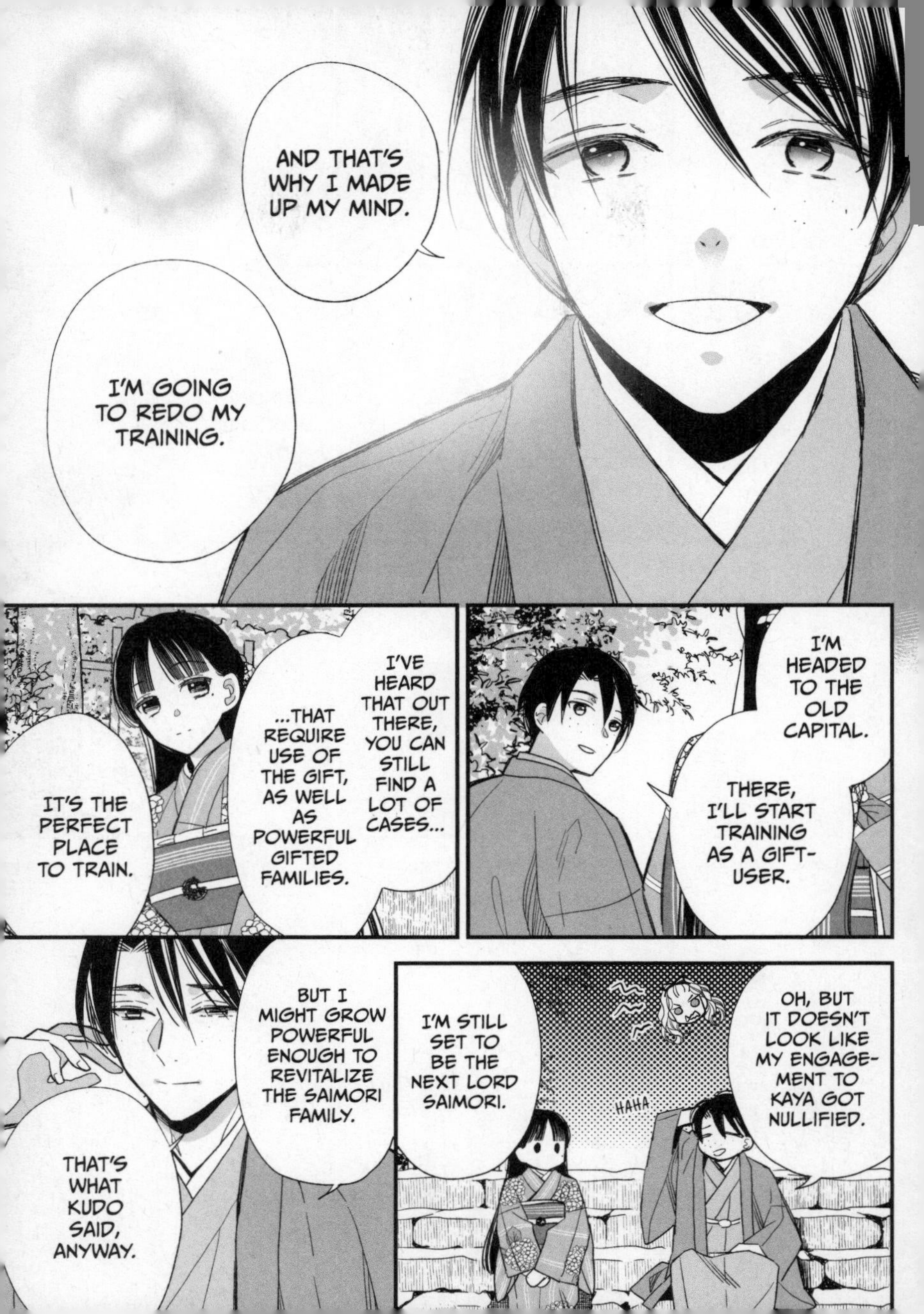
AND THAT'S WHY I MADE UP MY MIND.
I'M GOING TO REDO MY TRAINING.
I'M HEADED TO THE OLD CAPITAL.
THERE, I'LL START TRAINING AS A GIFT-USER.
I'VE HEARD THAT OUT THERE, YOU CAN STILL FIND A LOT OF CASES...
...THAT REQUIRE USE OF THE GIFT, AS WELL AS POWERFUL GIFTED FAMILIES.
IT'S THE PERFECT PLACE TO TRAIN.
OH, BUT IT DOESN'T LOOK LIKE MY ENGAGEMENT TO KAYA GOT NULLIFIED.
HAHA
I'M STILL SET TO BE THE NEXT LORD SAIMORI.
BUT I MIGHT GROW POWERFUL ENOUGH TO REVITALIZE THE SAIMORI FAMILY.
THAT'S WHAT KUDO SAID, ANYWAY.

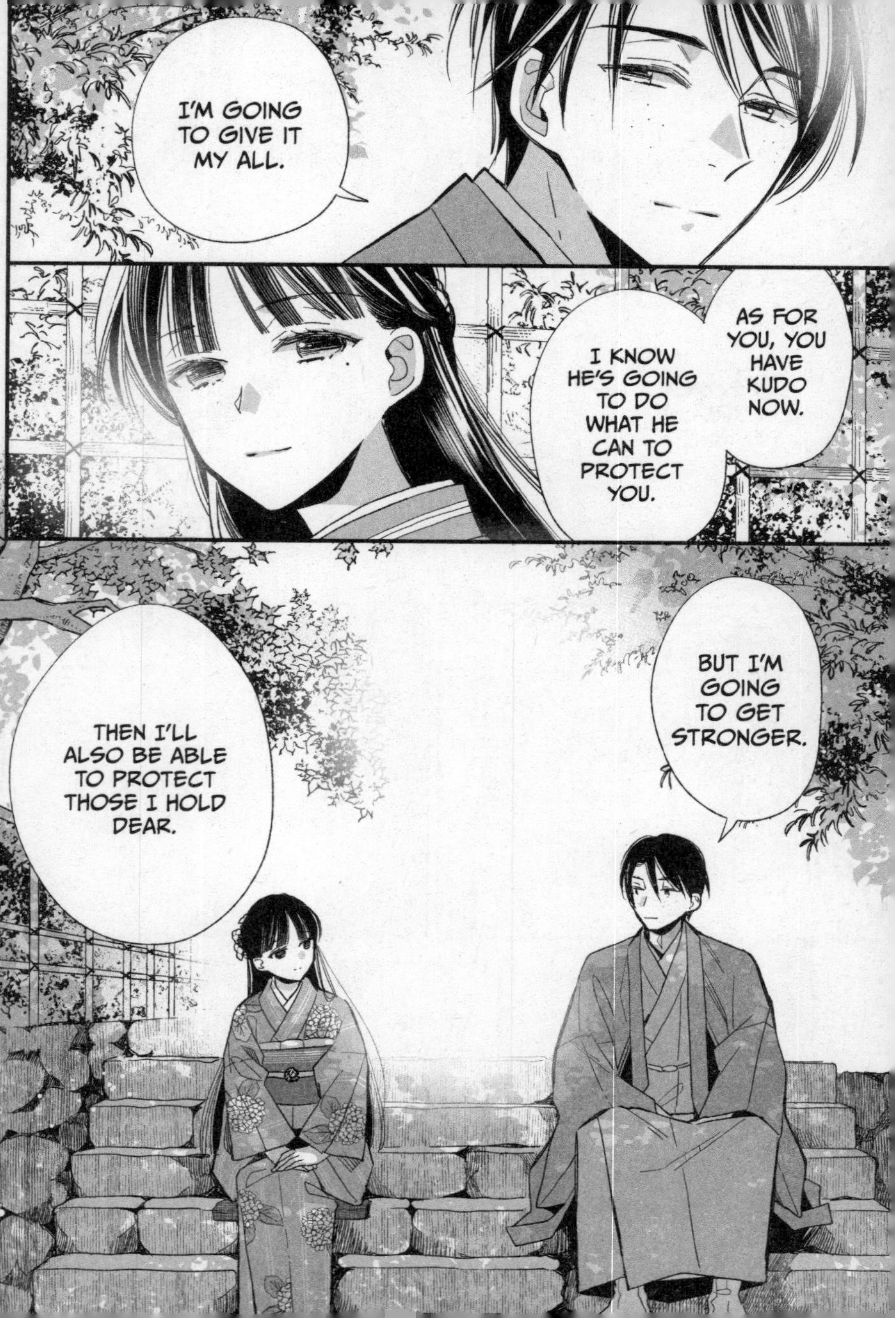
I'M GOING TO GIVE IT MY ALL.
AS FOR YOU, YOU HAVE KUDO NOW.
I KNOW HE'S GOING TO DO WHAT HE CAN TO PROTECT YOU.
BUT I'M GOING TO GET STRONGER.
THEN I'LL ALSO BE ABLE TO PROTECT THOSE I HOLD DEAR.

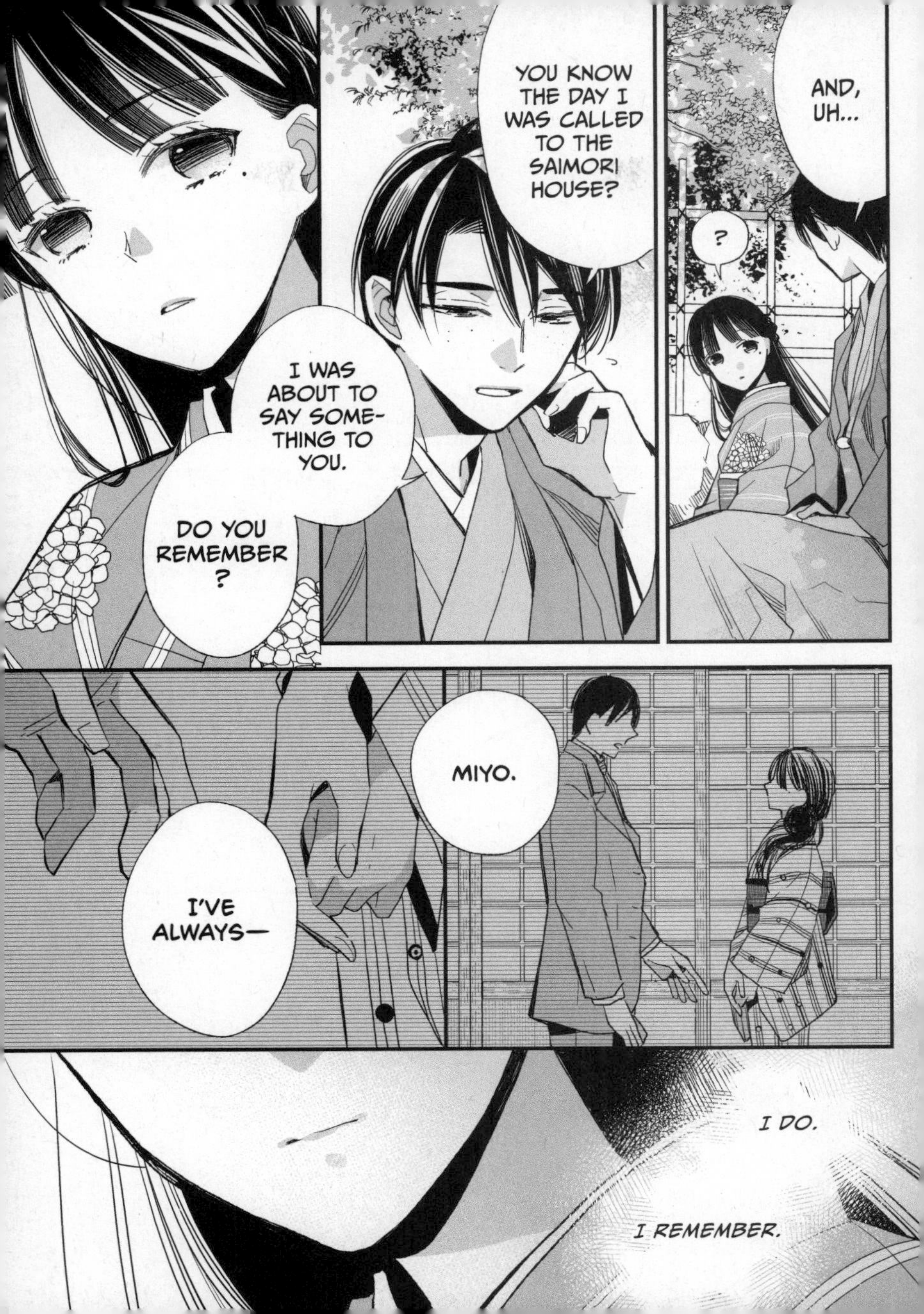
AND, UH...
?
YOU KNOW THE DAY I WAS CALLED TO THE SAIMORI HOUSE?
I WAS ABOUT TO SAY SOME-THING TO YOU.
DO YOU REMEMBER?
MIYO.
I'VE ALWAYS—
I DO.
I REMEMBER.

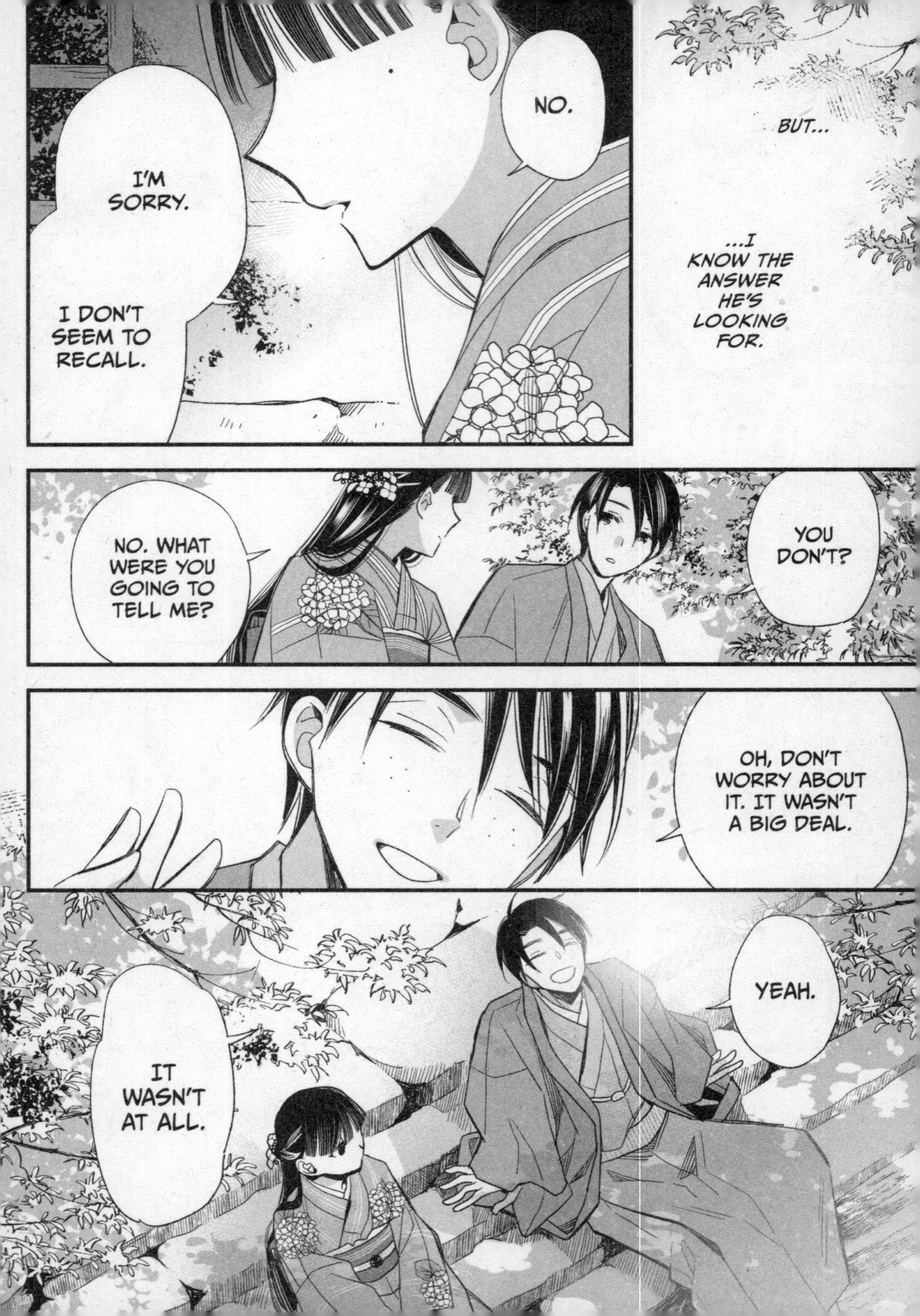
BUT...
...I KNOW THE ANSWER HE'S LOOKING FOR.
NO.
I'M SORRY.
I DON'T SEEM TO RECALL.
YOU DON'T?
NO. WHAT WERE YOU GOING TO TELL ME?
OH, DON'T WORRY ABOUT IT. IT WASN'T A BIG DEAL.
YEAH.
IT WASN'T AT ALL.

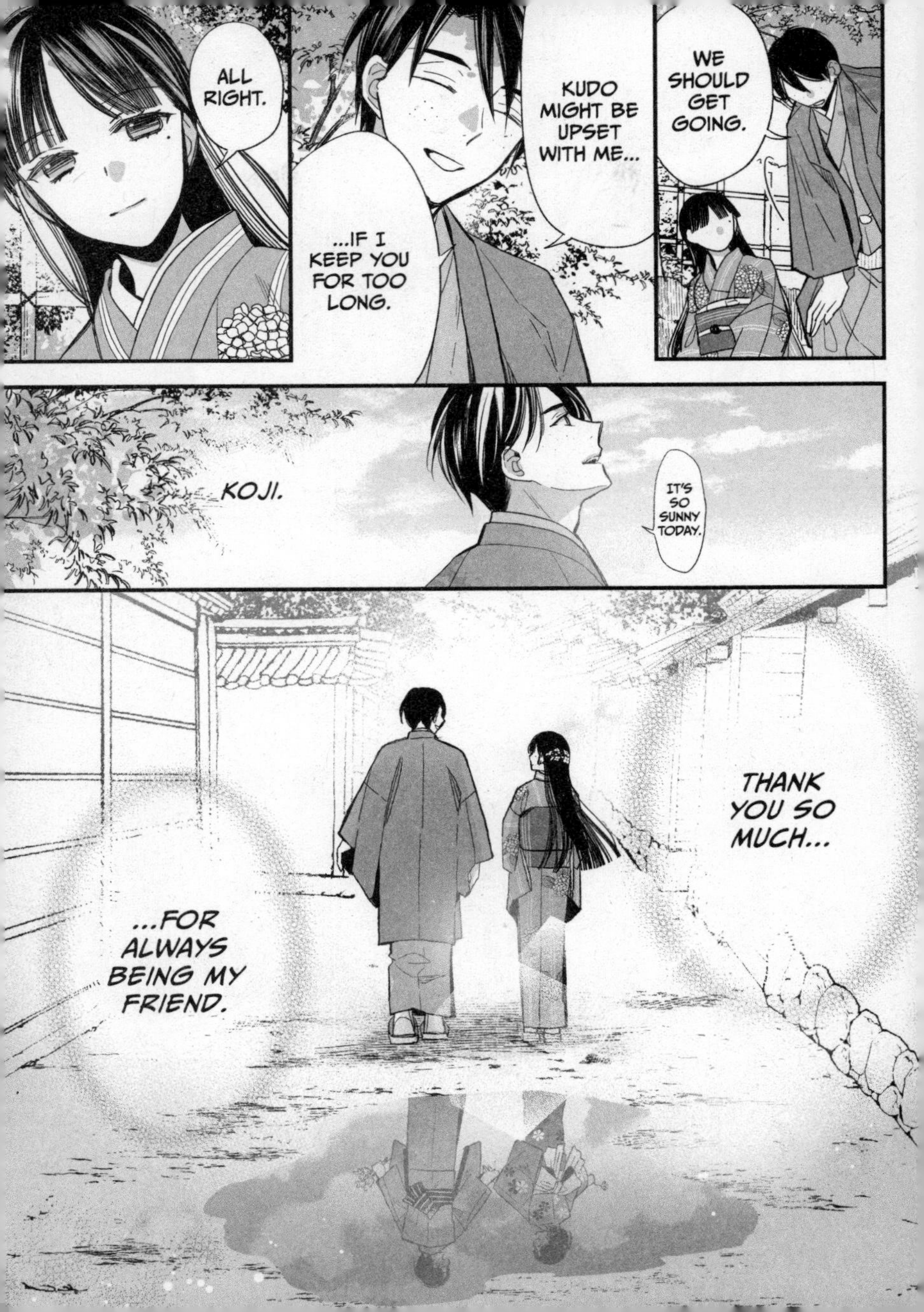
WE SHOULD GET GOING.
KUDO MIGHT BE UPSET WITH ME...
...IF I KEEP YOU FOR TOO LONG.
ALL RIGHT.
IT'S SO SUNNY TODAY.
KOJI.
THANK YOU SO MUCH...
...FOR ALWAYS BEING MY FRIEND.

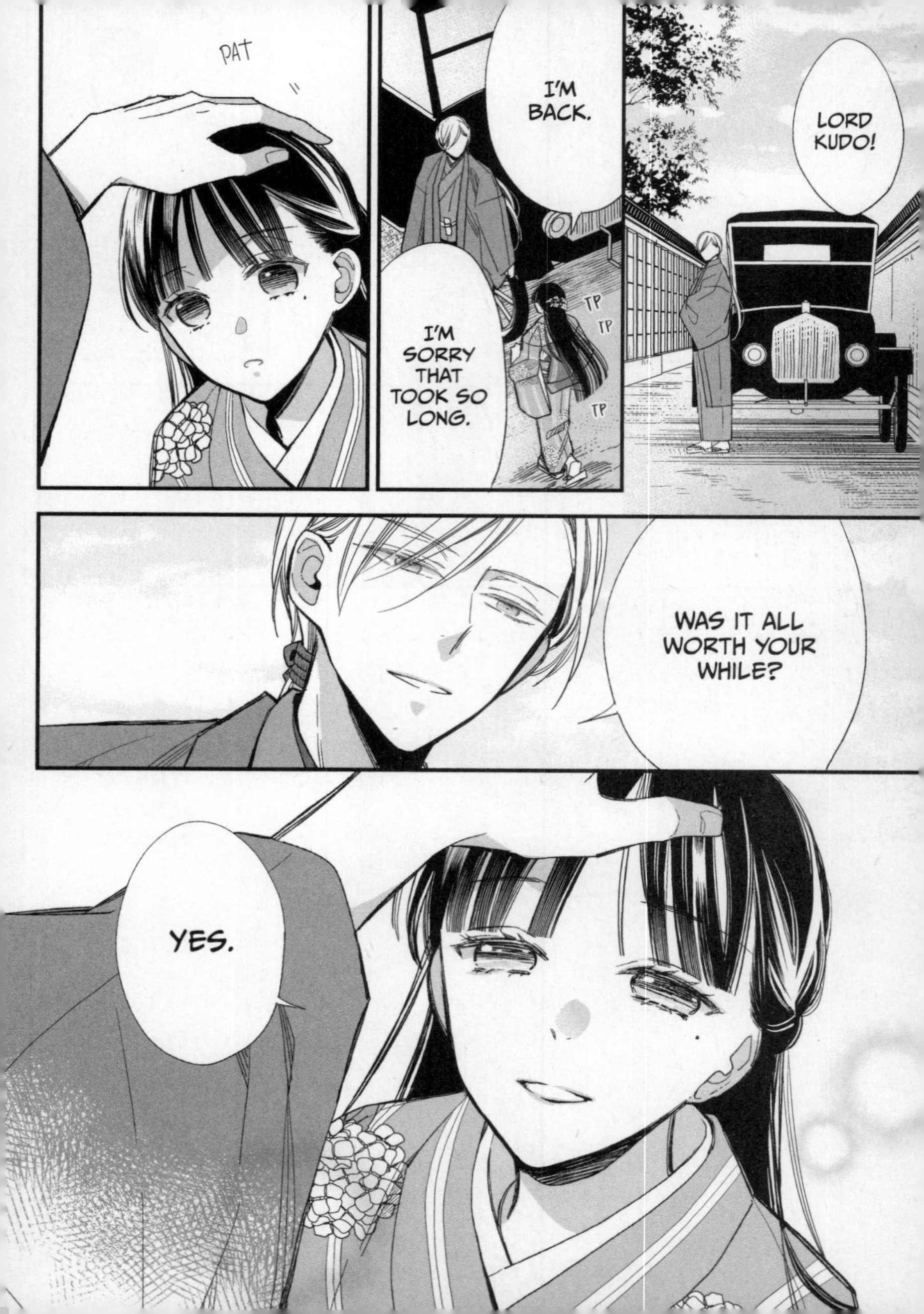
LORD KUDO!
I'M BACK.
TP
TP
TP
I'M SORRY THAT TOOK SO LONG.
PAT
WAS IT ALL WORTH YOUR WHILE?
YES.

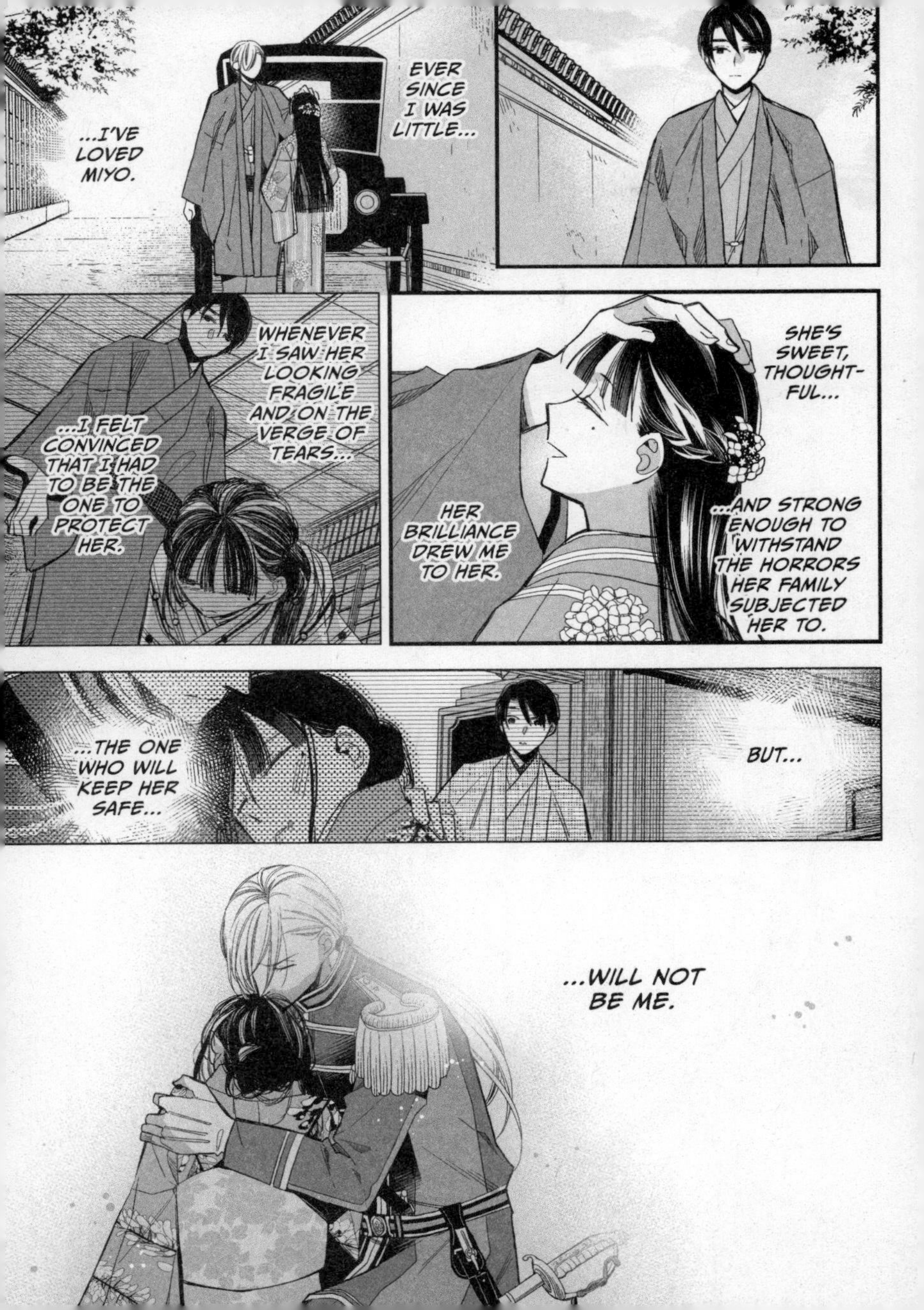
EVER SINCE I WAS LITTLE...
...I'VE LOVED MIYO.
SHE'S SWEET, THOUGHT-FUL...
...AND STRONG ENOUGH TO WITHSTAND THE HORRORS HER FAMILY SUBJECTED HER TO.
HER BRILLIANCE DREW ME TO HER.
WHENEVER I SAW HER LOOKING FRAGILE AND ON THE VERGE OF TEARS...
...I FELT CONVINCED THAT I HAD TO BE THE ONE TO PROTECT HER.
BUT...
...THE ONE WHO WILL KEEP HER SAFE...
...WILL NOT BE ME.

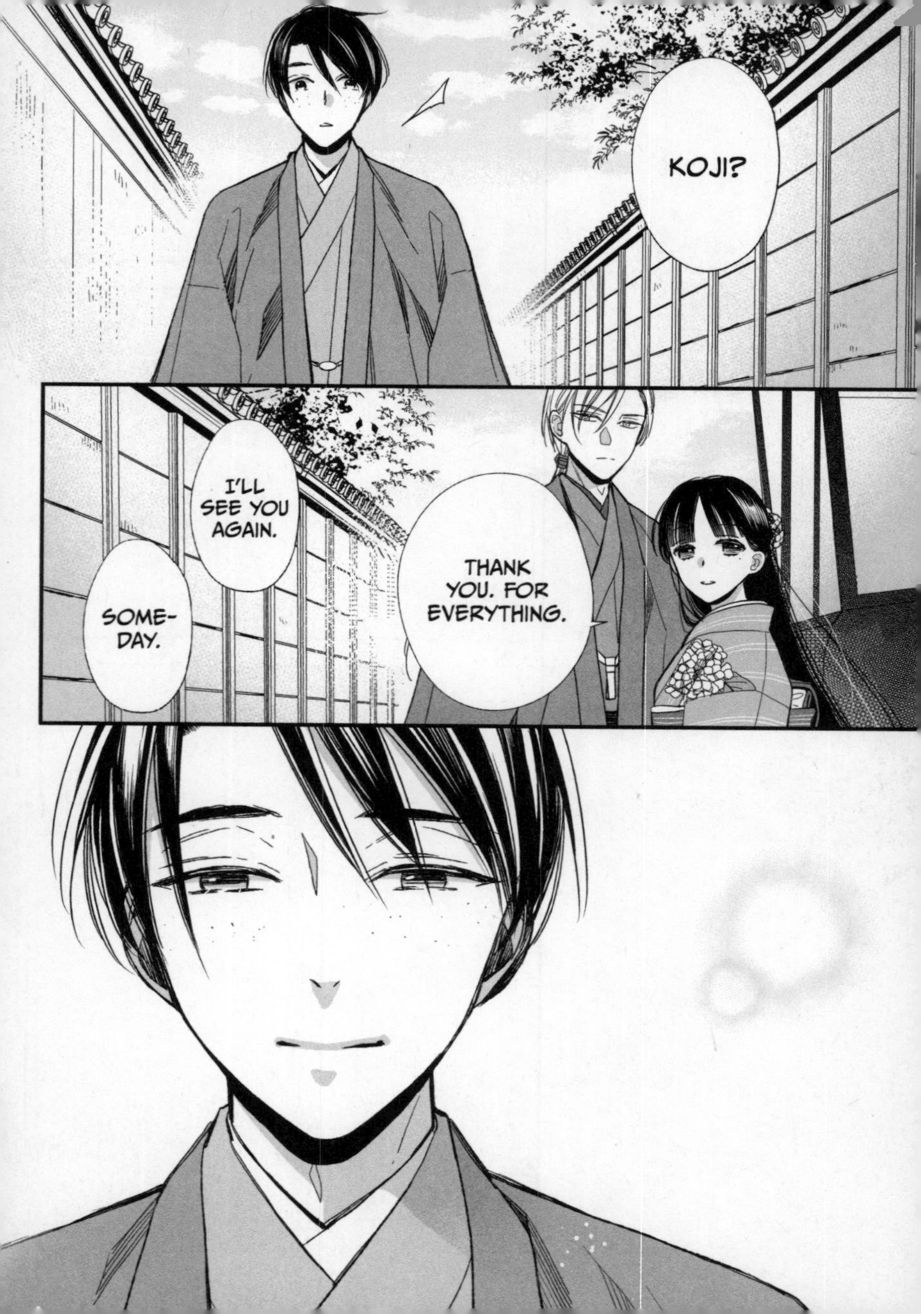
KOJI?
THANK YOU. FOR EVERYTHING.
I'LL SEE YOU AGAIN.
SOME-DAY.

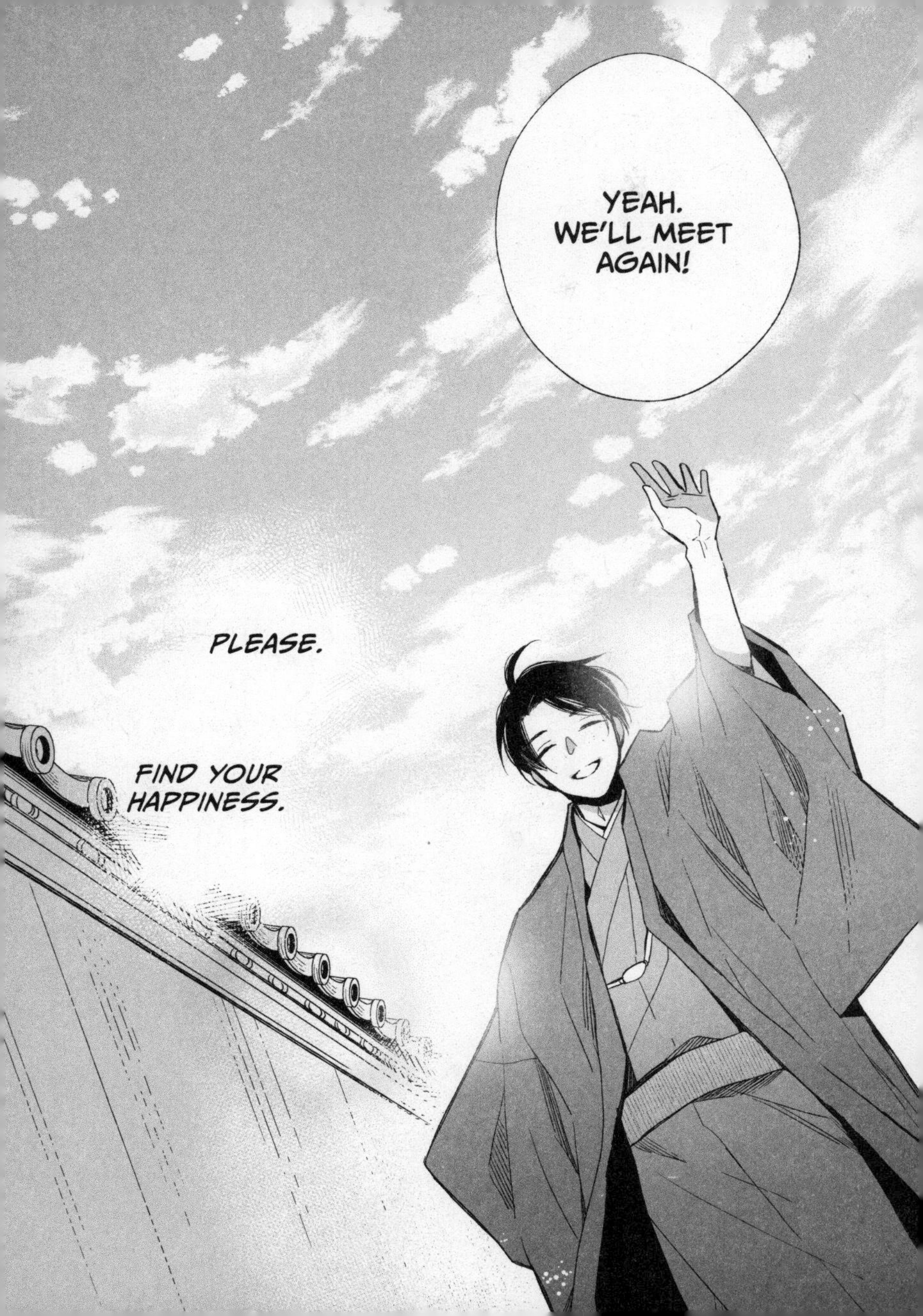
YEAH. WE'LL MEET AGAIN!
PLEASE.
FIND YOUR HAPPINESS.

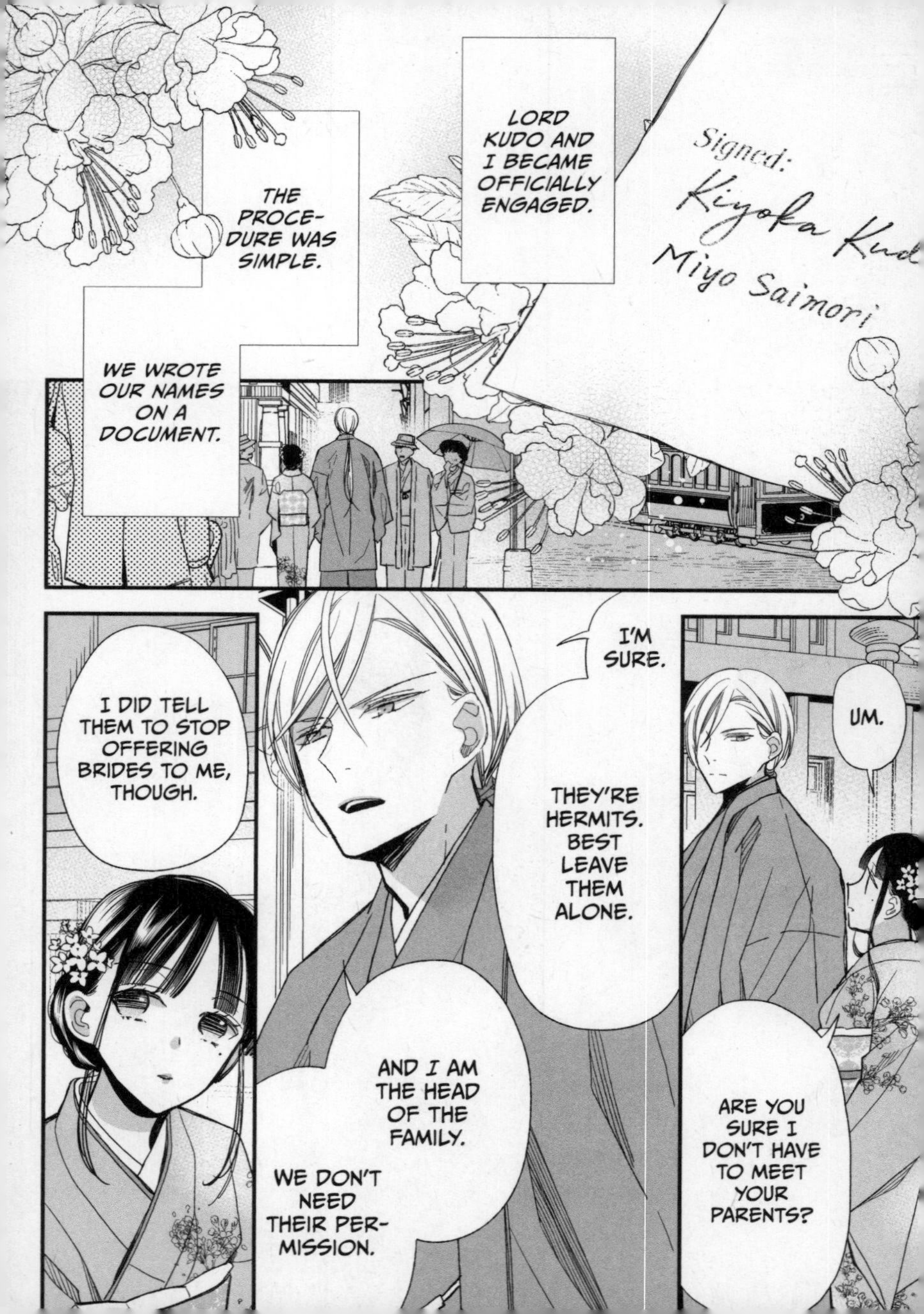
Signed:
Kiyoka Kud
Miyo Saimori
LORD KUDO AND I BECAME OFFICIALLY ENGAGED.
THE PROCE-DURE WAS SIMPLE.
WE WROTE OUR NAMES ON A DOCUMENT.
UM.
ARE YOU SURE I DON'T HAVE TO MEET YOUR PARENTS?
I'M SURE.
THEY'RE HERMITS. BEST LEAVE THEM ALONE.
AND I AM THE HEAD OF THE FAMILY.
WE DON'T NEED THEIR PER-MISSION.
I DID TELL THEM TO STOP OFFERING BRIDES TO ME, THOUGH.

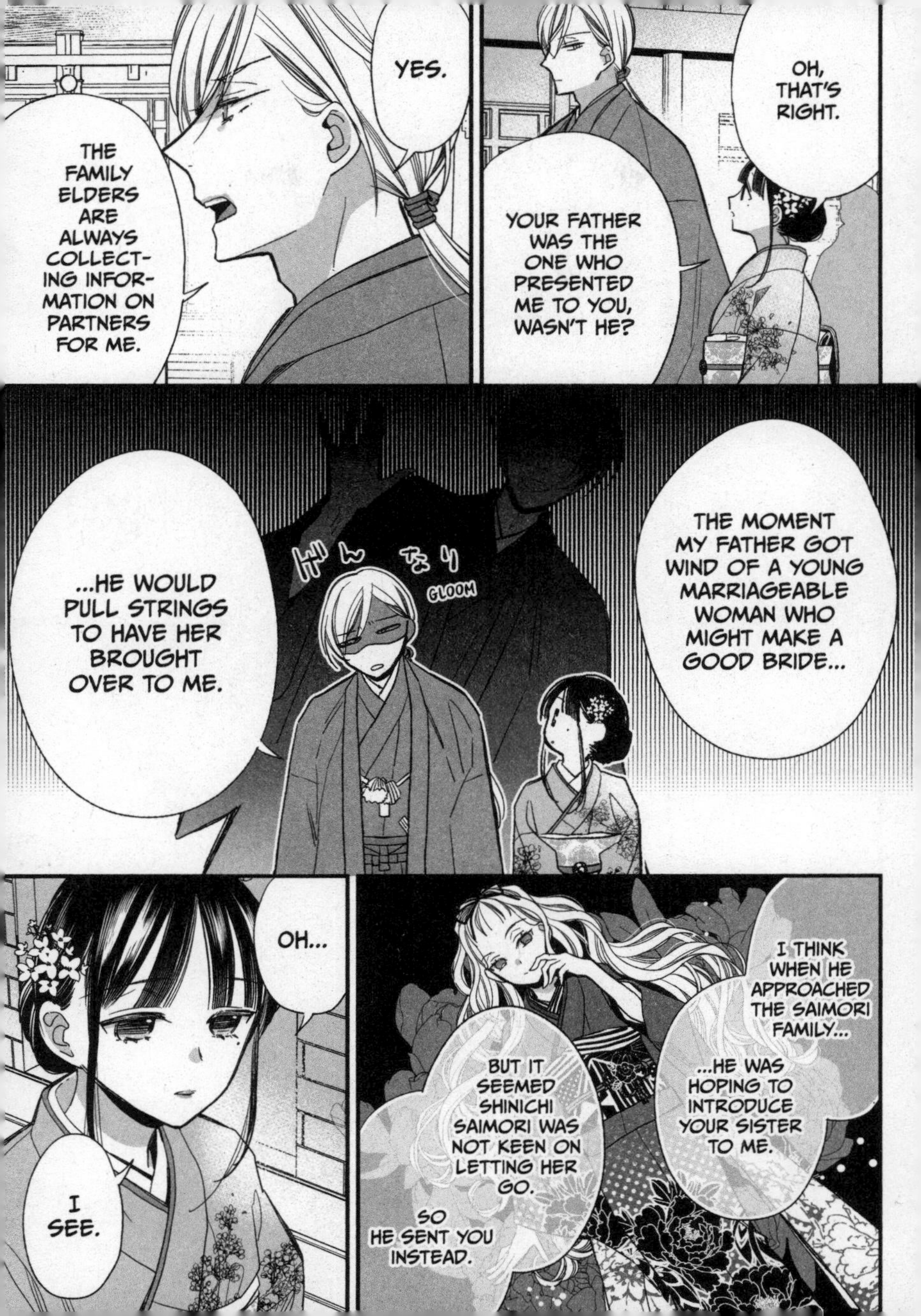
OH, THAT'S RIGHT.
YOUR FATHER WAS THE ONE WHO PRESENTED ME TO YOU, WASN'T HE?
YES.
THE FAMILY ELDERS ARE ALWAYS COLLECTING INFORMATION ON PARTNERS FOR ME.
THE MOMENT MY FATHER GOT WIND OF A YOUNG MARRIAGEABLE WOMAN WHO MIGHT MAKE A GOOD BRIDE...
げんなり
GLOOM
...HE WOULD PULL STRINGS TO HAVE HER BROUGHT OVER TO ME.
I THINK WHEN HE APPROACHED THE SAIMORI FAMILY...
...HE WAS HOPING TO INTRODUCE YOUR SISTER TO ME.
BUT IT SEEMED SHINICHI SAIMORI WAS NOT KEEN ON LETTING HER GO.
SO HE SENT YOU INSTEAD.
OH...
I SEE.

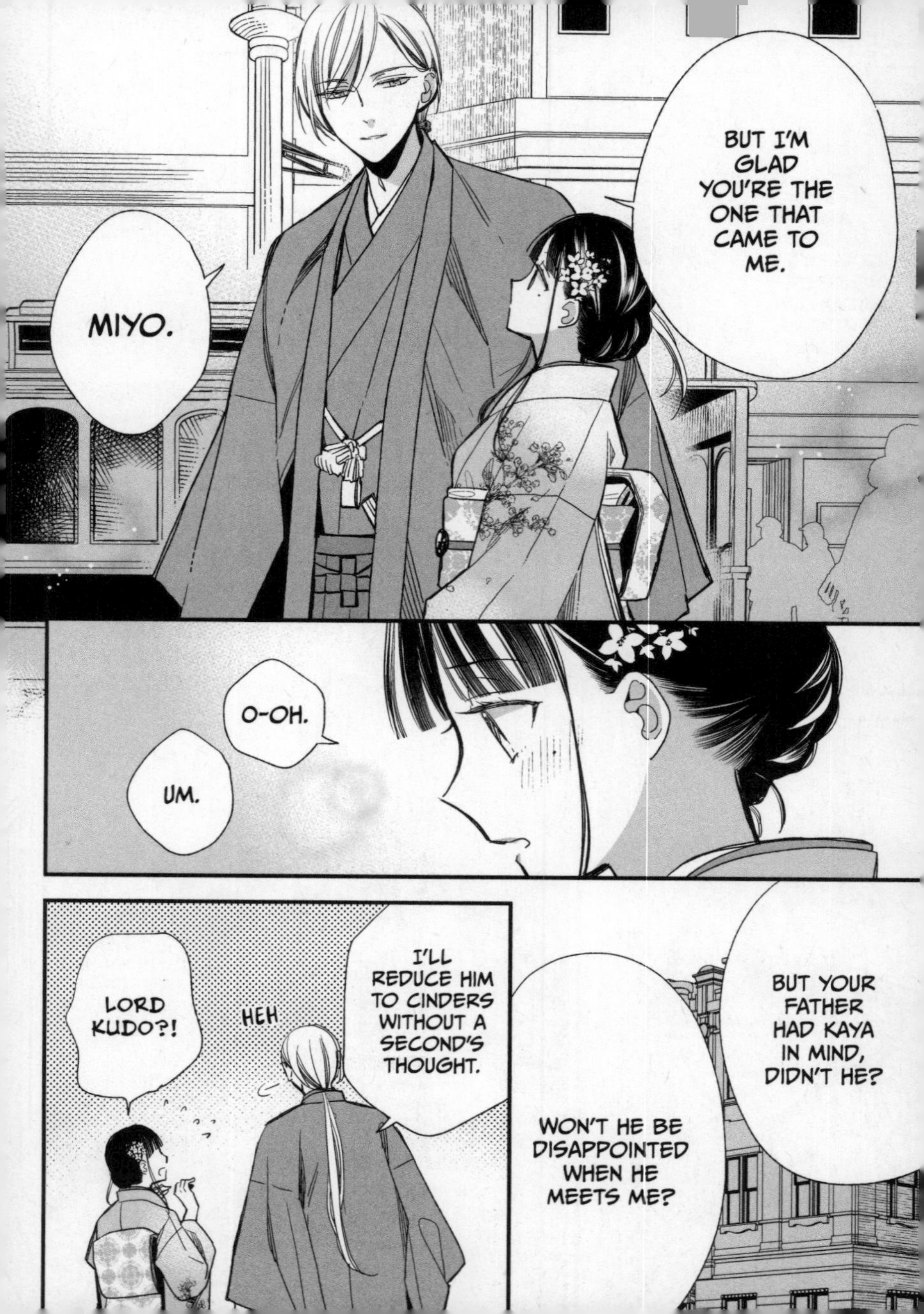
BUT I'M GLAD YOU'RE THE ONE THAT CAME TO ME.
MIYO.
O-OH.
UM.
BUT YOUR FATHER HAD KAYA IN MIND, DIDN'T HE?
WON'T HE BE DISAPPOINTED WHEN HE MEETS ME?
I'LL REDUCE HIM TO CINDERS WITHOUT A SECOND'S THOUGHT.
HEH
LORD KUDO?!

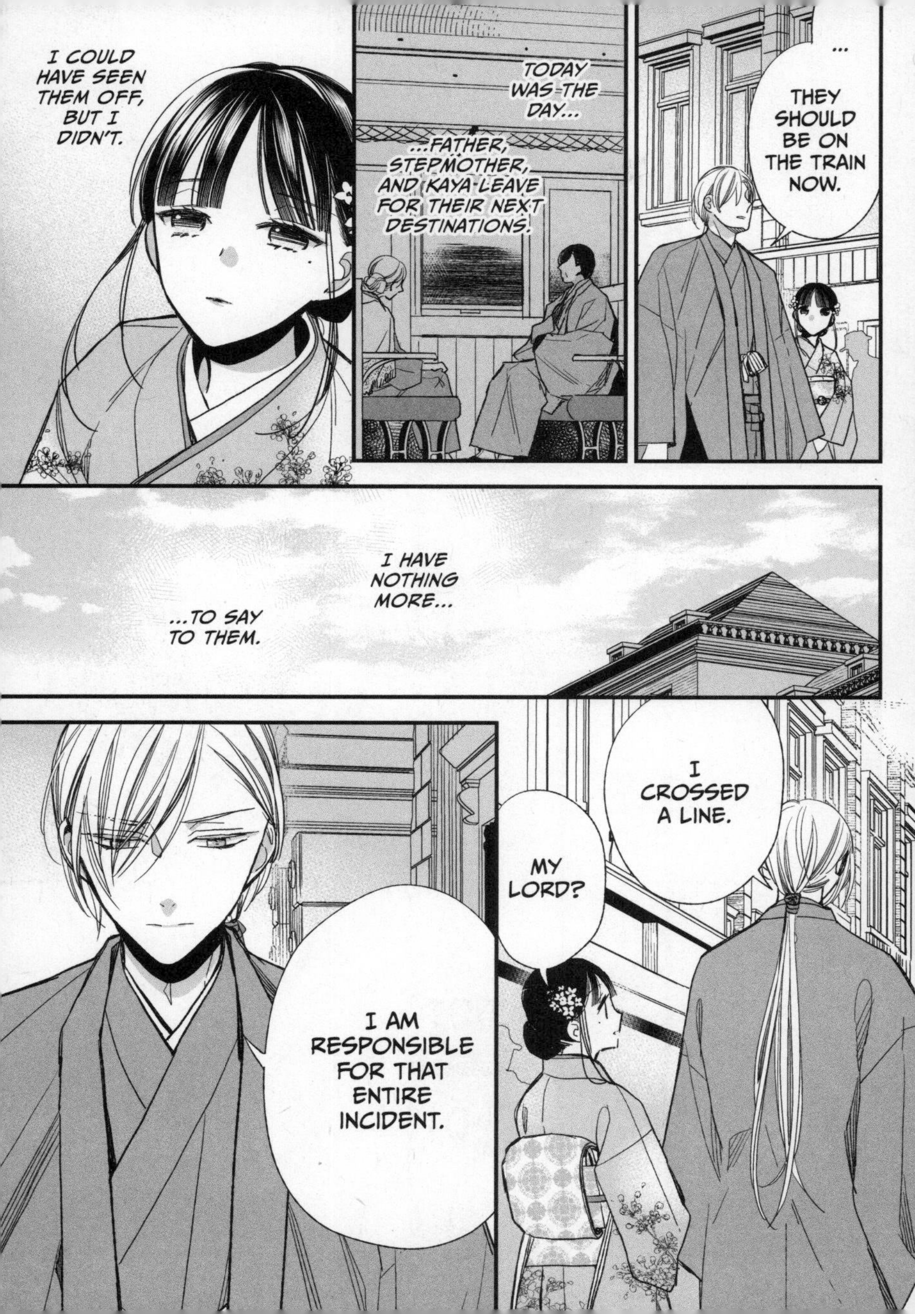
...
THEY SHOULD BE ON THE TRAIN NOW.
TODAY WAS THE DAY...
...FATHER, STEPMOTHER, AND KAYA LEAVE FOR THEIR NEXT DESTINATIONS.
I COULD HAVE SEEN THEM OFF, BUT I DIDN'T.
I HAVE NOTHING MORE...
...TO SAY TO THEM.
I CROSSED A LINE.
MY LORD?
I AM RESPONSIBLE FOR THAT ENTIRE INCIDENT.

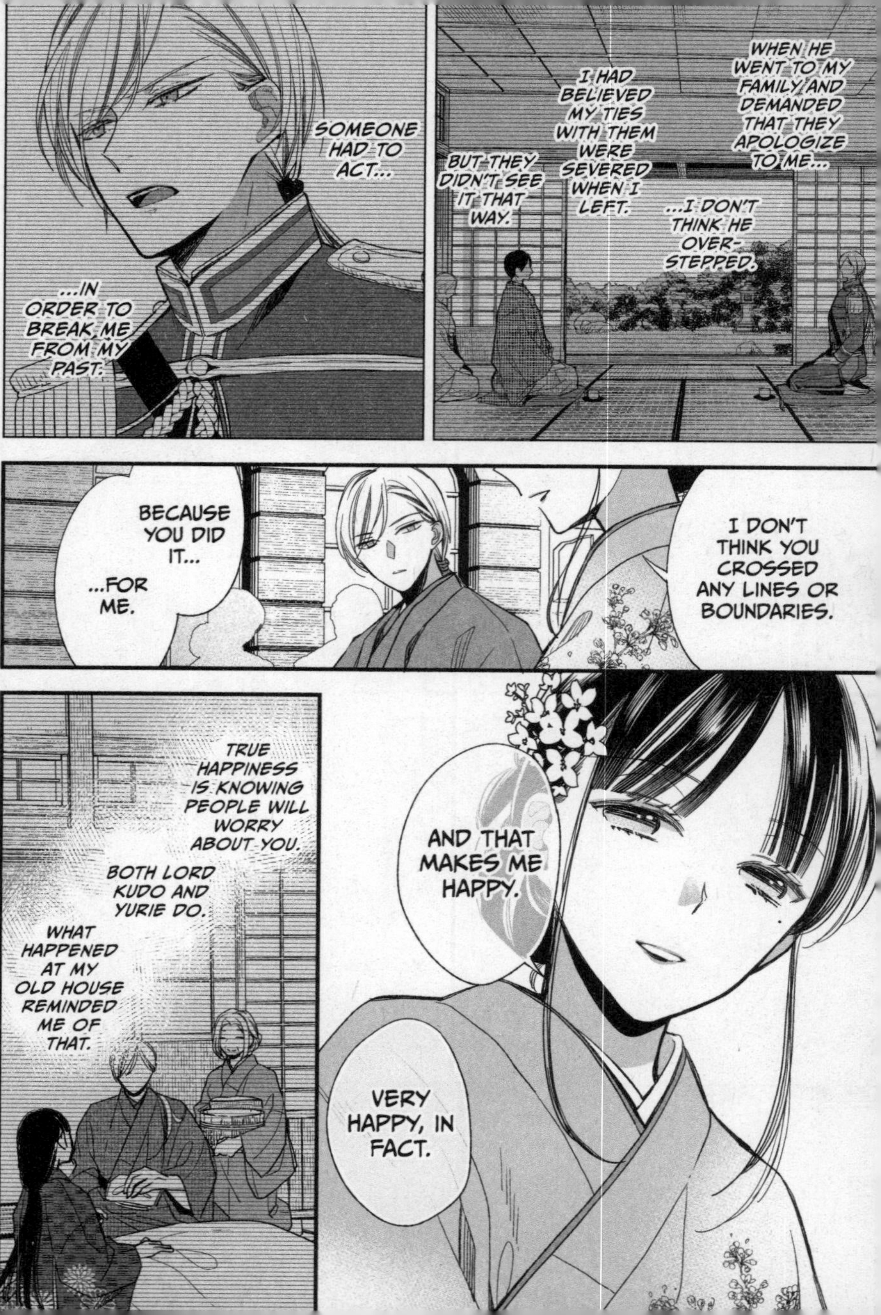
WHEN HE WENT TO MY FAMILY AND DEMANDED THAT THEY APOLOGIZE TO ME...
...I DON'T THINK HE OVER-STEPPED.
I HAD BELIEVED MY TIES WITH THEM WERE SEVERED WHEN I LEFT.
BUT THEY DIDN'T SEE IT THAT WAY.
SOMEONE HAD TO ACT...
...IN ORDER TO BREAK ME FROM MY PAST.
I DON'T THINK YOU CROSSED ANY LINES OR BOUNDARIES.
BECAUSE YOU DID IT...
...FOR ME.
AND THAT MAKES ME HAPPY.
VERY HAPPY, IN FACT.
TRUE HAPPINESS IS KNOWING PEOPLE WILL WORRY ABOUT YOU.
BOTH LORD KUDO AND YURIE DO.
WHAT HAPPENED AT MY OLD HOUSE REMINDED ME OF THAT.

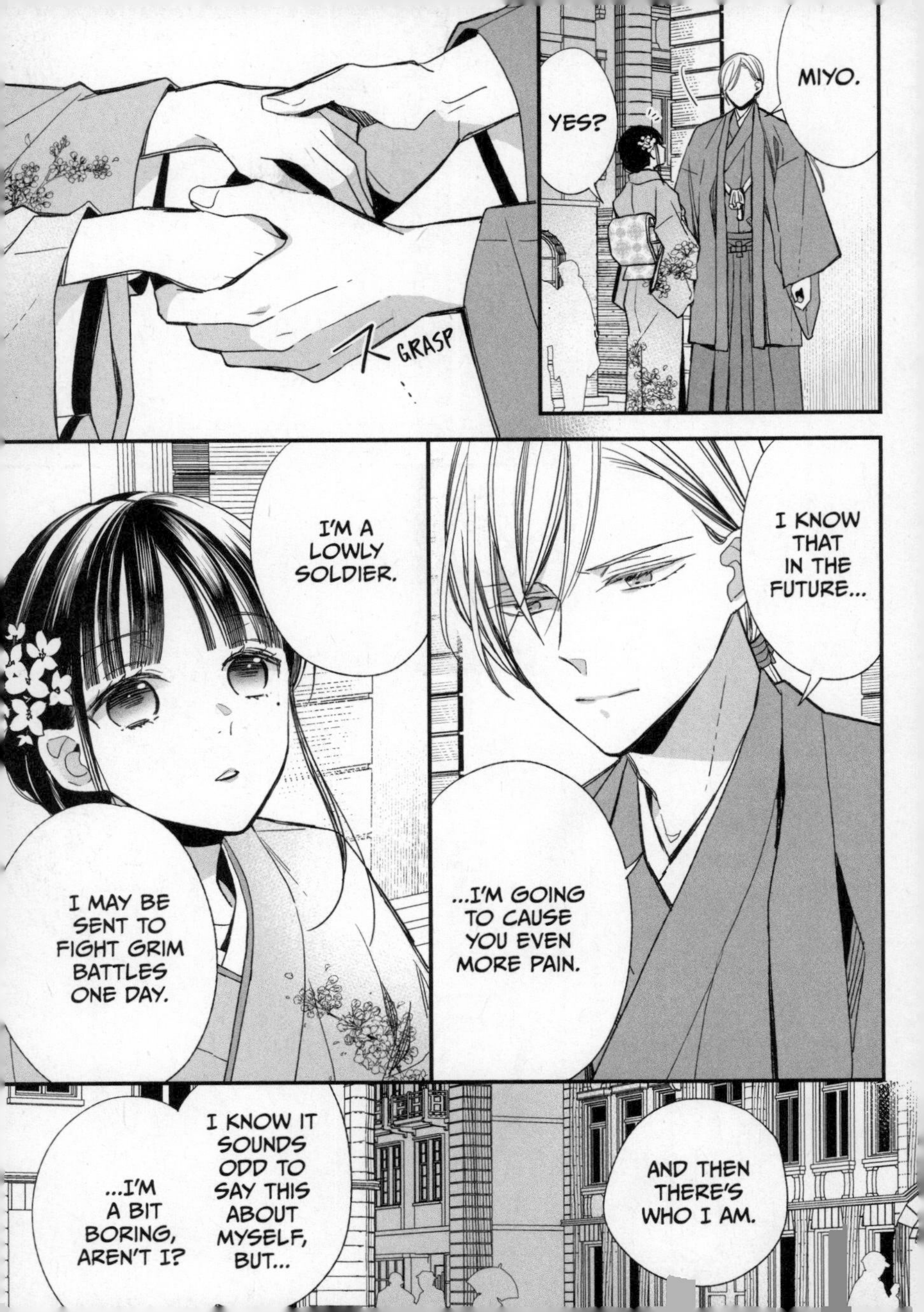
MIYO.
YES?
GRASP
I KNOW THAT IN THE FUTURE...
...I'M GOING TO CAUSE YOU EVEN MORE PAIN.
I'M A LOWLY SOLDIER.
I MAY BE SENT TO FIGHT GRIM BATTLES ONE DAY.
AND THEN THERE'S WHO I AM.
I KNOW IT SOUNDS ODD TO SAY THIS ABOUT MYSELF, BUT...
...I'M A BIT BORING, AREN'T I?

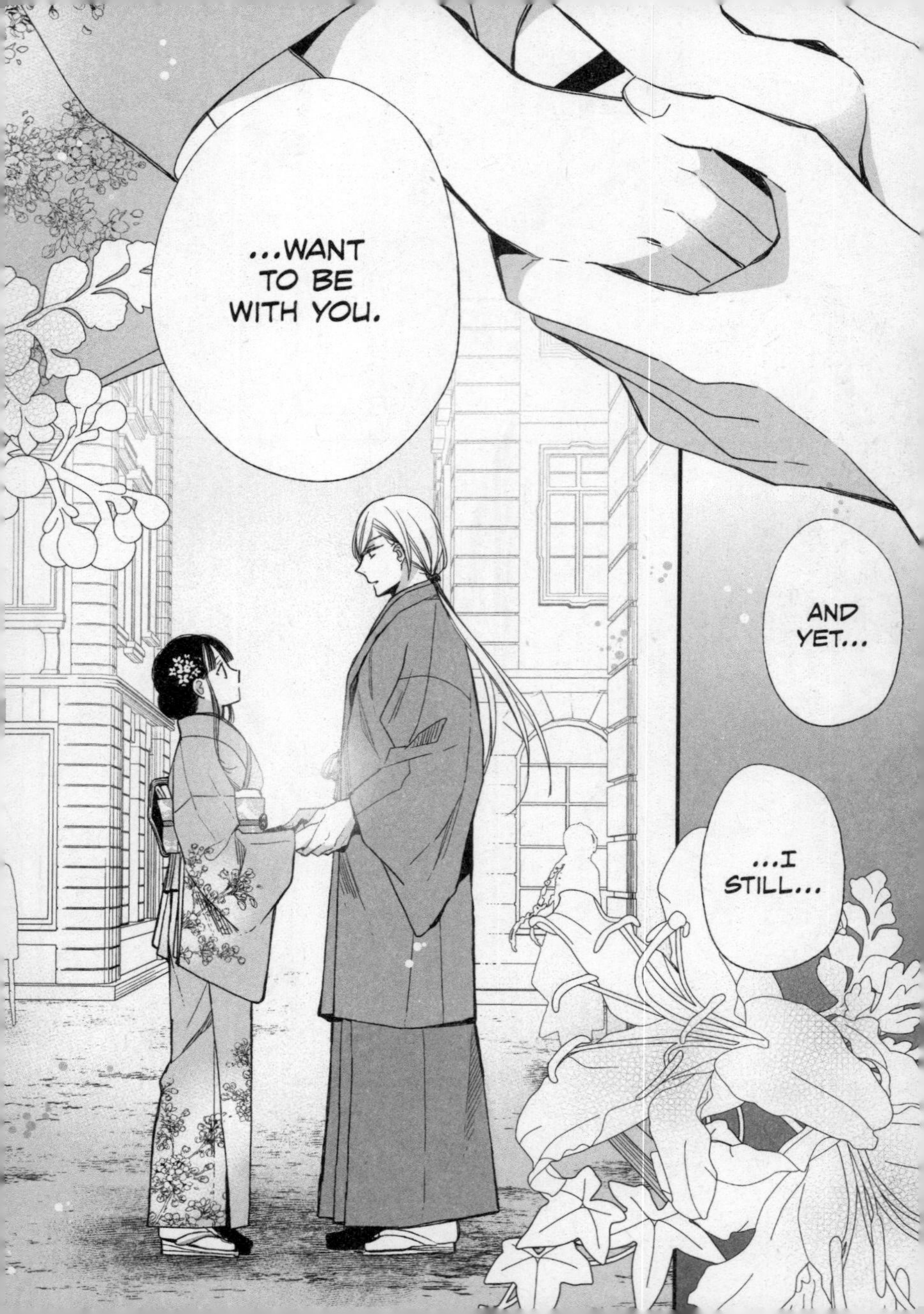
...WANT TO BE WITH YOU.
AND YET...
...I STILL...

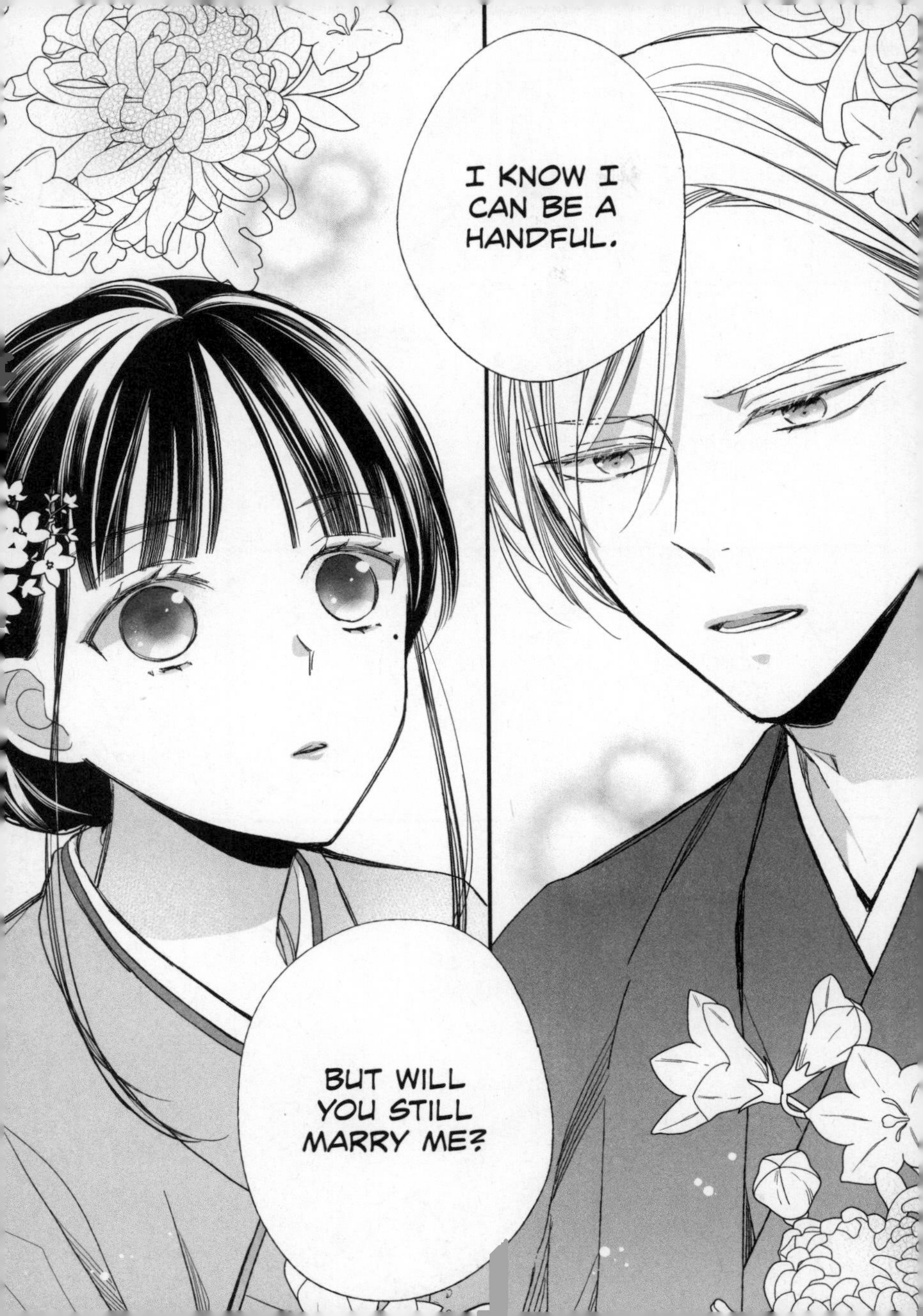
I KNOW I CAN BE A HANDFUL.
BUT WILL YOU STILL MARRY ME?

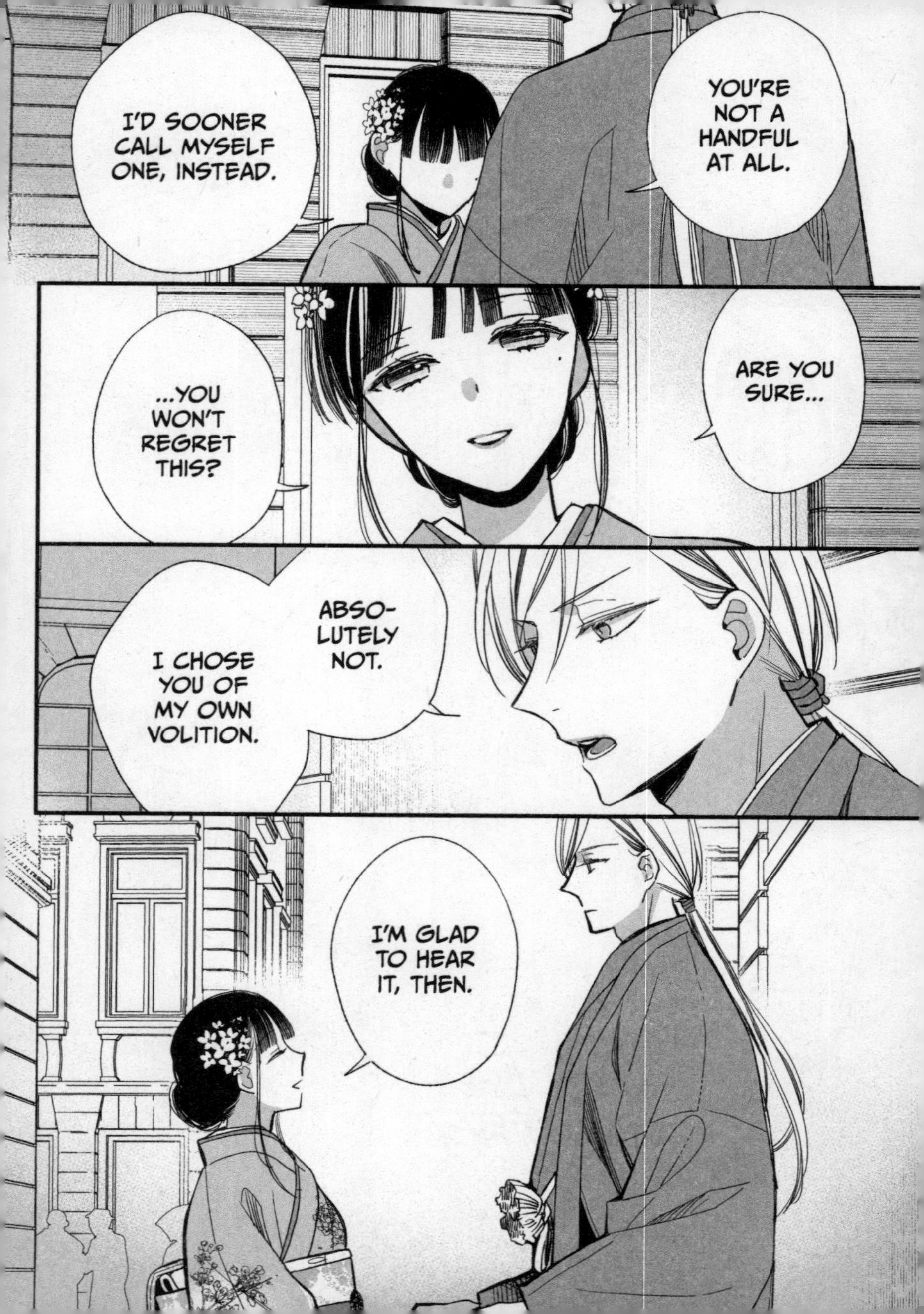
YOU'RE NOT A HANDFUL AT ALL.
I'D SOONER CALL MYSELF ONE, INSTEAD.
ARE YOU SURE...
...YOU WON'T REGRET THIS?
ABSO-LUTELY NOT.
I CHOSE YOU OF MY OWN VOLITION.
I'M GLAD TO HEAR IT, THEN.

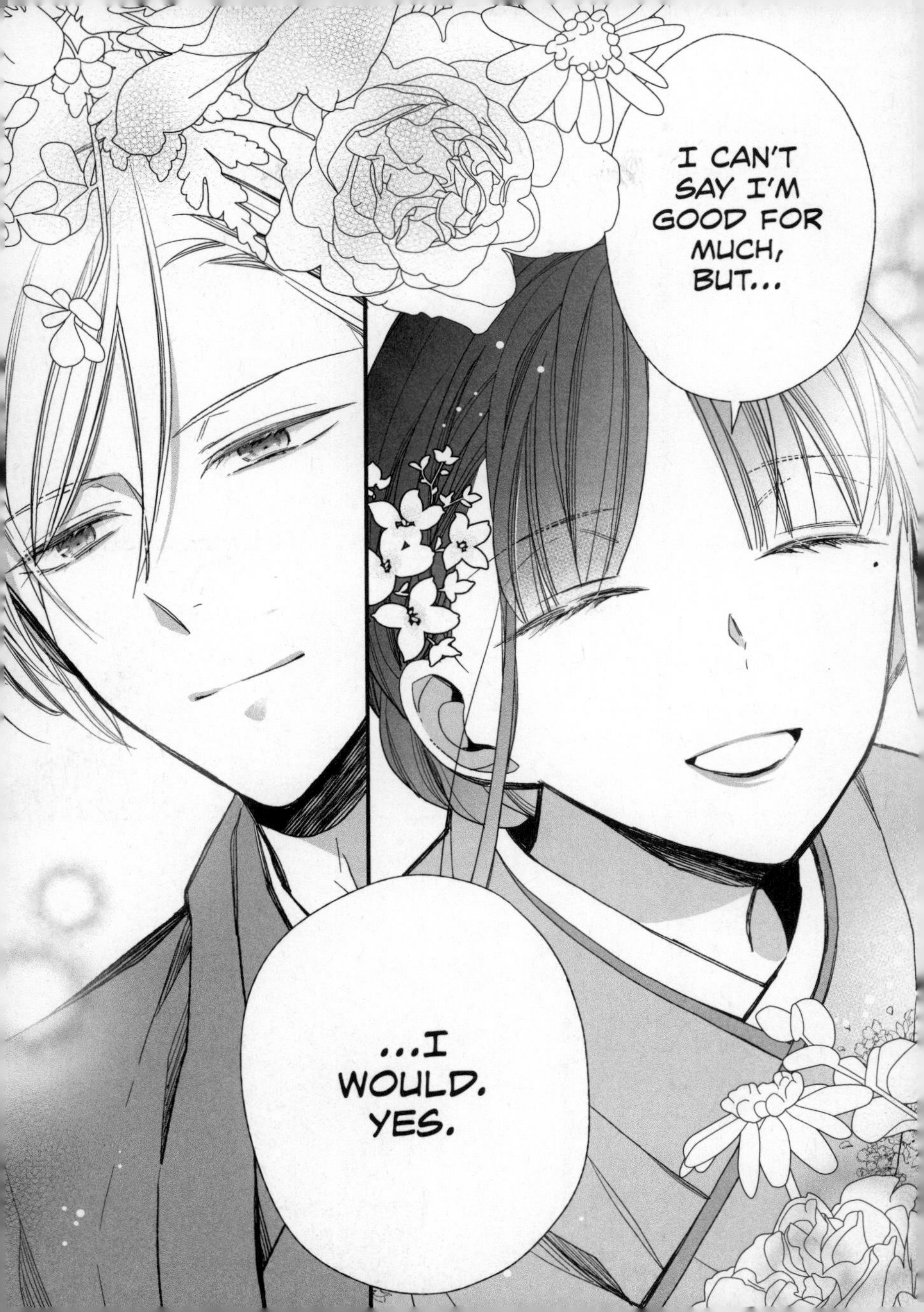
I CAN'T SAY I'M GOOD FOR MUCH, BUT...
...I WOULD. YES.

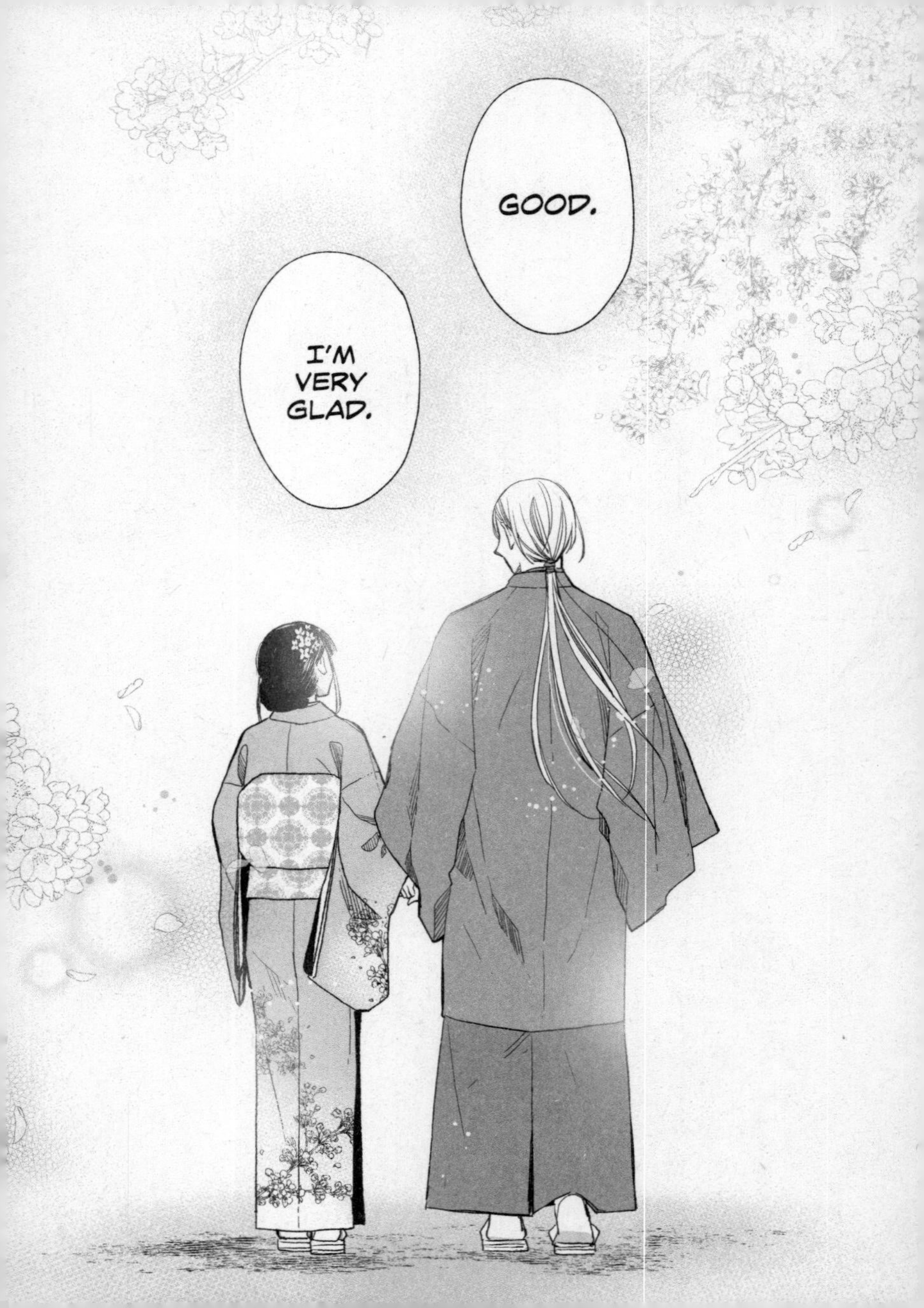
GOOD.
I'M VERY GLAD.

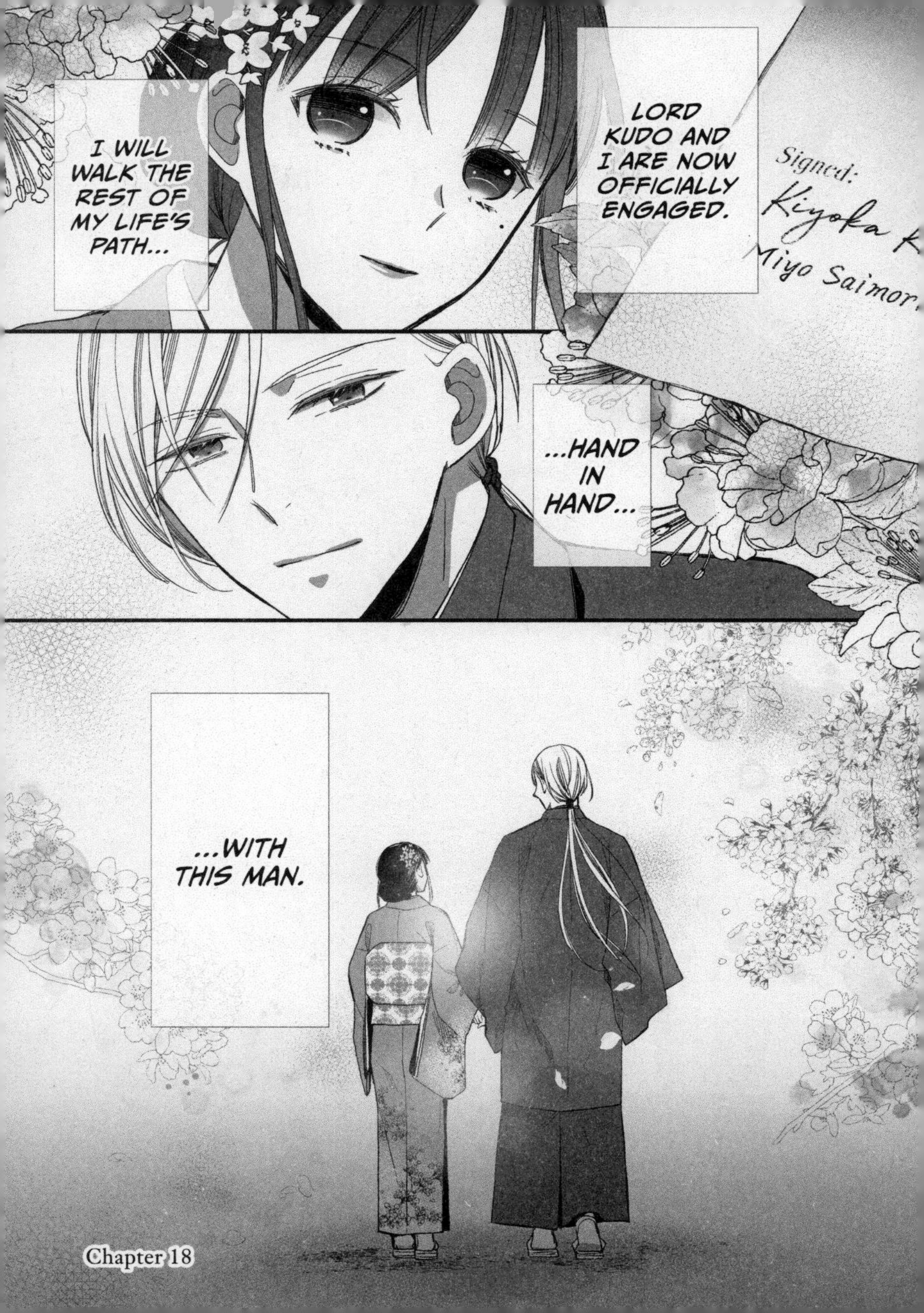
Signed:
Kiyoka K
Miyo Saimor
LORD KUDO AND I ARE NOW OFFICIALLY ENGAGED.
I WILL WALK THE REST OF MY LIFE'S PATH...
...HAND IN HAND...
...WITH THIS MAN.
Chapter 18

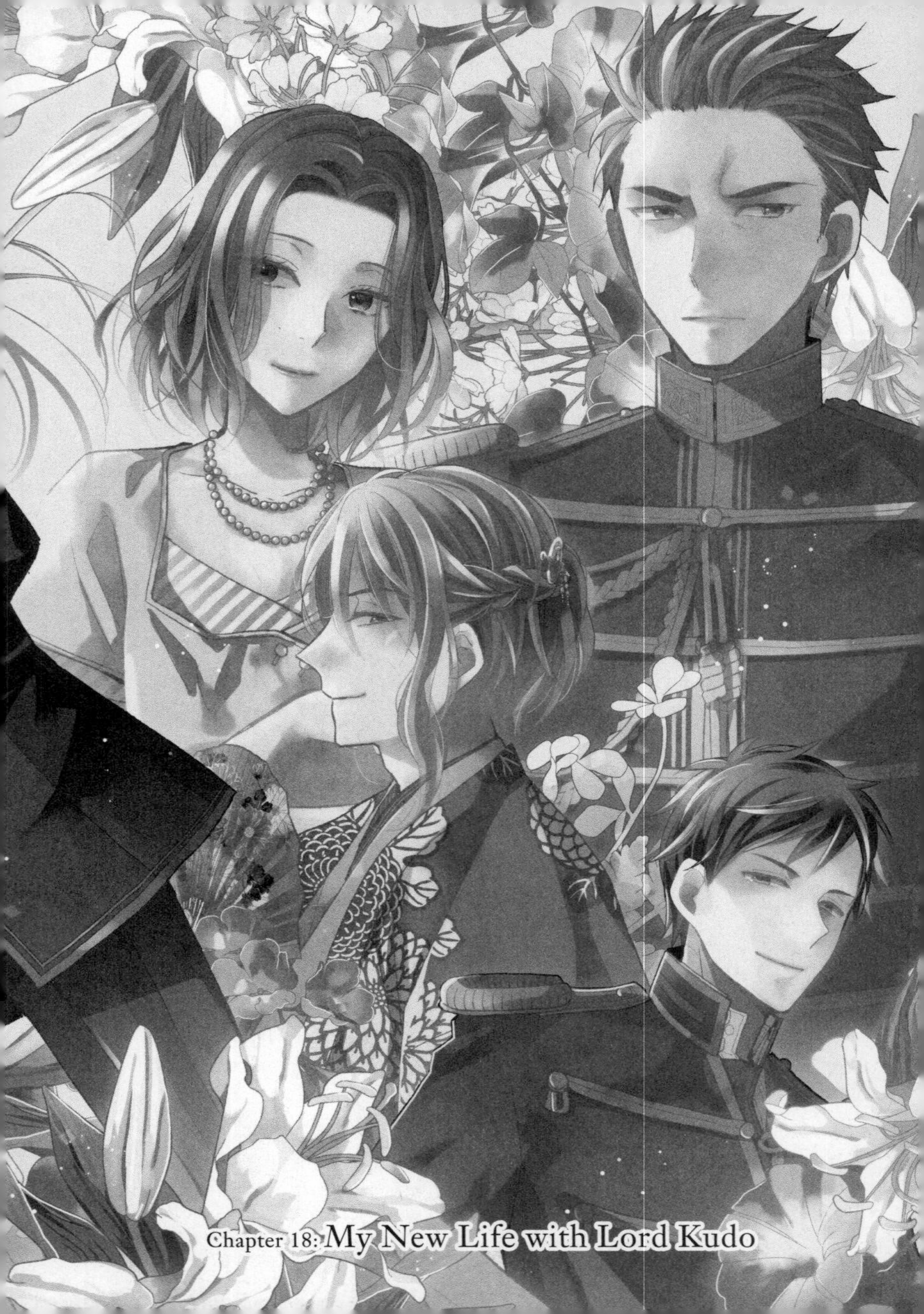

Chapter 18: My New Life with Lord Kudo

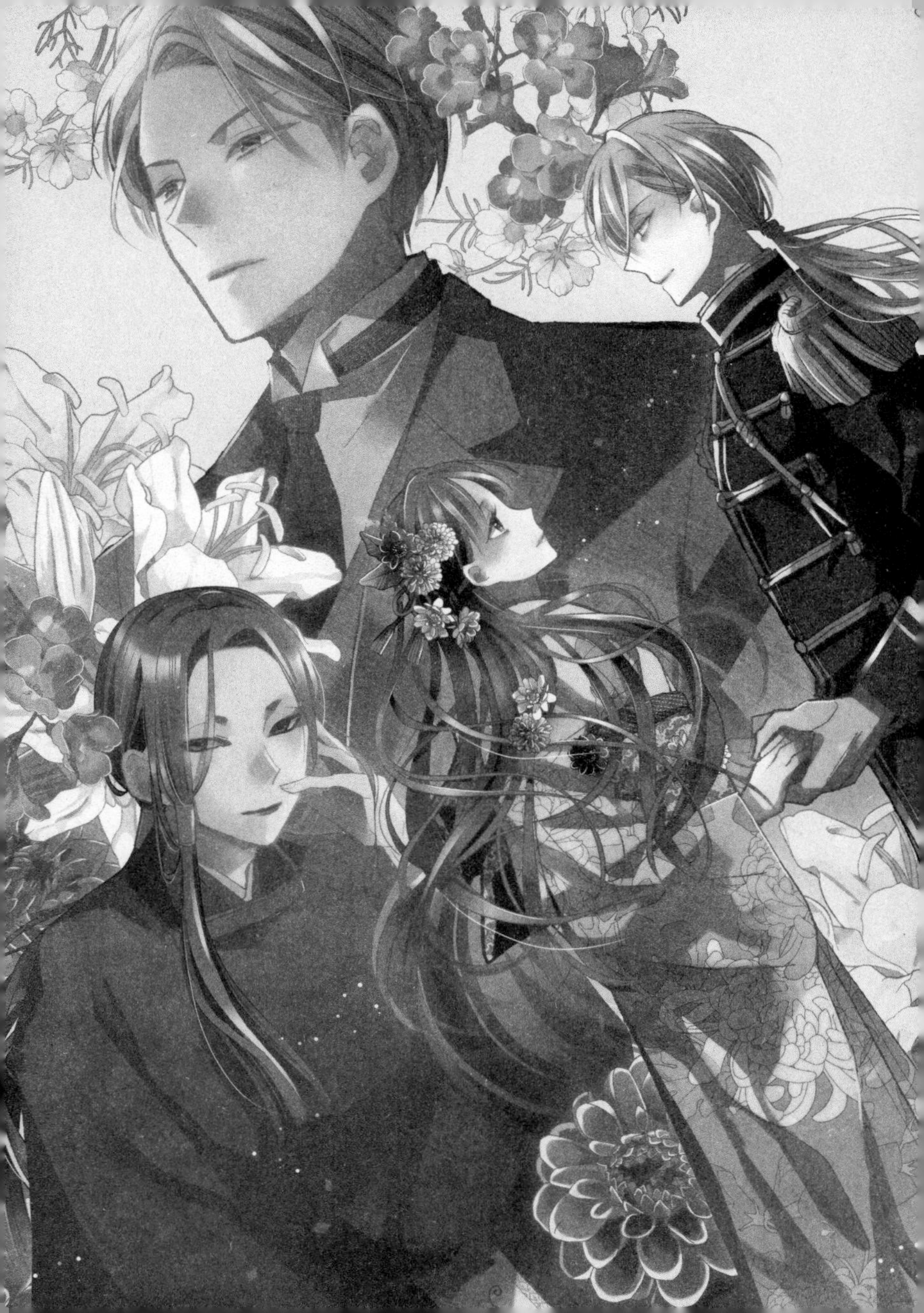

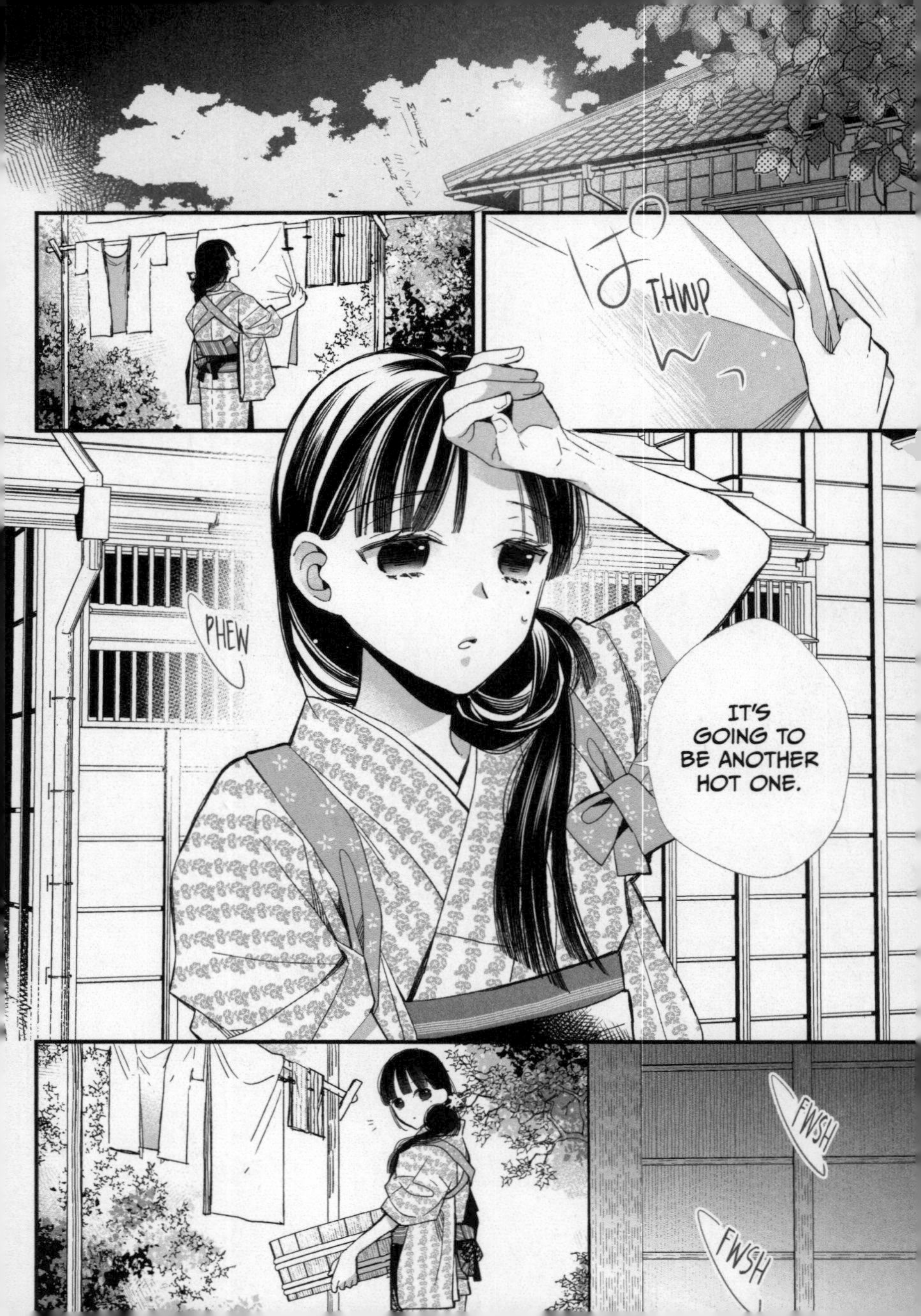
MEEEN
MEEN MEEN
THWP
PHEW
IT'S GOING TO BE ANOTHER HOT ONE.
FWSH
FWSH

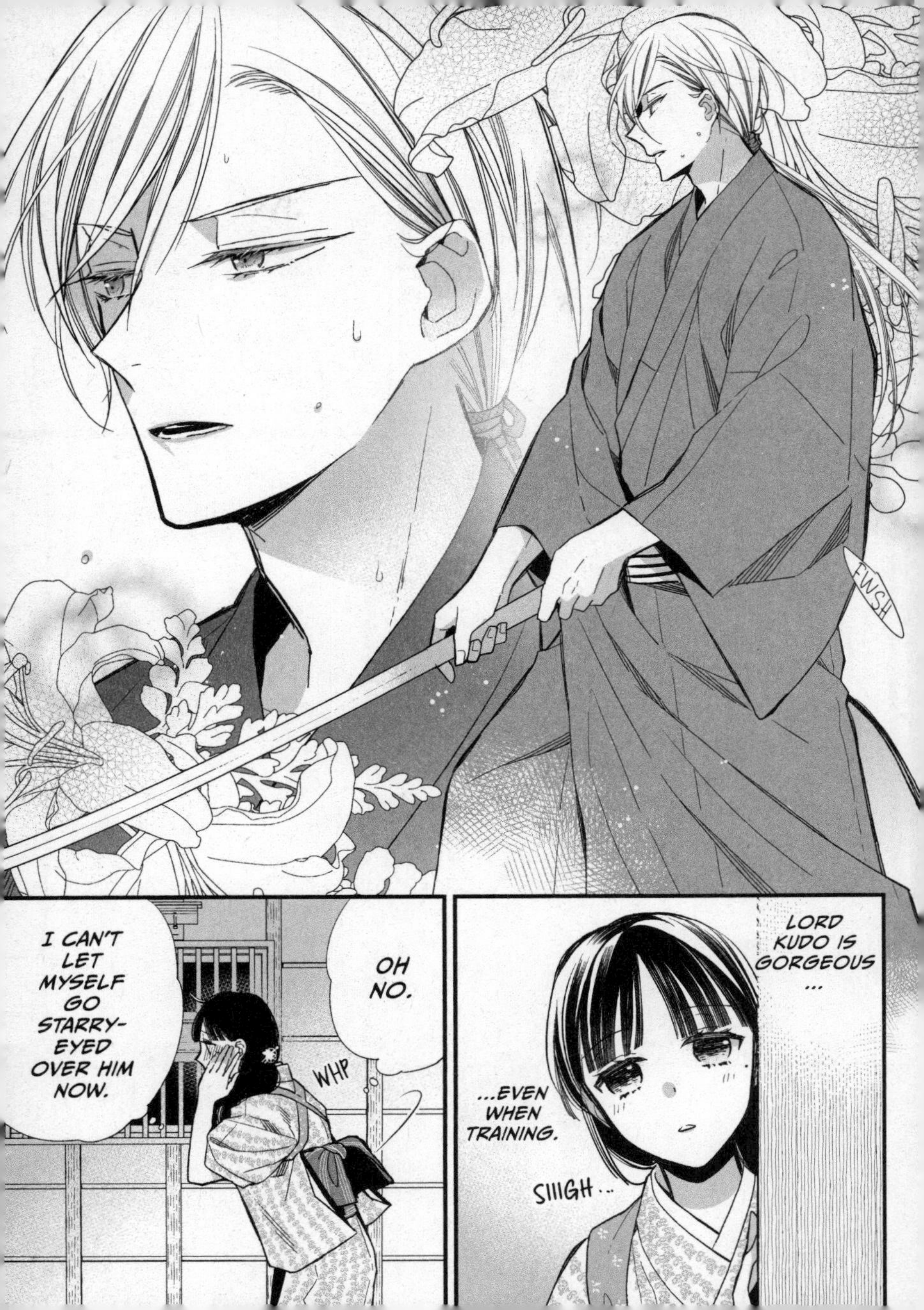
FWSH
LORD KUDO IS GORGEOUS ...
...EVEN WHEN TRAINING.
SIIIGH...
OH NO.
I CAN'T LET MYSELF GO STARRY-EYED OVER HIM NOW.
WHP

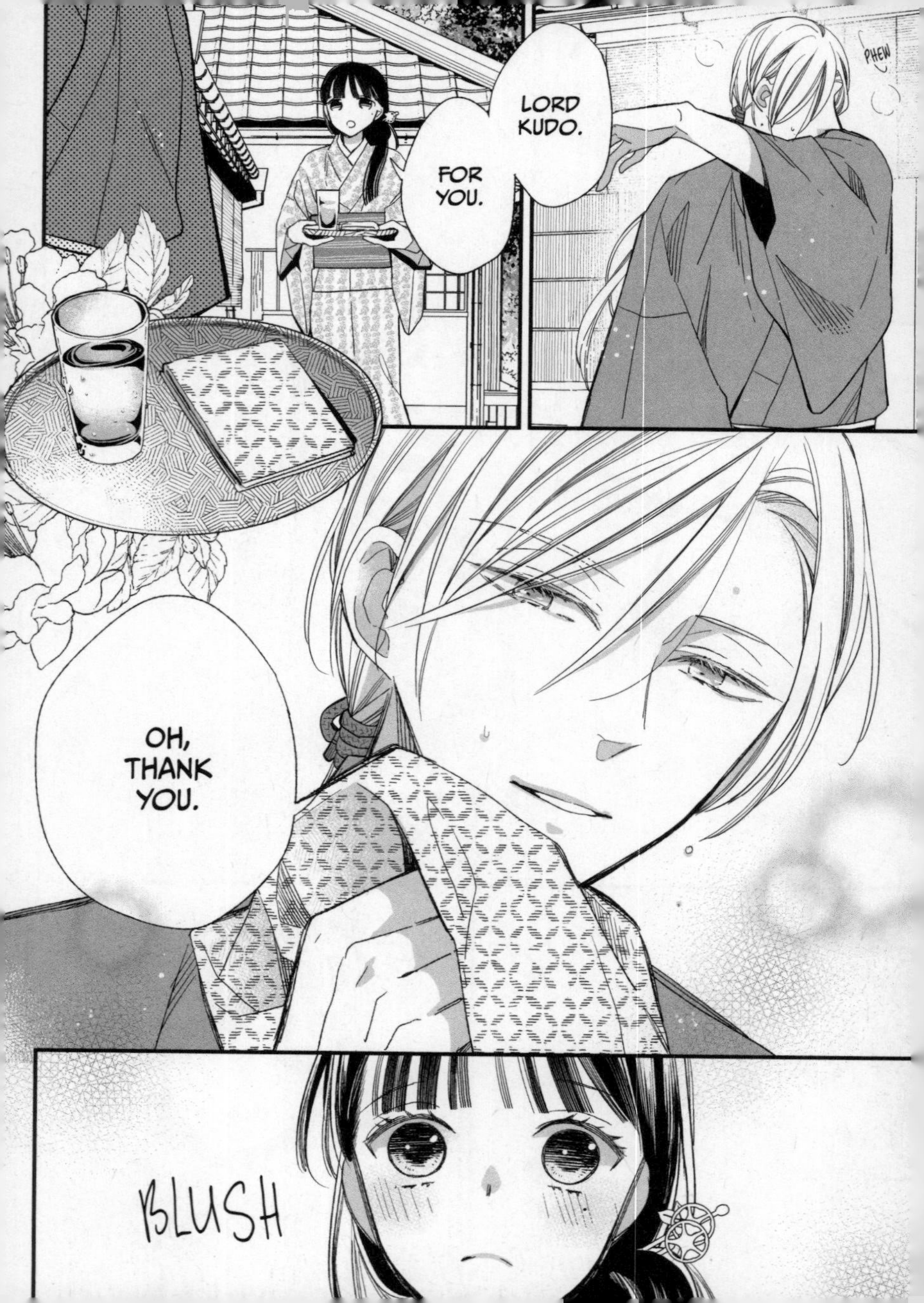
PHEW
LORD KUDO.
FOR YOU.
OH, THANK YOU.
BLUSH

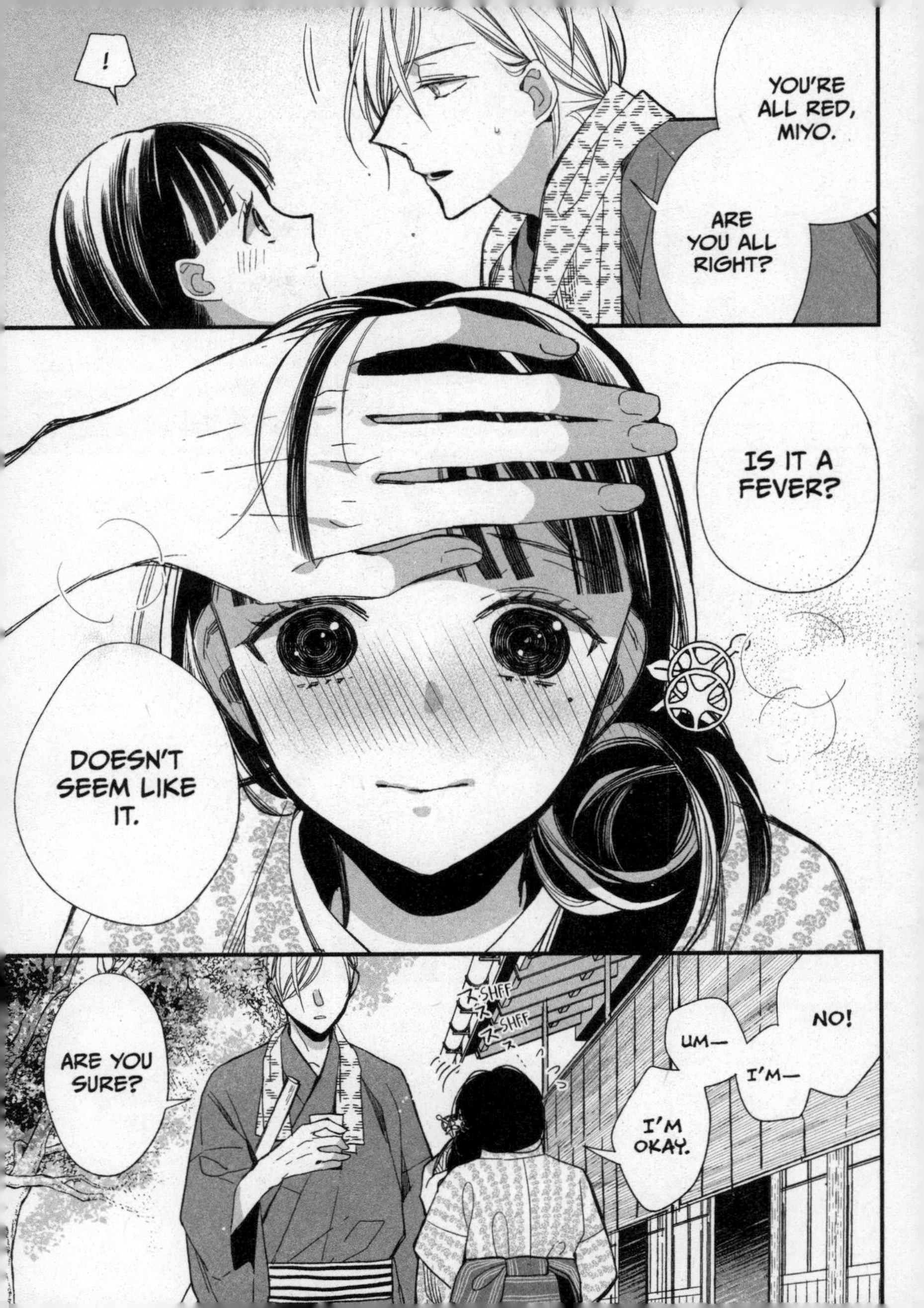
YOU'RE ALL RED, MIYO.
ARE YOU ALL RIGHT?
!
IS IT A FEVER?
DOESN'T SEEM LIKE IT.
NO!
UM—
I'M—
I'M OKAY.
SHFF
SHFF
ARE YOU SURE?

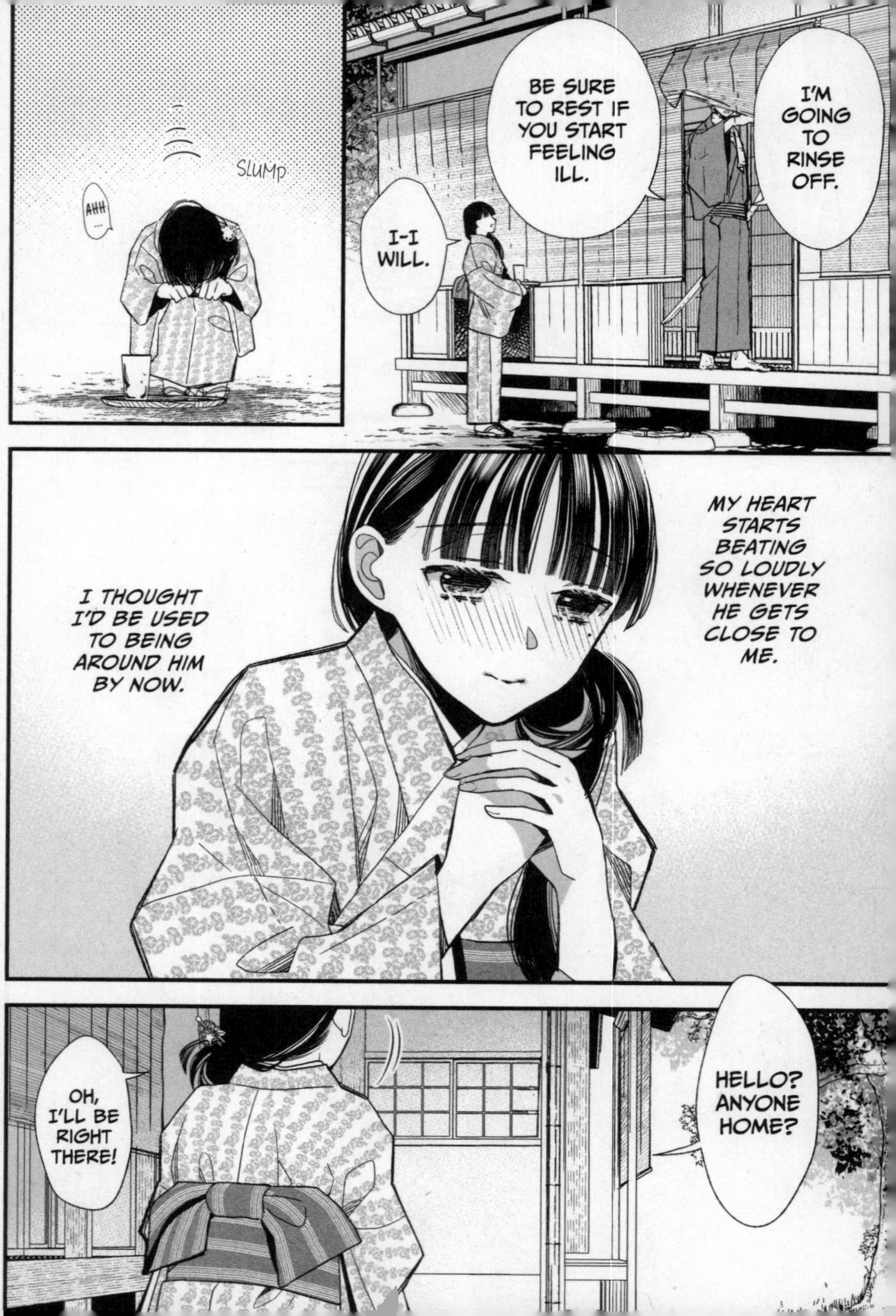
I'M GOING TO RINSE OFF.
BE SURE TO REST IF YOU START FEELING ILL.
I-I WILL.
SLUMP
AHH ...
MY HEART STARTS BEATING SO LOUDLY WHENEVER HE GETS CLOSE TO ME.
I THOUGHT I'D BE USED TO BEING AROUND HIM BY NOW.
HELLO? ANYONE HOME?
OH, I'LL BE RIGHT THERE!

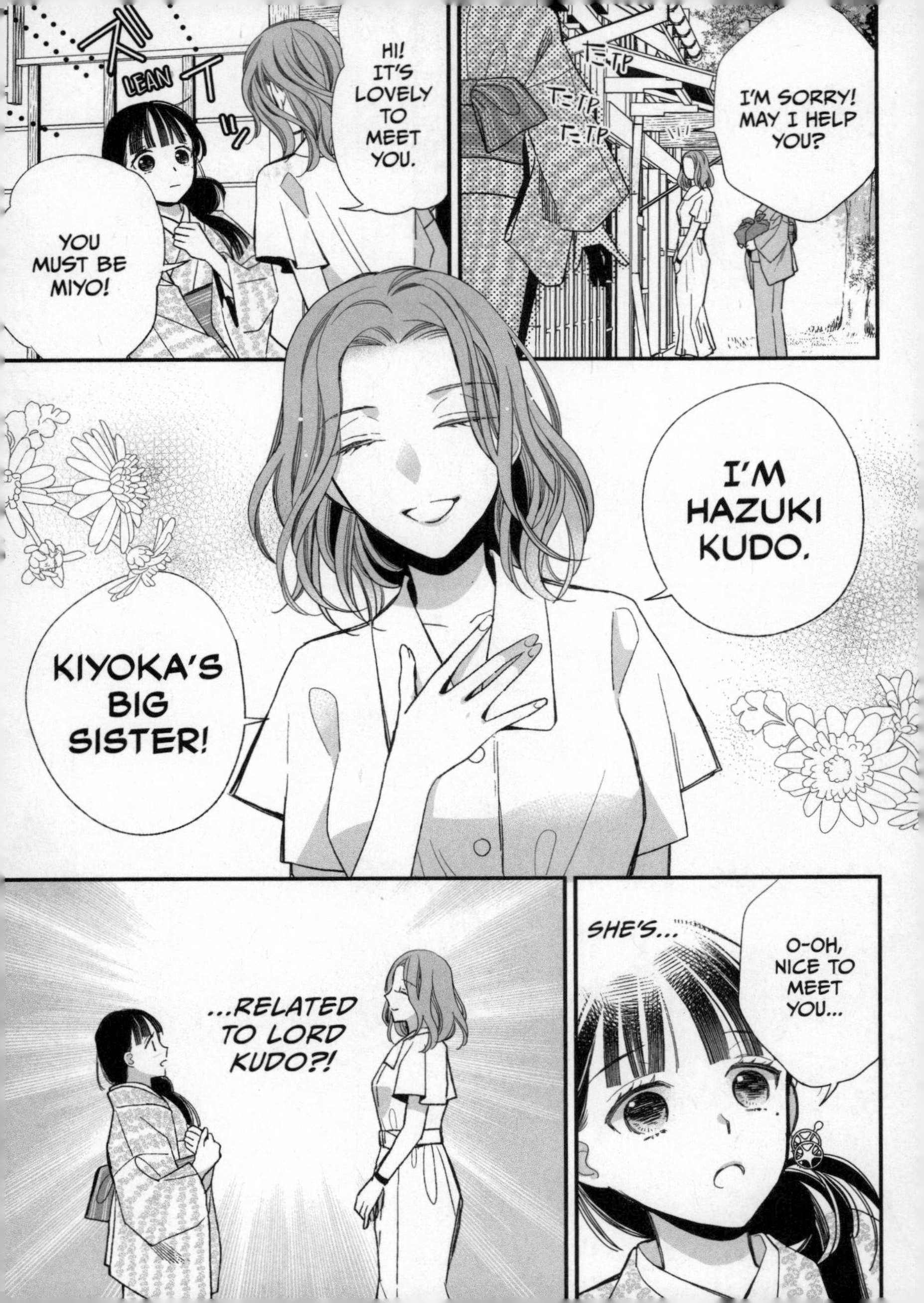
I'M SORRY! MAY I HELP YOU?
HI! IT'S LOVELY TO MEET YOU.
LEAN
YOU MUST BE MIYO!
I'M HAZUKI KUDO.
KIYOKA'S BIG SISTER!
O-OH, NICE TO MEET YOU...
SHE'S...
...RELATED TO LORD KUDO?!

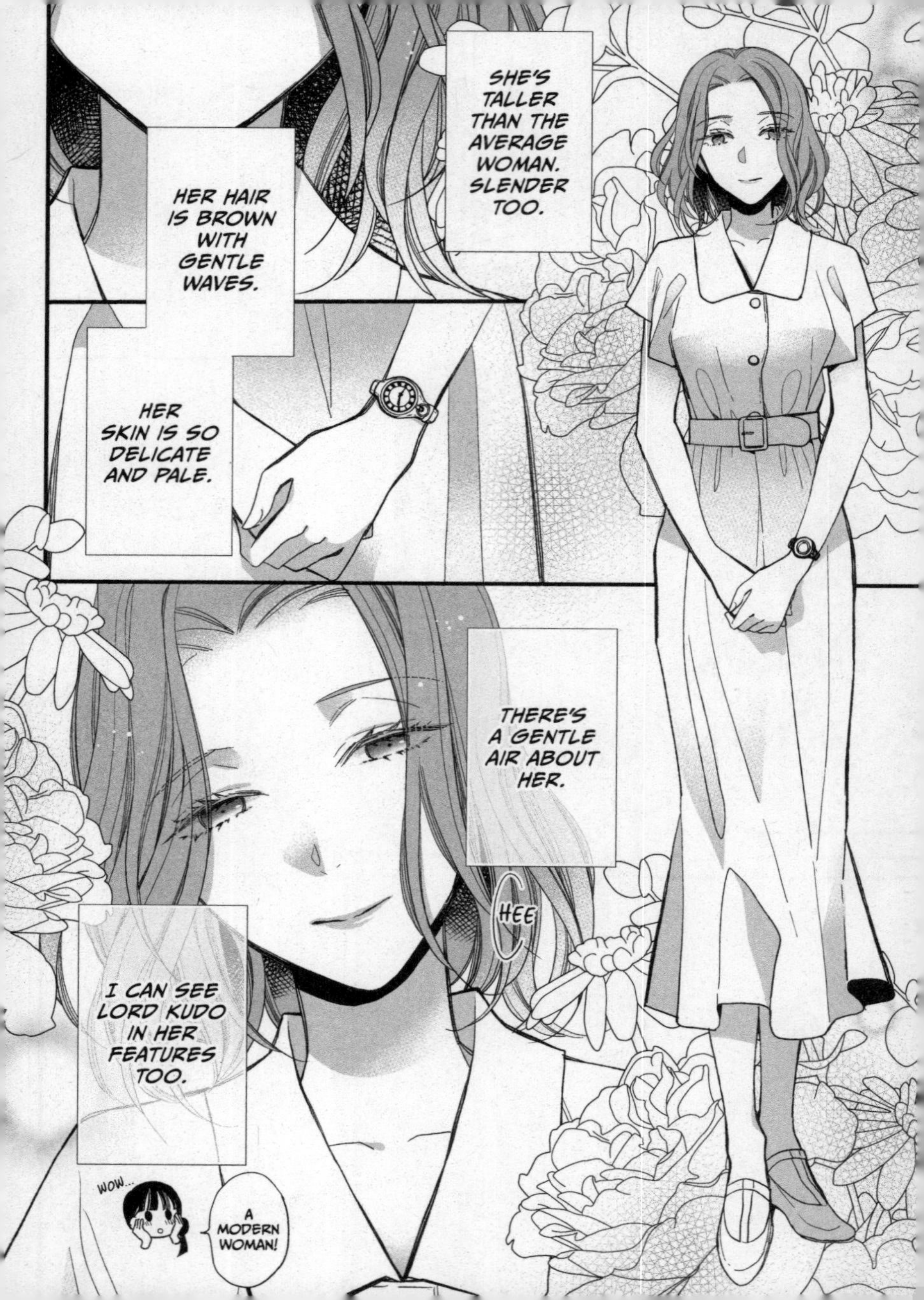
SHE'S TALLER THAN THE AVERAGE WOMAN. SLENDER TOO.
HER HAIR IS BROWN WITH GENTLE WAVES.
HER SKIN IS SO DELICATE AND PALE.
THERE'S A GENTLE AIR ABOUT HER.
CHEE
I CAN SEE LORD KUDO IN HER FEATURES TOO.
WOW...
A MODERN WOMAN!

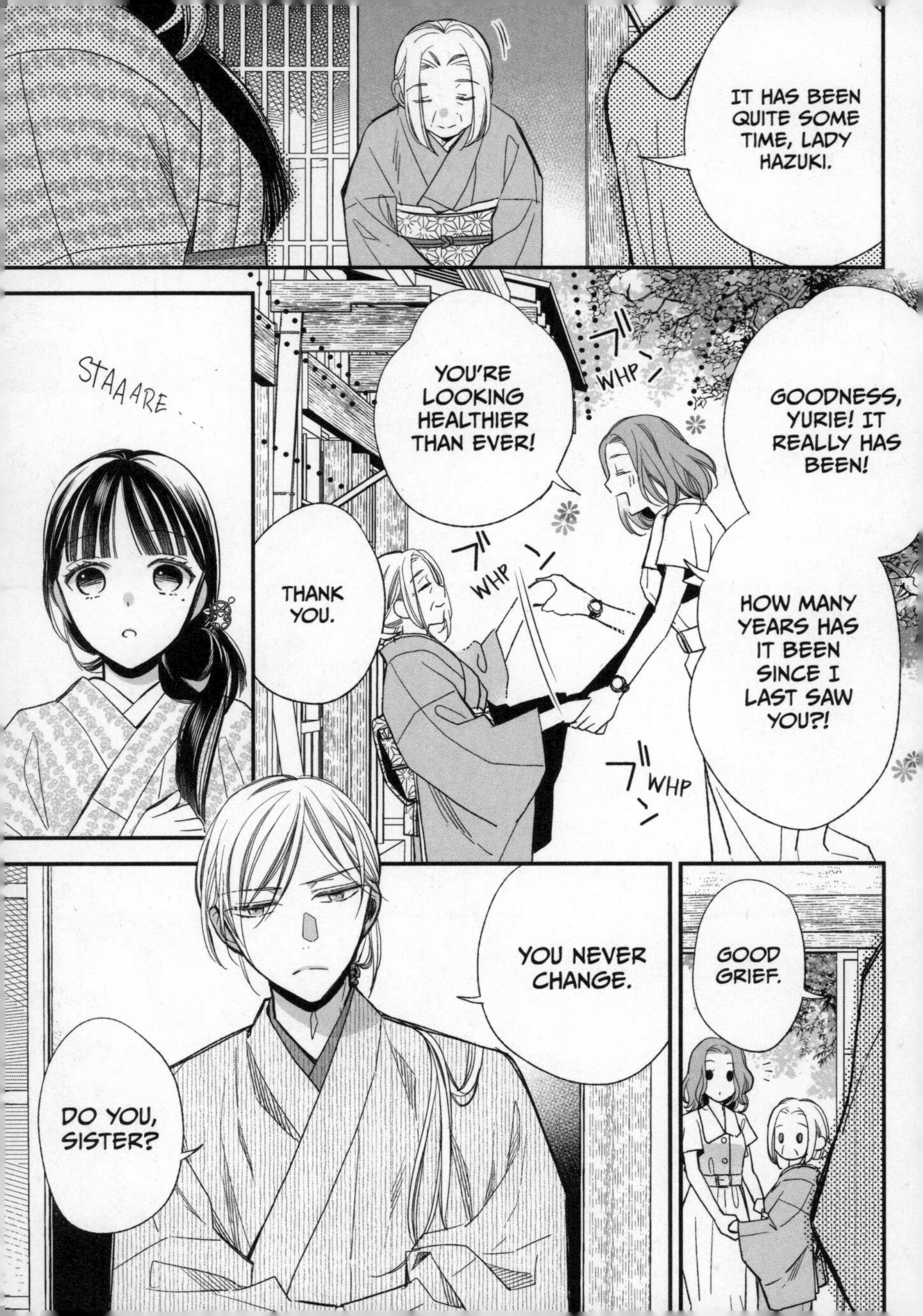
IT HAS BEEN QUITE SOME TIME, LADY HAZUKI.
GOODNESS, YURIE! IT REALLY HAS BEEN!
WHP
HOW MANY YEARS HAS IT BEEN SINCE I LAST SAW YOU?!
YOU'RE LOOKING HEALTHIER THAN EVER!
WHP
WHP
THANK YOU.
STAAARE...
GOOD GRIEF.
YOU NEVER CHANGE.
DO YOU, SISTER?

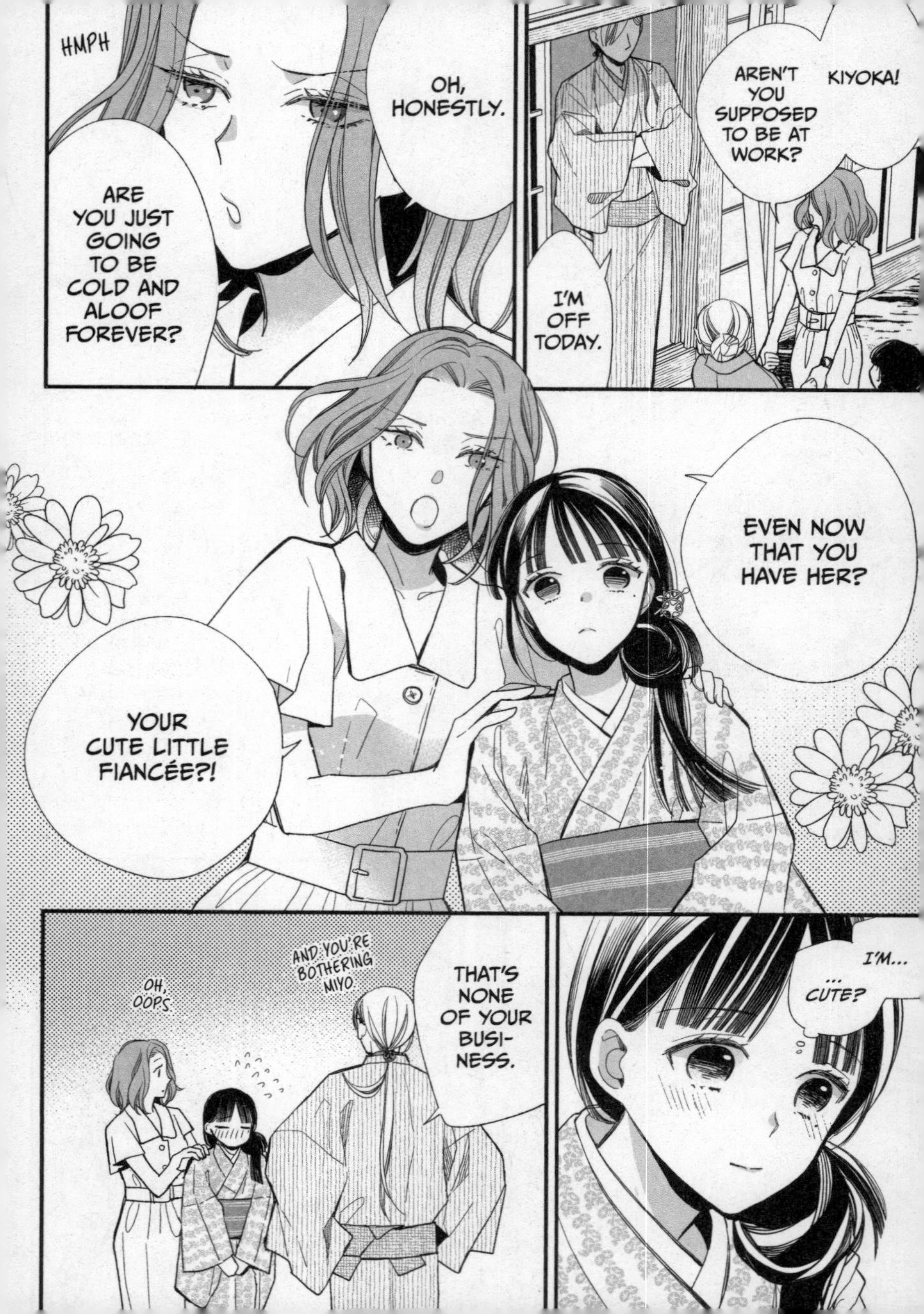
KIYOKA!
AREN'T YOU SUPPOSED TO BE AT WORK?
I'M OFF TODAY.
OH, HONESTLY.
HMPH
ARE YOU JUST GOING TO BE COLD AND ALOOF FOREVER?
EVEN NOW THAT YOU HAVE HER?
YOUR CUTE LITTLE FIANCÉE?!
I'M...
...CUTE?
THAT'S NONE OF YOUR BUSI-NESS.
AND YOU'RE BOTHERING MIYO.
OH, OOPS.

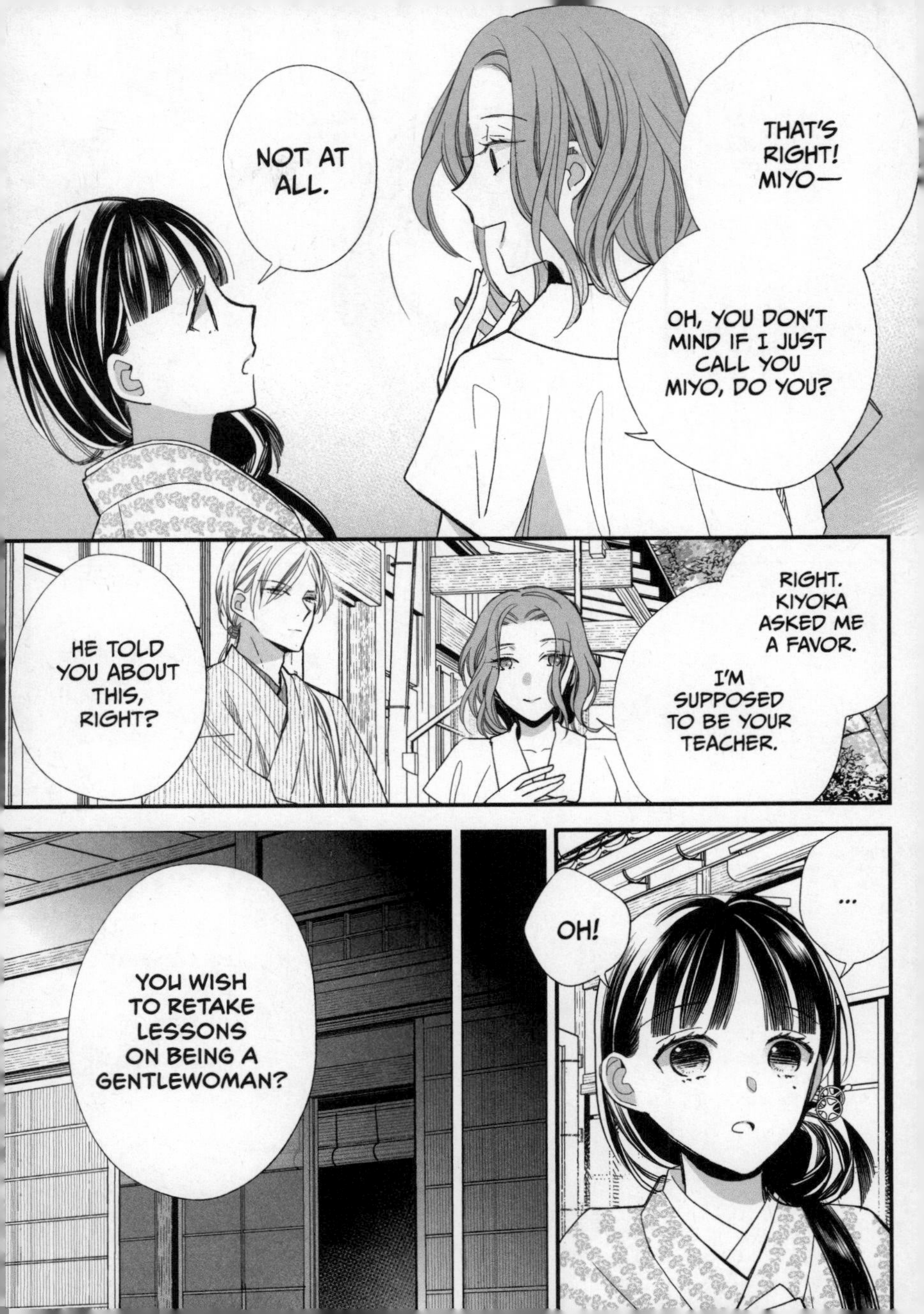
THAT'S RIGHT! MIYO—
OH, YOU DON'T MIND IF I JUST CALL YOU MIYO, DO YOU?
NOT AT ALL.
RIGHT. KIYOKA ASKED ME A FAVOR.
I'M SUPPOSED TO BE YOUR TEACHER.
HE TOLD YOU ABOUT THIS, RIGHT?
...
OH!
YOU WISH TO RETAKE LESSONS ON BEING A GENTLEWOMAN?

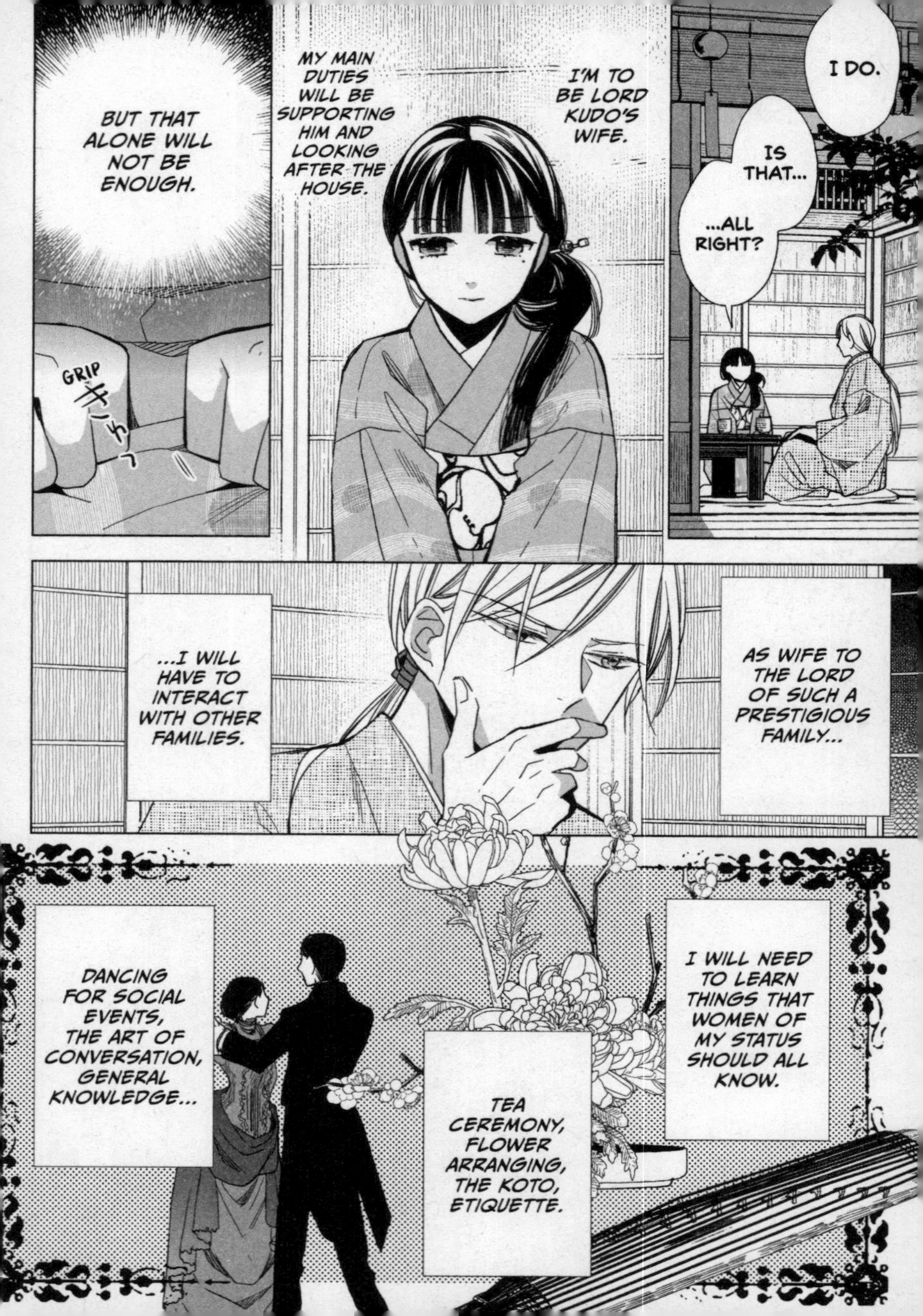
I DO.
IS THAT...
...ALL RIGHT?
I'M TO BE LORD KUDO'S WIFE.
MY MAIN DUTIES WILL BE SUPPORTING HIM AND LOOKING AFTER THE HOUSE.
BUT THAT ALONE WILL NOT BE ENOUGH.
GRIP
ギュッ
AS WIFE TO THE LORD OF SUCH A PRESTIGIOUS FAMILY...
...I WILL HAVE TO INTERACT WITH OTHER FAMILIES.
I WILL NEED TO LEARN THINGS THAT WOMEN OF MY STATUS SHOULD ALL KNOW.
TEA CEREMONY, FLOWER ARRANGING, THE KOTO, ETIQUETTE.
DANCING FOR SOCIAL EVENTS, THE ART OF CONVERSATION, GENERAL KNOWLEDGE...

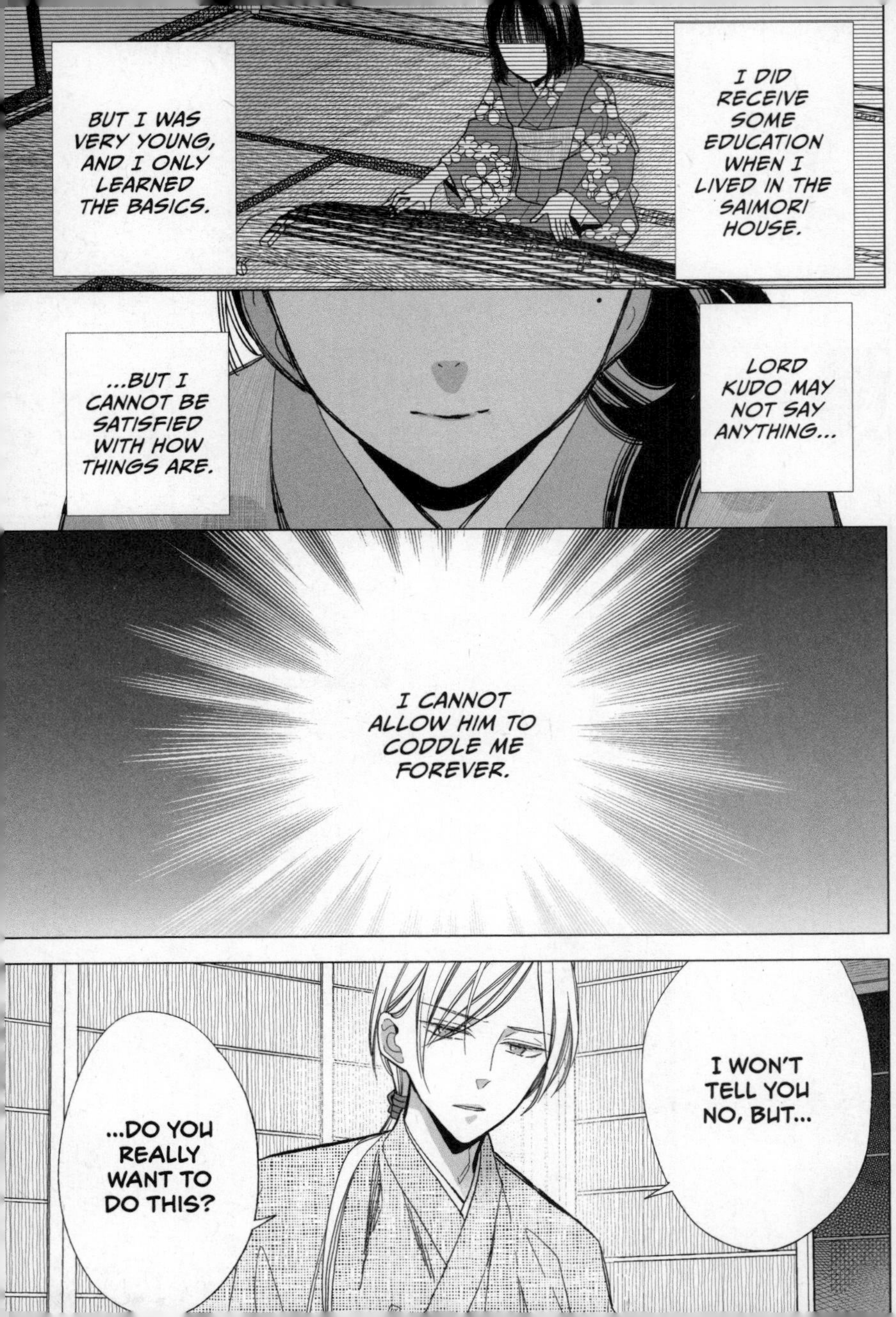
I DID RECEIVE SOME EDUCATION WHEN I LIVED IN THE SAIMORI HOUSE.
BUT I WAS VERY YOUNG, AND I ONLY LEARNED THE BASICS.
LORD KUDO MAY NOT SAY ANYTHING...
...BUT I CANNOT BE SATISFIED WITH HOW THINGS ARE.
I CANNOT ALLOW HIM TO CODDLE ME FOREVER.
I WON'T TELL YOU NO, BUT...
...DO YOU REALLY WANT TO DO THIS?

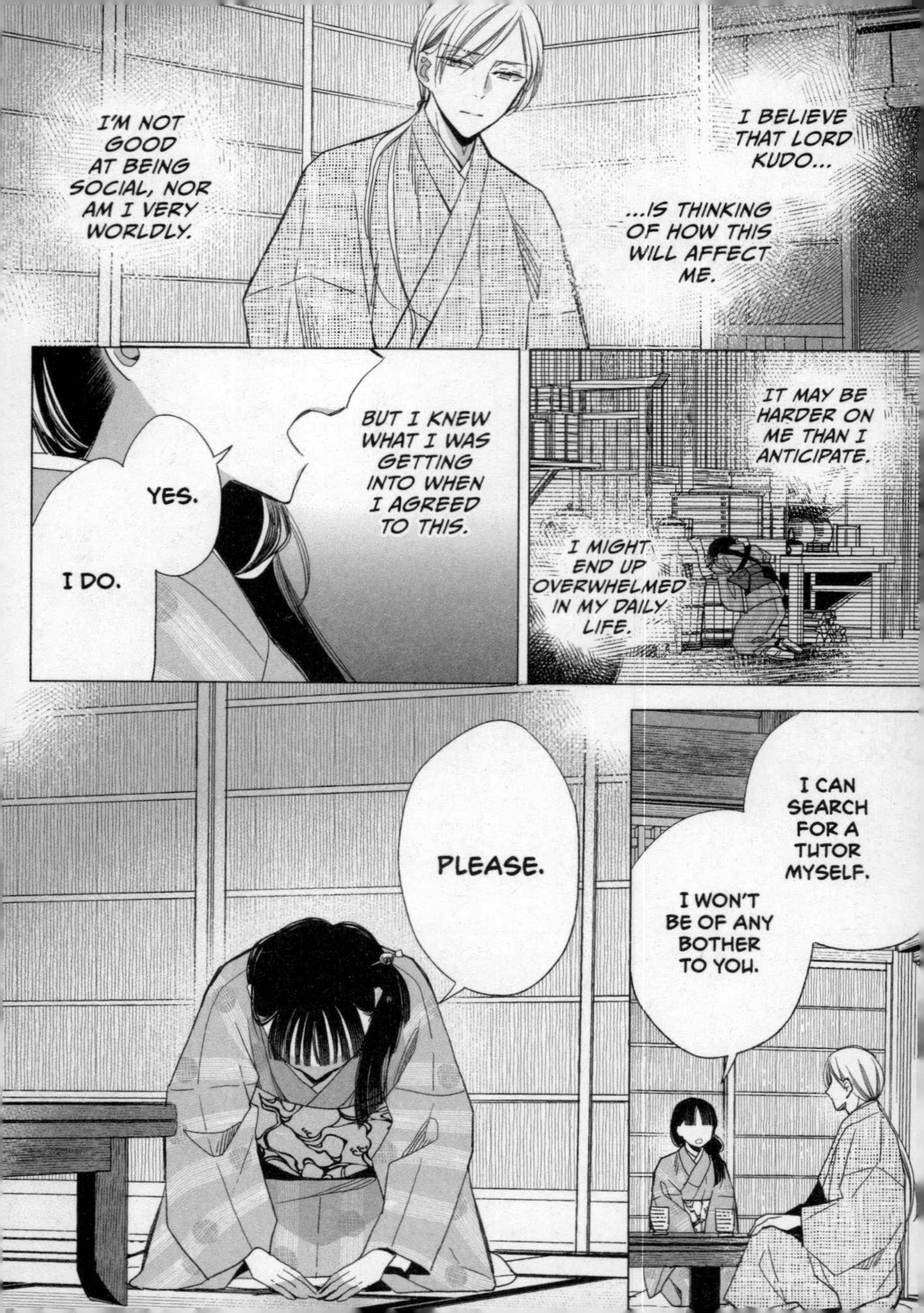
I BELIEVE THAT LORD KUDO...
...IS THINKING OF HOW THIS WILL AFFECT ME.
I'M NOT GOOD AT BEING SOCIAL, NOR AM I VERY WORLDLY.
IT MAY BE HARDER ON ME THAN I ANTICIPATE.
I MIGHT END UP OVERWHELMED IN MY DAILY LIFE.
BUT I KNEW WHAT I WAS GETTING INTO WHEN I AGREED TO THIS.
YES.
I DO.
I CAN SEARCH FOR A TUTOR MYSELF.
I WON'T BE OF ANY BOTHER TO YOU.
PLEASE.

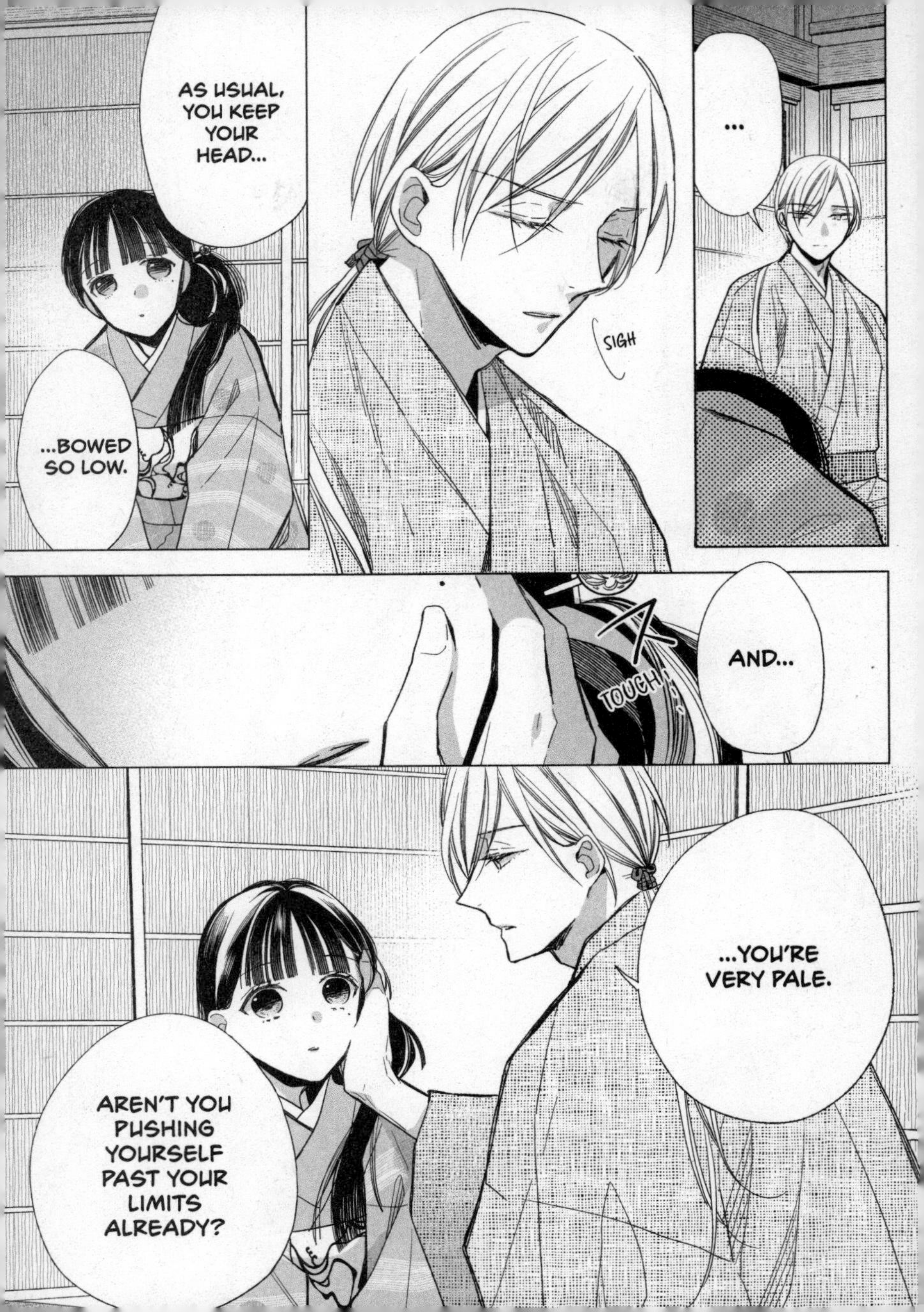
...
SIGH
AS USUAL, YOU KEEP YOUR HEAD...
...BOWED SO LOW.
AND...
TOUCH
...YOU'RE VERY PALE.
AREN'T YOU PUSHING YOURSELF PAST YOUR LIMITS ALREADY?

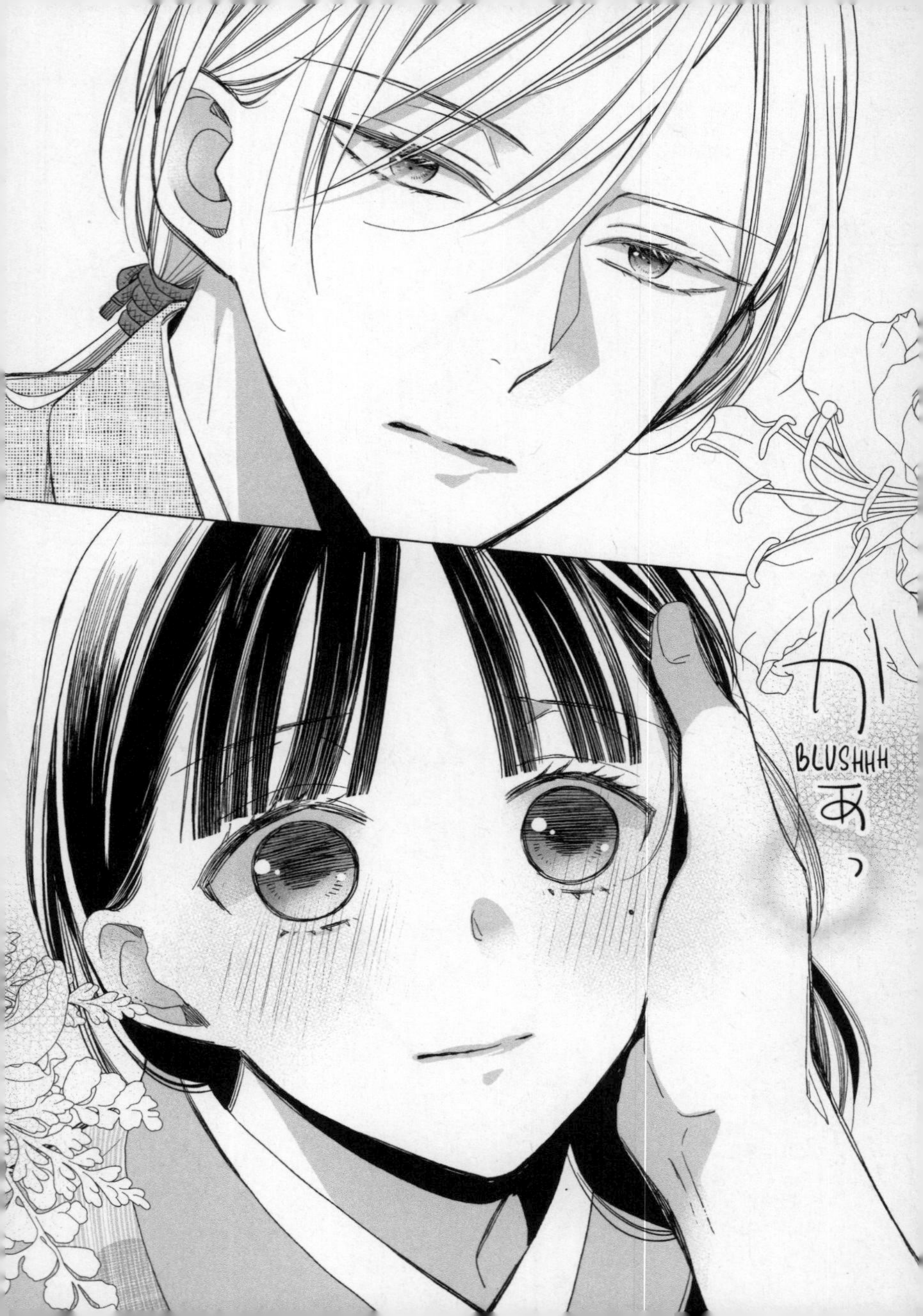
かあっ
BLUSHHH

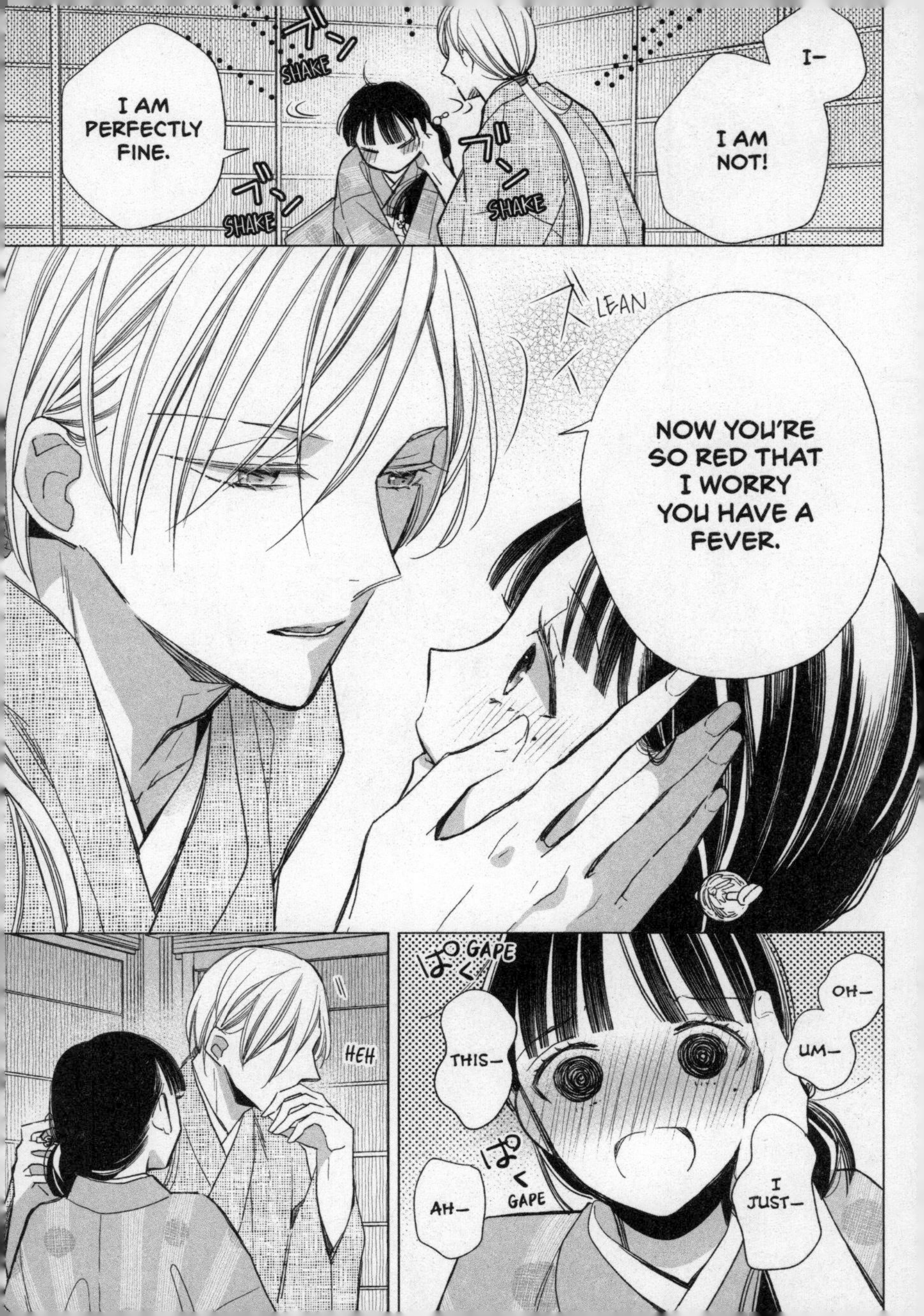
I— I AM NOT!
SHAKE
SHAKE
I AM PERFECTLY FINE.
SHAKE
LEAN
NOW YOU'RE SO RED THAT I WORRY YOU HAVE A FEVER.
ぱく GAPE
OH— UM—
I JUST—
THIS—
ぱく GAPE
AH—
HEH

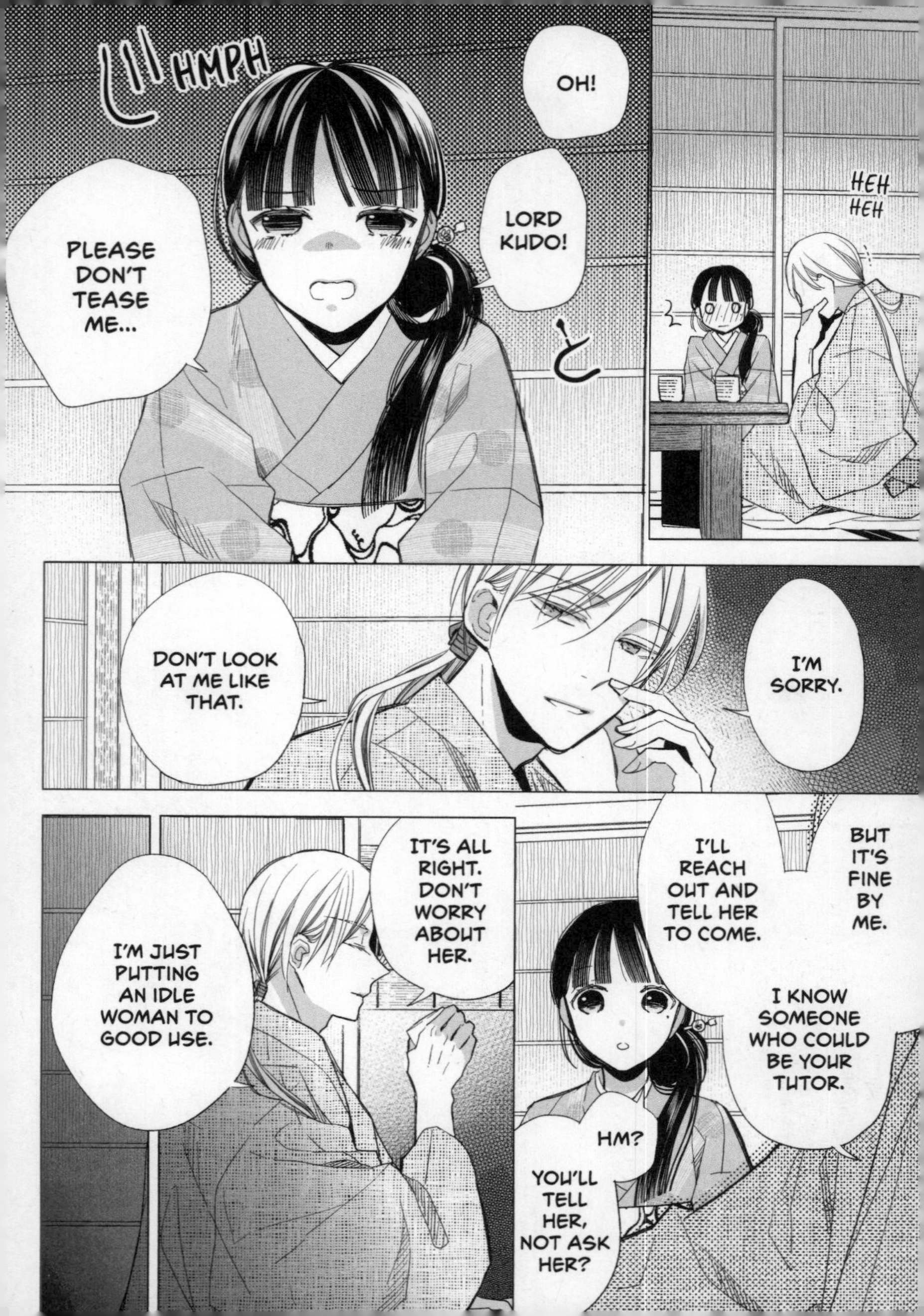
HEH HEH
OH!
LORD KUDO!
HMPH
PLEASE DON'T TEASE ME...
I'M SORRY.
DON'T LOOK AT ME LIKE THAT.
BUT IT'S FINE BY ME.
I'LL REACH OUT AND TELL HER TO COME.
I KNOW SOMEONE WHO COULD BE YOUR TUTOR.
HM?
YOU'LL TELL HER, NOT ASK HER?
IT'S ALL RIGHT. DON'T WORRY ABOUT HER.
I'M JUST PUTTING AN IDLE WOMAN TO GOOD USE.

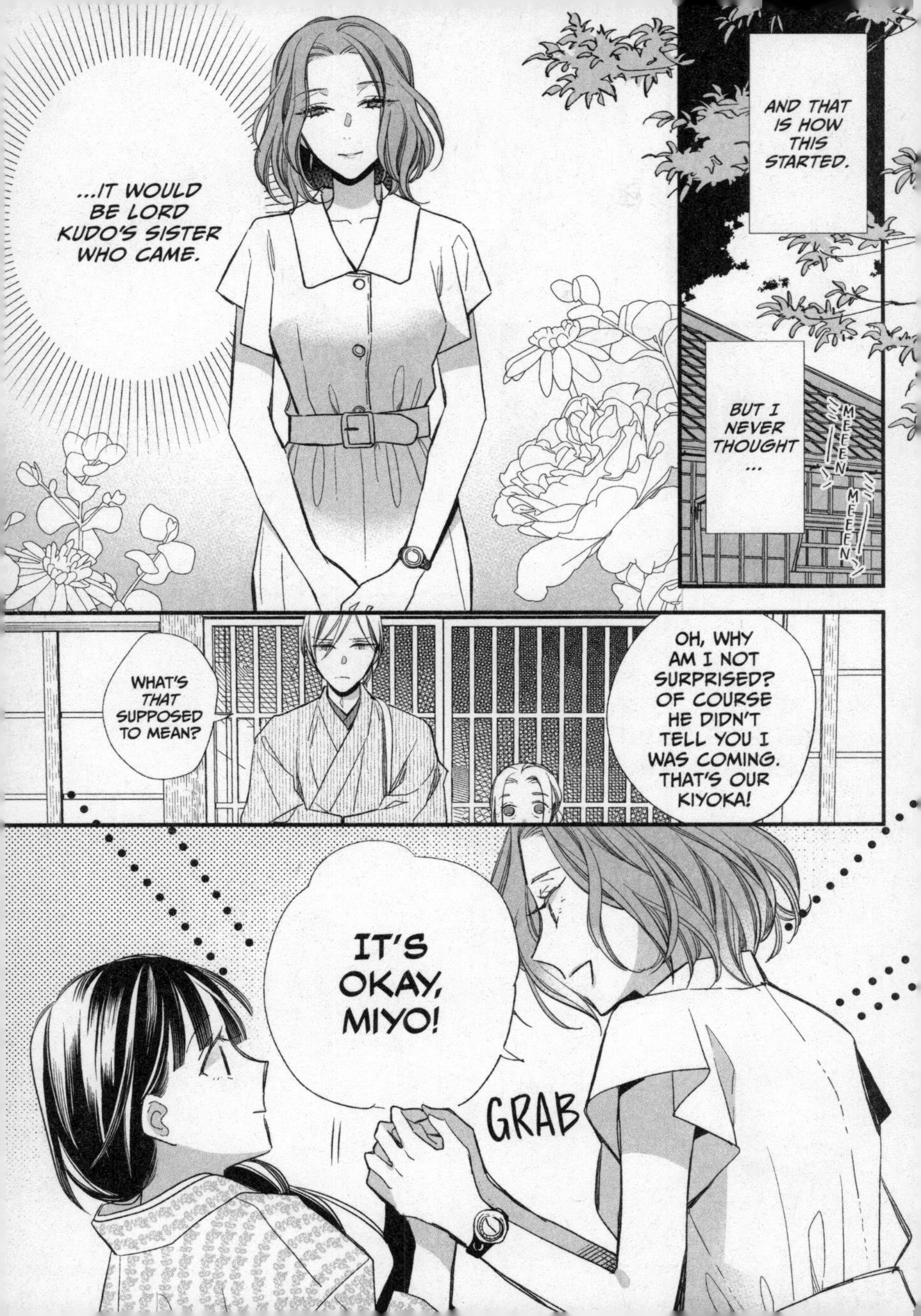
AND THAT IS HOW THIS STARTED.
BUT I NEVER THOUGHT...
MEEEN MEEEN
...IT WOULD BE LORD KUDO'S SISTER WHO CAME.
OH, WHY AM I NOT SURPRISED? OF COURSE HE DIDN'T TELL YOU I WAS COMING. THAT'S OUR KIYOKA!
WHAT'S THAT SUPPOSED TO MEAN?
IT'S OKAY, MIYO!
GRAB

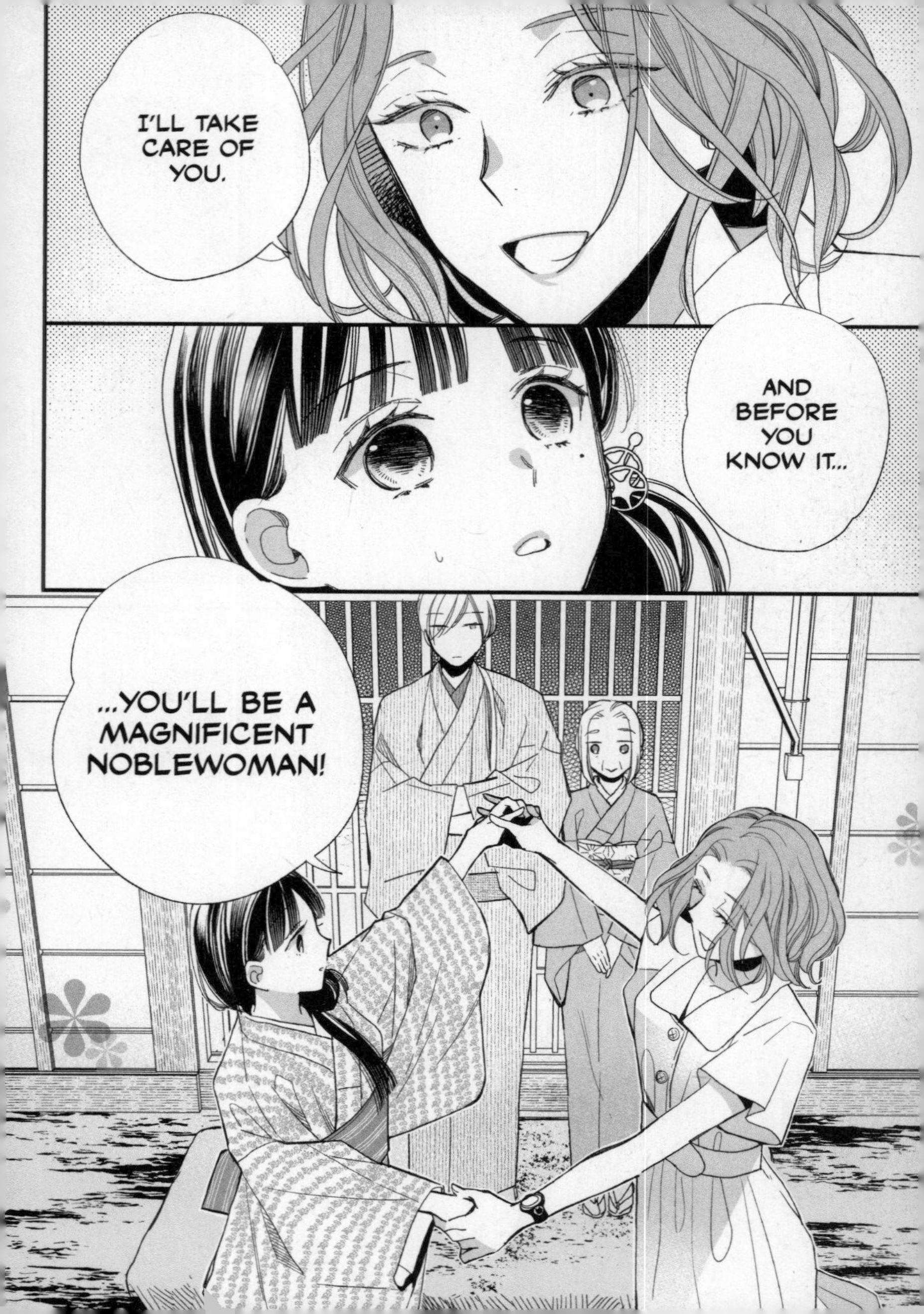
I'LL TAKE CARE OF YOU.
AND BEFORE YOU KNOW IT...
...YOU'LL BE A MAGNIFICENT NOBLEWOMAN!

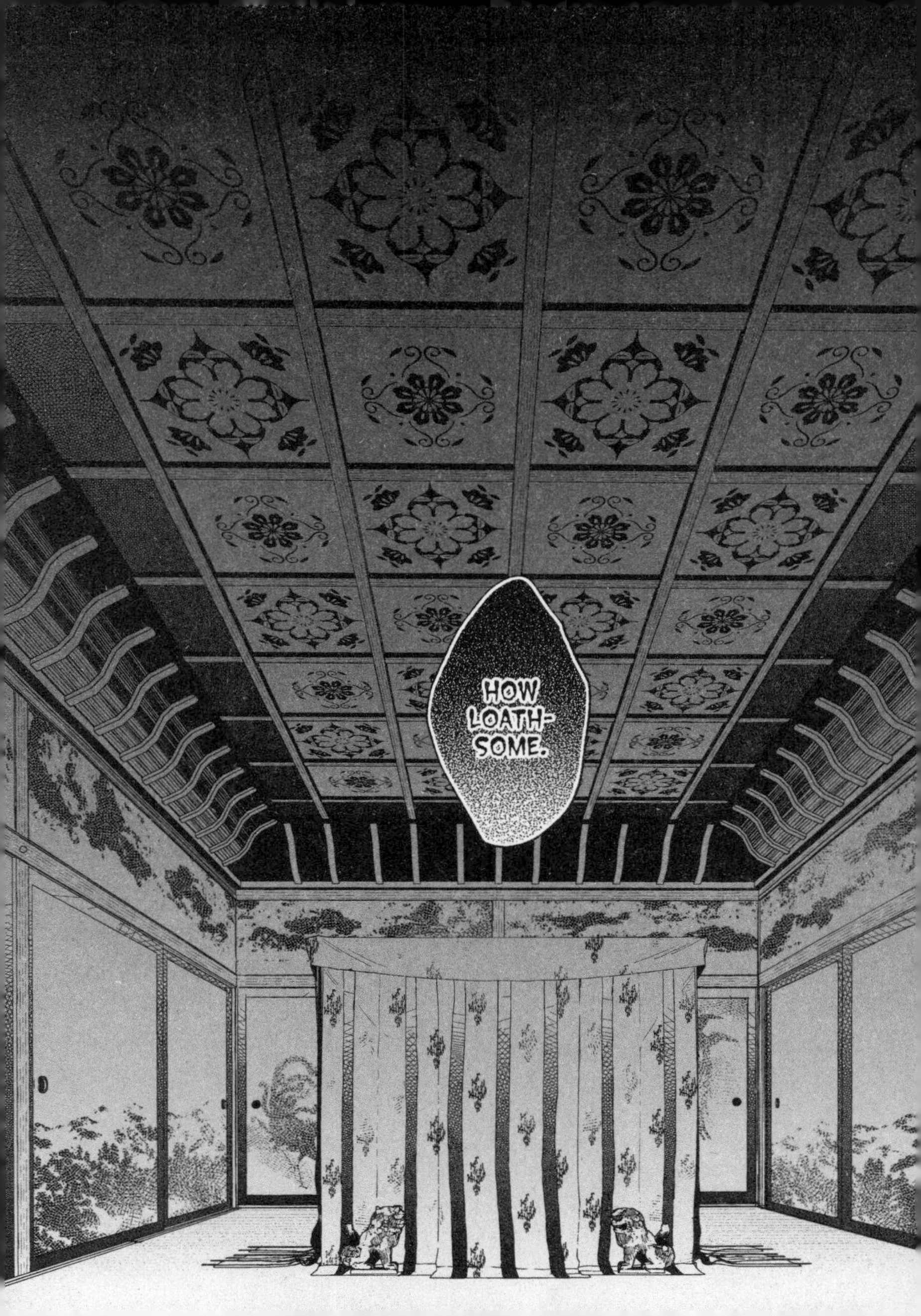
HOW LOATH-SOME.

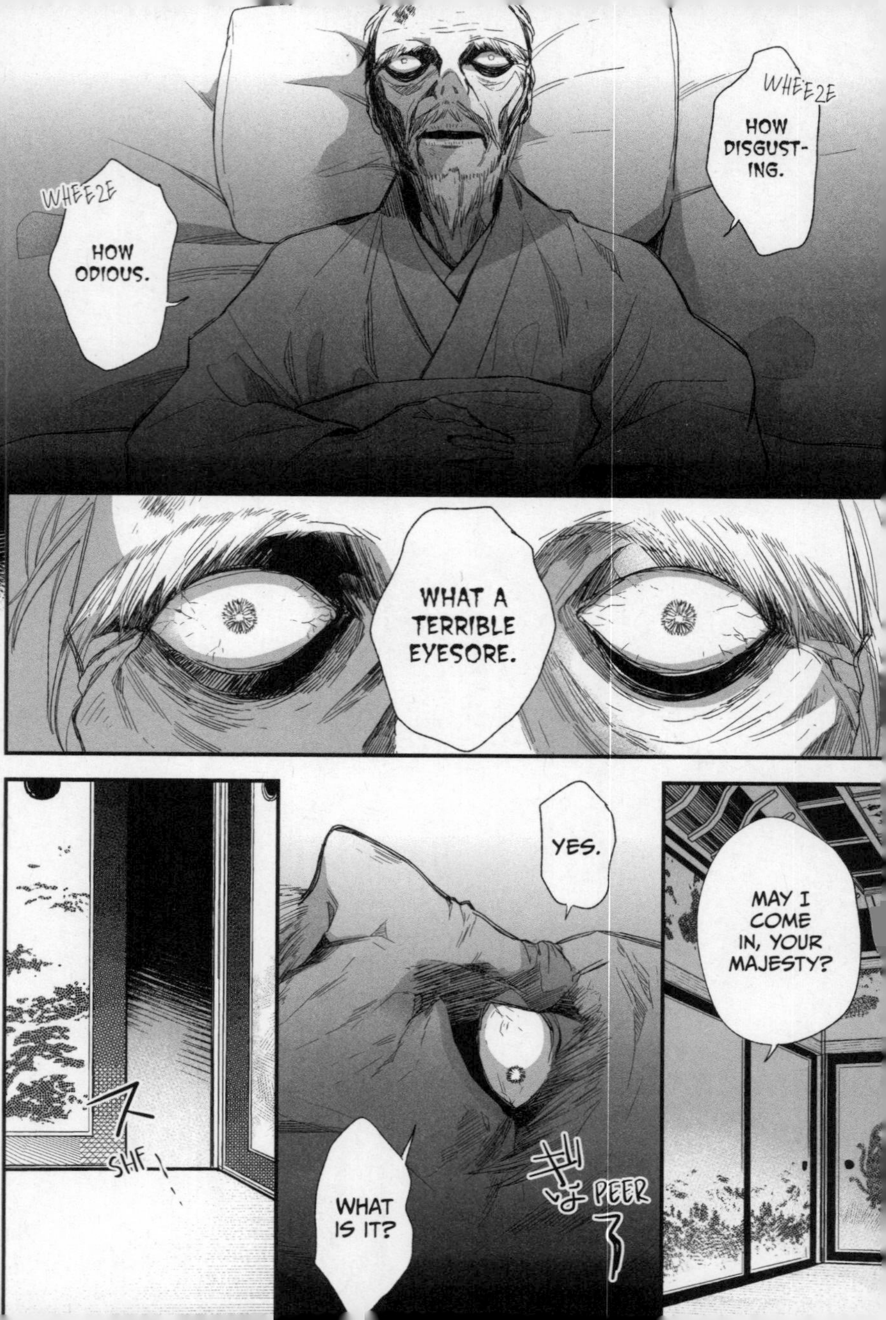
WHEEZE
HOW DISGUST-ING.
WHEEZE
HOW ODIOUS.
WHAT A TERRIBLE EYESORE.
MAY I COME IN, YOUR MAJESTY?
YES.
PEER
WHAT IS IT?
SHF

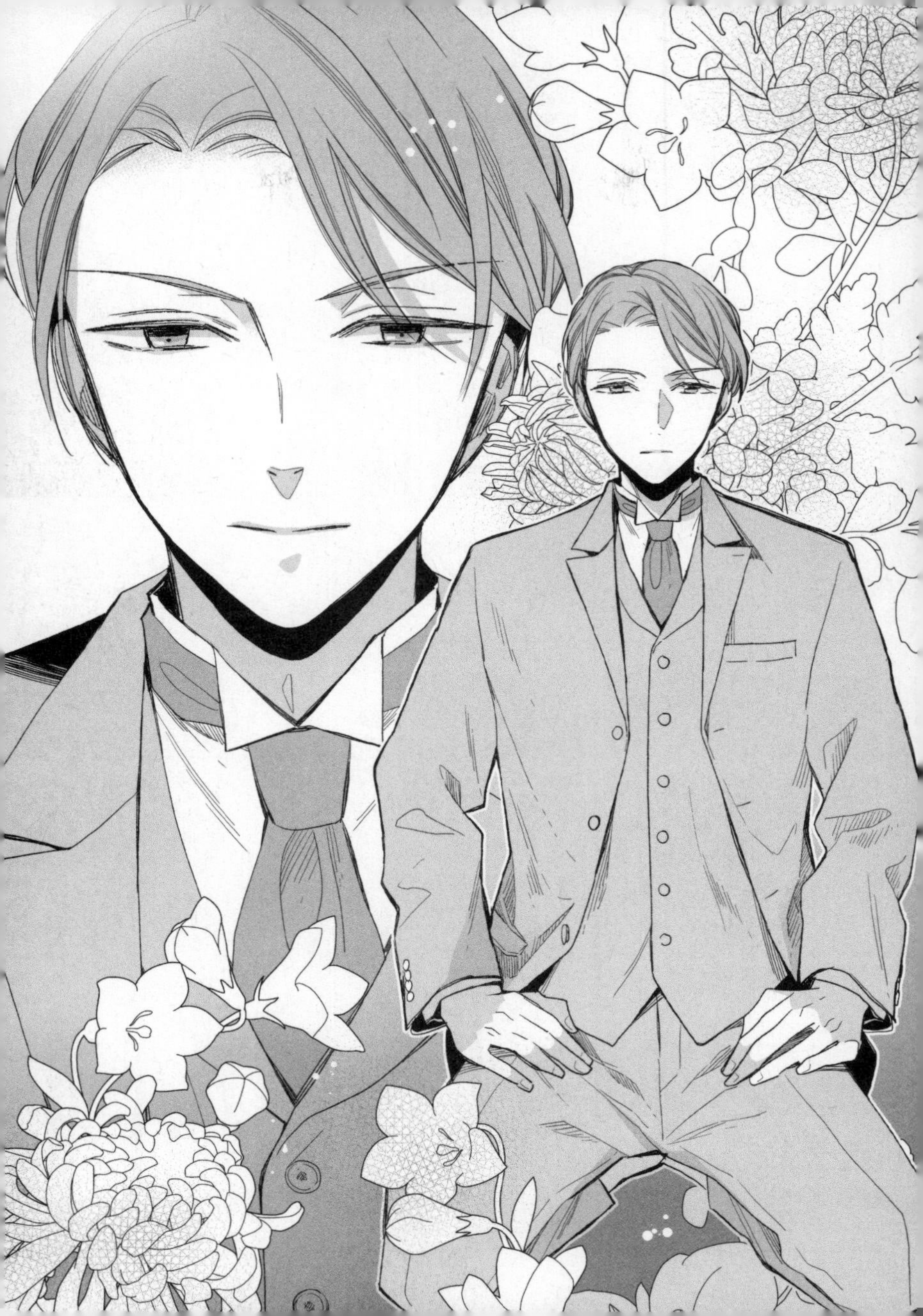

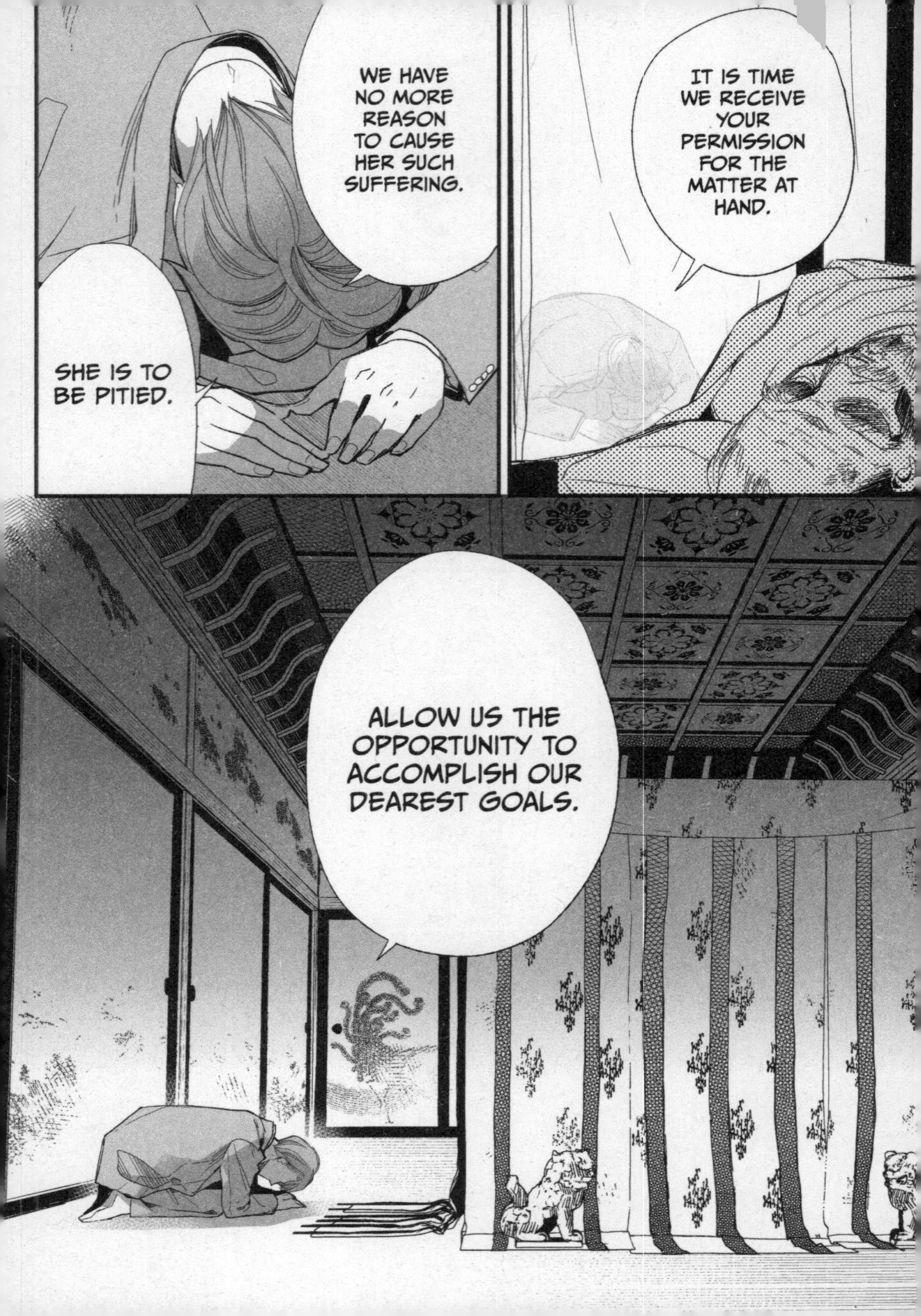
IT IS TIME WE RECEIVE YOUR PERMISSION FOR THE MATTER AT HAND.
WE HAVE NO MORE REASON TO CAUSE HER SUCH SUFFERING.
SHE IS TO BE PITIED.
ALLOW US THE OPPORTUNITY TO ACCOMPLISH OUR DEAREST GOALS.

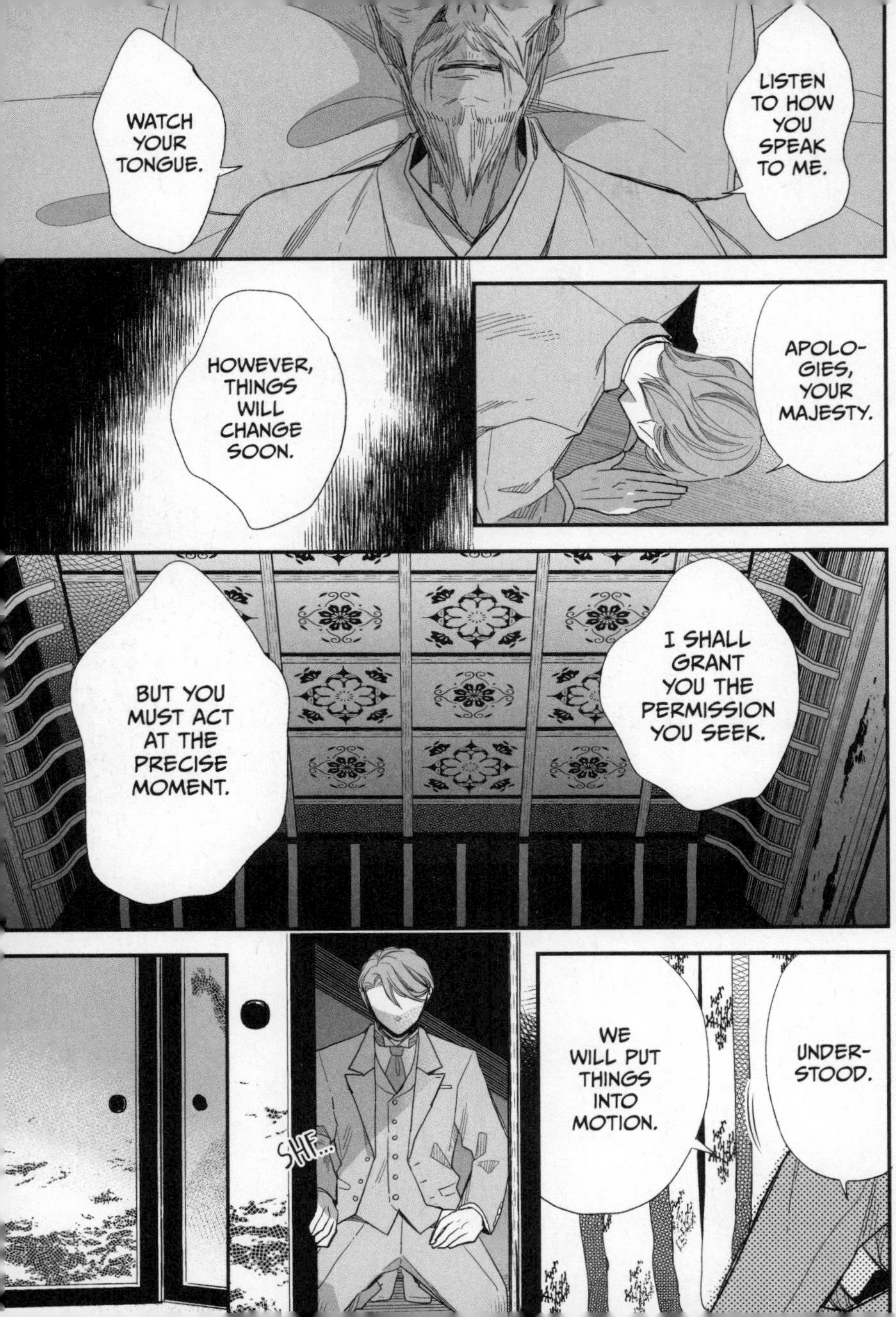
LISTEN TO HOW YOU SPEAK TO ME.
WATCH YOUR TONGUE.
APOLOGIES, YOUR MAJESTY.
HOWEVER, THINGS WILL CHANGE SOON.
I SHALL GRANT YOU THE PERMISSION YOU SEEK.
BUT YOU MUST ACT AT THE PRECISE MOMENT.
UNDER-STOOD.
WE WILL PUT THINGS INTO MOTION.
SHF...

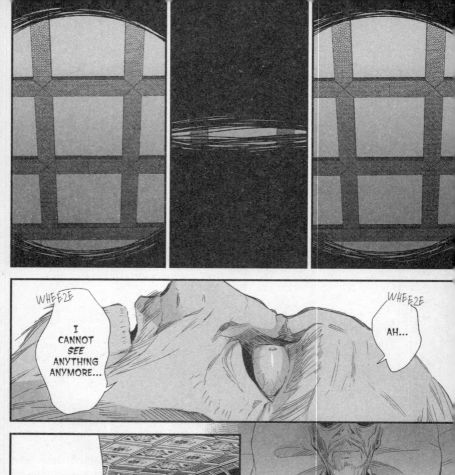

WHEEZE

I CANNOT *SEE* ANYTHING ANYMORE...

WHEEZE

AH...

DO YOU NEED ME, YOUR MAJESTY?

TIIING

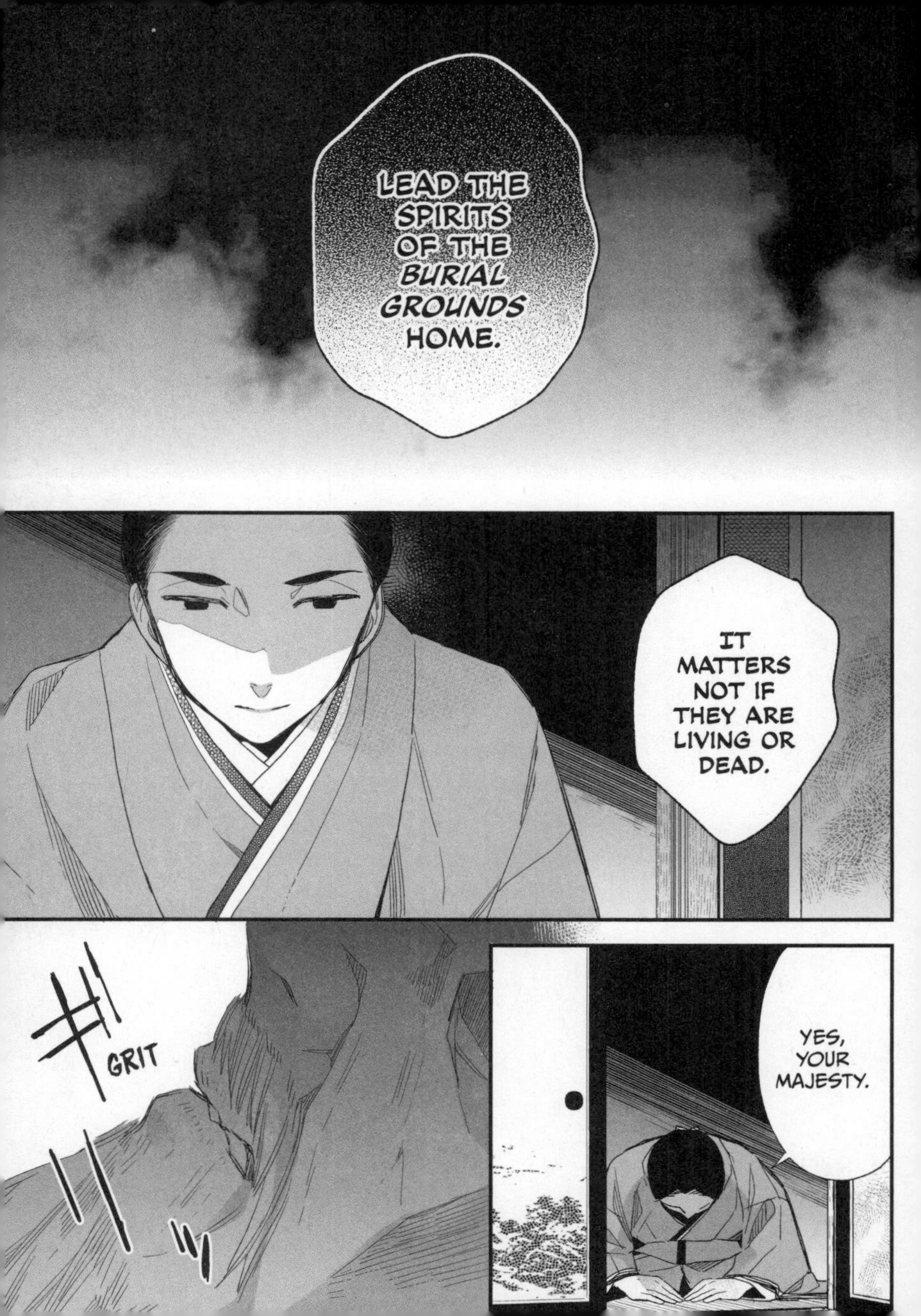
LEAD THE SPIRITS OF THE BURIAL GROUNDS HOME.
IT MATTERS NOT IF THEY ARE LIVING OR DEAD.
YES, YOUR MAJESTY.
GRIT

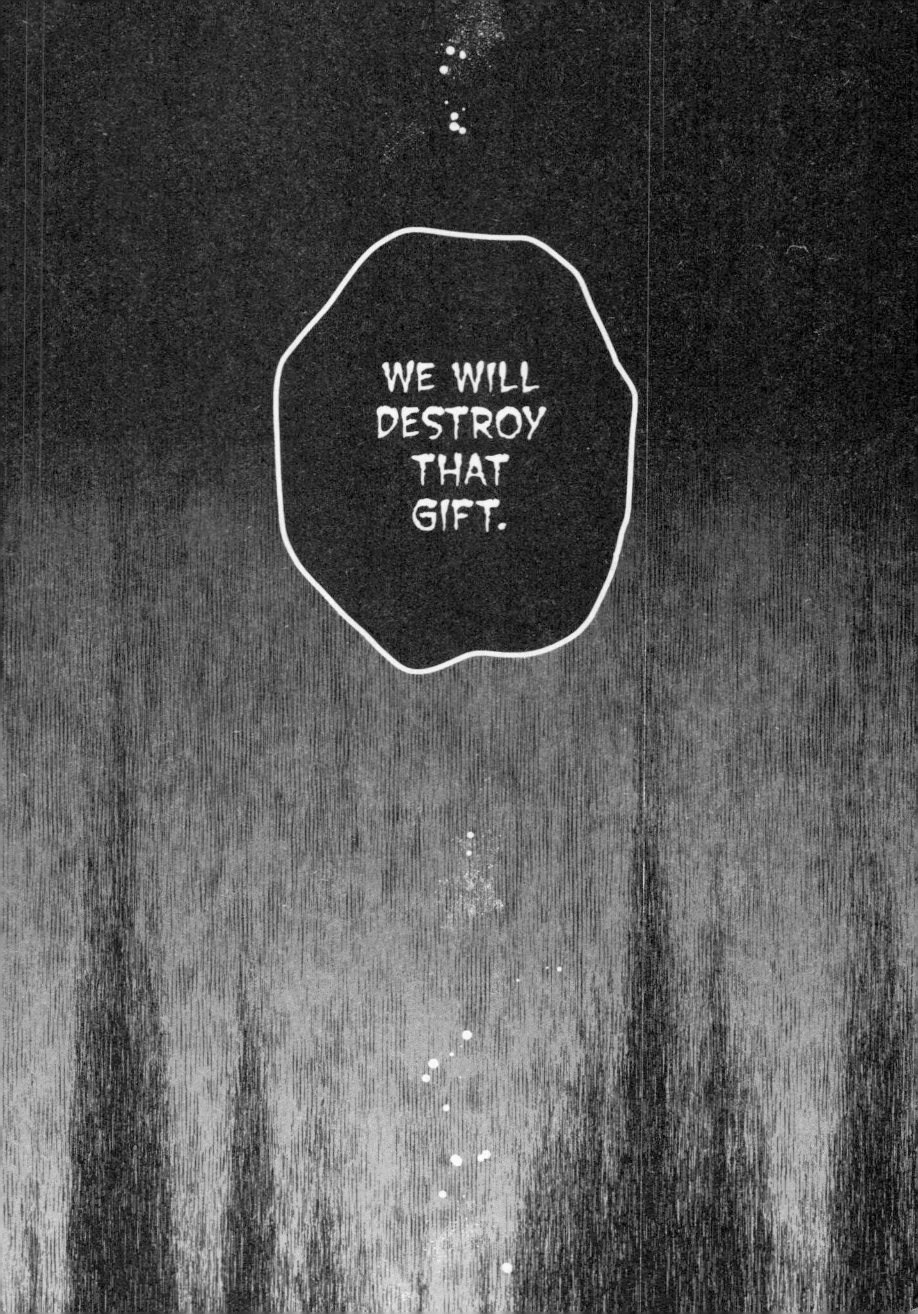
WE WILL DESTROY THAT GIFT.

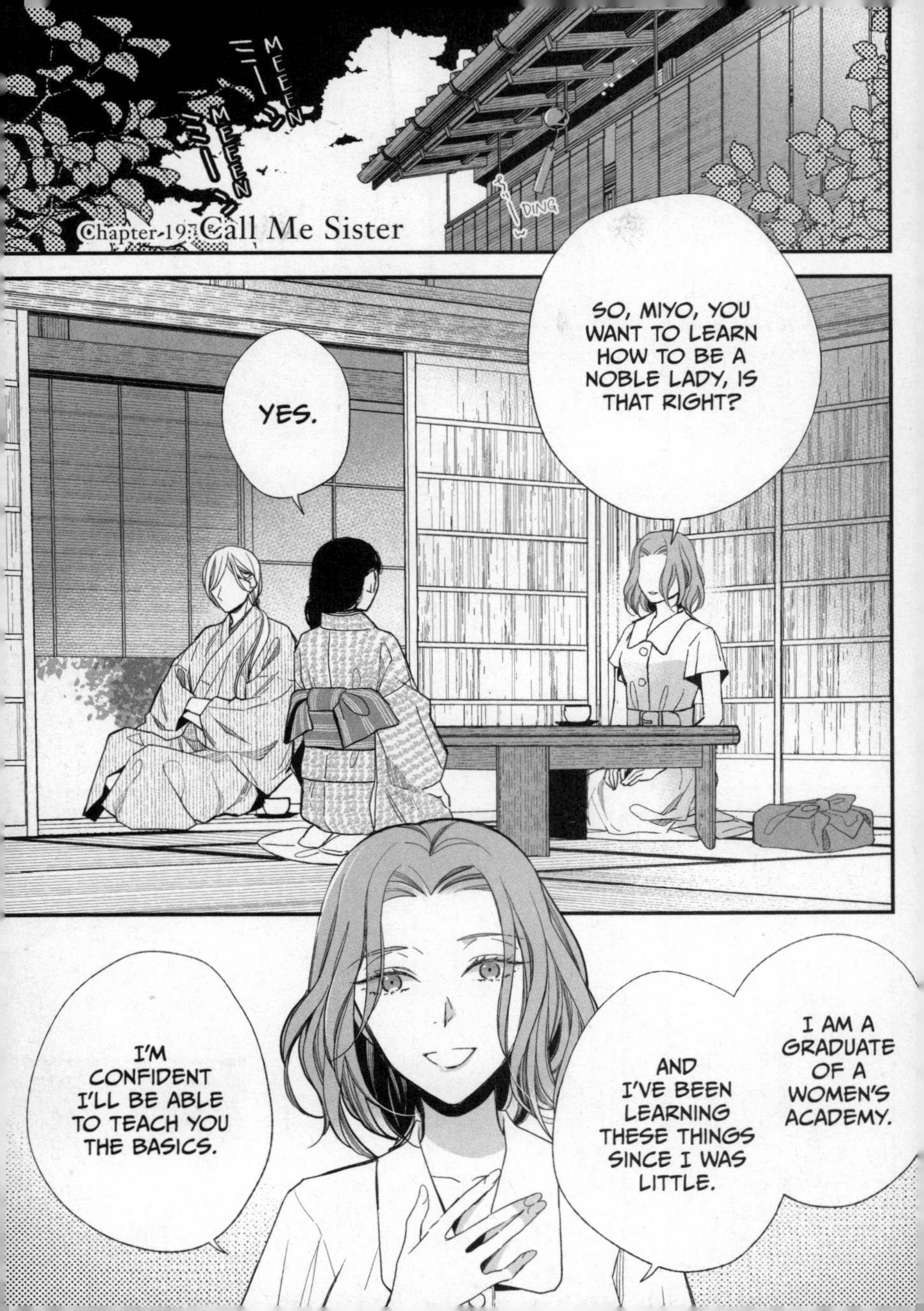
MEEEEN
MEEEEN
DING
Chapter 19: Call Me Sister
SO, MIYO, YOU WANT TO LEARN HOW TO BE A NOBLE LADY, IS THAT RIGHT?
YES.
I AM A GRADUATE OF A WOMEN'S ACADEMY.
AND I'VE BEEN LEARNING THESE THINGS SINCE I WAS LITTLE.
I'M CONFIDENT I'LL BE ABLE TO TEACH YOU THE BASICS.

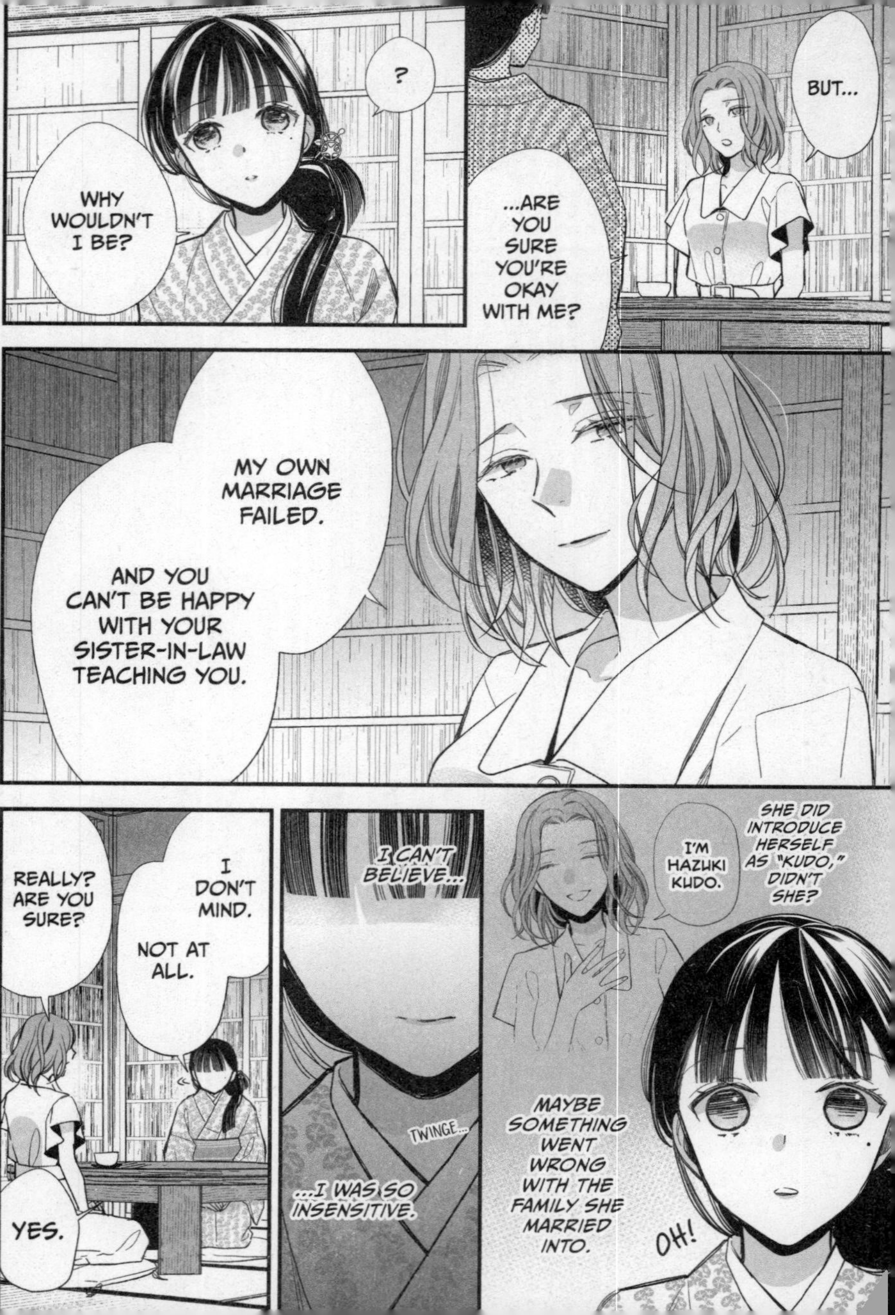
BUT...
...ARE YOU SURE YOU'RE OKAY WITH ME?
?
WHY WOULDN'T I BE?
MY OWN MARRIAGE FAILED.
AND YOU CAN'T BE HAPPY WITH YOUR SISTER-IN-LAW TEACHING YOU.
SHE DID INTRODUCE HERSELF AS "KUDO," DIDN'T SHE?
I'M HAZUKI KUDO.
MAYBE SOMETHING WENT WRONG WITH THE FAMILY SHE MARRIED INTO.
OH!
I CAN'T BELIEVE...
TWINGE...
...I WAS SO INSENSITIVE.
I DON'T MIND.
NOT AT ALL.
REALLY? ARE YOU SURE?
YES.

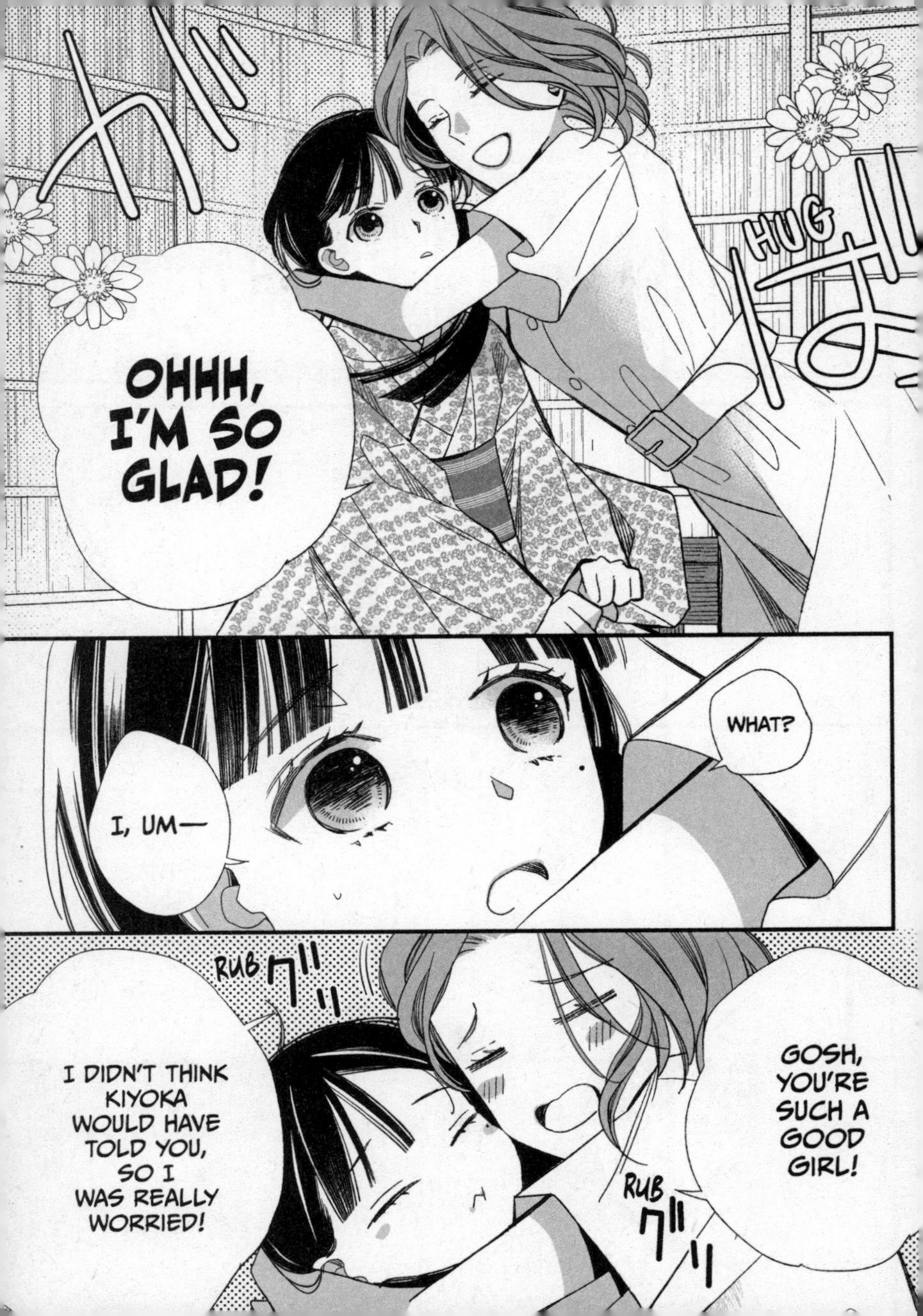
HUG
OHHH, I'M SO GLAD!
WHAT?
I, UM—
RUB
RUB
GOSH, YOU'RE SUCH A GOOD GIRL!
I DIDN'T THINK KIYOKA WOULD HAVE TOLD YOU, SO I WAS REALLY WORRIED!

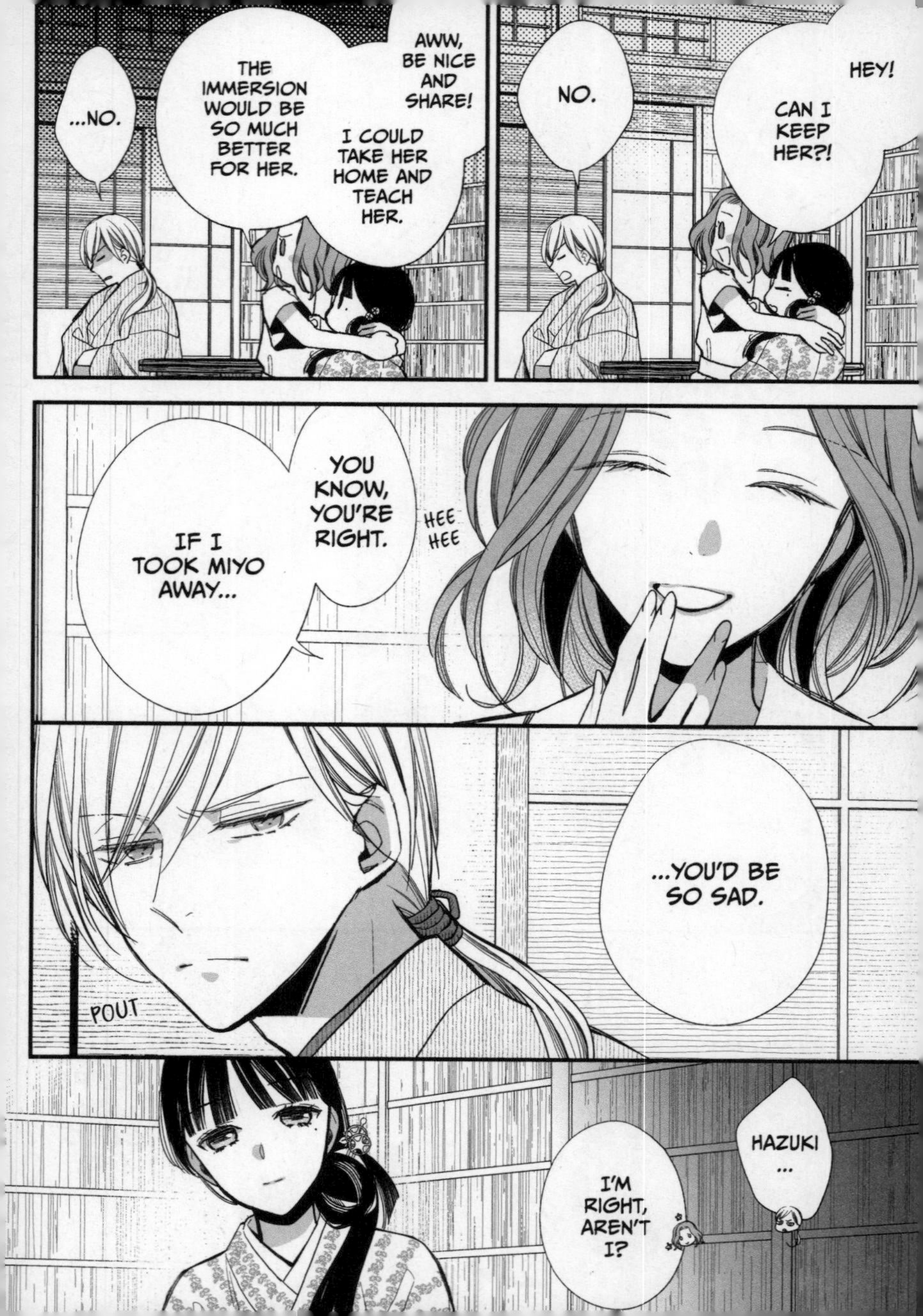
HEY!
CAN I KEEP HER?!
NO.
AWW, BE NICE AND SHARE!
I COULD TAKE HER HOME AND TEACH HER.
THE IMMERSION WOULD BE SO MUCH BETTER FOR HER.
...NO.
YOU KNOW, YOU'RE RIGHT.
HEE HEE
IF I TOOK MIYO AWAY...
...YOU'D BE SO SAD.
POUT
HAZUKI...
I'M RIGHT, AREN'T I?

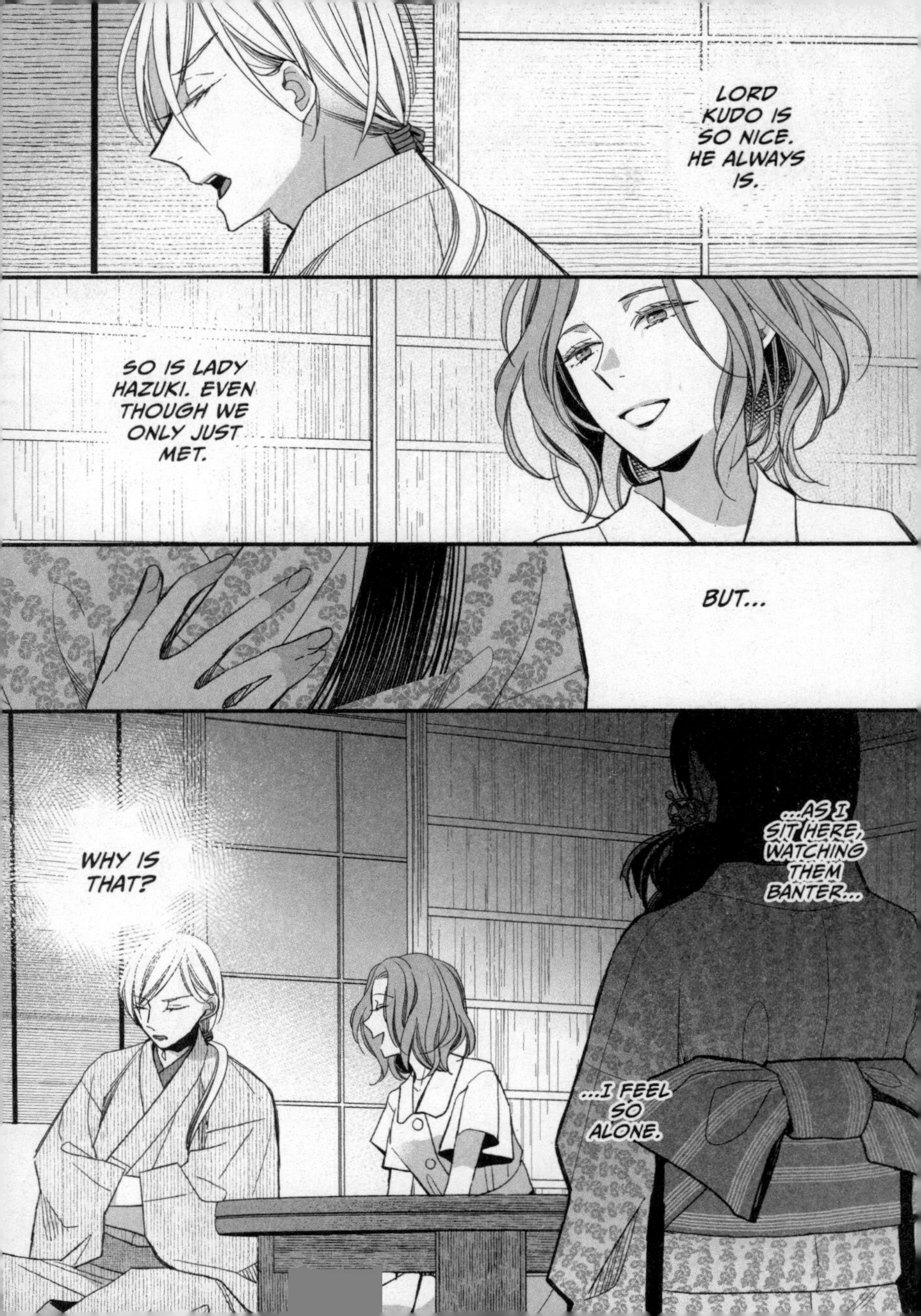
LORD KUDO IS SO NICE. HE ALWAYS IS.
SO IS LADY HAZUKI. EVEN THOUGH WE ONLY JUST MET.
BUT...
...AS I SIT HERE, WATCHING THEM BANTER...
...I FEEL SO ALONE.
WHY IS THAT?

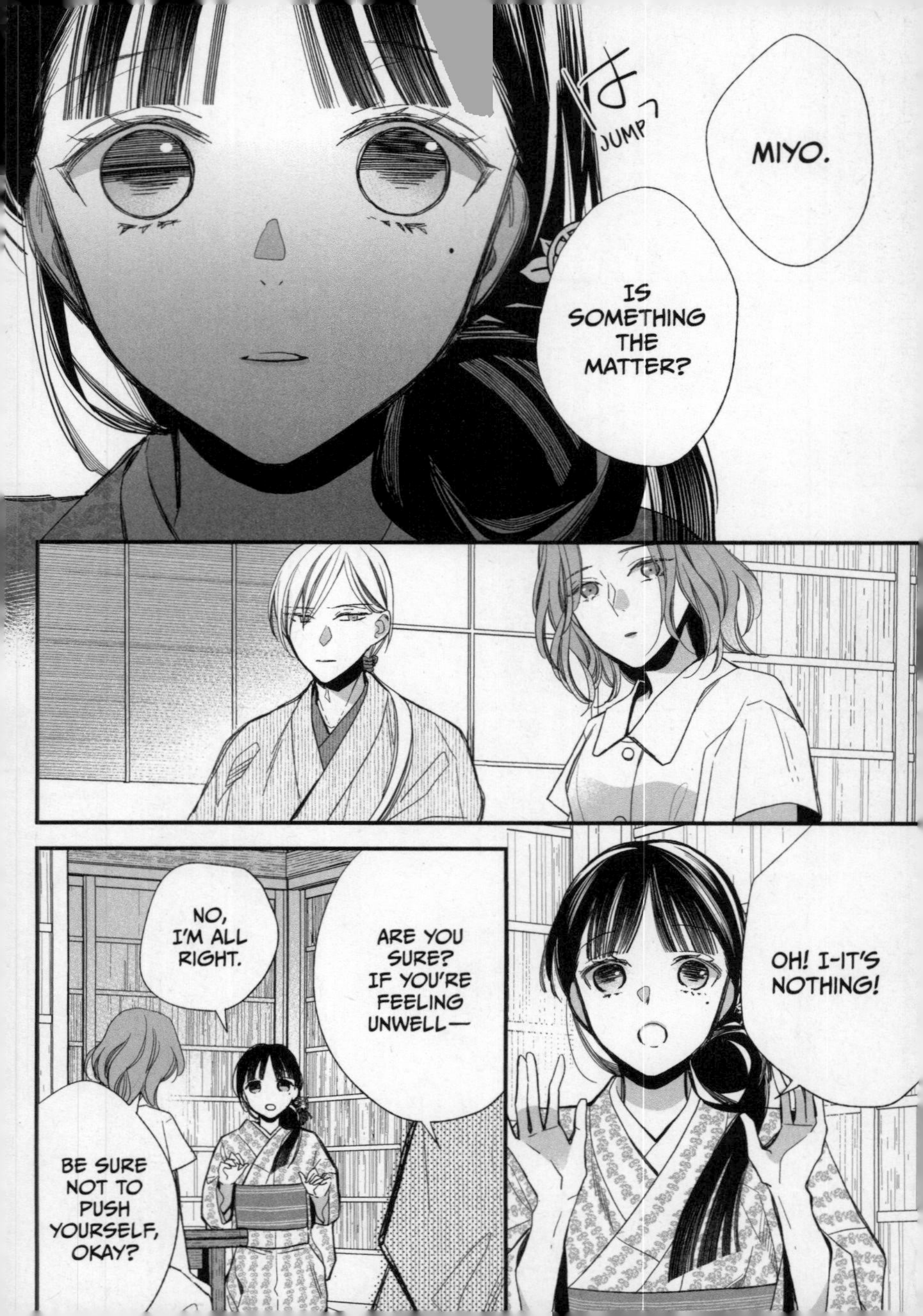
MIYO.
は JUMP
IS SOMETHING THE MATTER?
OH! I-IT'S NOTHING!
ARE YOU SURE? IF YOU'RE FEELING UNWELL—
NO, I'M ALL RIGHT.
BE SURE NOT TO PUSH YOURSELF, OKAY?

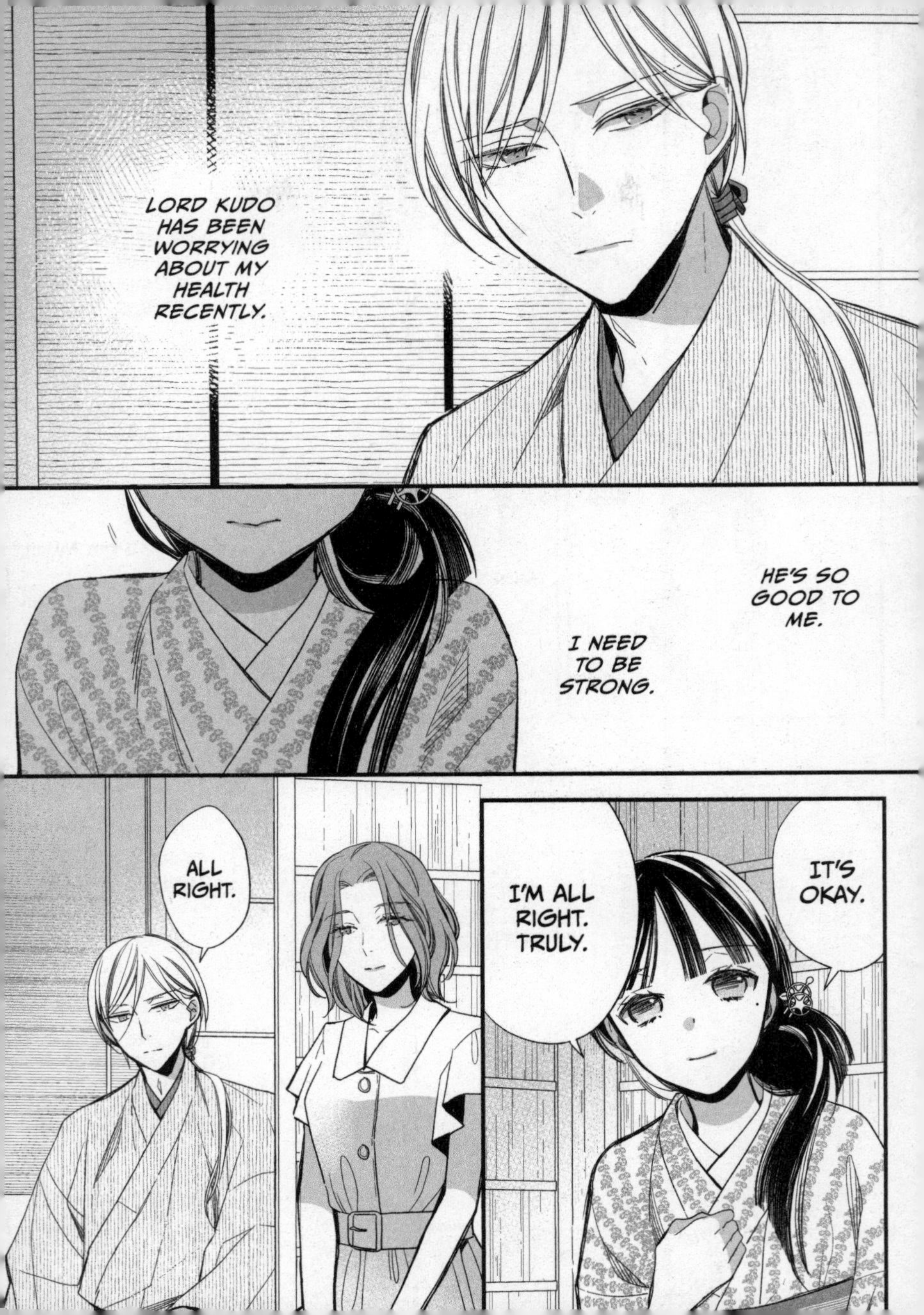
LORD KUDO HAS BEEN WORRYING ABOUT MY HEALTH RECENTLY.
HE'S SO GOOD TO ME.
I NEED TO BE STRONG.
IT'S OKAY.
I'M ALL RIGHT. TRULY.
ALL RIGHT.

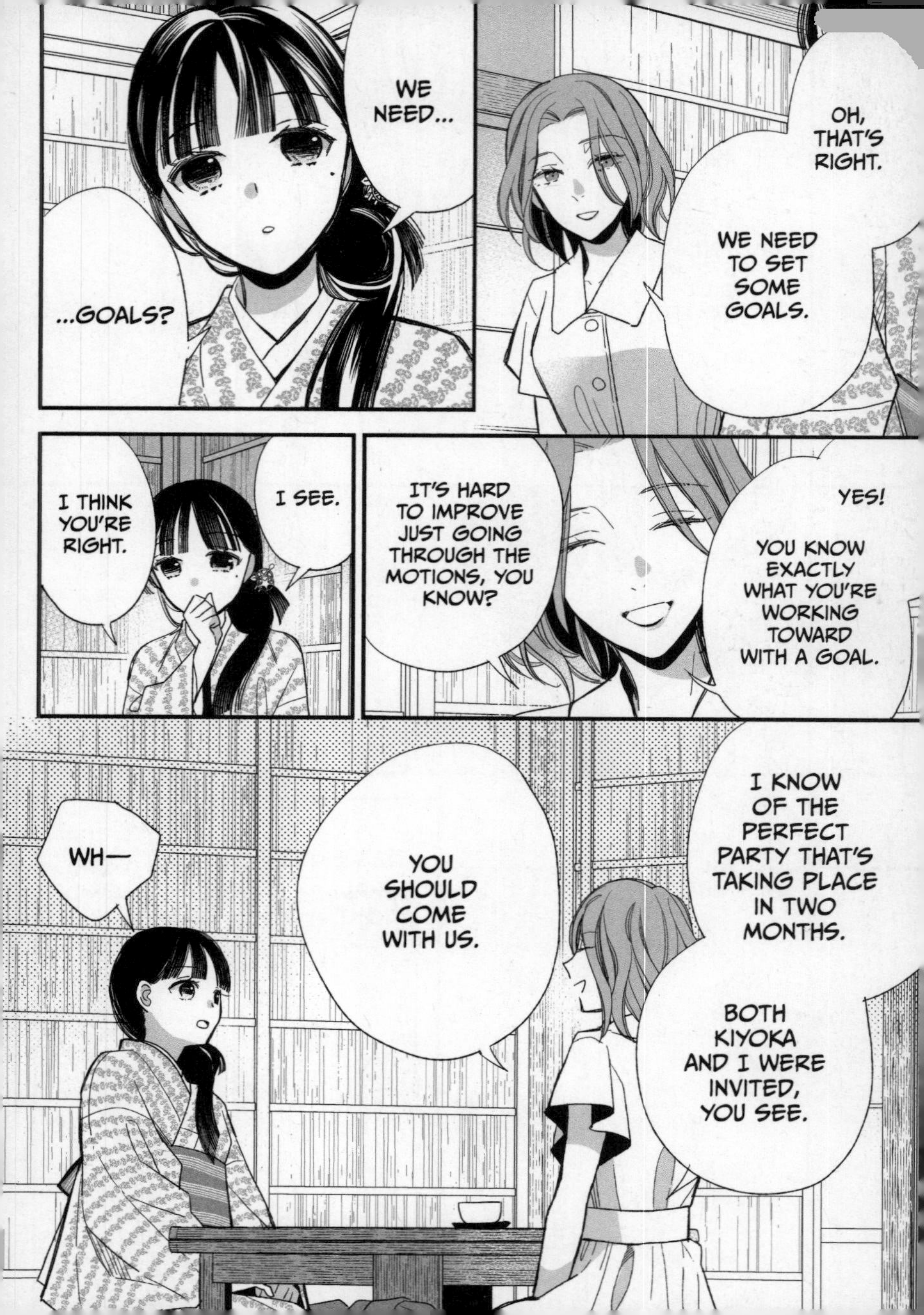
OH, THAT'S RIGHT.
WE NEED TO SET SOME GOALS.
WE NEED...
...GOALS?
YES!
YOU KNOW EXACTLY WHAT YOU'RE WORKING TOWARD WITH A GOAL.
IT'S HARD TO IMPROVE JUST GOING THROUGH THE MOTIONS, YOU KNOW?
I SEE.
I THINK YOU'RE RIGHT.
I KNOW OF THE PERFECT PARTY THAT'S TAKING PLACE IN TWO MONTHS.
BOTH KIYOKA AND I WERE INVITED, YOU SEE.
YOU SHOULD COME WITH US.
WH—

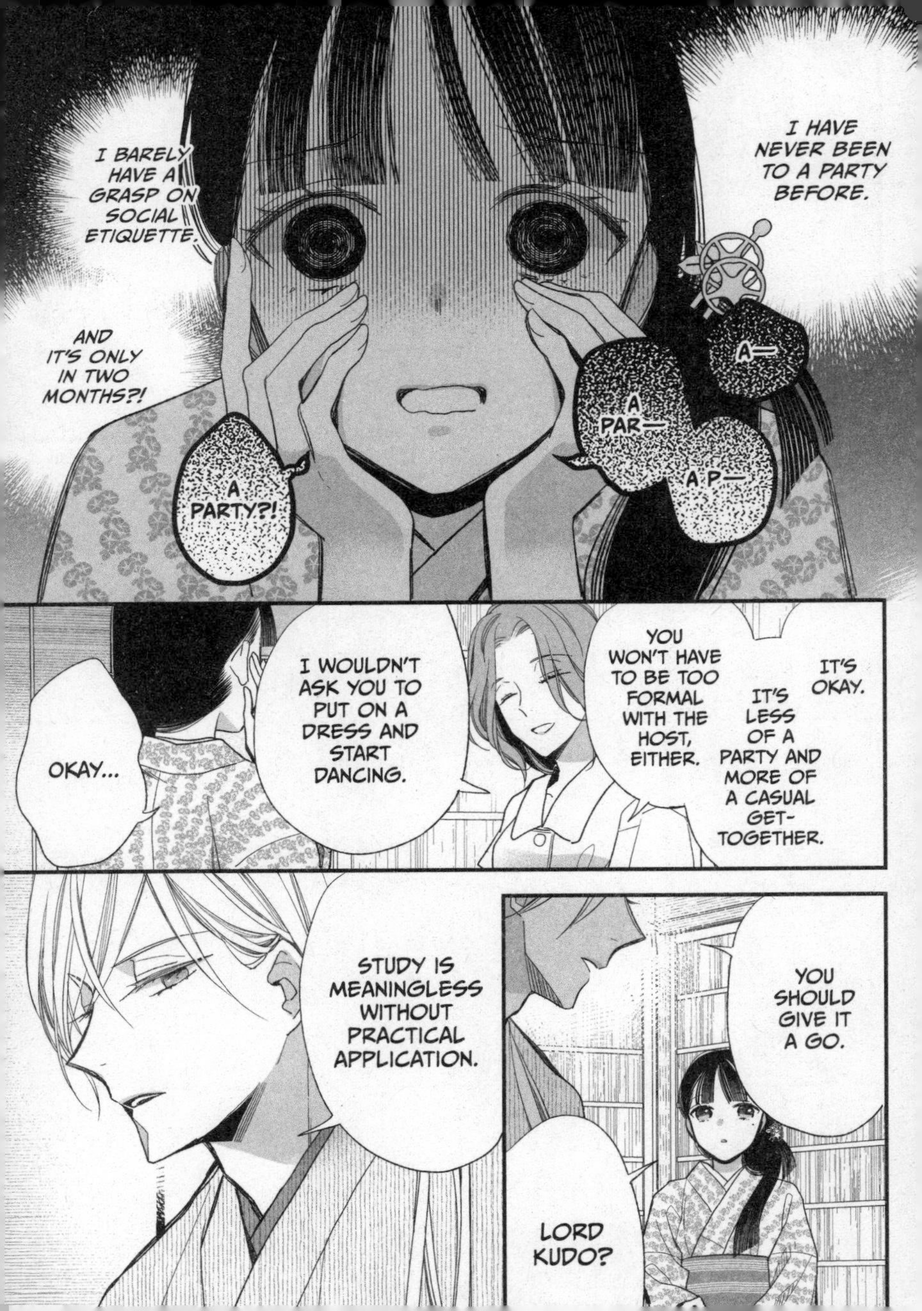
I HAVE NEVER BEEN TO A PARTY BEFORE.
I BARELY HAVE A GRASP ON SOCIAL ETIQUETTE.
A—
A PAR—
A P—
AND IT'S ONLY IN TWO MONTHS?!
A PARTY?!
IT'S OKAY.
IT'S LESS OF A PARTY AND MORE OF A CASUAL GET-TOGETHER.
YOU WON'T HAVE TO BE TOO FORMAL WITH THE HOST, EITHER.
I WOULDN'T ASK YOU TO PUT ON A DRESS AND START DANCING.
OKAY...
YOU SHOULD GIVE IT A GO.
LORD KUDO?
STUDY IS MEANINGLESS WITHOUT PRACTICAL APPLICATION.

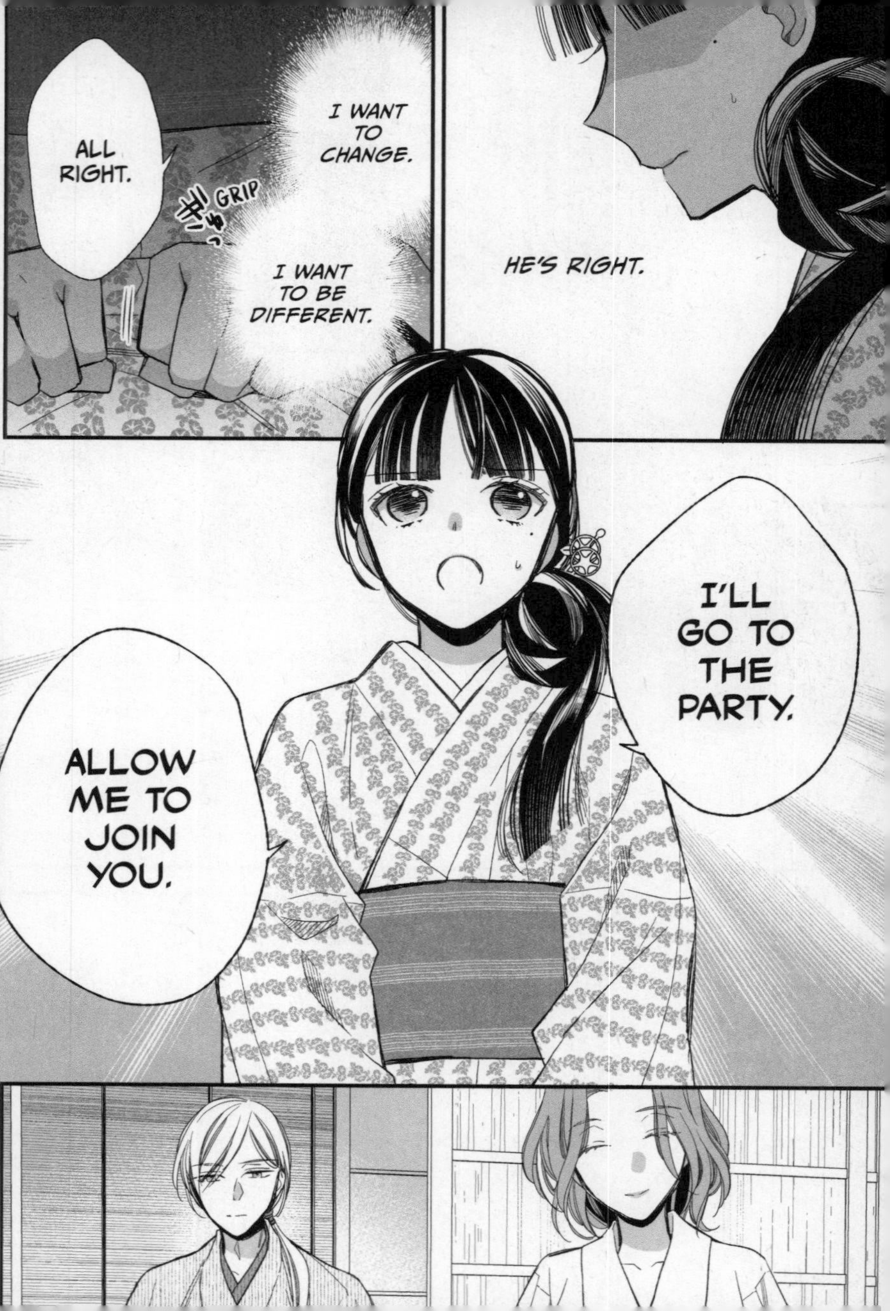
HE'S RIGHT.
I WANT TO CHANGE.
I WANT TO BE DIFFERENT.
GRIP
ALL RIGHT.
I'LL GO TO THE PARTY.
ALLOW ME TO JOIN YOU.

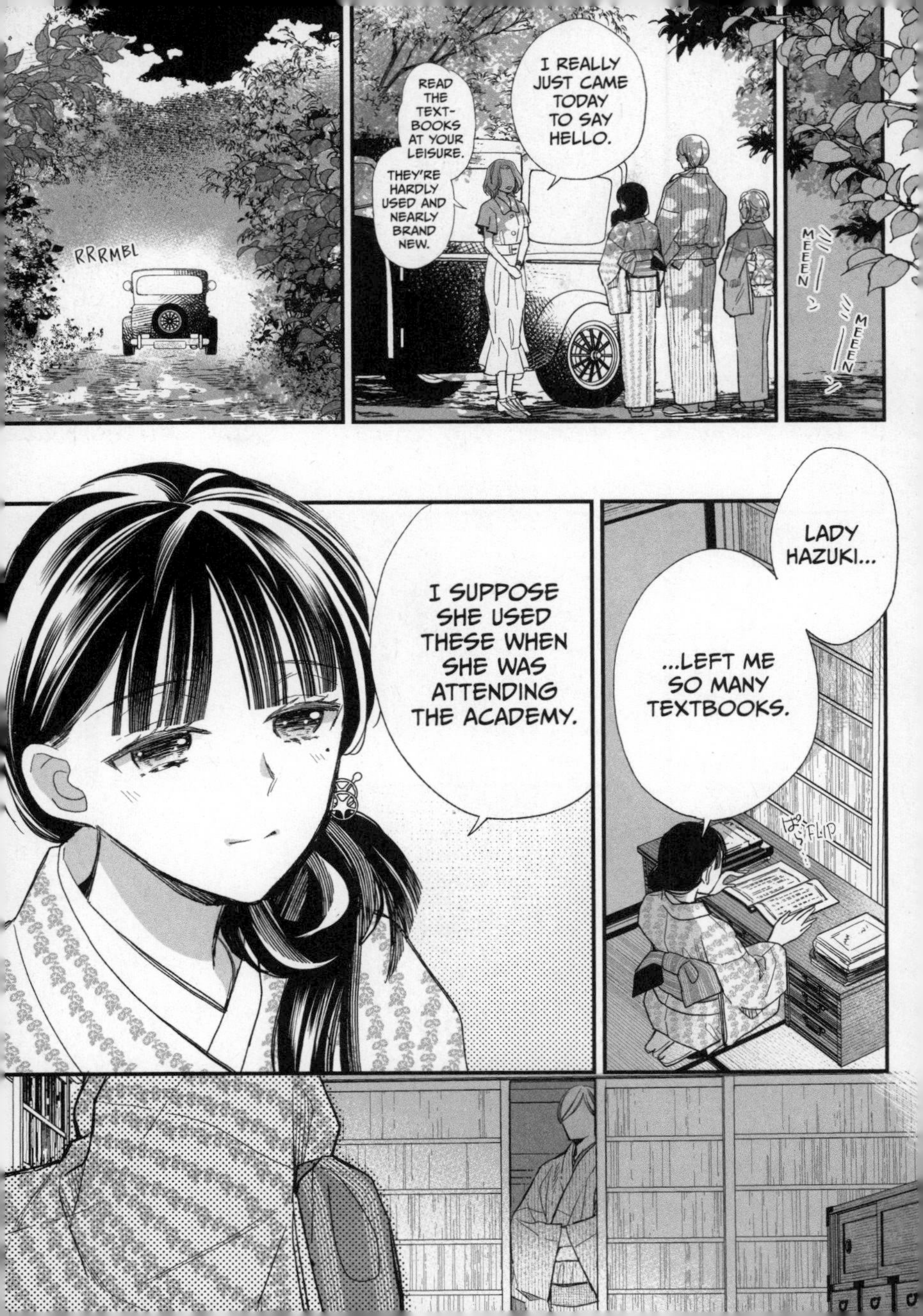
MEEEN
MEEEN
I REALLY JUST CAME TODAY TO SAY HELLO.
READ THE TEXT-BOOKS AT YOUR LEISURE.
THEY'RE HARDLY USED AND NEARLY BRAND NEW.
RRRMBL
LADY HAZUKI...
...LEFT ME SO MANY TEXTBOOKS.
FLIP
I SUPPOSE SHE USED THESE WHEN SHE WAS ATTENDING THE ACADEMY.

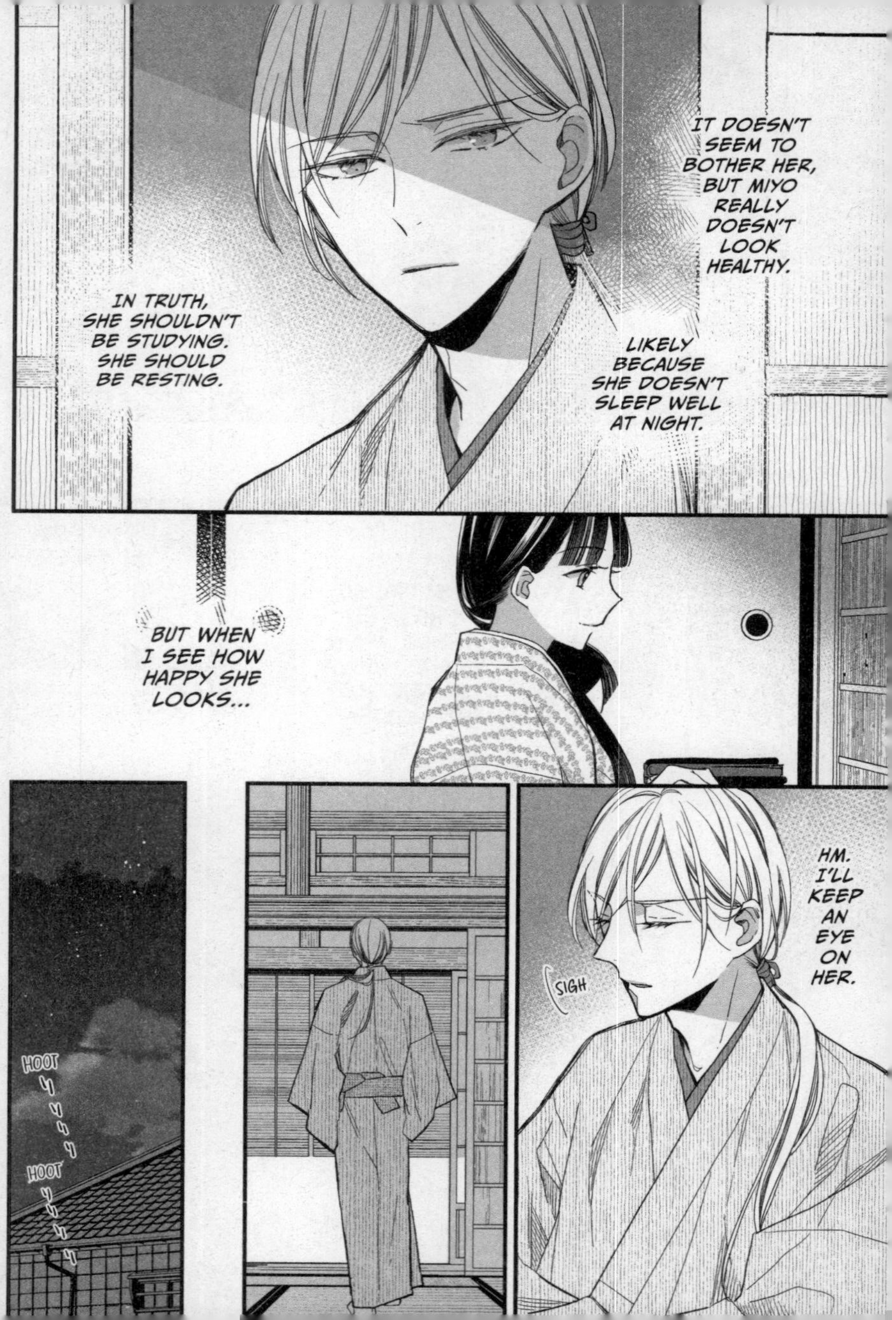
IT DOESN'T SEEM TO BOTHER HER, BUT MIYO REALLY DOESN'T LOOK HEALTHY.
LIKELY BECAUSE SHE DOESN'T SLEEP WELL AT NIGHT.
IN TRUTH, SHE SHOULDN'T BE STUDYING. SHE SHOULD BE RESTING.
BUT WHEN I SEE HOW HAPPY SHE LOOKS...
HM. I'LL KEEP AN EYE ON HER.
SIGH
HOOT
HOOT

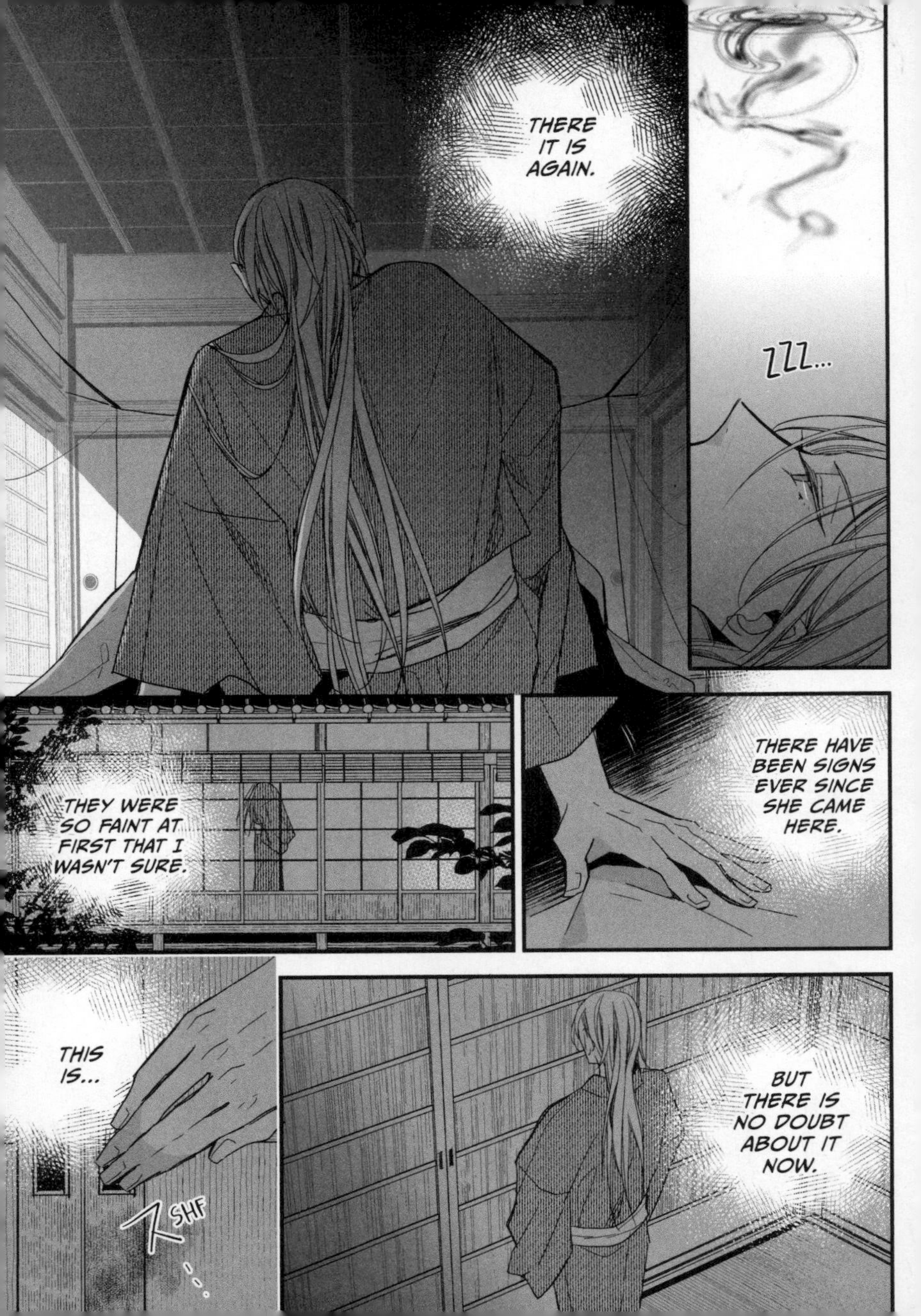
ZZZ...
THERE IT IS AGAIN.
THERE HAVE BEEN SIGNS EVER SINCE SHE CAME HERE.
THEY WERE SO FAINT AT FIRST THAT I WASN'T SURE.
BUT THERE IS NO DOUBT ABOUT IT NOW.
THIS IS...
SHF
...

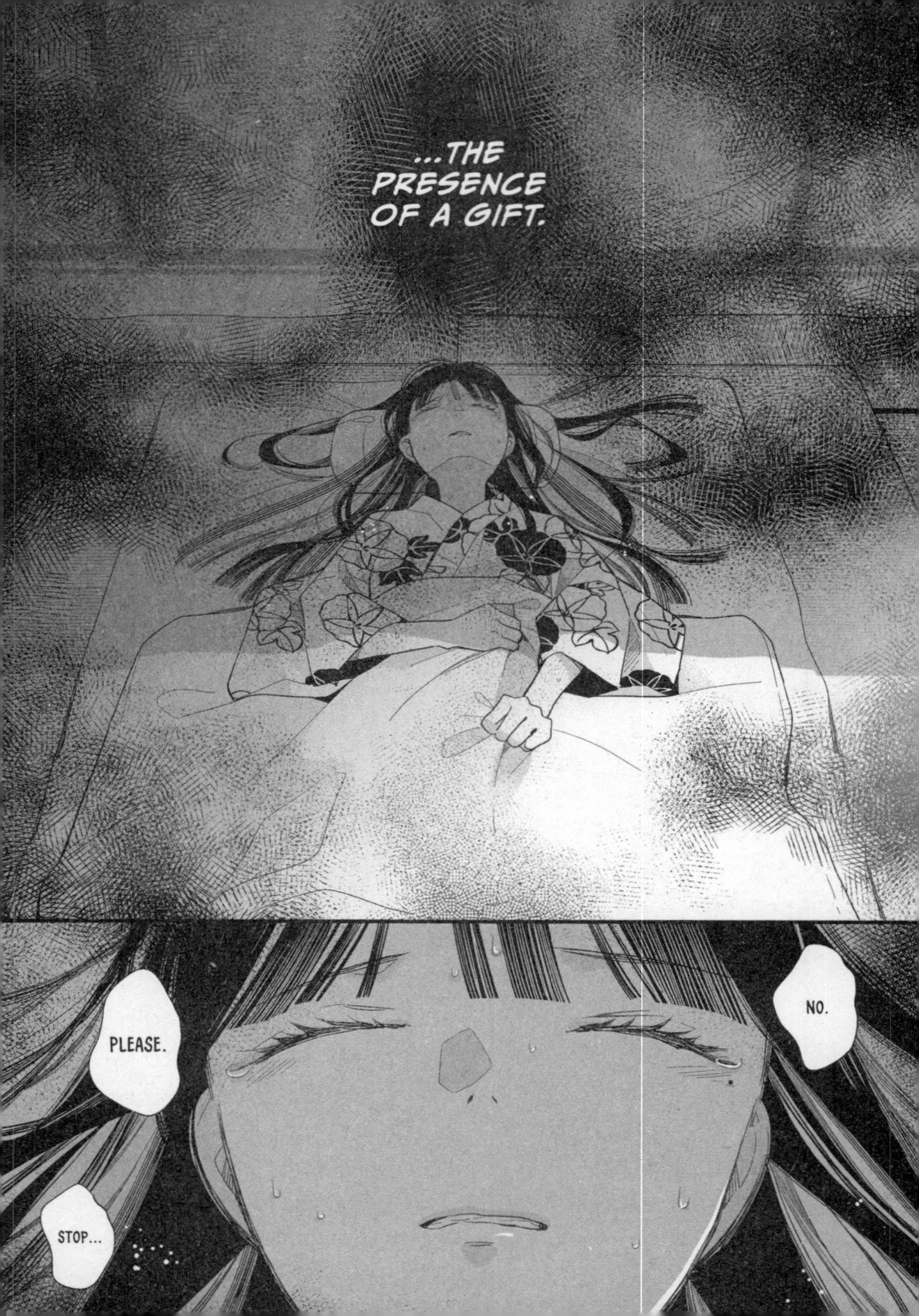
...THE PRESENCE OF A GIFT.
NO.
PLEASE.
STOP...

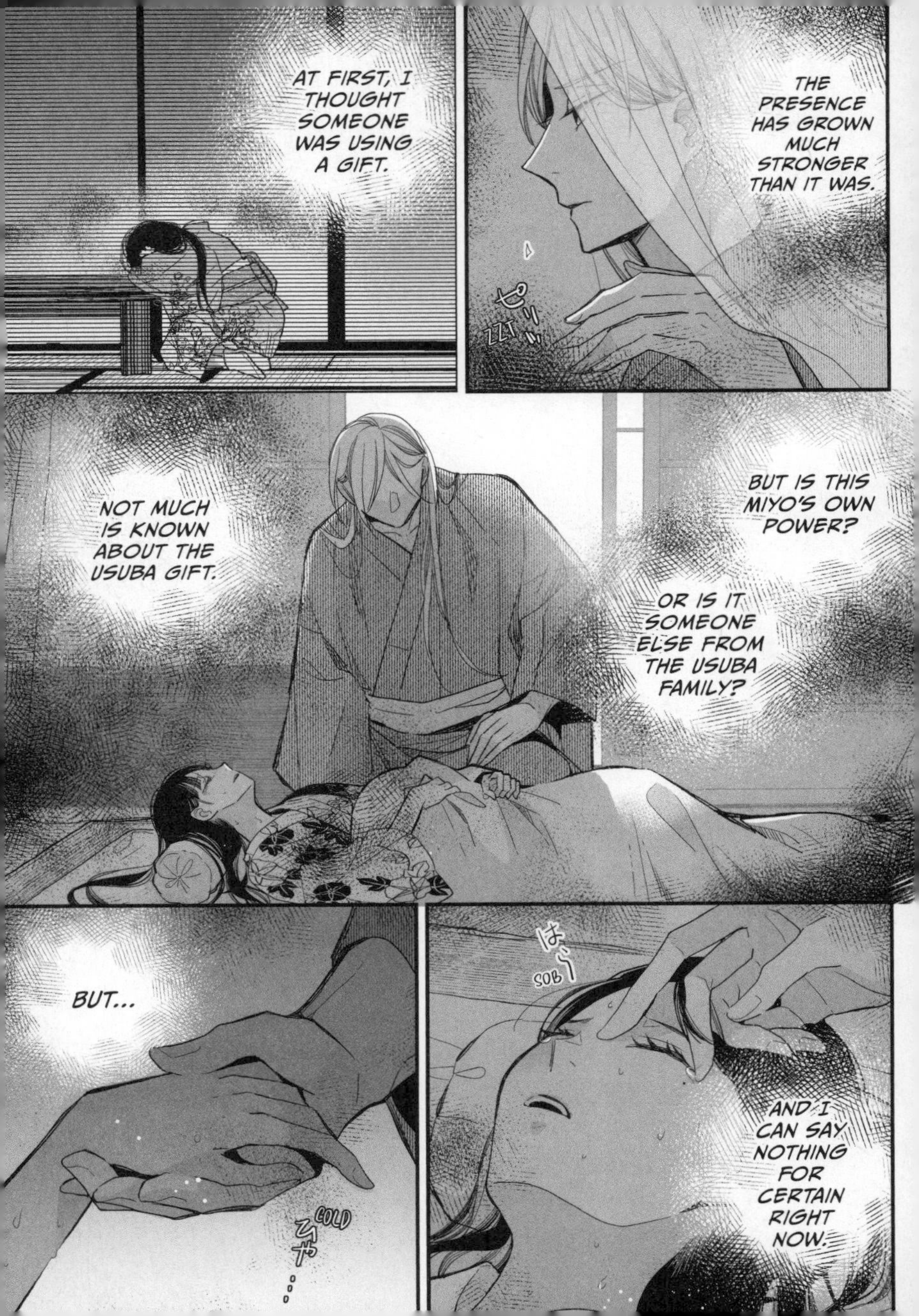
THE PRESENCE HAS GROWN MUCH STRONGER THAN IT WAS.
ピリッ
ZZT
AT FIRST, I THOUGHT SOMEONE WAS USING A GIFT.
BUT IS THIS MIYO'S OWN POWER?
OR IS IT SOMEONE ELSE FROM THE USUBA FAMILY?
NOT MUCH IS KNOWN ABOUT THE USUBA GIFT.
はっ
SOB
AND I CAN SAY NOTHING FOR CERTAIN RIGHT NOW.
BUT...
COLD
ひや...

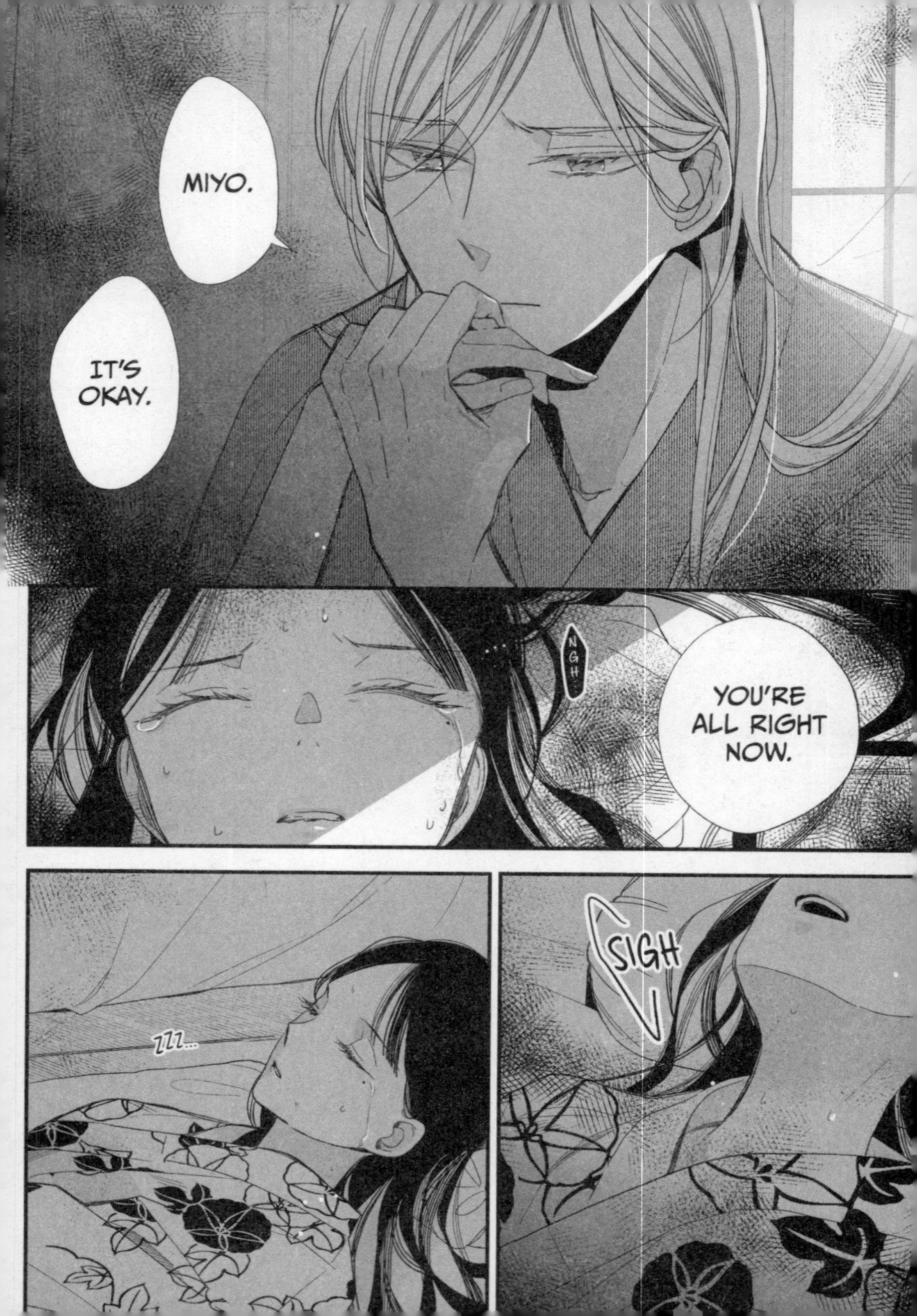
MIYO.
IT'S OKAY.
YOU'RE ALL RIGHT NOW.
NGH...
SIGH
ZZZ...

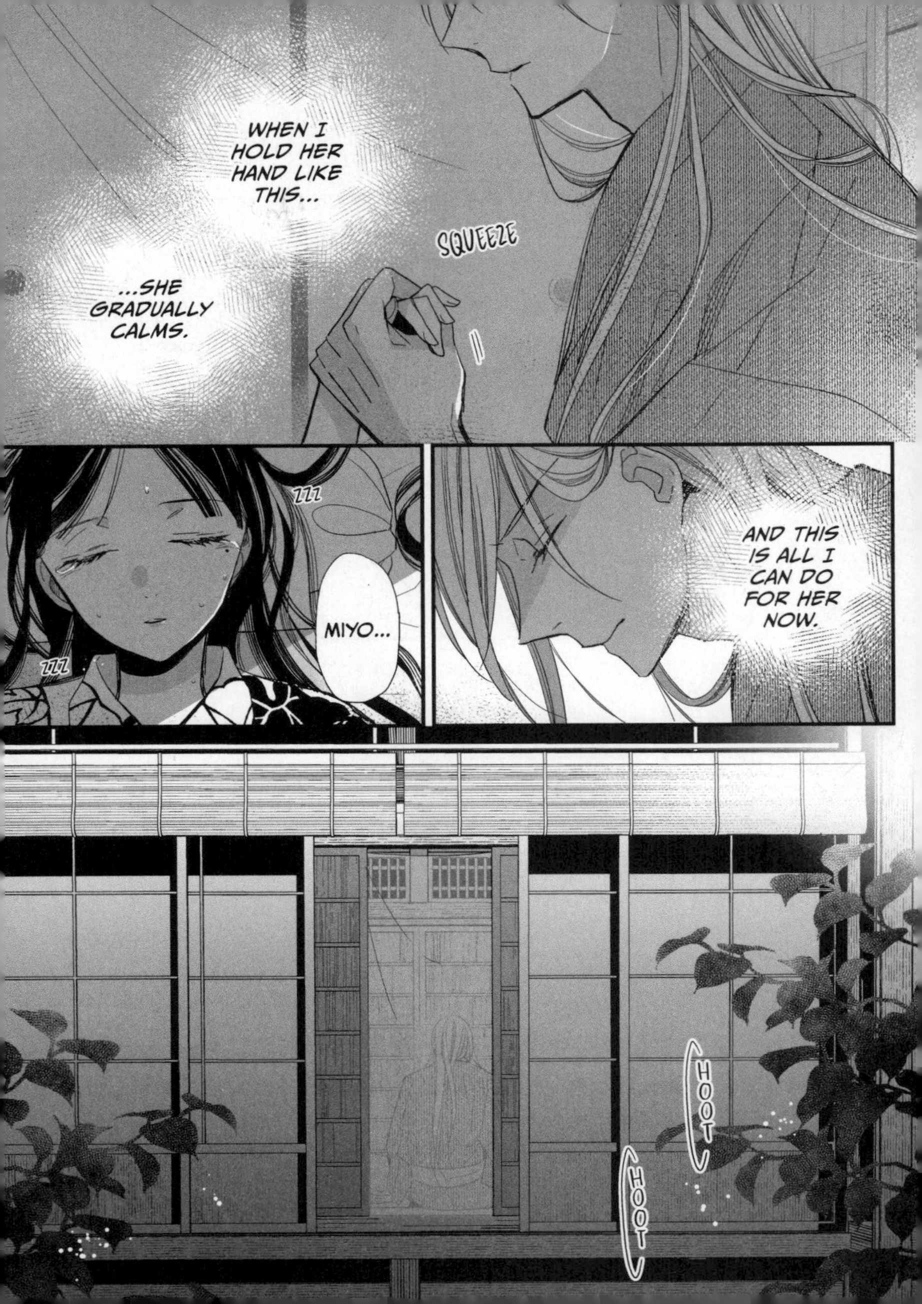
WHEN I HOLD HER HAND LIKE THIS...
SQUEEZE
...SHE GRADUALLY CALMS.
AND THIS IS ALL I CAN DO FOR HER NOW.
ZZZ
MIYO...
ZZZ
HOOT
HOOT

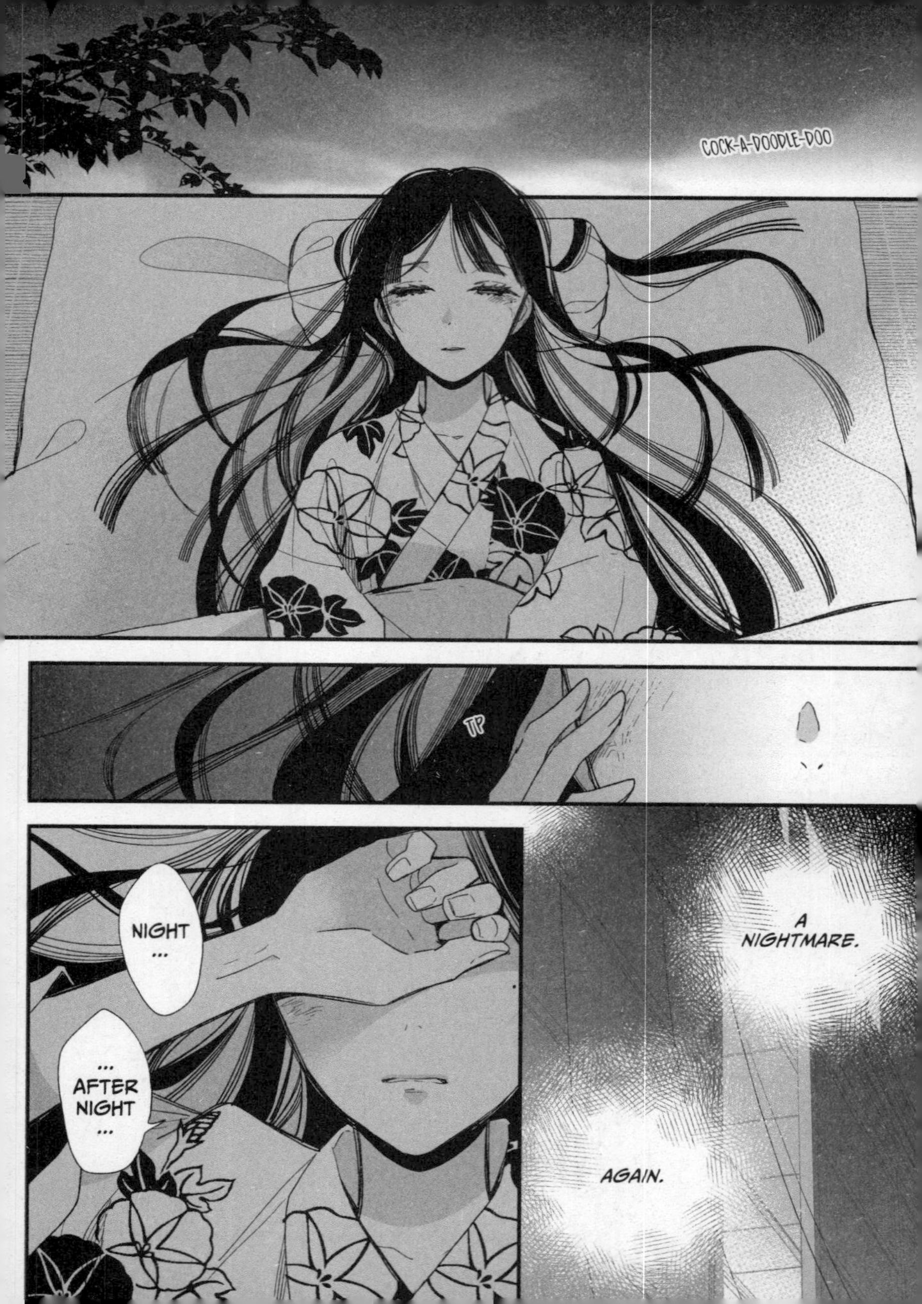
COCK-A-DOODLE-DOO
TP
A NIGHTMARE.
AGAIN.
NIGHT...
...AFTER NIGHT...

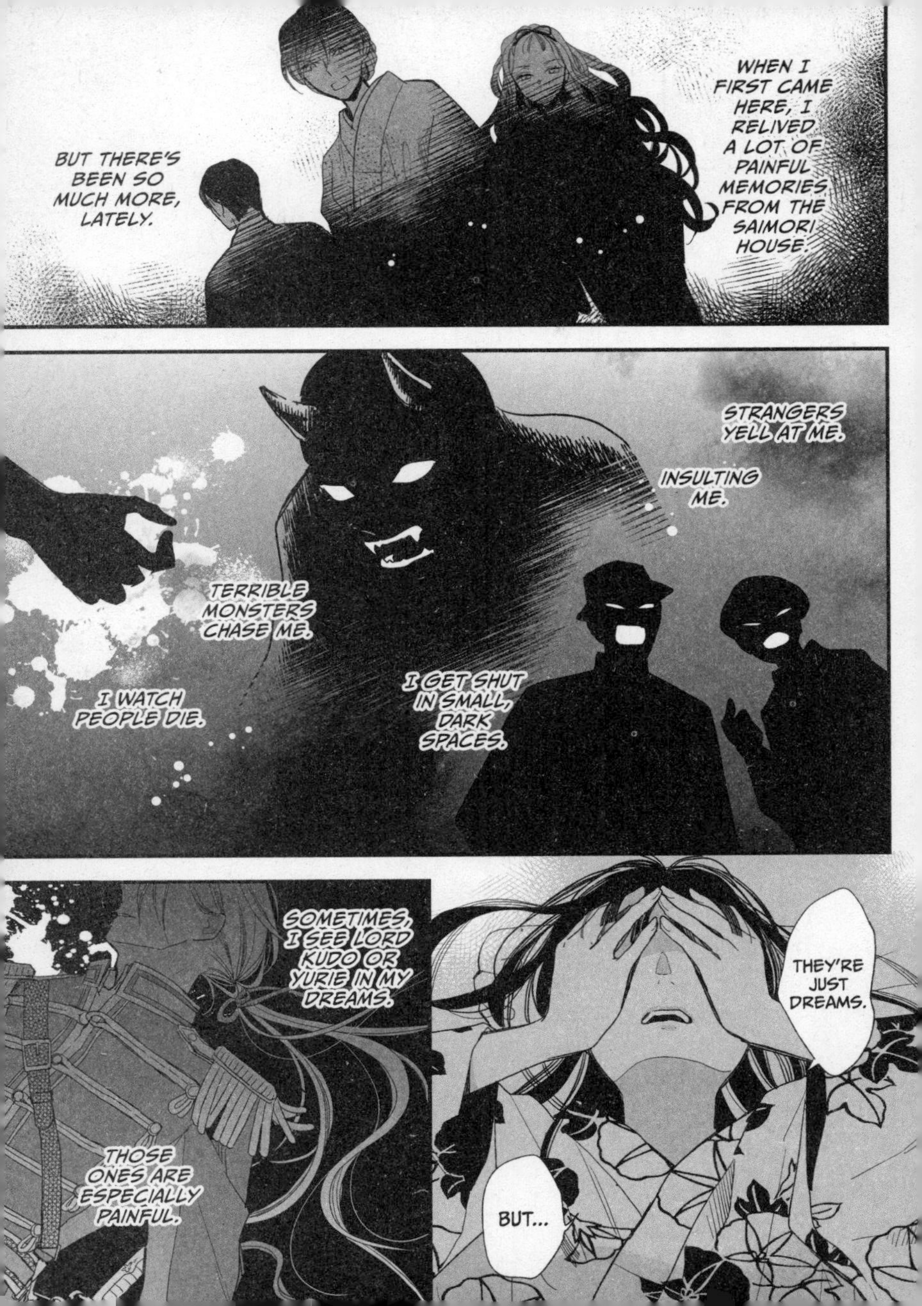
WHEN I FIRST CAME HERE, I RELIVED A LOT OF PAINFUL MEMORIES FROM THE SAIMORI HOUSE.
BUT THERE'S BEEN SO MUCH MORE, LATELY.
STRANGERS YELL AT ME.
INSULTING ME.
TERRIBLE MONSTERS CHASE ME.
I GET SHUT IN SMALL, DARK SPACES.
I WATCH PEOPLE DIE.
THEY'RE JUST DREAMS.
BUT...
SOMETIMES, I SEE LORD KUDO OR YURIE IN MY DREAMS.
THOSE ONES ARE ESPECIALLY PAINFUL.

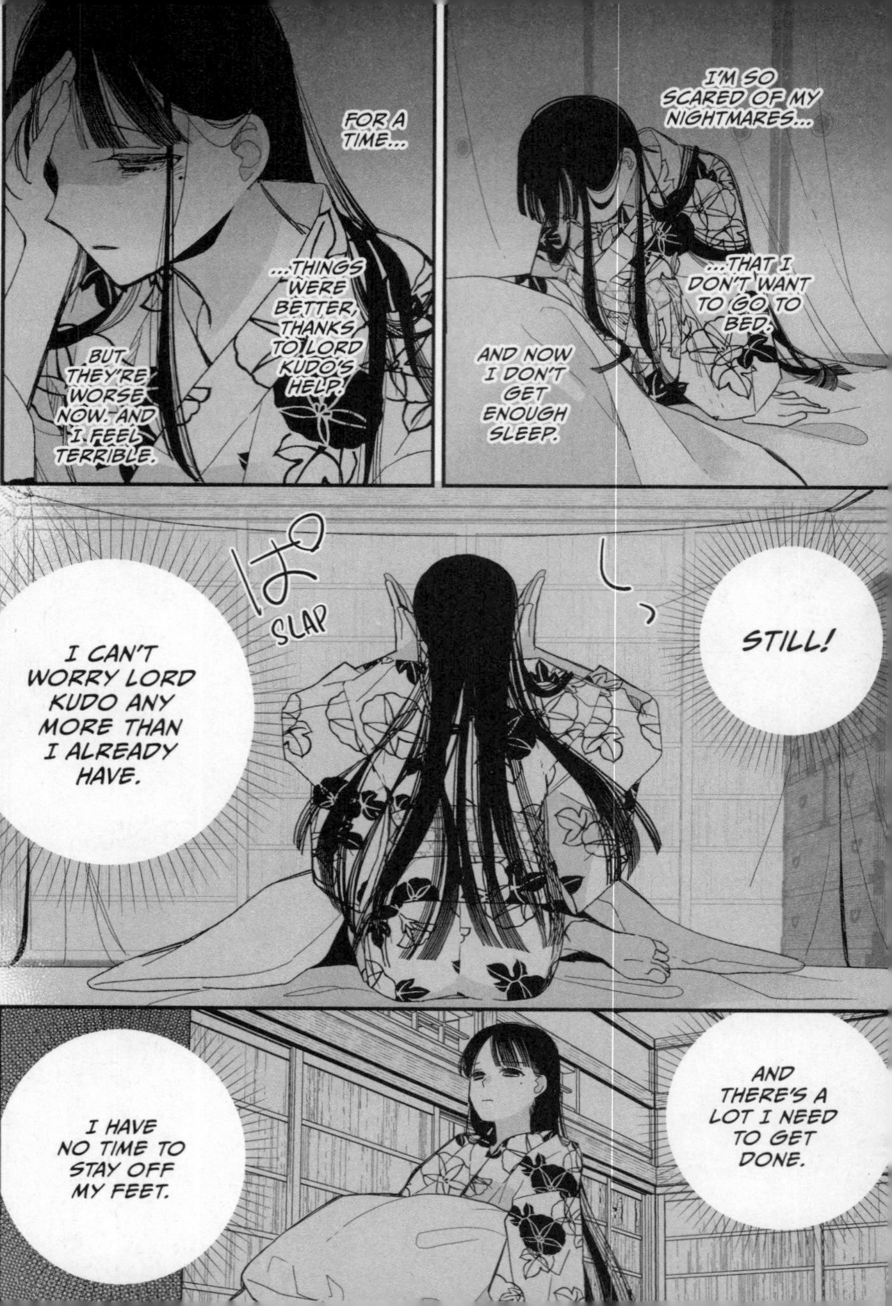
I'M SO SCARED OF MY NIGHTMARES...
...THAT I DON'T WANT TO GO TO BED.
AND NOW I DON'T GET ENOUGH SLEEP.
FOR A TIME...
...THINGS WERE BETTER, THANKS TO LORD KUDO'S HELP.
BUT THEY'RE WORSE NOW. AND I FEEL TERRIBLE.
STILL!
ぱし
SLAP
I CAN'T WORRY LORD KUDO ANY MORE THAN I ALREADY HAVE.
AND THERE'S A LOT I NEED TO GET DONE.
I HAVE NO TIME TO STAY OFF MY FEET.

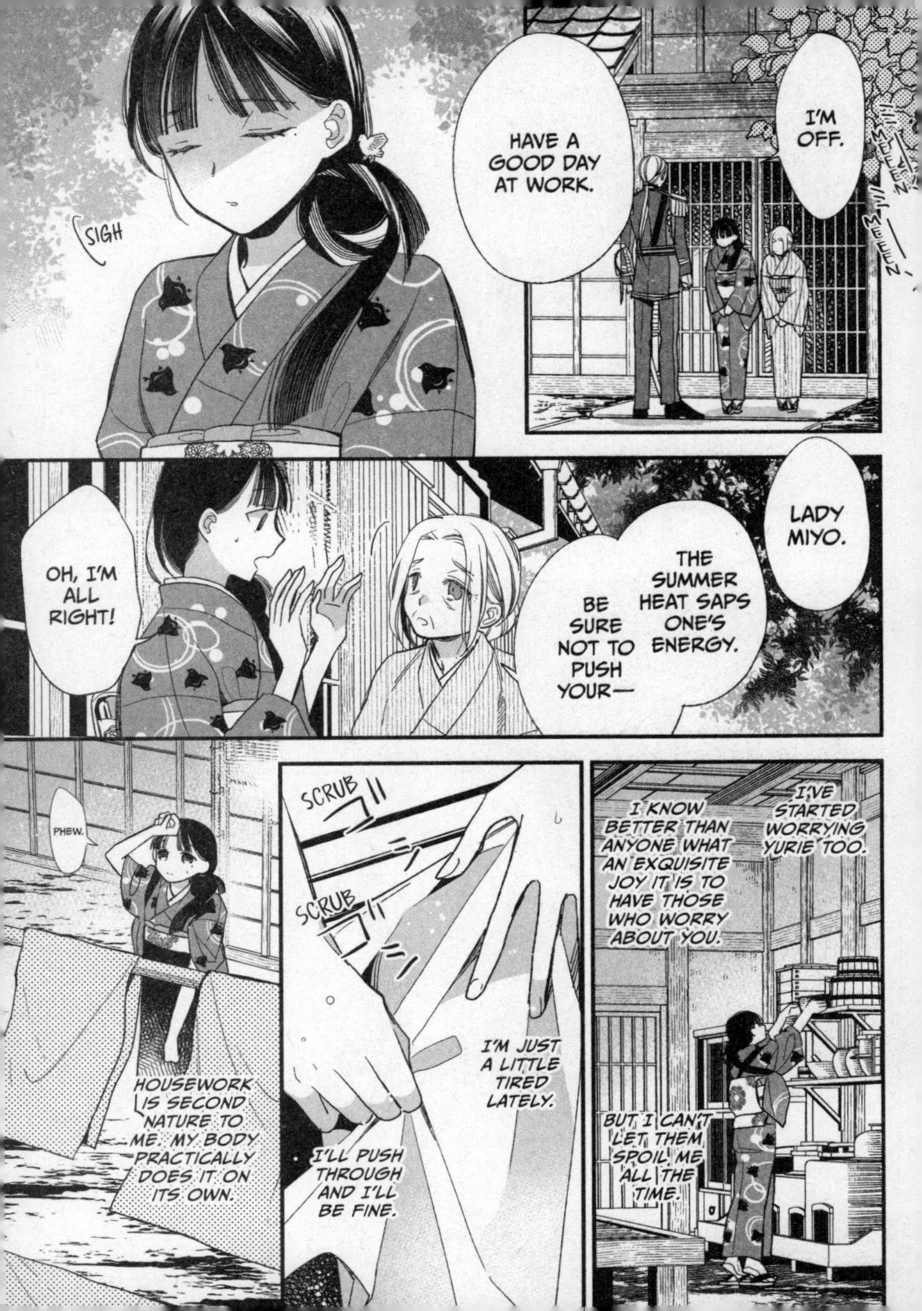
MEEEN
MEEEN
I'M OFF.
HAVE A GOOD DAY AT WORK.
SIGH
LADY MIYO.
THE SUMMER HEAT SAPS ONE'S ENERGY.
BE SURE NOT TO PUSH YOUR—
OH, I'M ALL RIGHT!
I'VE STARTED WORRYING YURIE TOO.
I KNOW BETTER THAN ANYONE WHAT AN EXQUISITE JOY IT IS TO HAVE THOSE WHO WORRY ABOUT YOU.
BUT I CAN'T LET THEM SPOIL ME ALL THE TIME.
SCRUB
SCRUB
I'M JUST A LITTLE TIRED LATELY.
I'LL PUSH THROUGH AND I'LL BE FINE.
PHEW.
HOUSEWORK IS SECOND NATURE TO ME. MY BODY PRACTICALLY DOES IT ON ITS OWN.

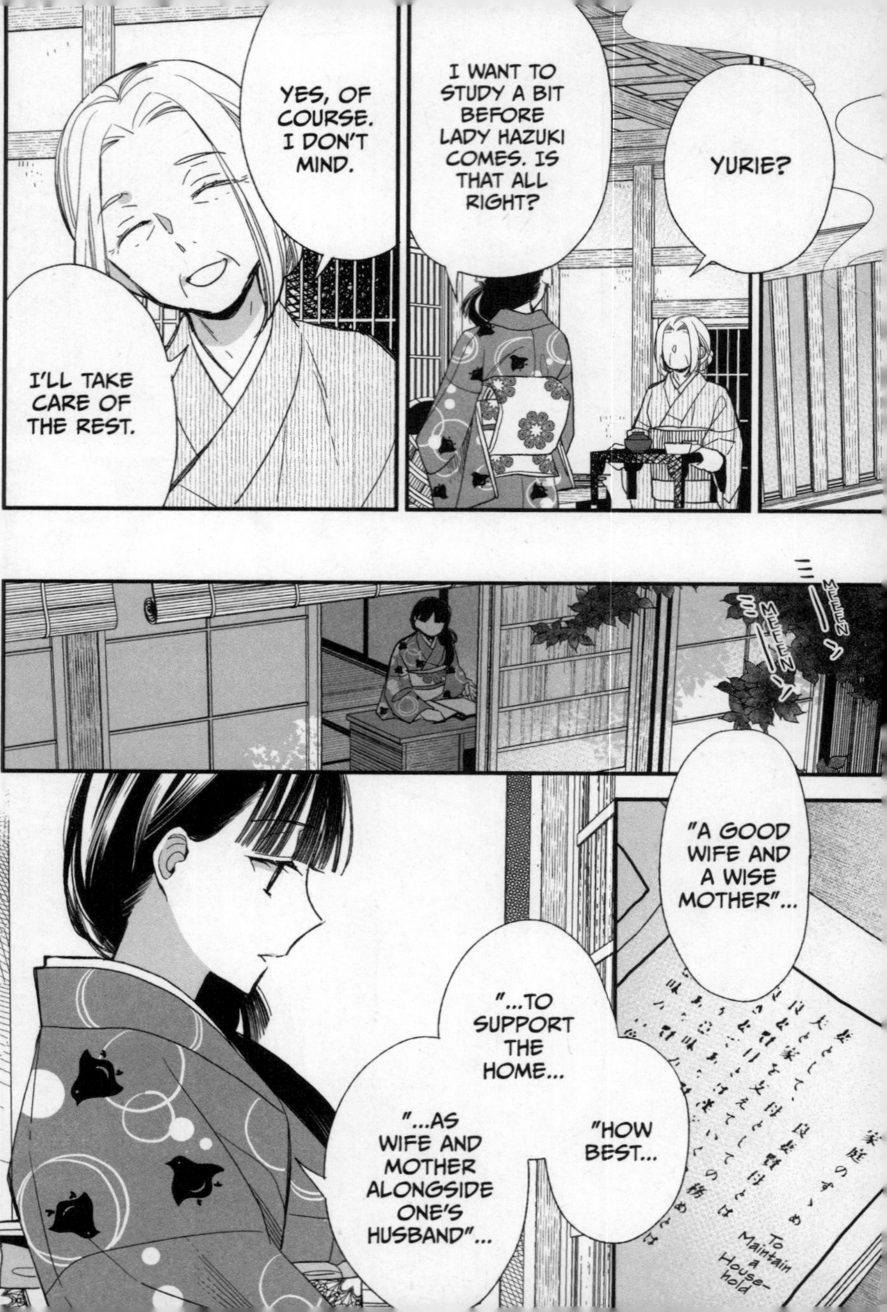
YURIE?
I WANT TO STUDY A BIT BEFORE LADY HAZUKI COMES. IS THAT ALL RIGHT?
YES, OF COURSE. I DON'T MIND.
I'LL TAKE CARE OF THE REST.
MEEEN
MEEEN
"A GOOD WIFE AND A WISE MOTHER"...
"...TO SUPPORT THE HOME...
"HOW BEST...
"...AS WIFE AND MOTHER ALONGSIDE ONE'S HUSBAND"...
家庭のすゝめ
To Maintain a House-hold

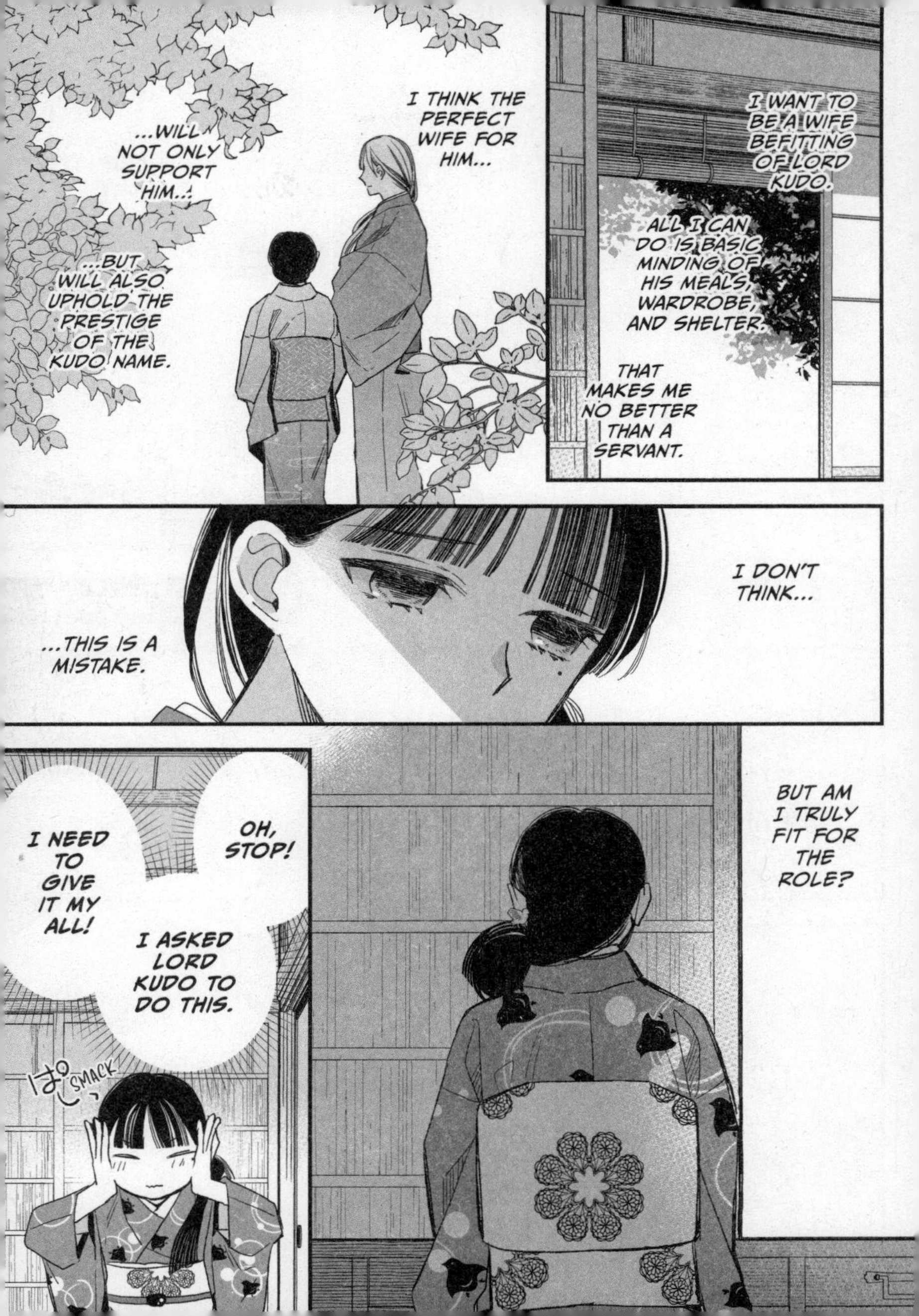
I WANT TO BE A WIFE BEFITTING OF LORD KUDO.
ALL I CAN DO IS BASIC MINDING OF HIS MEALS, WARDROBE, AND SHELTER.
THAT MAKES ME NO BETTER THAN A SERVANT.
I THINK THE PERFECT WIFE FOR HIM...
...WILL NOT ONLY SUPPORT HIM...
...BUT WILL ALSO UPHOLD THE PRESTIGE OF THE KUDO NAME.
I DON'T THINK...
...THIS IS A MISTAKE.
BUT AM I TRULY FIT FOR THE ROLE?
OH, STOP!
I ASKED LORD KUDO TO DO THIS.
I NEED TO GIVE IT MY ALL!
SMACK

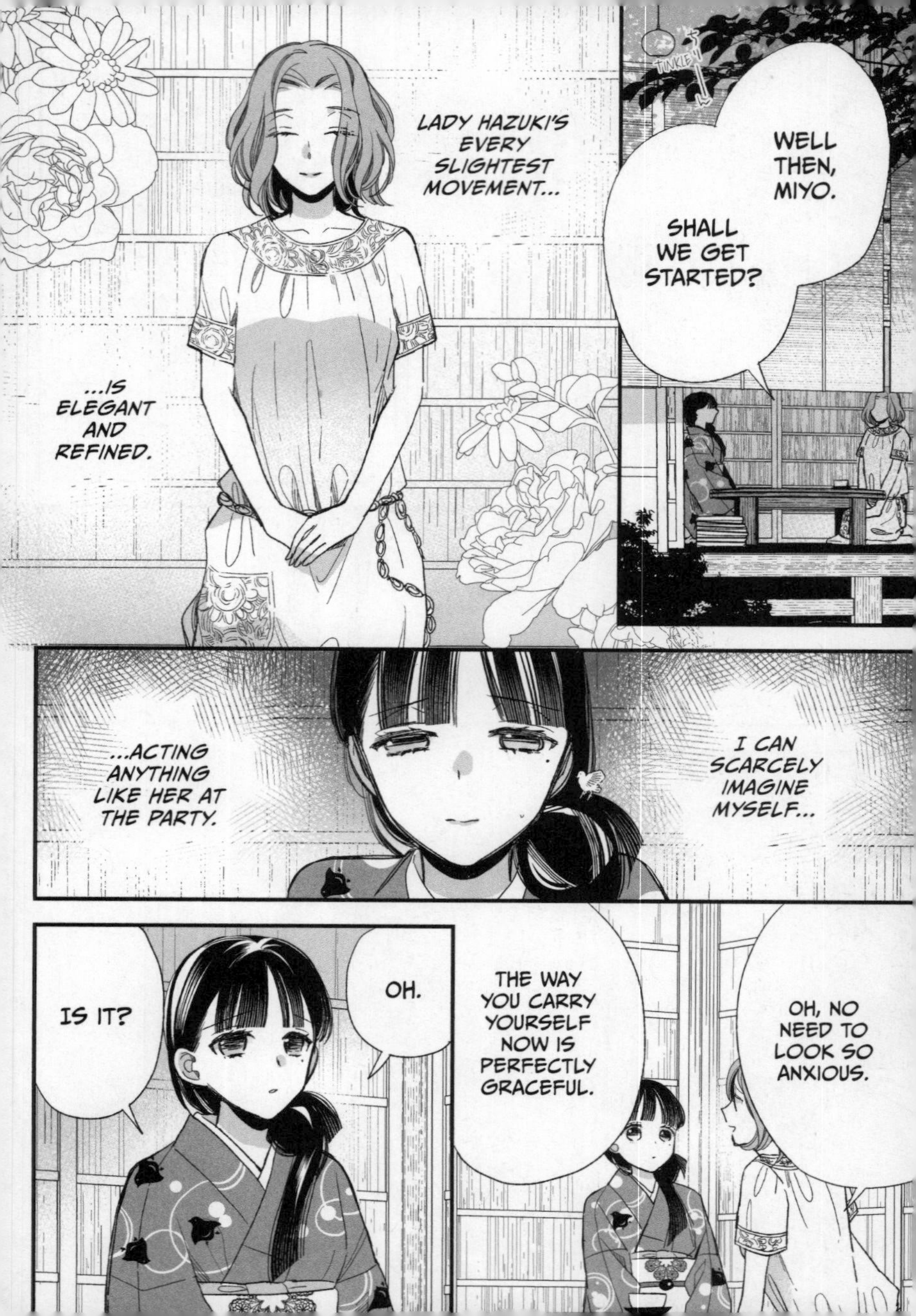
TINKLE
WELL THEN, MIYO.
SHALL WE GET STARTED?
LADY HAZUKI'S EVERY SLIGHTEST MOVEMENT...
...IS ELEGANT AND REFINED.
I CAN SCARCELY IMAGINE MYSELF...
...ACTING ANYTHING LIKE HER AT THE PARTY.
OH, NO NEED TO LOOK SO ANXIOUS.
THE WAY YOU CARRY YOURSELF NOW IS PERFECTLY GRACEFUL.
OH.
IS IT?

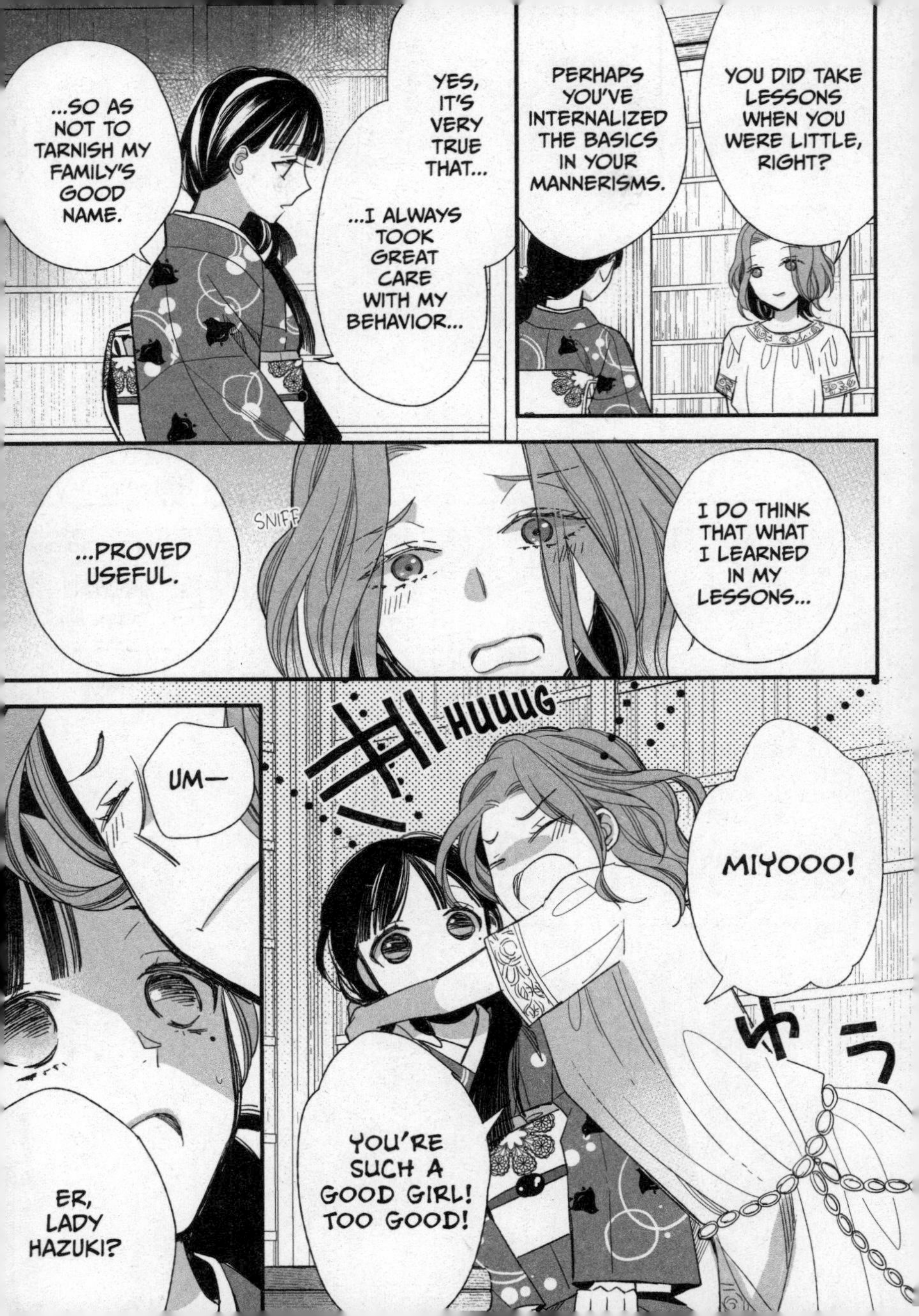

YOU DID TAKE LESSONS WHEN YOU WERE LITTLE, RIGHT?
PERHAPS YOU'VE INTERNALIZED THE BASICS IN YOUR MANNERISMS.
YES, IT'S VERY TRUE THAT...
...I ALWAYS TOOK GREAT CARE WITH MY BEHAVIOR...
...SO AS NOT TO TARNISH MY FAMILY'S GOOD NAME.
I DO THINK THAT WHAT I LEARNED IN MY LESSONS...
SNIFF
...PROVED USEFUL.
HUUUG
MIYOOO!
YOU'RE SUCH A GOOD GIRL! TOO GOOD!
UM—
ER, LADY HAZUKI?

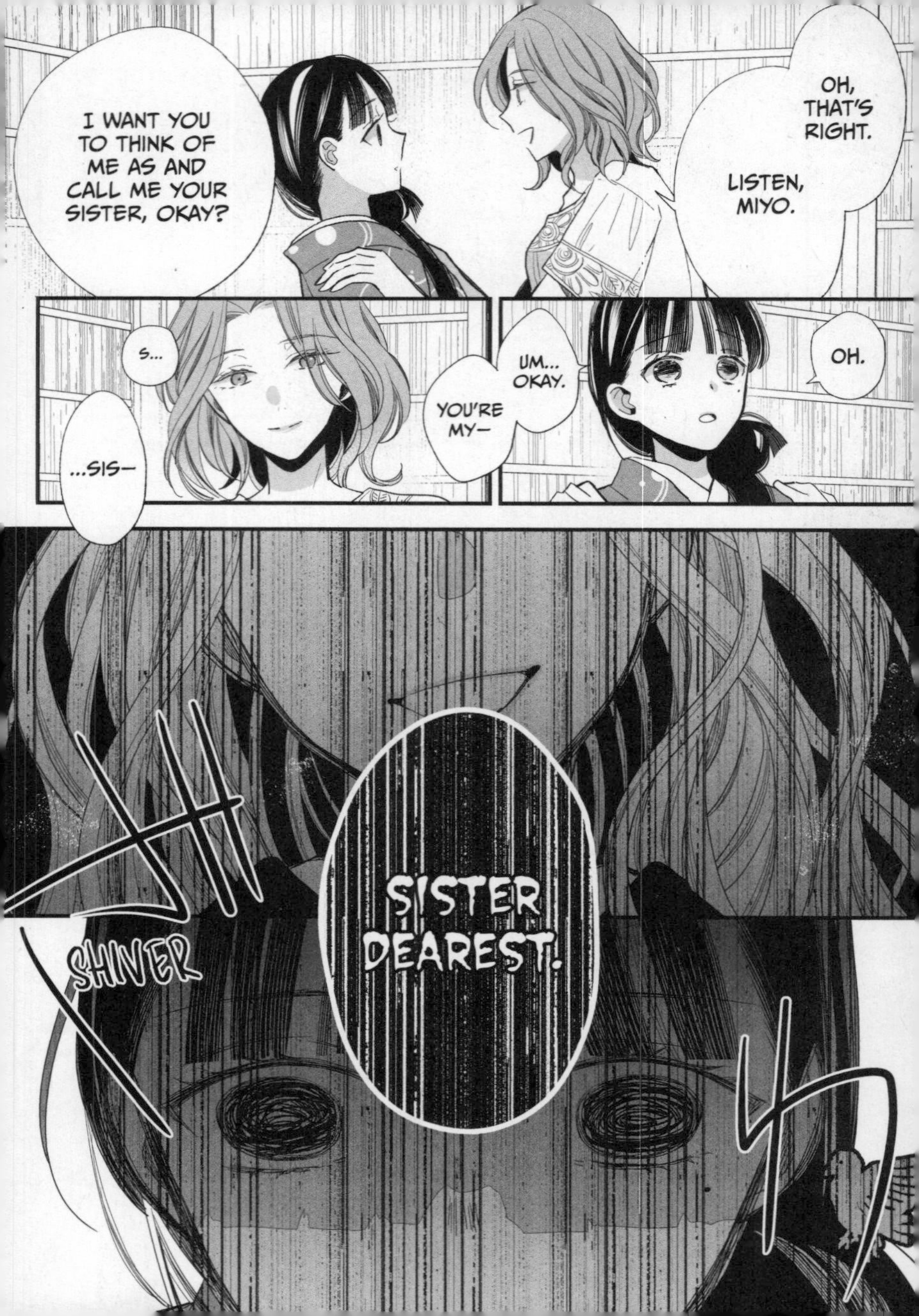
OH, THAT'S RIGHT.
LISTEN, MIYO.
I WANT YOU TO THINK OF ME AS AND CALL ME YOUR SISTER, OKAY?
OH.
UM... OKAY.
YOU'RE MY—
S...
...SIS—
SISTER DEAREST.
SHIVER

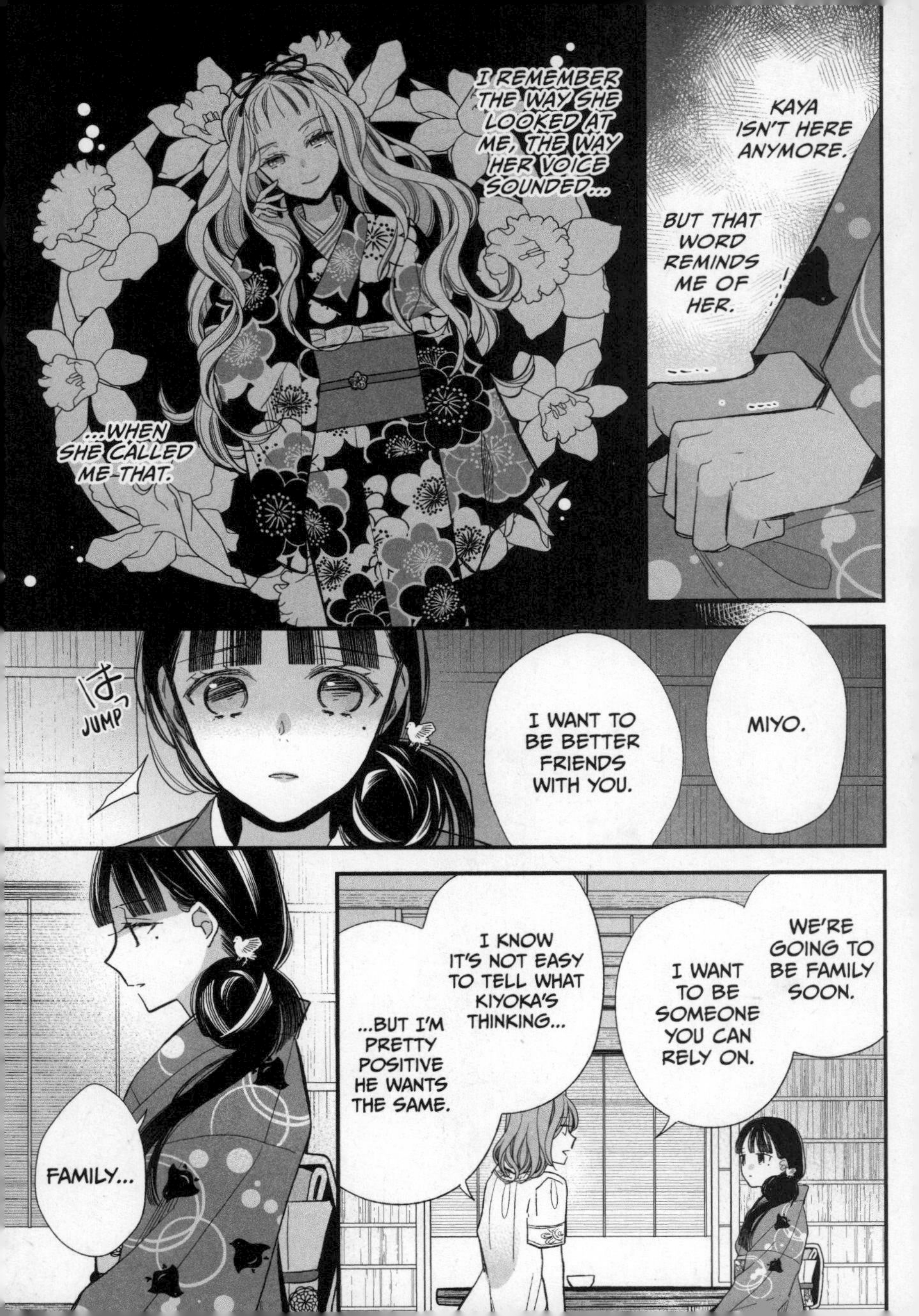
KAYA ISN'T HERE ANYMORE.
BUT THAT WORD REMINDS ME OF HER.
I REMEMBER THE WAY SHE LOOKED AT ME, THE WAY HER VOICE SOUNDED...
...WHEN SHE CALLED ME THAT.
MIYO.
I WANT TO BE BETTER FRIENDS WITH YOU.
はっ
JUMP
WE'RE GOING TO BE FAMILY SOON.
I WANT TO BE SOMEONE YOU CAN RELY ON.
I KNOW IT'S NOT EASY TO TELL WHAT KIYOKA'S THINKING...
...BUT I'M PRETTY POSITIVE HE WANTS THE SAME.
FAMILY...

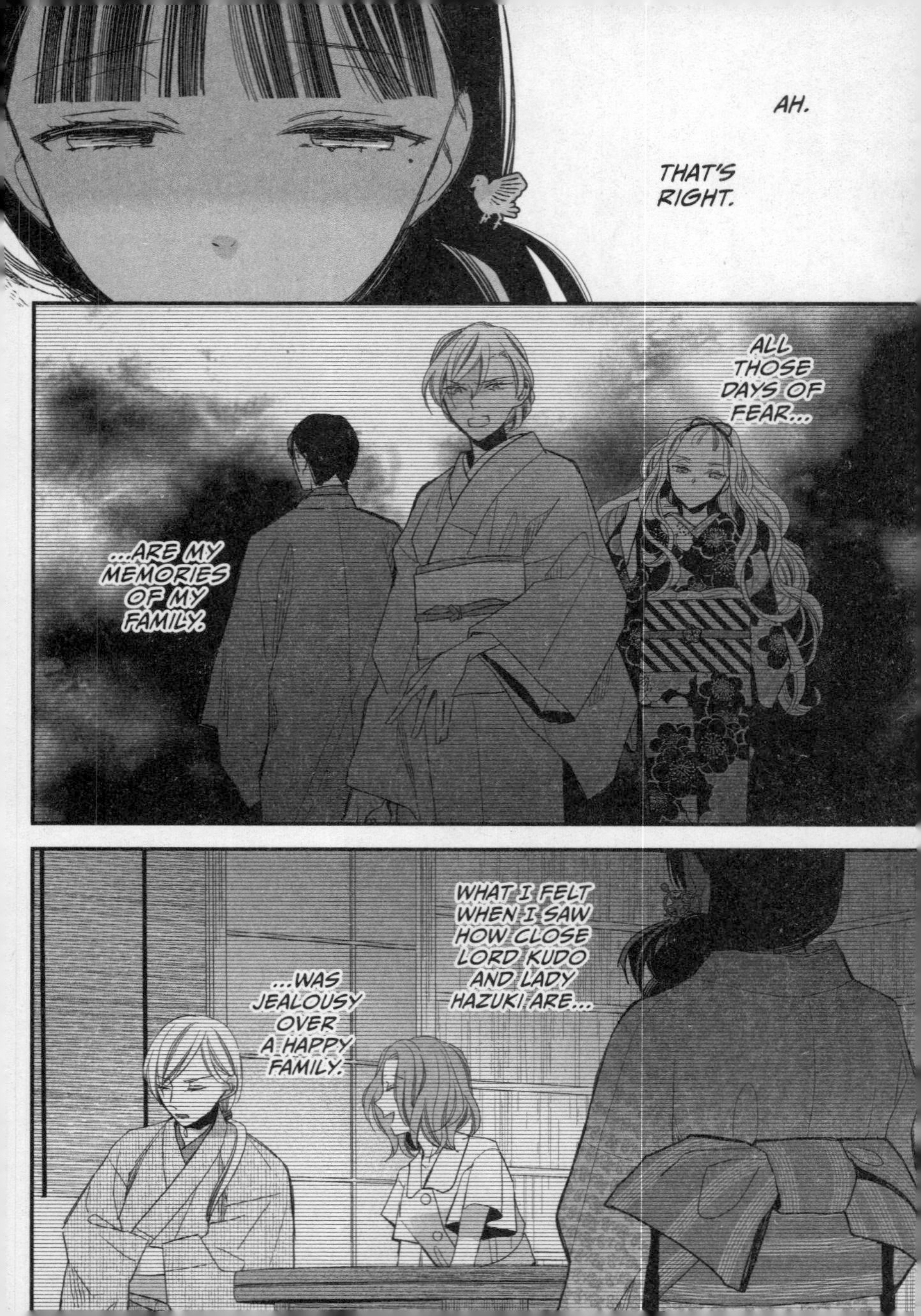
AH.
THAT'S RIGHT.
ALL THOSE DAYS OF FEAR...
...ARE MY MEMORIES OF MY FAMILY.
WHAT I FELT WHEN I SAW HOW CLOSE LORD KUDO AND LADY HAZUKI ARE...
...WAS JEALOUSY OVER A HAPPY FAMILY.

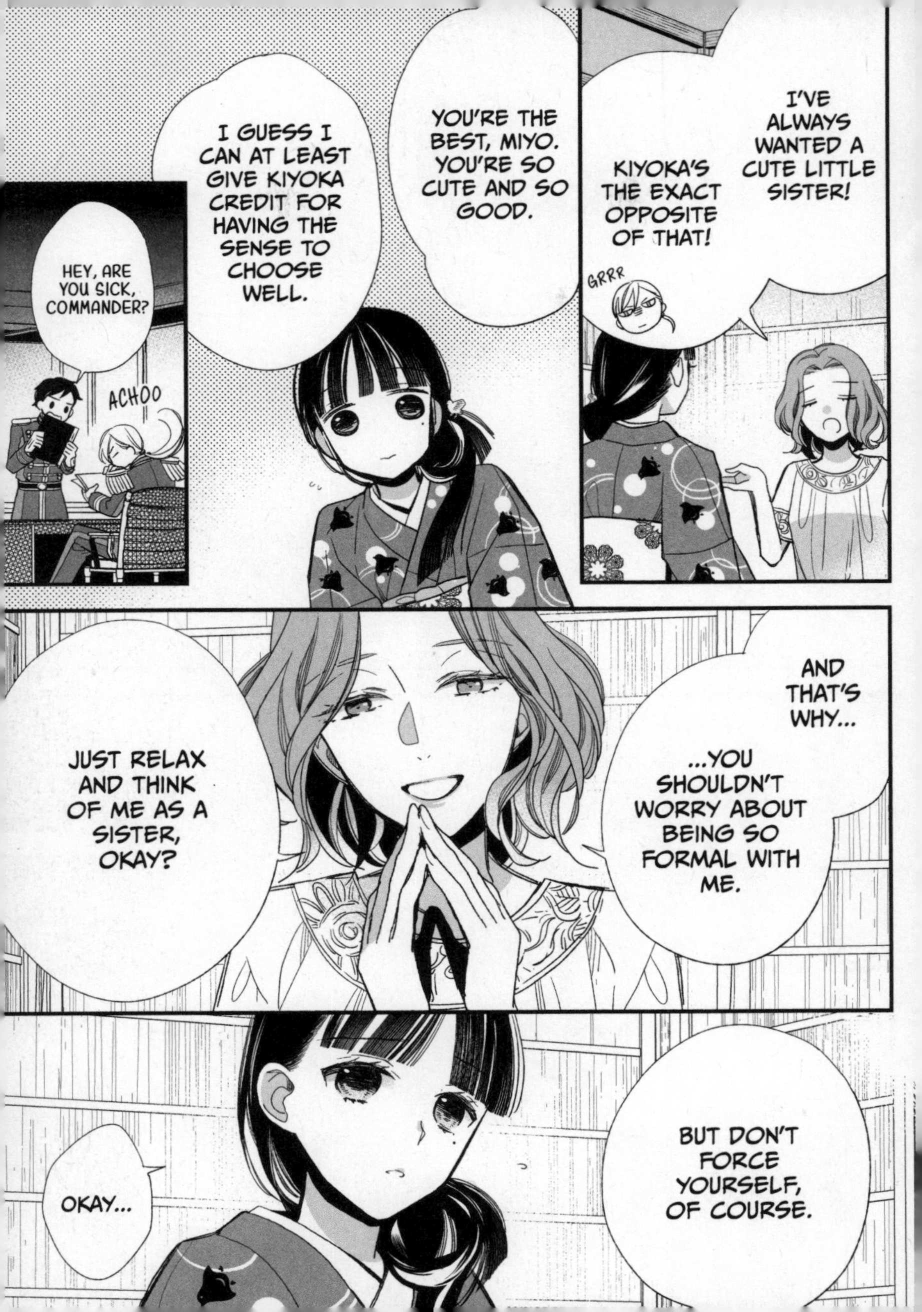
I'VE ALWAYS WANTED A CUTE LITTLE SISTER!
KIYOKA'S THE EXACT OPPOSITE OF THAT!
GRRR
YOU'RE THE BEST, MIYO. YOU'RE SO CUTE AND SO GOOD.
I GUESS I CAN AT LEAST GIVE KIYOKA CREDIT FOR HAVING THE SENSE TO CHOOSE WELL.
HEY, ARE YOU SICK, COMMANDER?
ACHOO
AND THAT'S WHY...
...YOU SHOULDN'T WORRY ABOUT BEING SO FORMAL WITH ME.
JUST RELAX AND THINK OF ME AS A SISTER, OKAY?
BUT DON'T FORCE YOURSELF, OF COURSE.
OKAY...

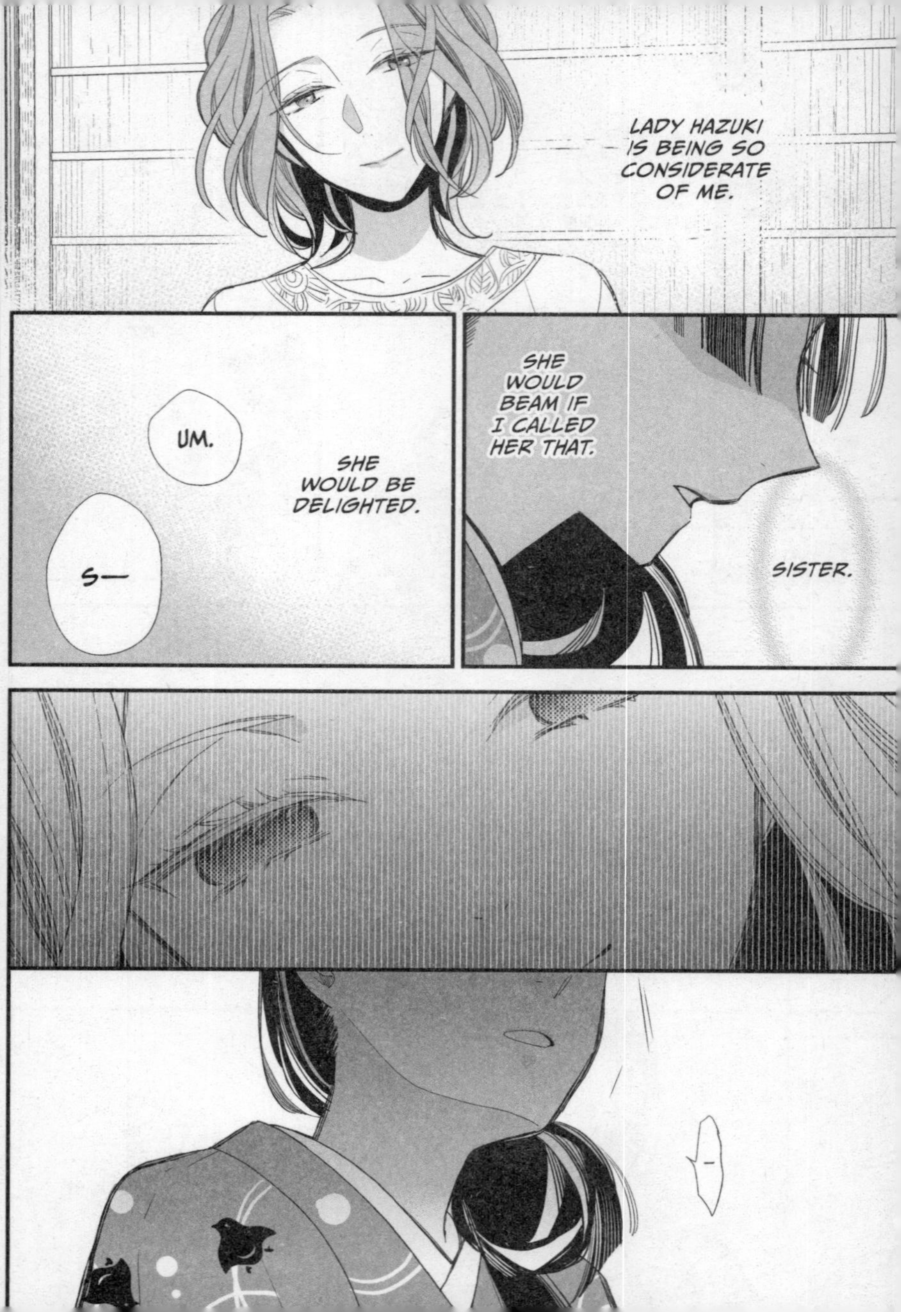
LADY HAZUKI IS BEING SO CONSIDERATE OF ME.
SHE WOULD BEAM IF I CALLED HER THAT.
SISTER.
SHE WOULD BE DELIGHTED.
UM.
S—
—

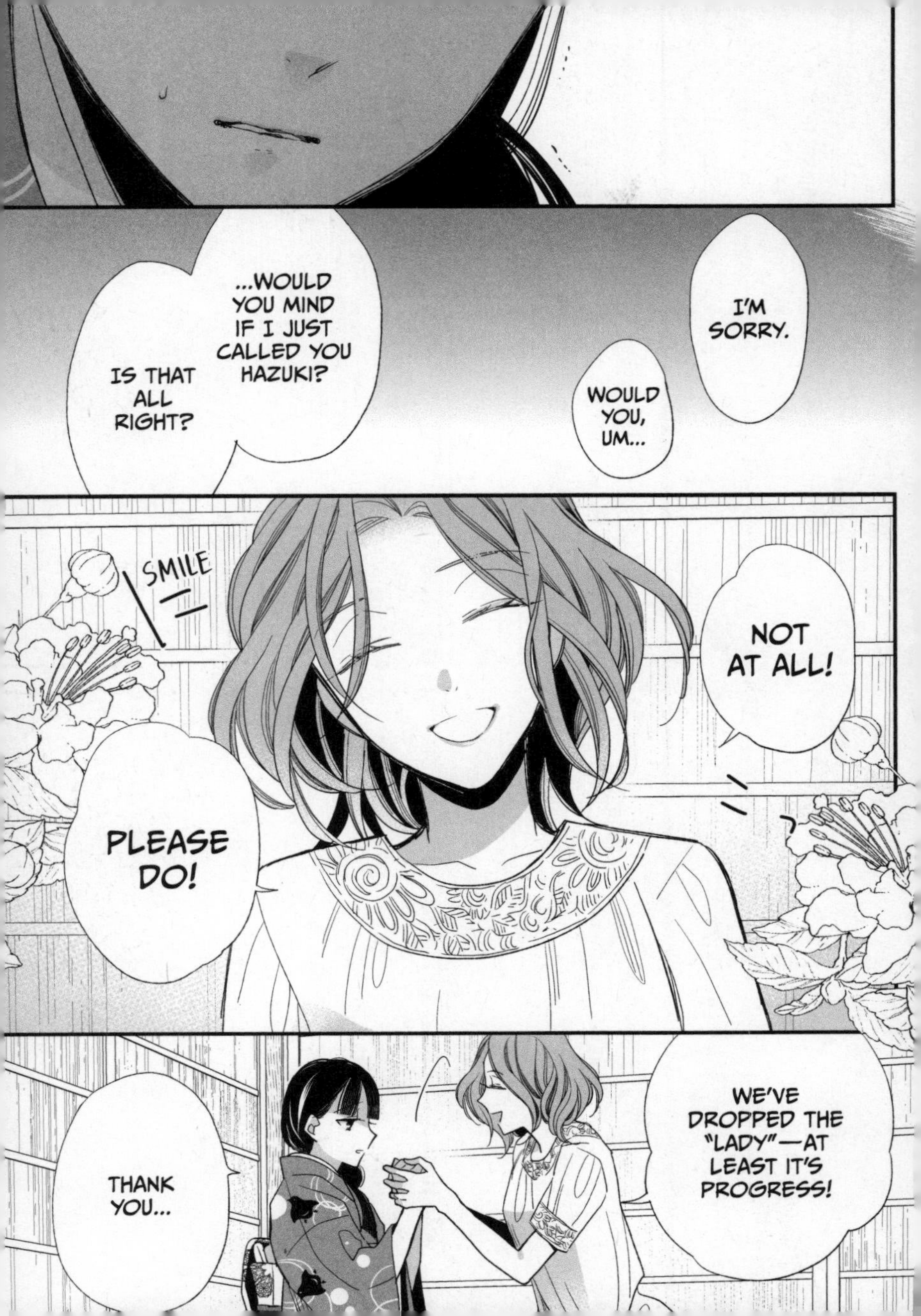
I'M SORRY.
WOULD YOU, UM...
...WOULD YOU MIND IF I JUST CALLED YOU HAZUKI?
IS THAT ALL RIGHT?
NOT AT ALL!
SMILE
PLEASE DO!
WE'VE DROPPED THE "LADY"—AT LEAST IT'S PROGRESS!
THANK YOU...

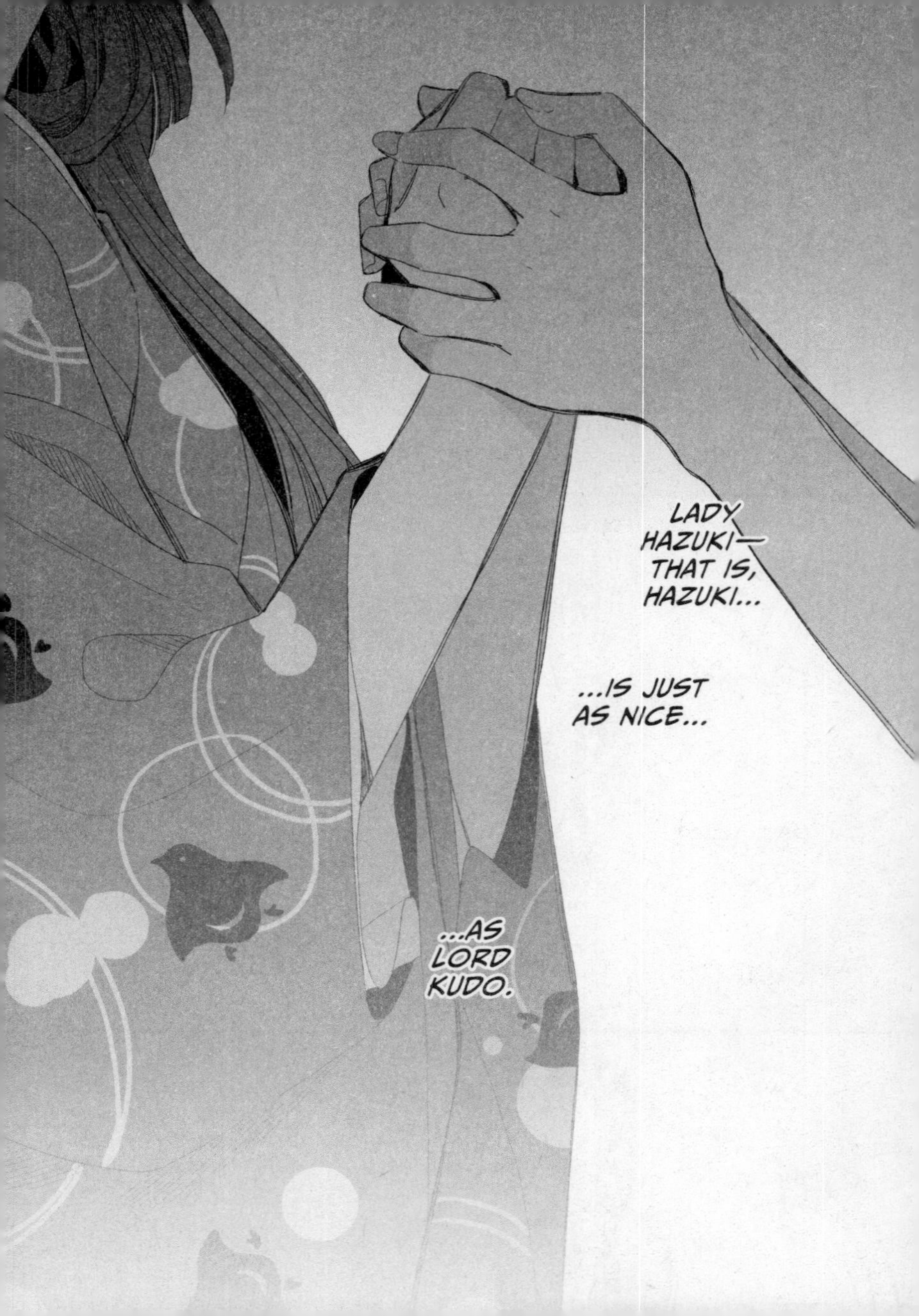
LADY HAZUKI— THAT IS, HAZUKI...
...IS JUST AS NICE...
...AS LORD KUDO.

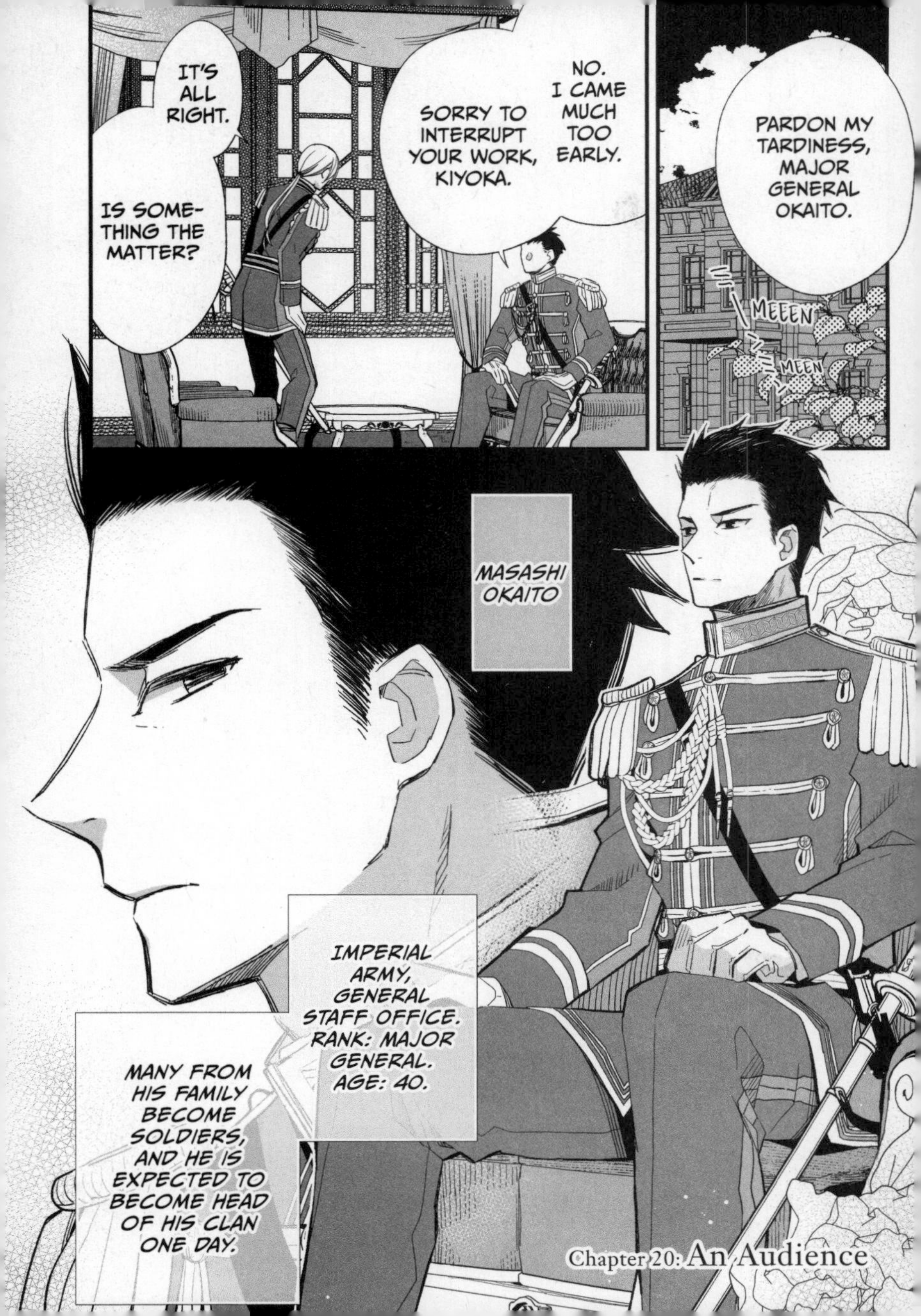
PARDON MY TARDINESS, MAJOR GENERAL OKAITO.
MEEEN
MEEN
NO. I CAME MUCH TOO EARLY.
SORRY TO INTERRUPT YOUR WORK, KIYOKA.
IT'S ALL RIGHT.
IS SOMETHING THE MATTER?
MASASHI OKAITO
IMPERIAL ARMY, GENERAL STAFF OFFICE. RANK: MAJOR GENERAL. AGE: 40.
MANY FROM HIS FAMILY BECOME SOLDIERS, AND HE IS EXPECTED TO BECOME HEAD OF HIS CLAN ONE DAY.
Chapter 20: An Audience

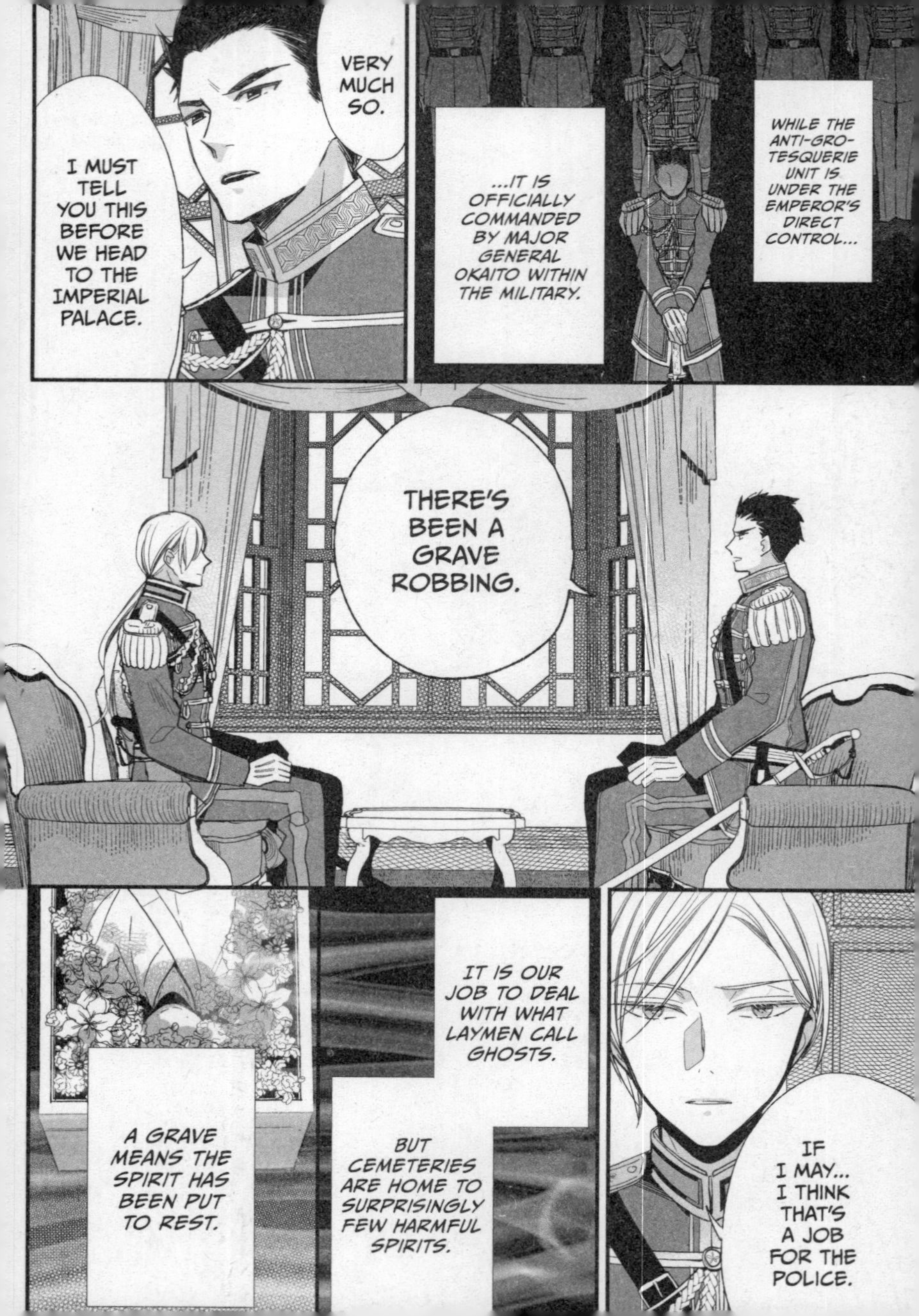
WHILE THE ANTI-GRO-TESQUERIE UNIT IS UNDER THE EMPEROR'S DIRECT CONTROL...
...IT IS OFFICIALLY COMMANDED BY MAJOR GENERAL OKAITO WITHIN THE MILITARY.
VERY MUCH SO.
I MUST TELL YOU THIS BEFORE WE HEAD TO THE IMPERIAL PALACE.
THERE'S BEEN A GRAVE ROBBING.
IF I MAY... I THINK THAT'S A JOB FOR THE POLICE.
IT IS OUR JOB TO DEAL WITH WHAT LAYMEN CALL GHOSTS.
BUT CEMETERIES ARE HOME TO SURPRISINGLY FEW HARMFUL SPIRITS.
A GRAVE MEANS THE SPIRIT HAS BEEN PUT TO REST.

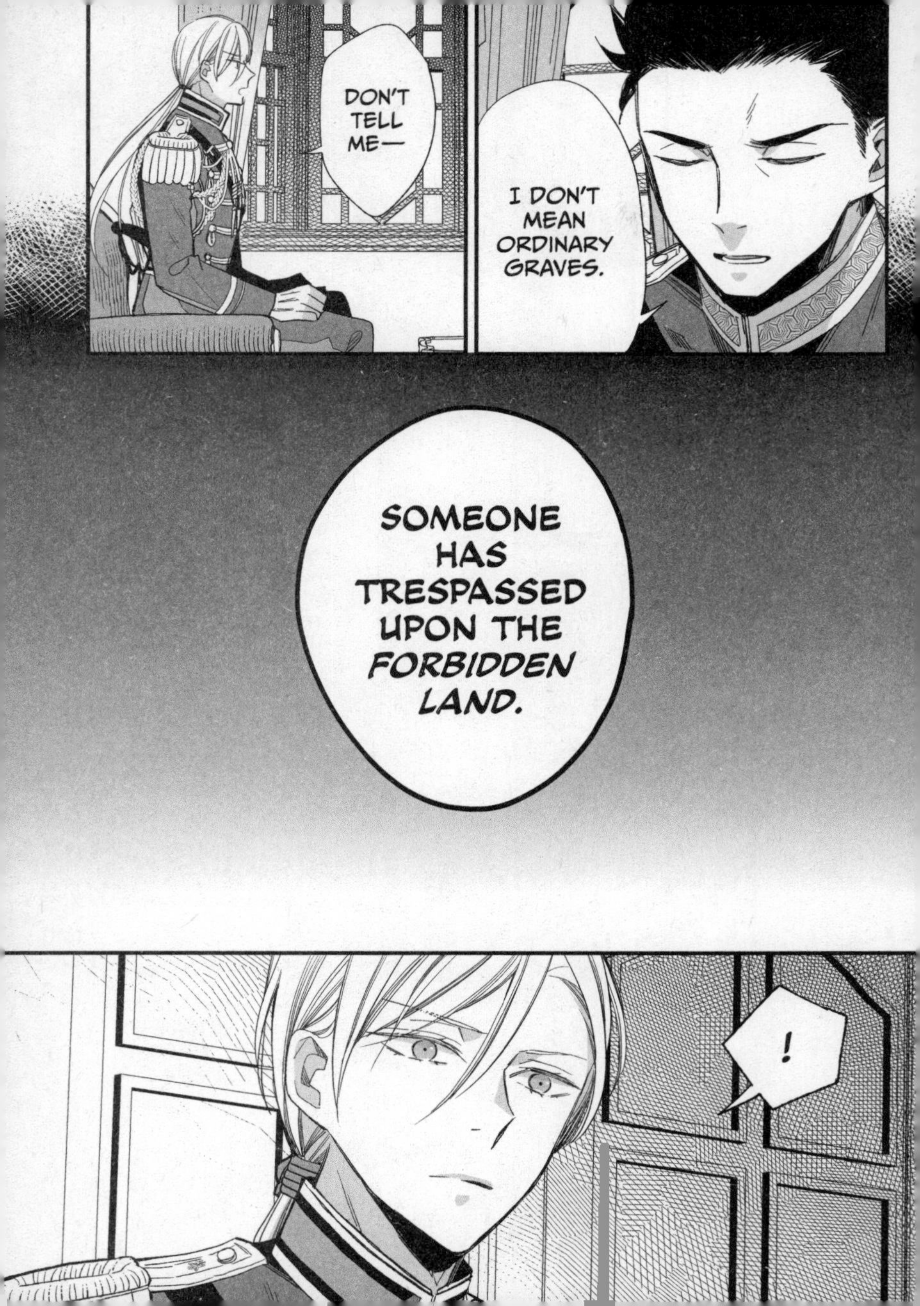
I DON'T MEAN ORDINARY GRAVES.
DON'T TELL ME—
SOMEONE HAS TRESPASSED UPON THE *FORBIDDEN* LAND.
!

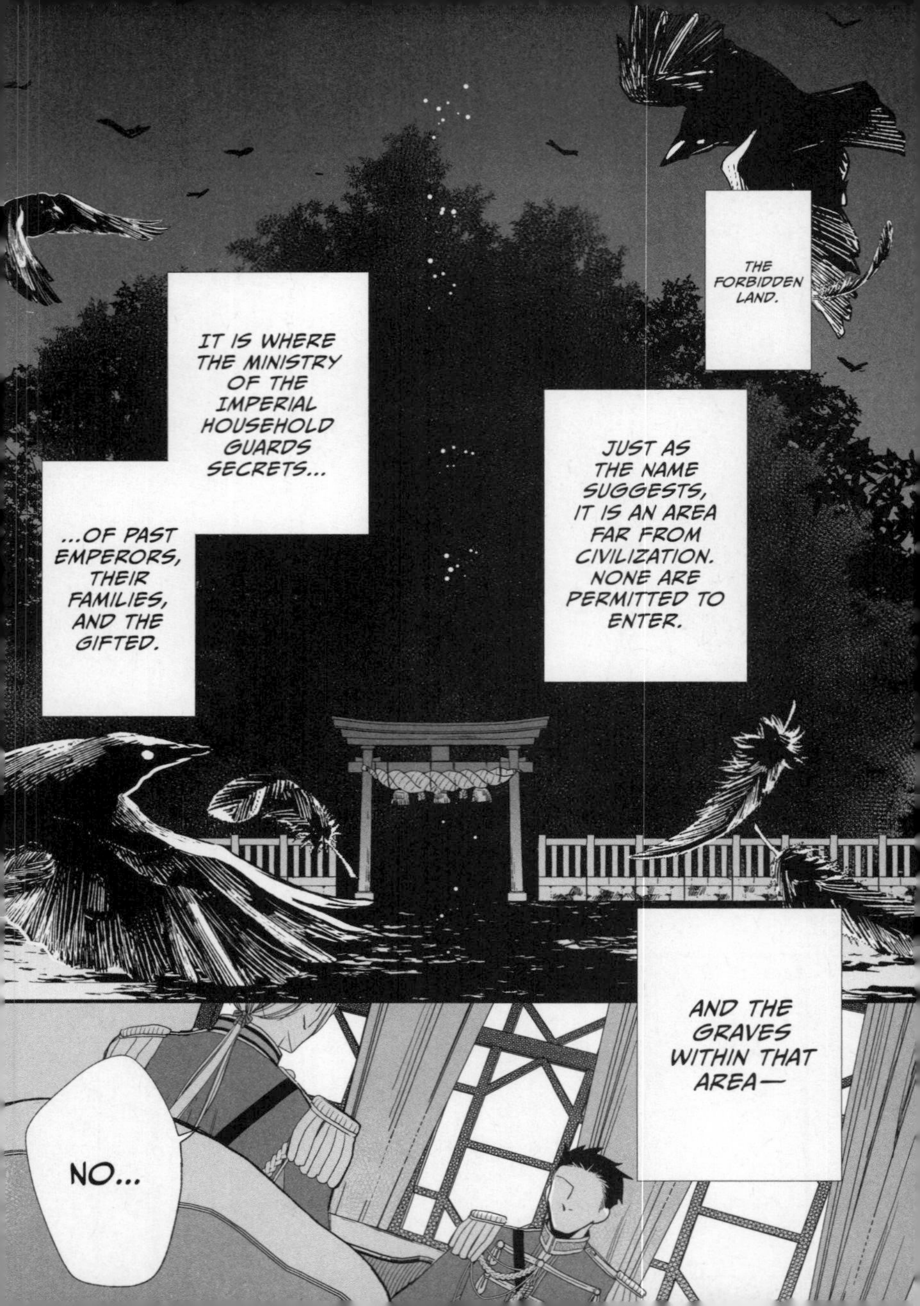

THE FORBIDDEN LAND.
JUST AS THE NAME SUGGESTS, IT IS AN AREA FAR FROM CIVILIZATION. NONE ARE PERMITTED TO ENTER.
IT IS WHERE THE MINISTRY OF THE IMPERIAL HOUSEHOLD GUARDS SECRETS...
...OF PAST EMPERORS, THEIR FAMILIES, AND THE GIFTED.
AND THE GRAVES WITHIN THAT AREA—
NO...

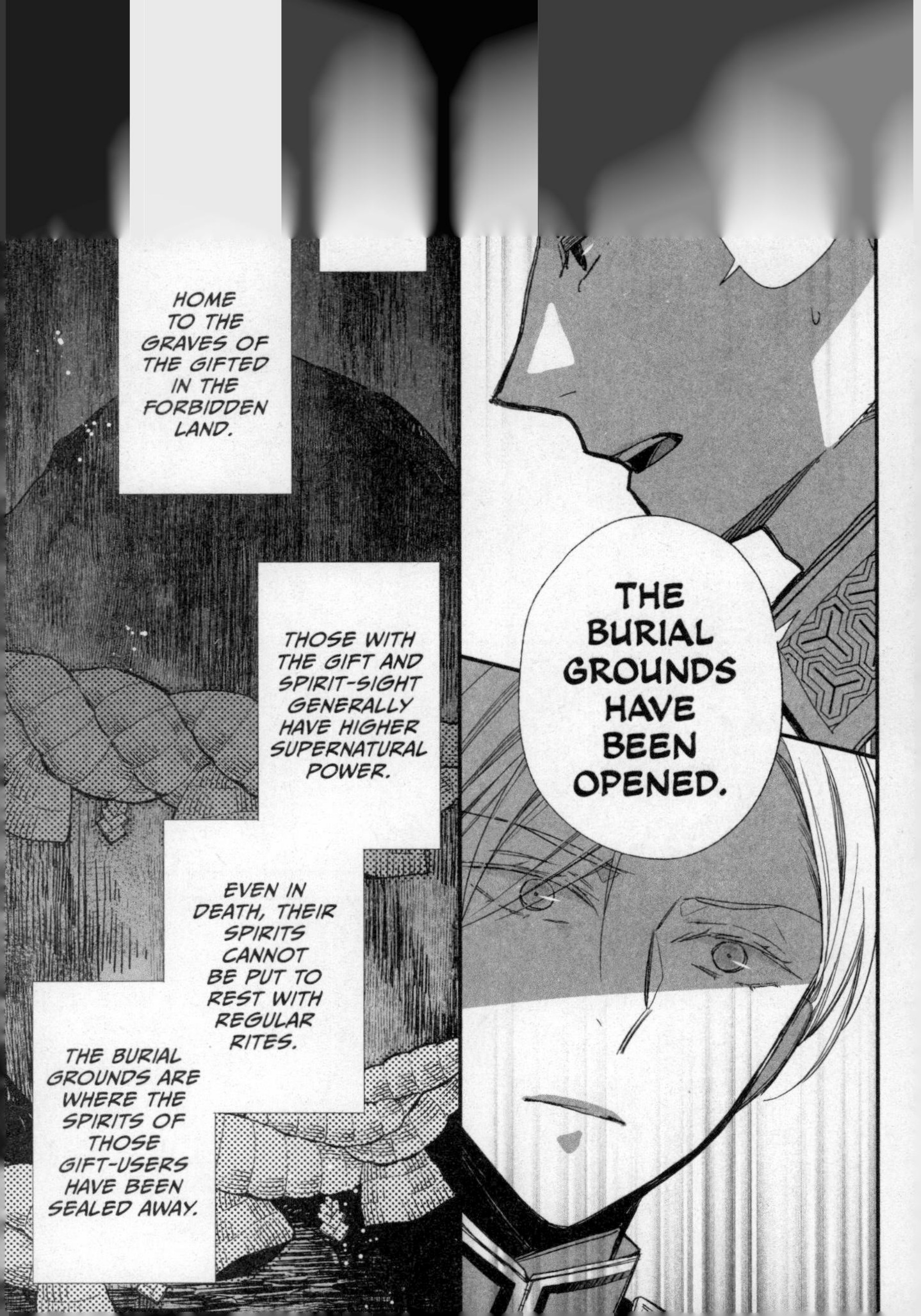
THE BURIAL GROUNDS HAVE BEEN OPENED.
HOME TO THE GRAVES OF THE GIFTED IN THE FORBIDDEN LAND.
THOSE WITH THE GIFT AND SPIRIT-SIGHT GENERALLY HAVE HIGHER SUPERNATURAL POWER.
EVEN IN DEATH, THEIR SPIRITS CANNOT BE PUT TO REST WITH REGULAR RITES.
THE BURIAL GROUNDS ARE WHERE THE SPIRITS OF THOSE GIFT-USERS HAVE BEEN SEALED AWAY.

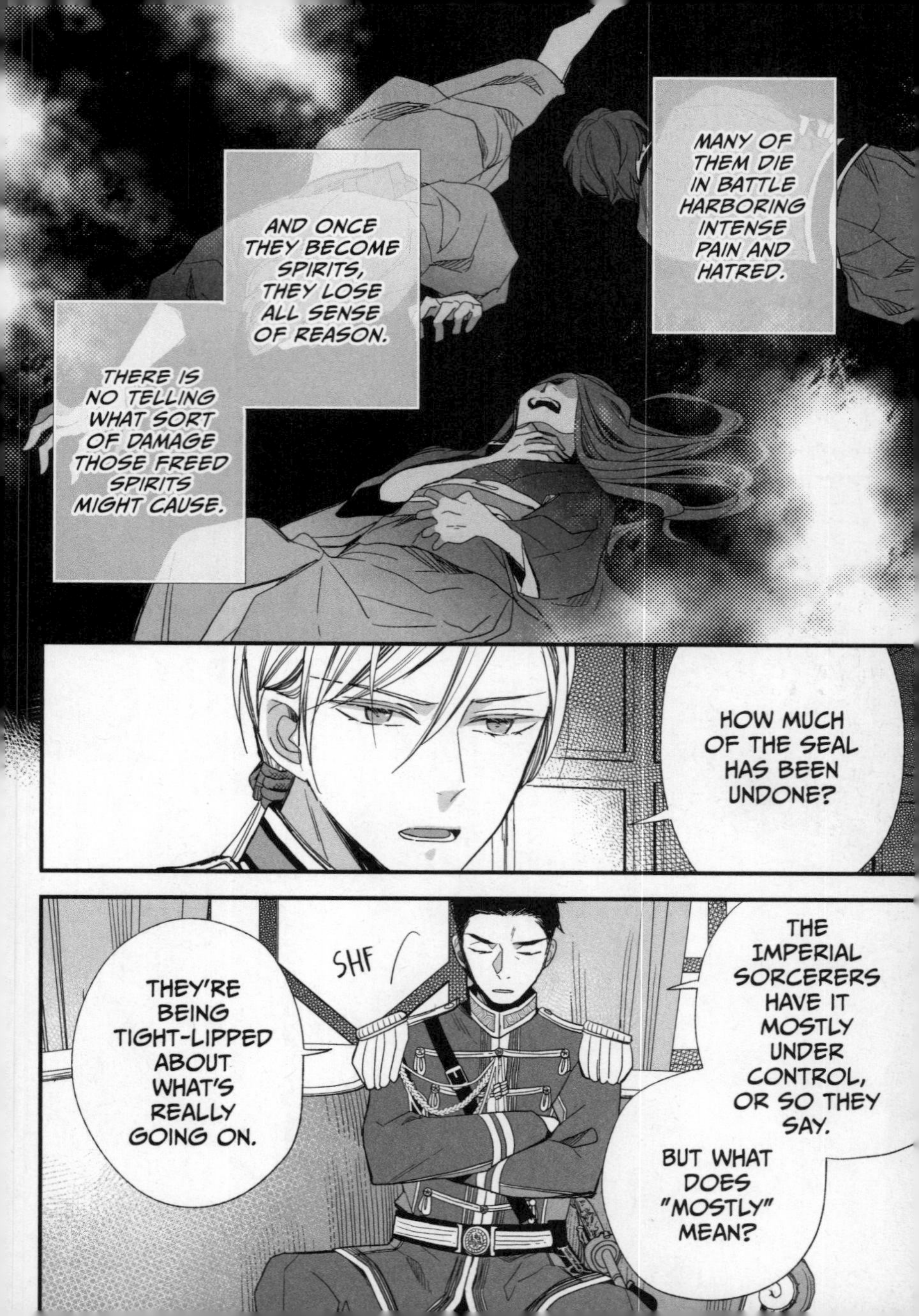
MANY OF THEM DIE IN BATTLE HARBORING INTENSE PAIN AND HATRED.
AND ONCE THEY BECOME SPIRITS, THEY LOSE ALL SENSE OF REASON.
THERE IS NO TELLING WHAT SORT OF DAMAGE THOSE FREED SPIRITS MIGHT CAUSE.
HOW MUCH OF THE SEAL HAS BEEN UNDONE?
THE IMPERIAL SORCERERS HAVE IT MOSTLY UNDER CONTROL, OR SO THEY SAY.
BUT WHAT DOES "MOSTLY" MEAN?
SHF
THEY'RE BEING TIGHT-LIPPED ABOUT WHAT'S REALLY GOING ON.

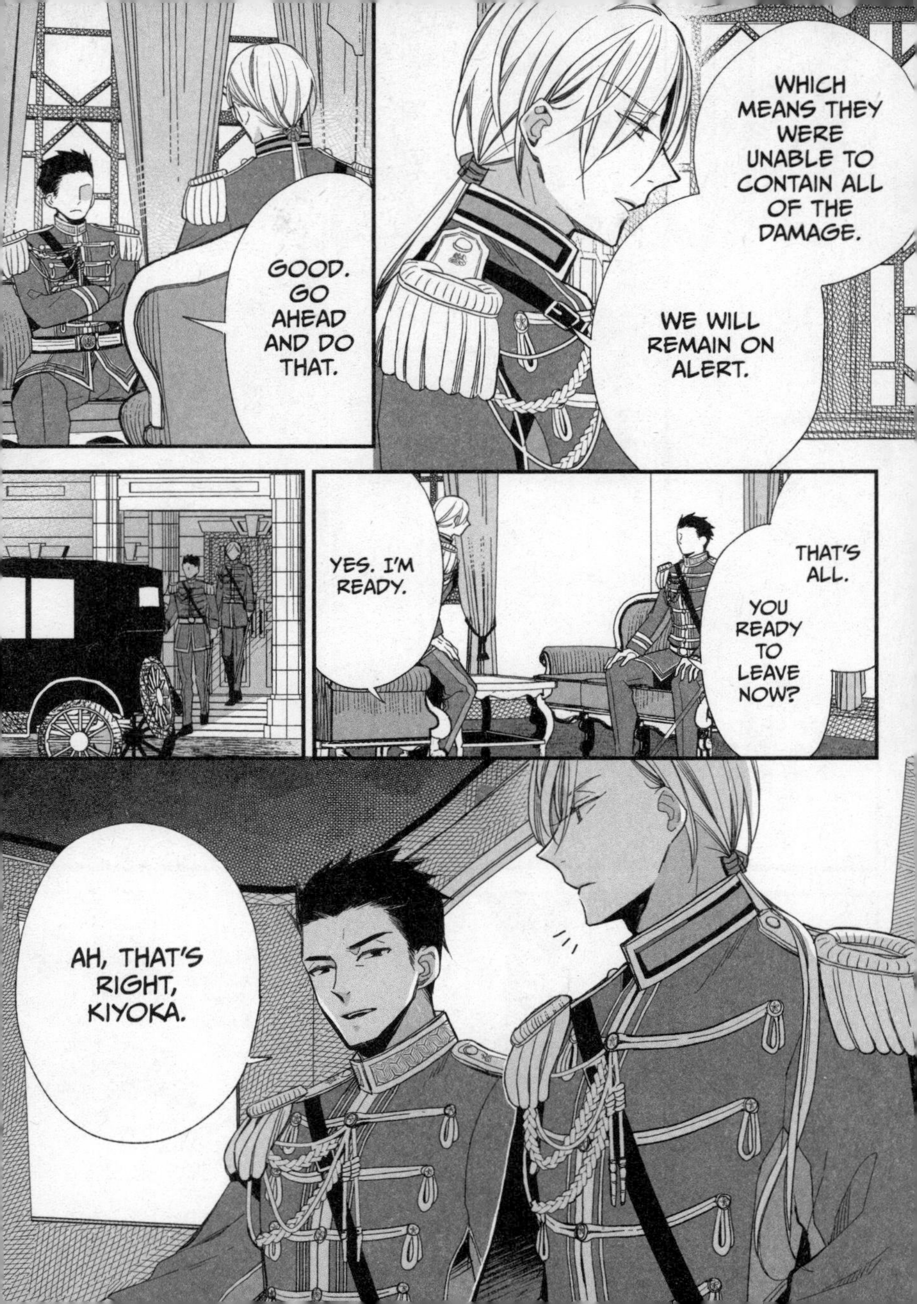
WHICH MEANS THEY WERE UNABLE TO CONTAIN ALL OF THE DAMAGE.
WE WILL REMAIN ON ALERT.
GOOD. GO AHEAD AND DO THAT.
THAT'S ALL.
YOU READY TO LEAVE NOW?
YES. I'M READY.
AH, THAT'S RIGHT, KIYOKA.

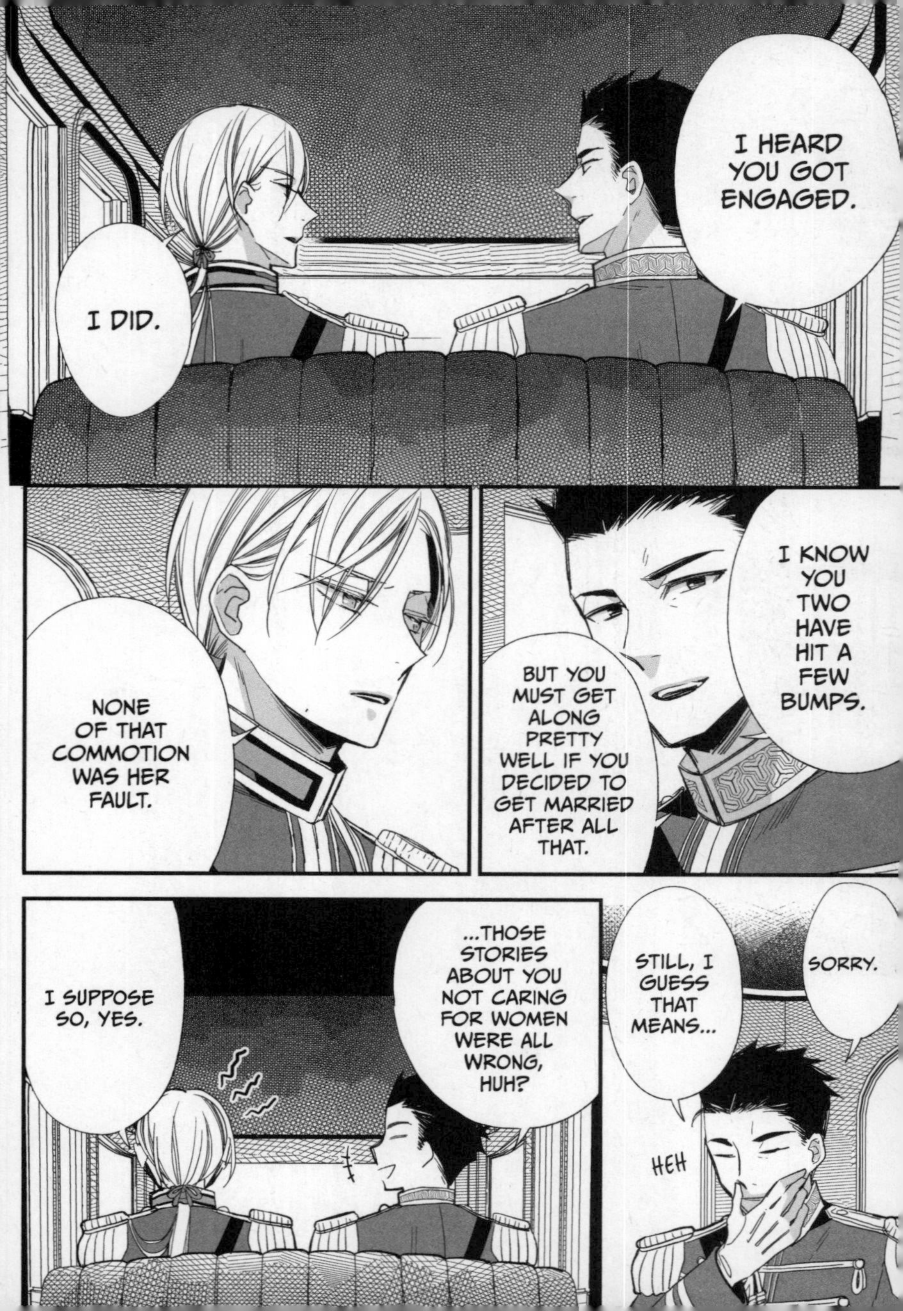
I HEARD YOU GOT ENGAGED.
I DID.
I KNOW YOU TWO HAVE HIT A FEW BUMPS.
BUT YOU MUST GET ALONG PRETTY WELL IF YOU DECIDED TO GET MARRIED AFTER ALL THAT.
NONE OF THAT COMMOTION WAS HER FAULT.
SORRY.
STILL, I GUESS THAT MEANS...
HEH
...THOSE STORIES ABOUT YOU NOT CARING FOR WOMEN WERE ALL WRONG, HUH?
I SUPPOSE SO, YES.

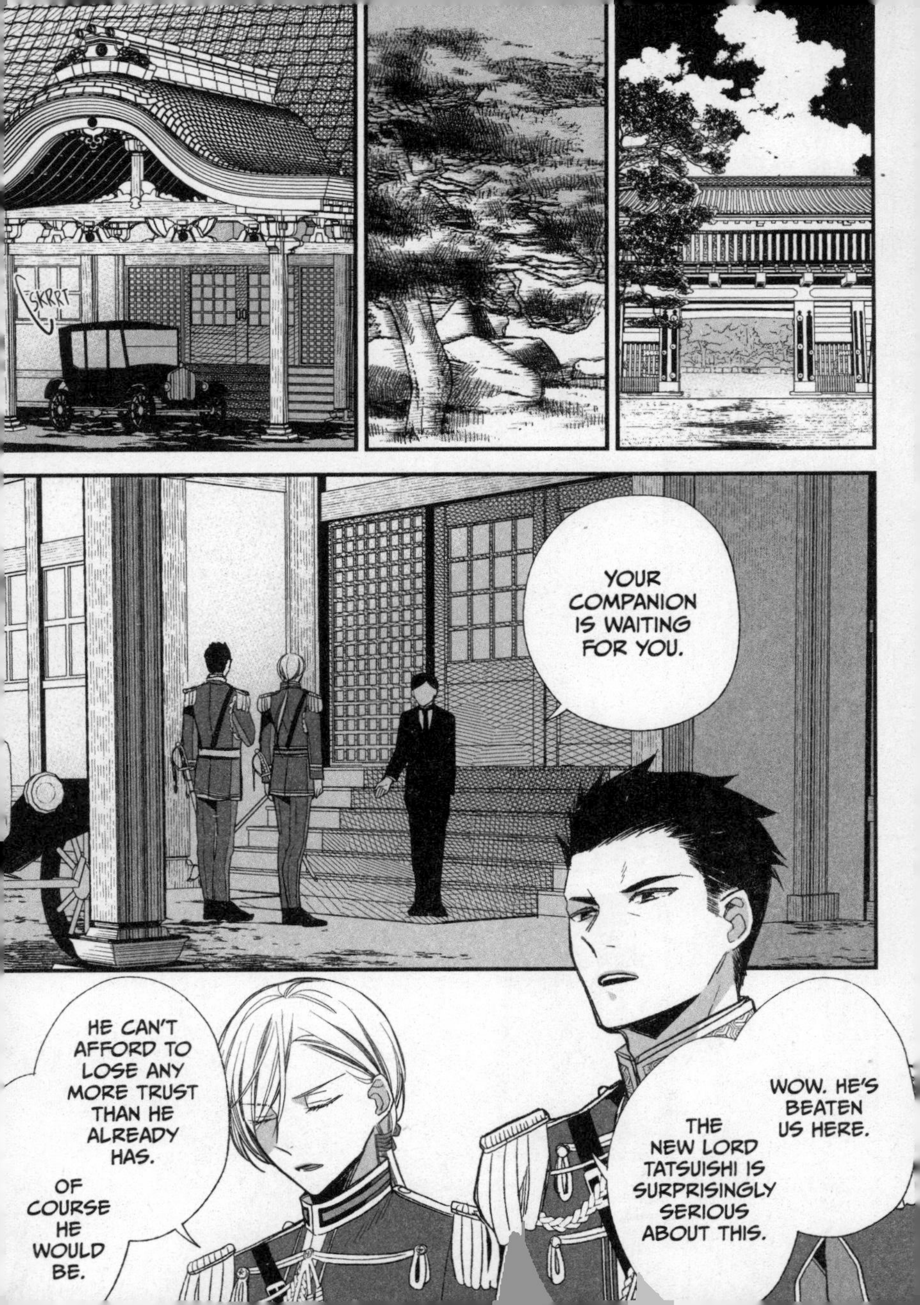
SKRRT
YOUR COMPANION IS WAITING FOR YOU.
WOW. HE'S BEATEN US HERE.
THE NEW LORD TATSUISHI IS SURPRISINGLY SERIOUS ABOUT THIS.
HE CAN'T AFFORD TO LOSE ANY MORE TRUST THAN HE ALREADY HAS.
OF COURSE HE WOULD BE.

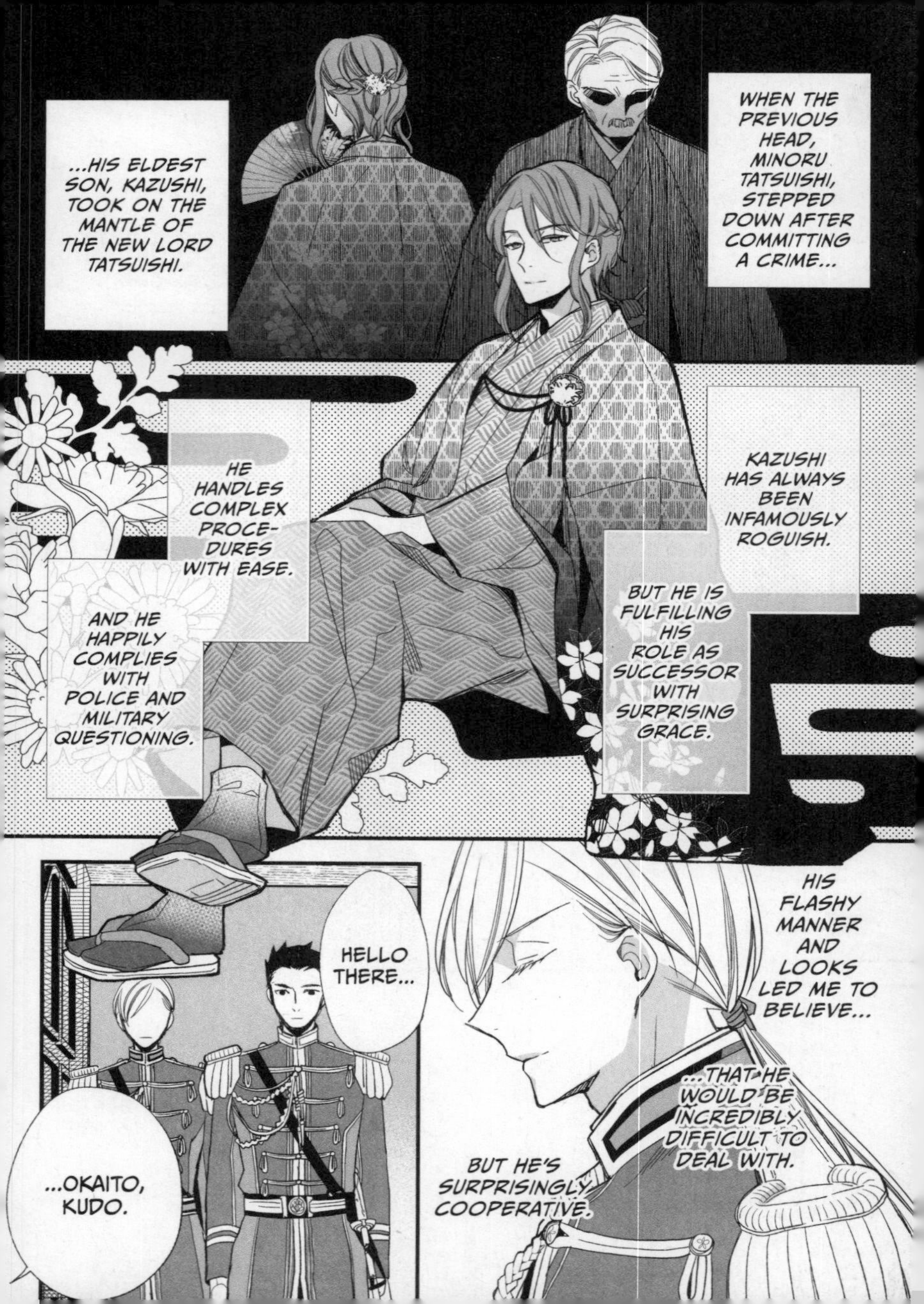
WHEN THE PREVIOUS HEAD, MINORU TATSUISHI, STEPPED DOWN AFTER COMMITTING A CRIME...
...HIS ELDEST SON, KAZUSHI, TOOK ON THE MANTLE OF THE NEW LORD TATSUISHI.
KAZUSHI HAS ALWAYS BEEN INFAMOUSLY ROGUISH.
BUT HE IS FULFILLING HIS ROLE AS SUCCESSOR WITH SURPRISING GRACE.
HE HANDLES COMPLEX PROCE-DURES WITH EASE.
AND HE HAPPILY COMPLIES WITH POLICE AND MILITARY QUESTIONING.
HIS FLASHY MANNER AND LOOKS LED ME TO BELIEVE...
...THAT HE WOULD BE INCREDIBLY DIFFICULT TO DEAL WITH.
BUT HE'S SURPRISINGLY COOPERATIVE.
HELLO THERE...
...OKAITO, KUDO.

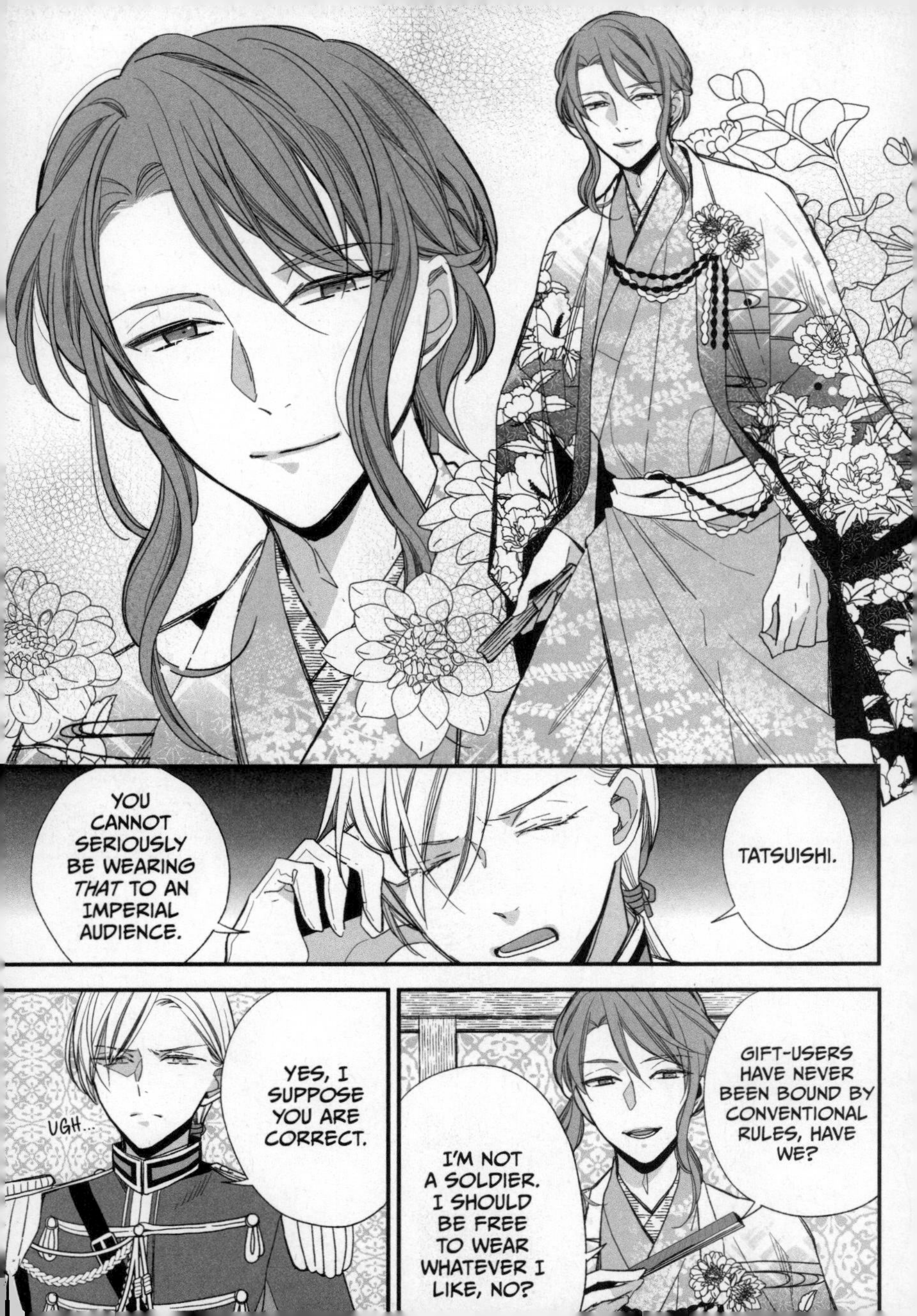
TATSUISHI.
YOU CANNOT SERIOUSLY BE WEARING *THAT* TO AN IMPERIAL AUDIENCE.
GIFT-USERS HAVE NEVER BEEN BOUND BY CONVENTIONAL RULES, HAVE WE?
I'M NOT A SOLDIER. I SHOULD BE FREE TO WEAR WHATEVER I LIKE, NO?
YES, I SUPPOSE YOU ARE CORRECT.
UGH...

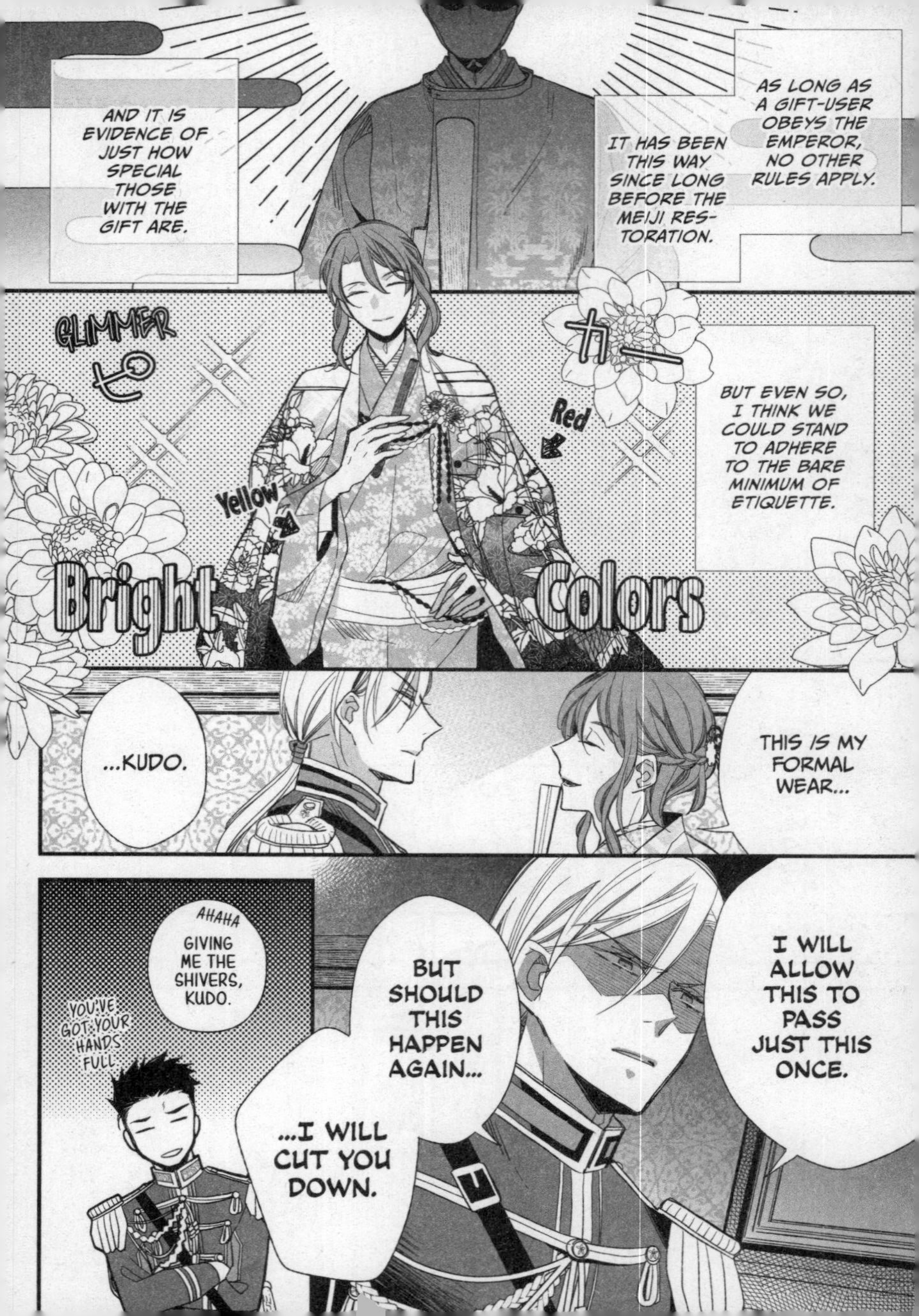
AS LONG AS A GIFT-USER OBEYS THE EMPEROR, NO OTHER RULES APPLY.
IT HAS BEEN THIS WAY SINCE LONG BEFORE THE MEIJI RESTORATION.
AND IT IS EVIDENCE OF JUST HOW SPECIAL THOSE WITH THE GIFT ARE.
BUT EVEN SO, I THINK WE COULD STAND TO ADHERE TO THE BARE MINIMUM OF ETIQUETTE.
Red
Yellow
GLIMMER
Bright Colors
THIS IS MY FORMAL WEAR...
...KUDO.
I WILL ALLOW THIS TO PASS JUST THIS ONCE.
BUT SHOULD THIS HAPPEN AGAIN...
...I WILL CUT YOU DOWN.
AHAHA
GIVING ME THE SHIVERS, KUDO.
YOU'VE GOT YOUR HANDS FULL

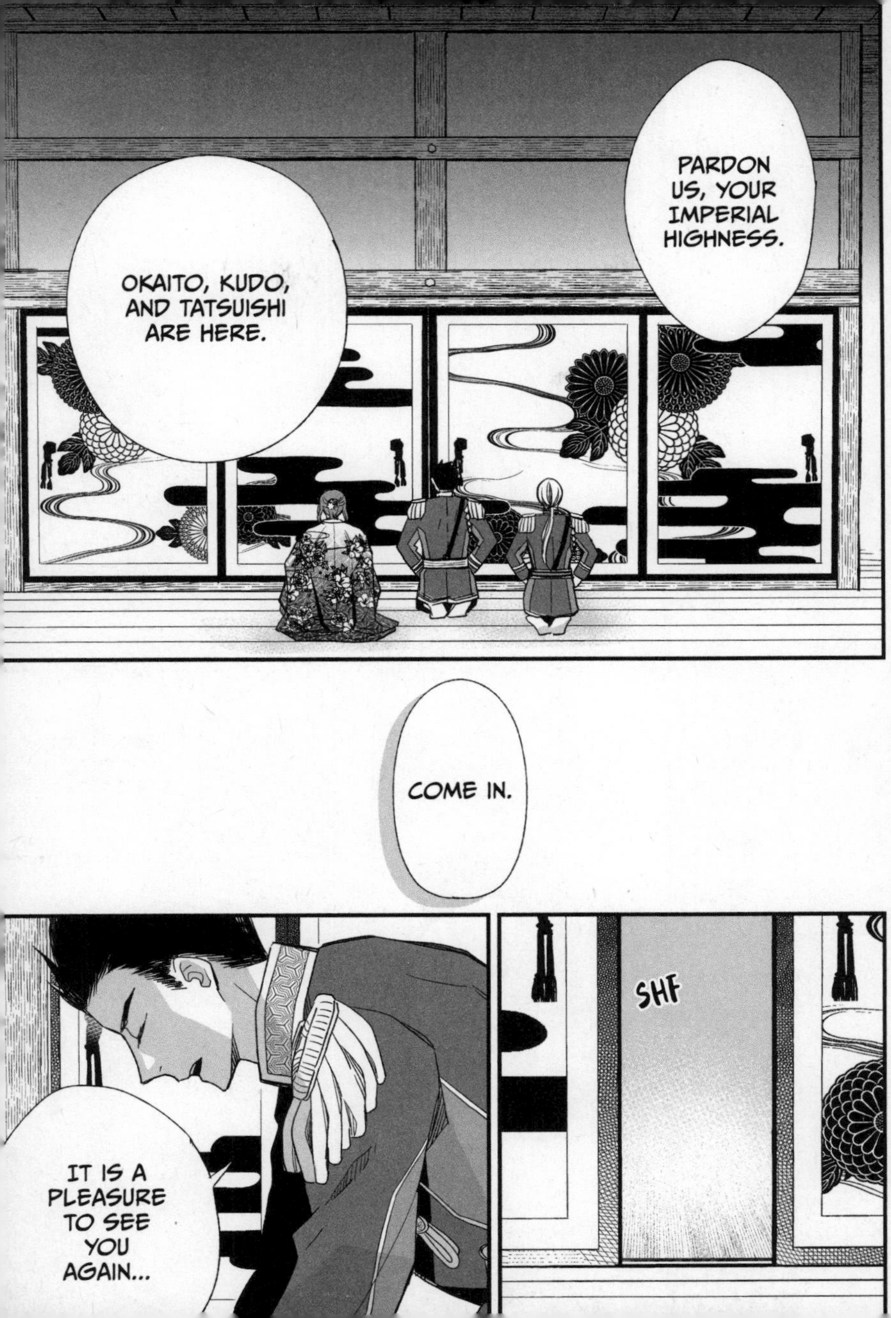
PARDON US, YOUR IMPERIAL HIGHNESS.
OKAITO, KUDO, AND TATSUISHI ARE HERE.
COME IN.
SHF
IT IS A PLEASURE TO SEE YOU AGAIN...

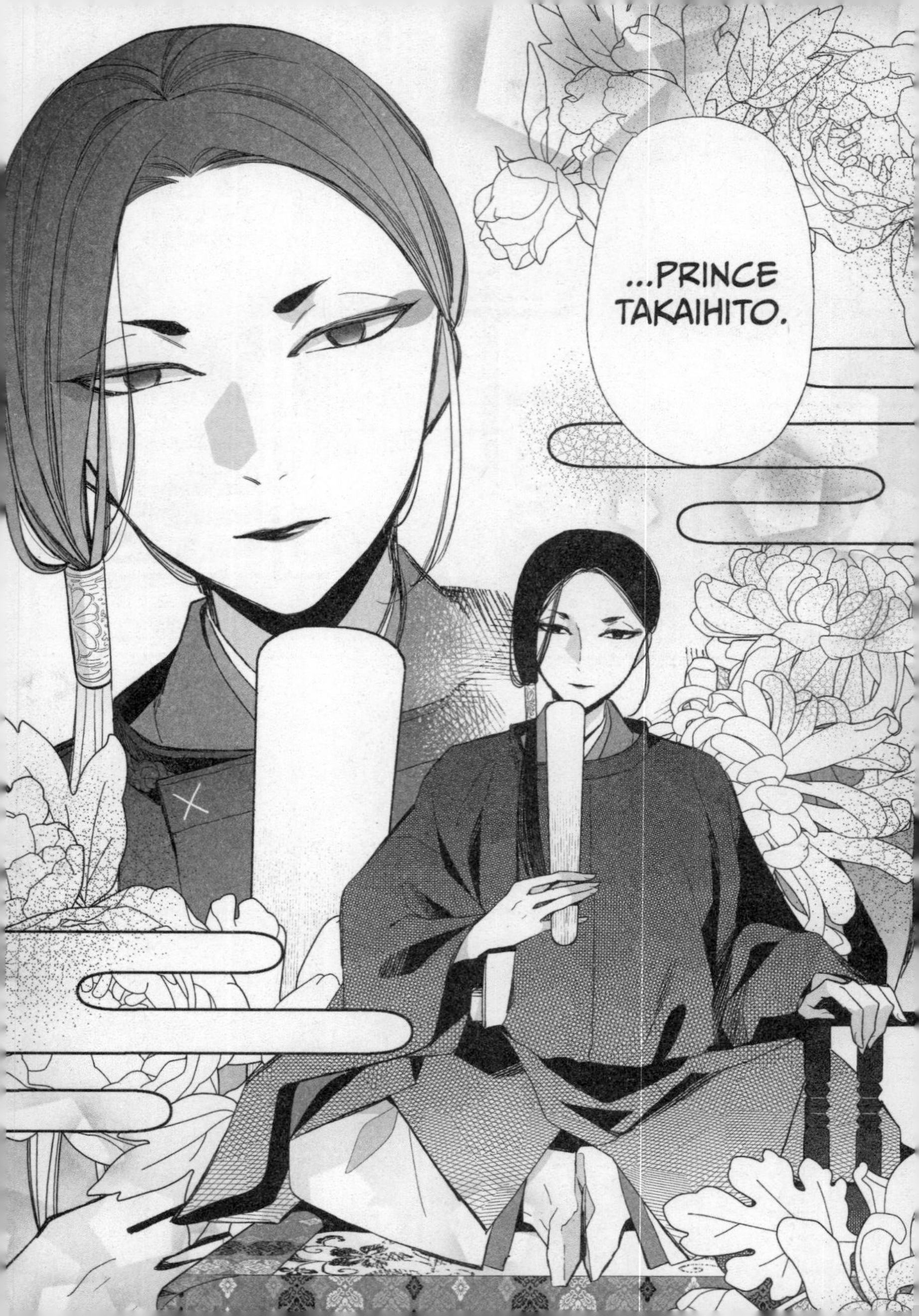
...PRINCE TAKAIHITO.

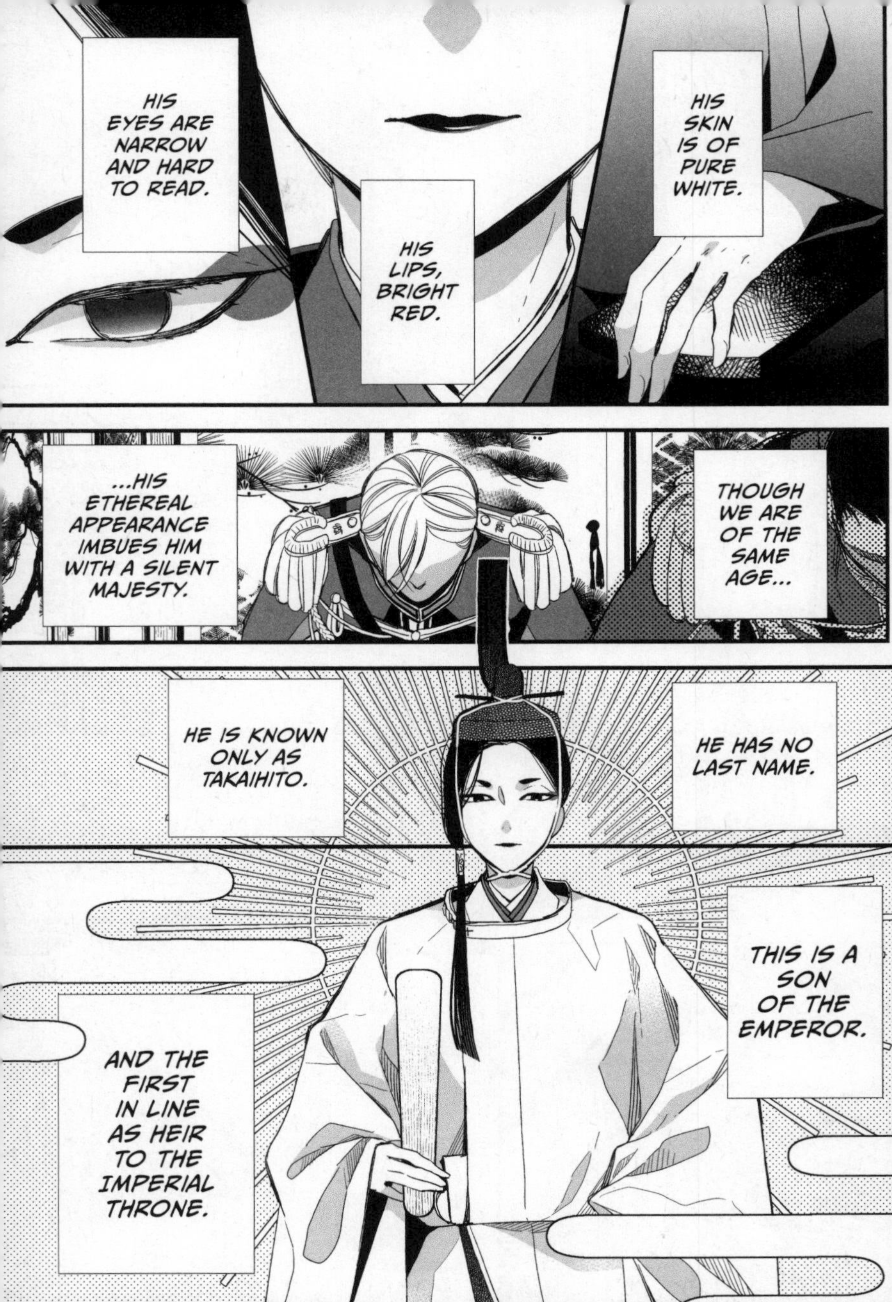
HIS SKIN IS OF PURE WHITE.
HIS LIPS, BRIGHT RED.
HIS EYES ARE NARROW AND HARD TO READ.
THOUGH WE ARE OF THE SAME AGE...
...HIS ETHEREAL APPEARANCE IMBUES HIM WITH A SILENT MAJESTY.
HE HAS NO LAST NAME.
HE IS KNOWN ONLY AS TAKAIHITO.
THIS IS A SON OF THE EMPEROR.
AND THE FIRST IN LINE AS HEIR TO THE IMPERIAL THRONE.

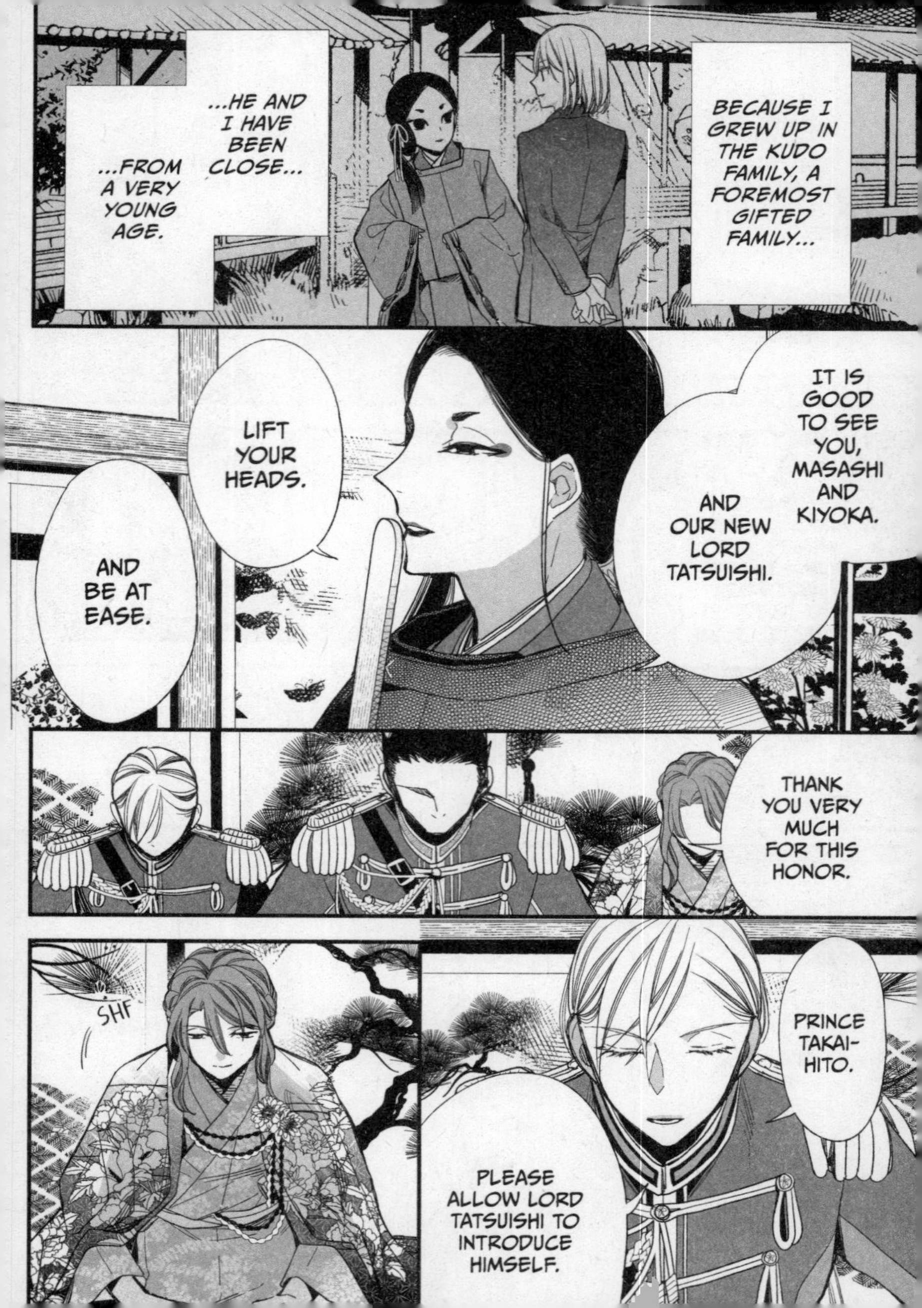
BECAUSE I GREW UP IN THE KUDO FAMILY, A FOREMOST GIFTED FAMILY...
...HE AND I HAVE BEEN CLOSE...
...FROM A VERY YOUNG AGE.
IT IS GOOD TO SEE YOU, MASASHI AND KIYOKA.
AND OUR NEW LORD TATSUISHI.
LIFT YOUR HEADS.
AND BE AT EASE.
THANK YOU VERY MUCH FOR THIS HONOR.
PRINCE TAKAI-HITO.
PLEASE ALLOW LORD TATSUISHI TO INTRODUCE HIMSELF.
SHF

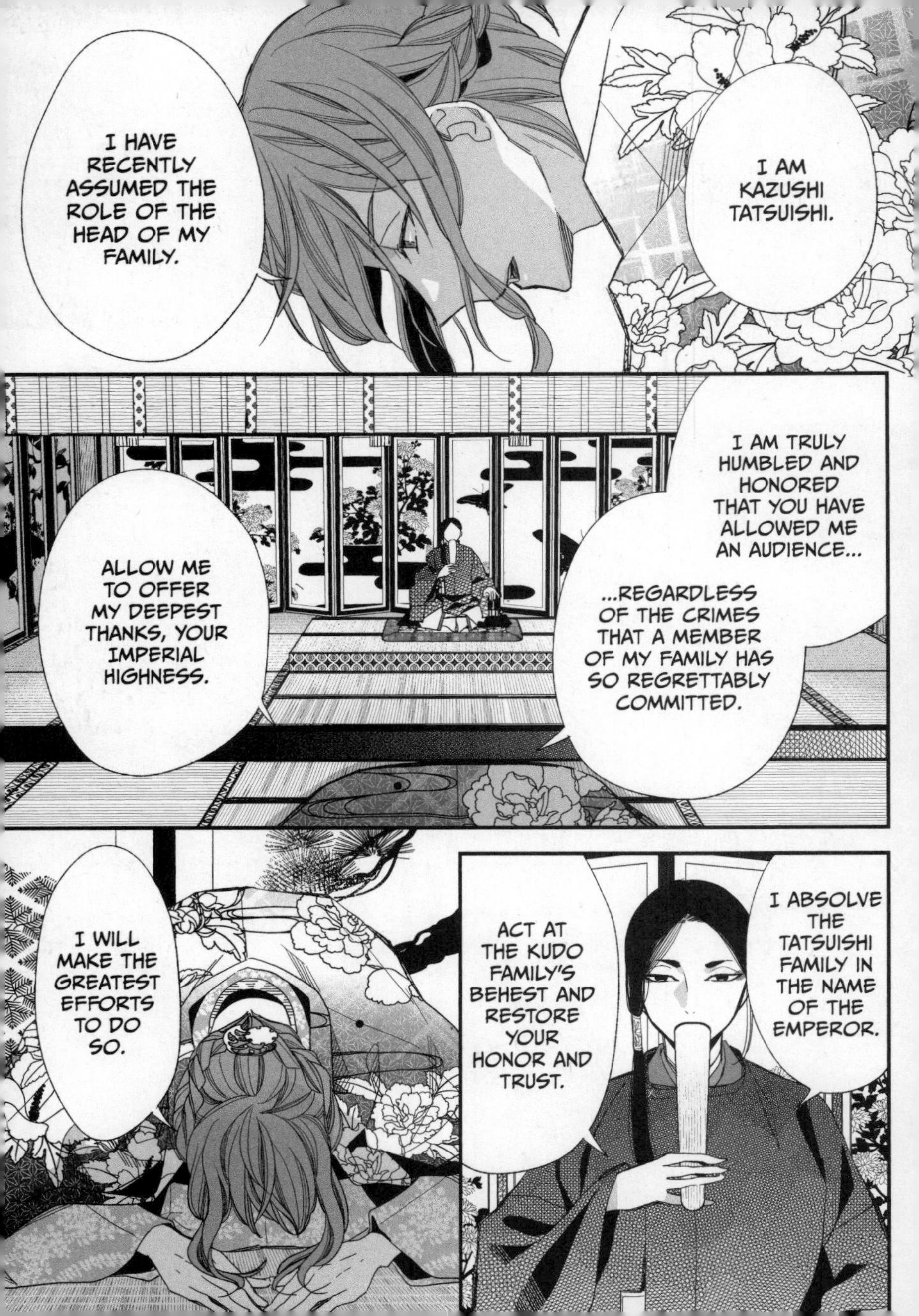
I AM KAZUSHI TATSUISHI.
I HAVE RECENTLY ASSUMED THE ROLE OF THE HEAD OF MY FAMILY.
I AM TRULY HUMBLED AND HONORED THAT YOU HAVE ALLOWED ME AN AUDIENCE...
...REGARDLESS OF THE CRIMES THAT A MEMBER OF MY FAMILY HAS SO REGRETTABLY COMMITTED.
ALLOW ME TO OFFER MY DEEPEST THANKS, YOUR IMPERIAL HIGHNESS.
I ABSOLVE THE TATSUISHI FAMILY IN THE NAME OF THE EMPEROR.
ACT AT THE KUDO FAMILY'S BEHEST AND RESTORE YOUR HONOR AND TRUST.
I WILL MAKE THE GREATEST EFFORTS TO DO SO.

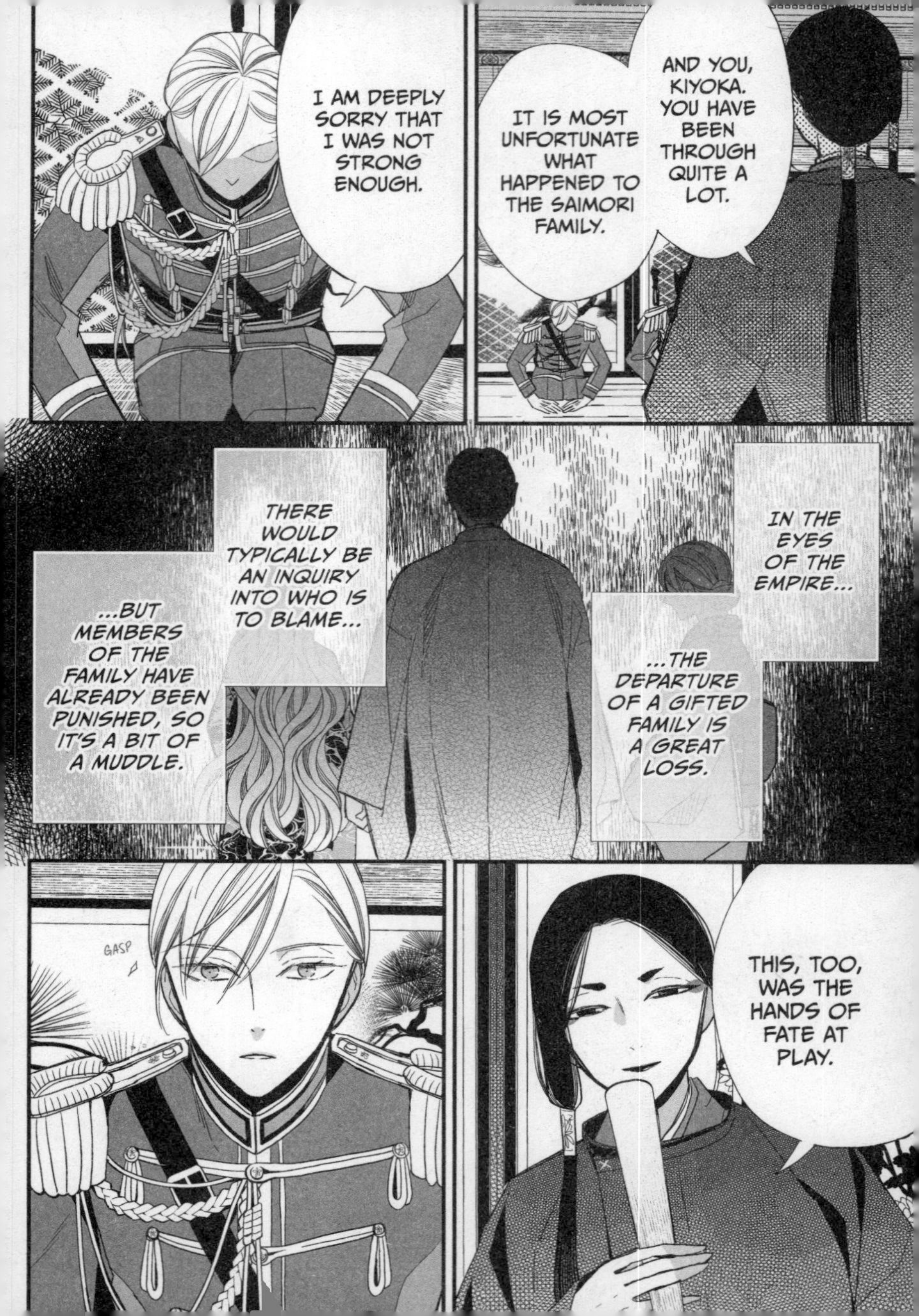
AND YOU, KIYOKA. YOU HAVE BEEN THROUGH QUITE A LOT.
IT IS MOST UNFORTUNATE WHAT HAPPENED TO THE SAIMORI FAMILY.
I AM DEEPLY SORRY THAT I WAS NOT STRONG ENOUGH.
IN THE EYES OF THE EMPIRE...
...THE DEPARTURE OF A GIFTED FAMILY IS A GREAT LOSS.
THERE WOULD TYPICALLY BE AN INQUIRY INTO WHO IS TO BLAME...
...BUT MEMBERS OF THE FAMILY HAVE ALREADY BEEN PUNISHED, SO IT'S A BIT OF A MUDDLE.
THIS, TOO, WAS THE HANDS OF FATE AT PLAY.
GASP

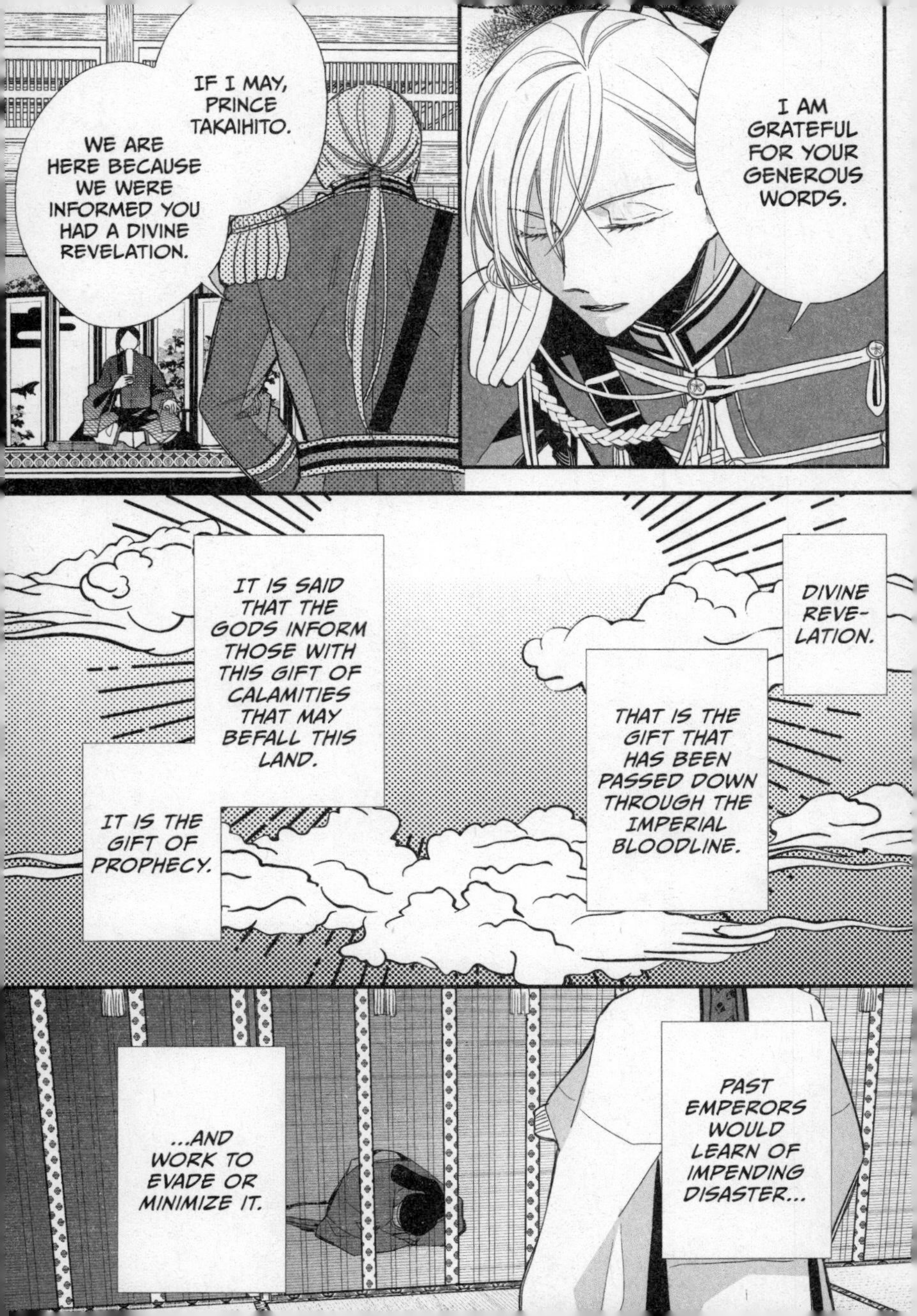
I AM GRATEFUL FOR YOUR GENEROUS WORDS.
IF I MAY, PRINCE TAKAIHITO.
WE ARE HERE BECAUSE WE WERE INFORMED YOU HAD A DIVINE REVELATION.
DIVINE REVE-LATION.
THAT IS THE GIFT THAT HAS BEEN PASSED DOWN THROUGH THE IMPERIAL BLOODLINE.
IT IS SAID THAT THE GODS INFORM THOSE WITH THIS GIFT OF CALAMITIES THAT MAY BEFALL THIS LAND.
IT IS THE GIFT OF PROPHECY.
PAST EMPERORS WOULD LEARN OF IMPENDING DISASTER...
...AND WORK TO EVADE OR MINIMIZE IT.

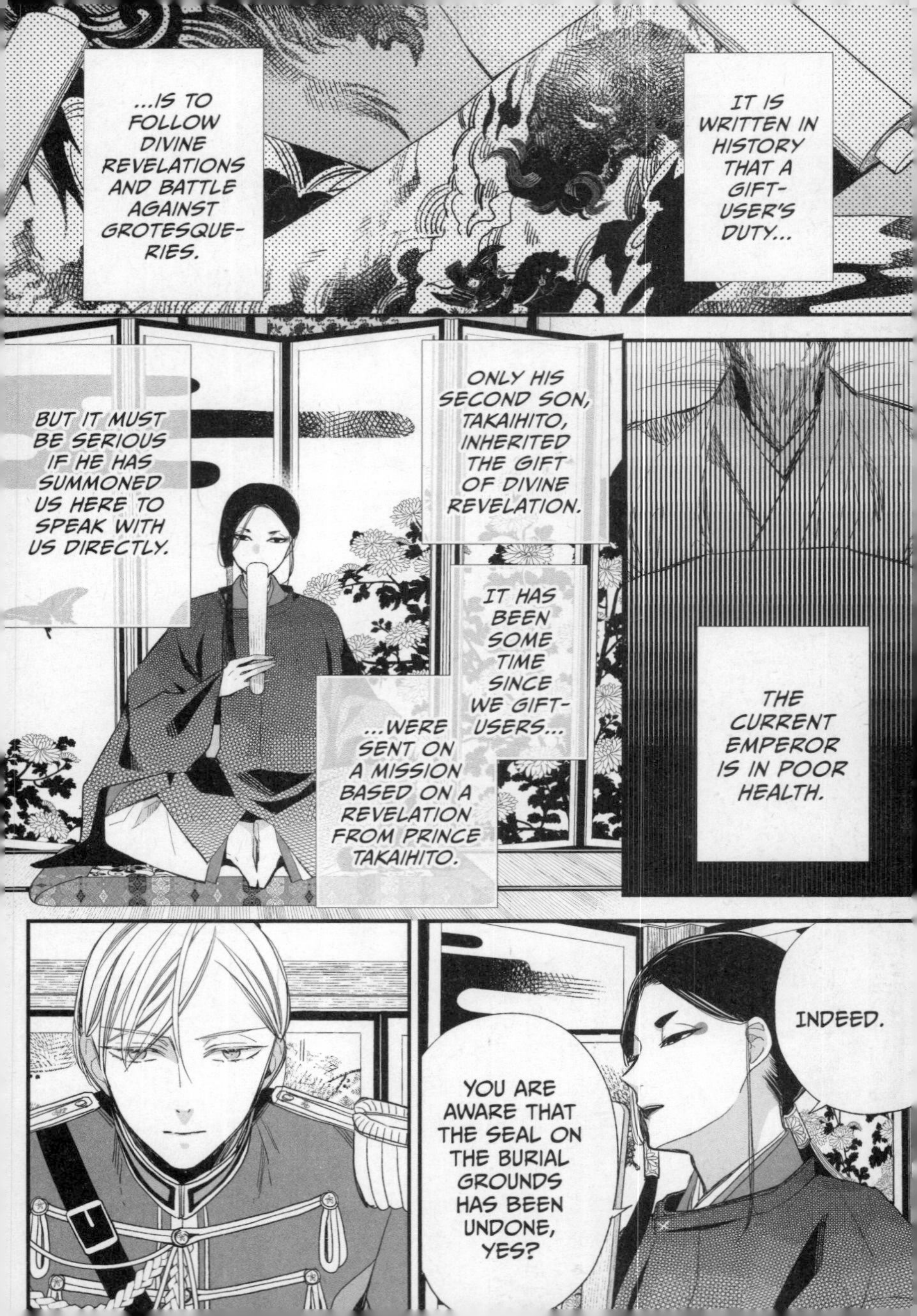
IT IS WRITTEN IN HISTORY THAT A GIFT-USER'S DUTY...
...IS TO FOLLOW DIVINE REVELATIONS AND BATTLE AGAINST GROTESQUERIES.
THE CURRENT EMPEROR IS IN POOR HEALTH.
ONLY HIS SECOND SON, TAKAIHITO, INHERITED THE GIFT OF DIVINE REVELATION.
IT HAS BEEN SOME TIME SINCE WE GIFT-USERS...
...WERE SENT ON A MISSION BASED ON A REVELATION FROM PRINCE TAKAIHITO.
BUT IT MUST BE SERIOUS IF HE HAS SUMMONED US HERE TO SPEAK WITH US DIRECTLY.
YOU ARE AWARE THAT THE SEAL ON THE BURIAL GROUNDS HAS BEEN UNDONE, YES?
INDEED.

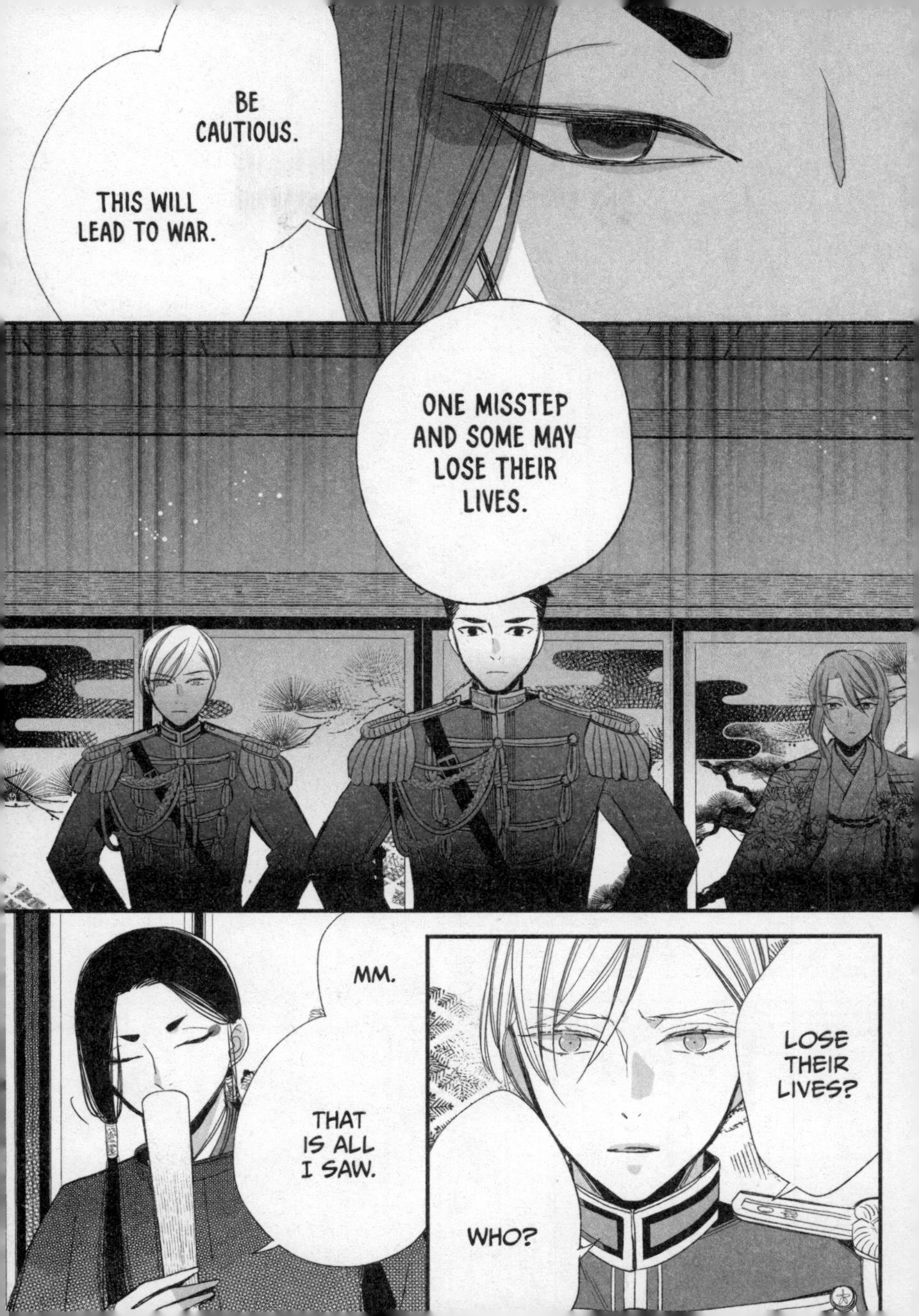
BE CAUTIOUS.
THIS WILL LEAD TO WAR.
ONE MISSTEP AND SOME MAY LOSE THEIR LIVES.
LOSE THEIR LIVES?
WHO?
MM.
THAT IS ALL I SAW.

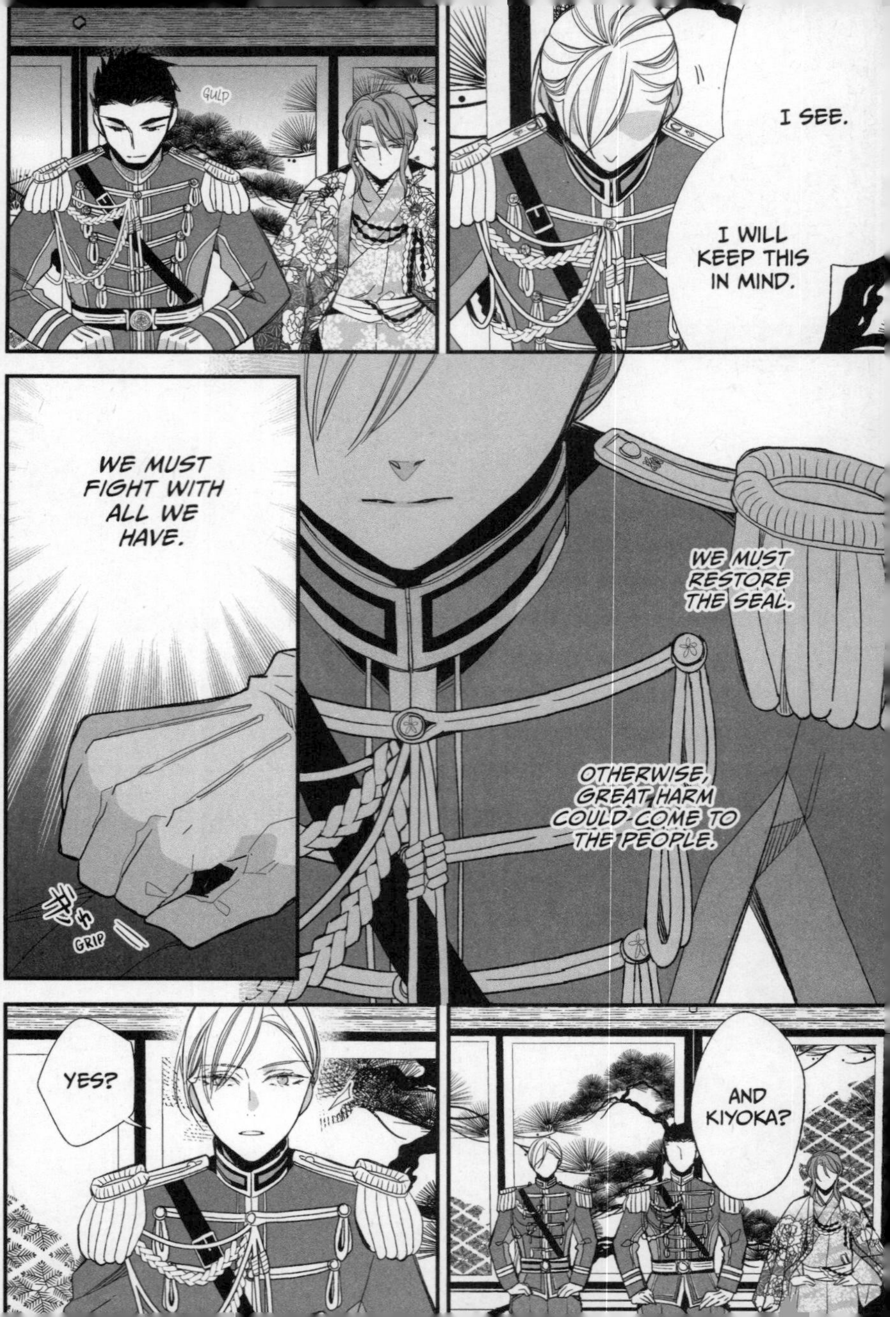
I SEE.
I WILL KEEP THIS IN MIND.
GULP
WE MUST RESTORE THE SEAL.
OTHERWISE, GREAT HARM COULD COME TO THE PEOPLE.
WE MUST FIGHT WITH ALL WE HAVE.
GRIP
AND KIYOKA?
YES?

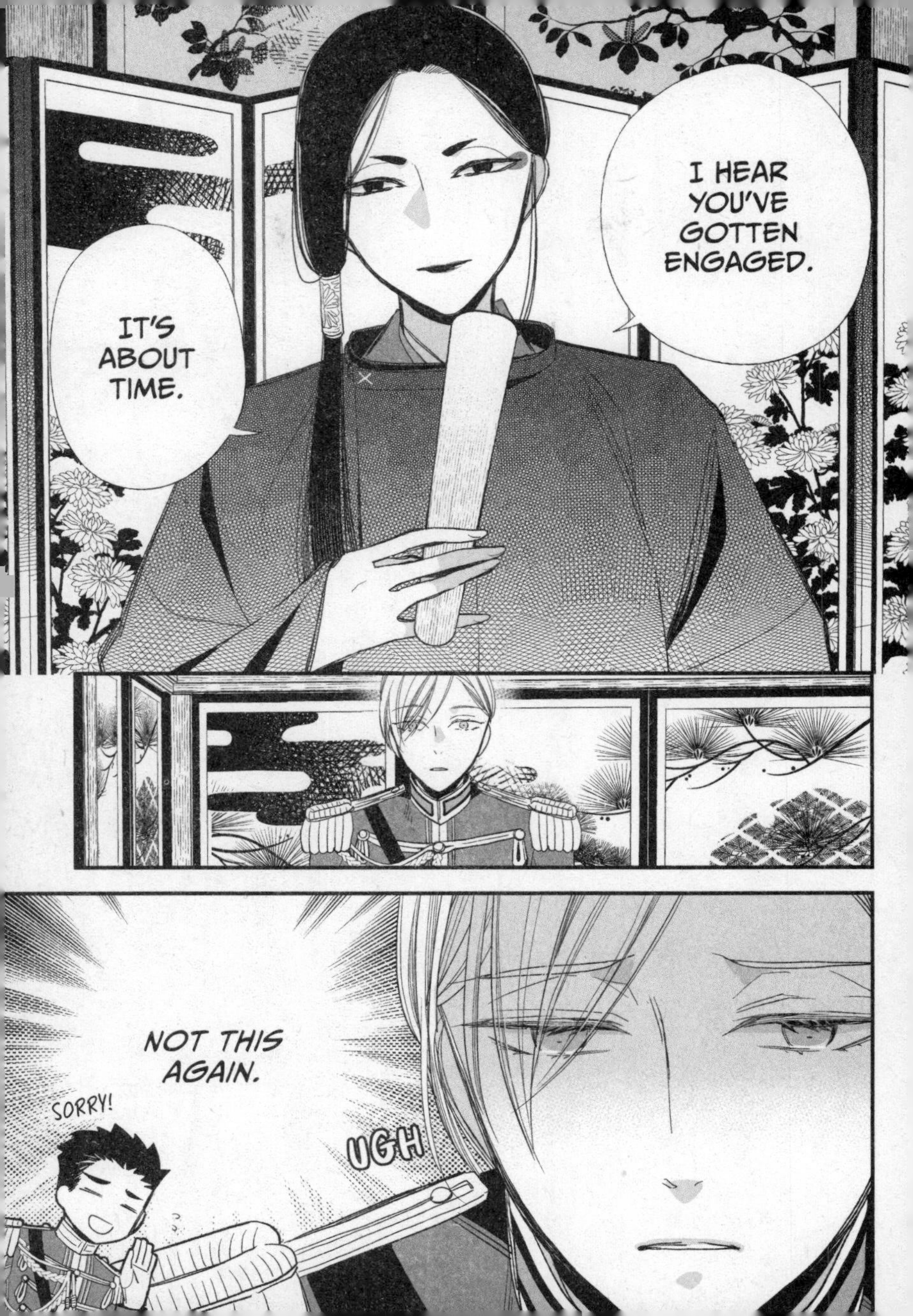
I HEAR YOU'VE GOTTEN ENGAGED.
IT'S ABOUT TIME.
NOT THIS AGAIN.
UGH
SORRY!

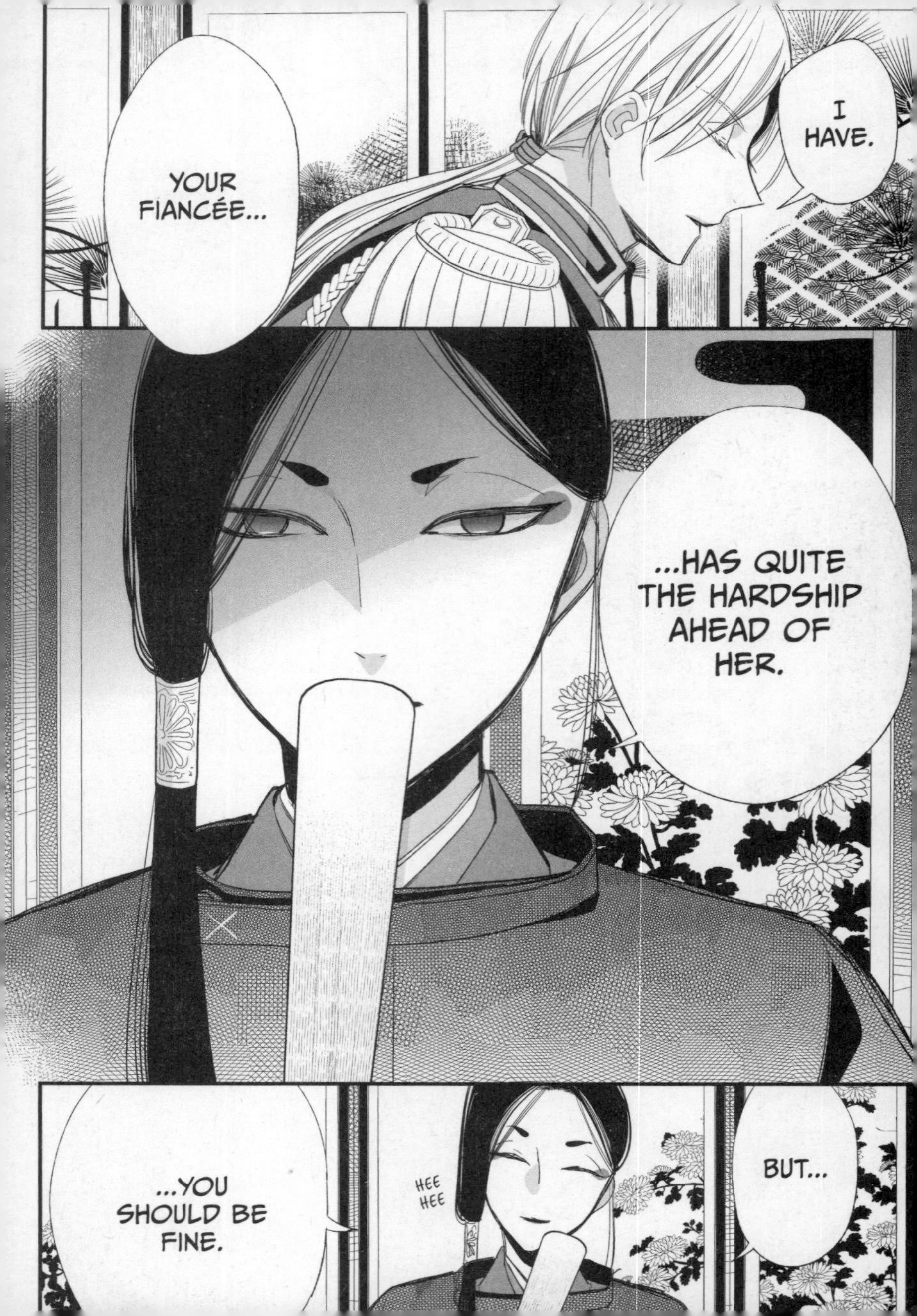
I HAVE.
YOUR FIANCÉE...
...HAS QUITE THE HARDSHIP AHEAD OF HER.
BUT...
HEE HEE
...YOU SHOULD BE FINE.

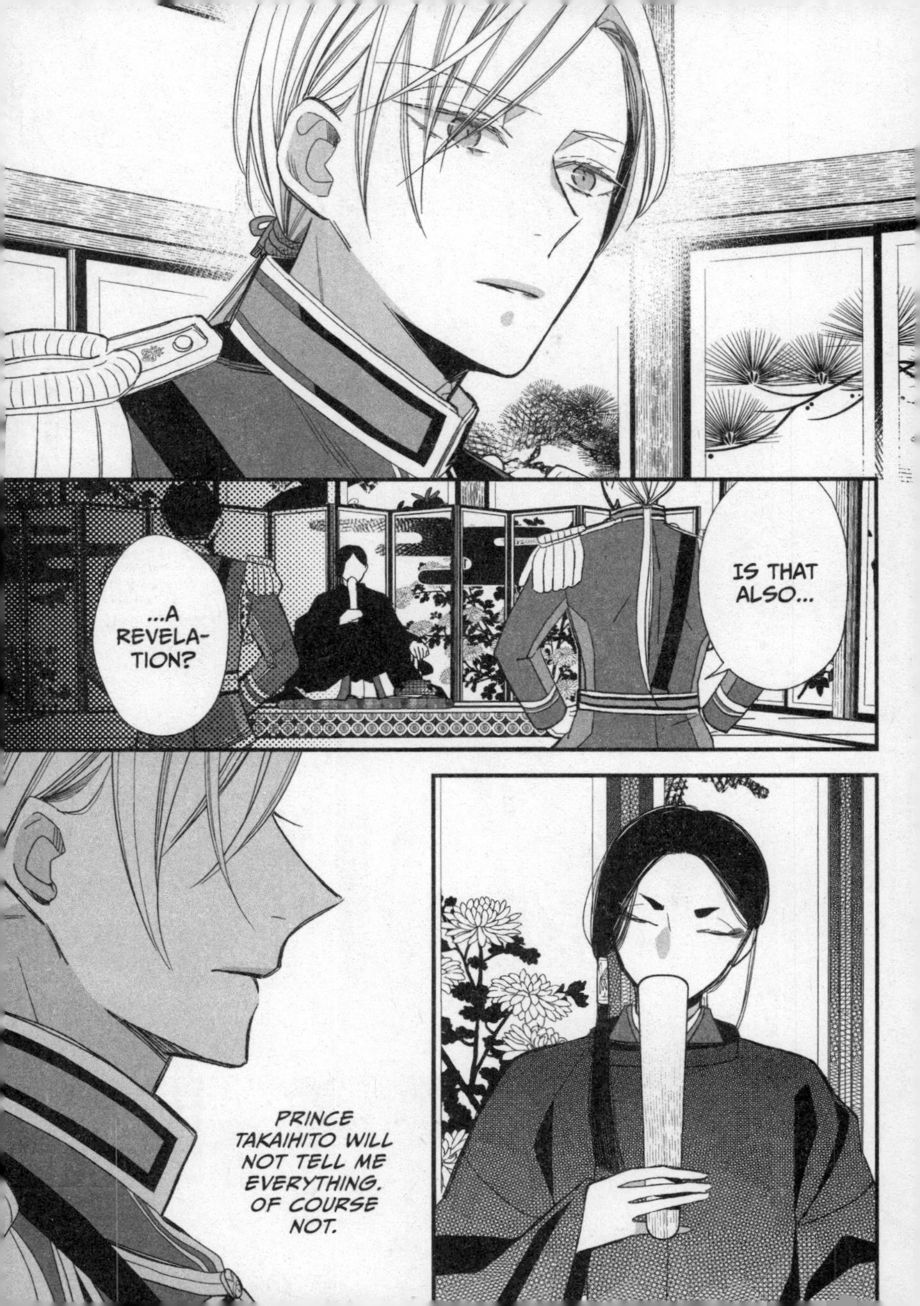
IS THAT ALSO...
...A REVELATION?
PRINCE TAKAIHITO WILL NOT TELL ME EVERYTHING. OF COURSE NOT.

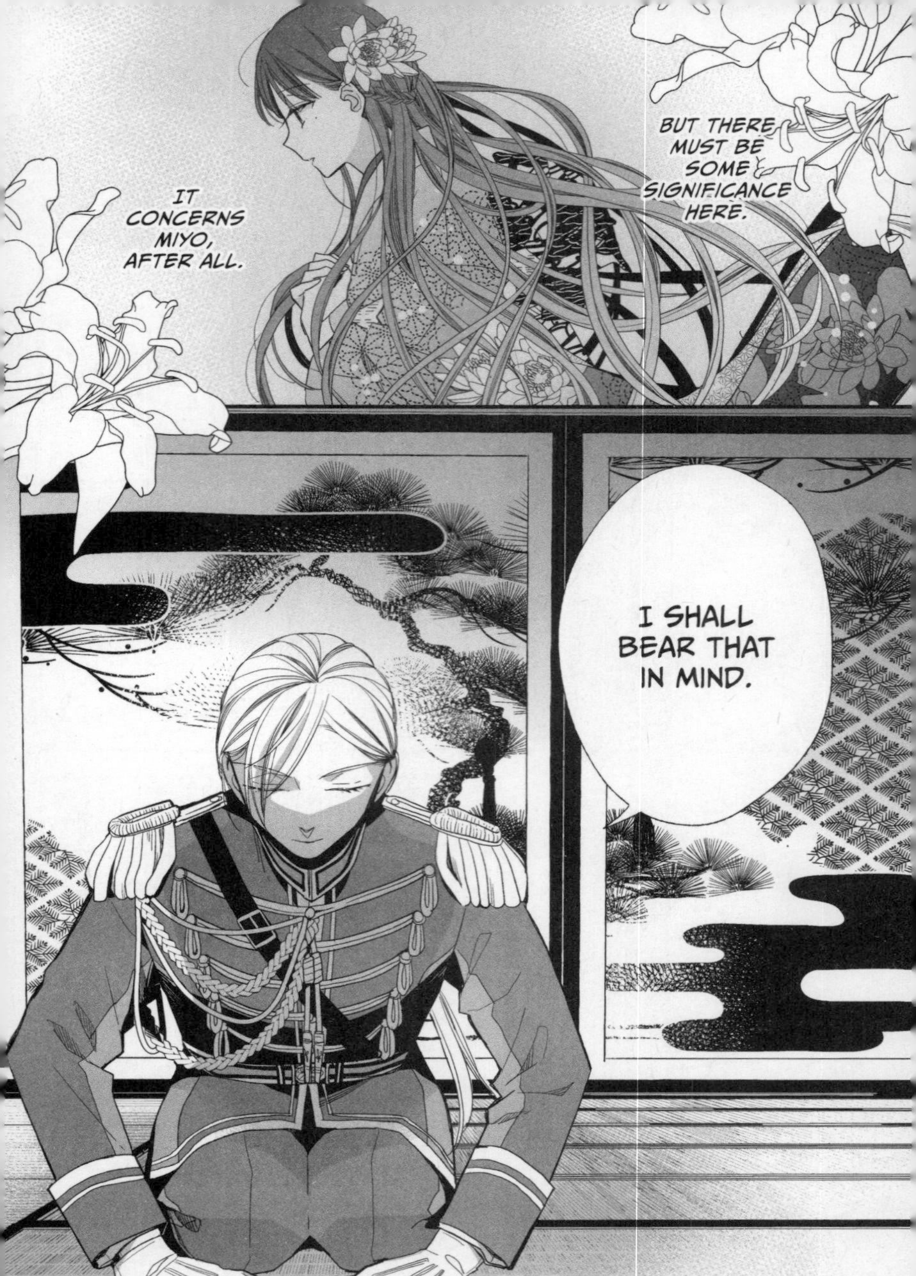
BUT THERE MUST BE SOME SIGNIFICANCE HERE.
IT CONCERNS MIYO, AFTER ALL.
I SHALL BEAR THAT IN MIND.

My Happy Marriage, Vol. 3 • END

MY HAPPY MARRIAGE

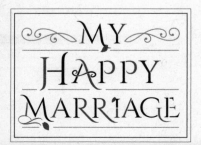

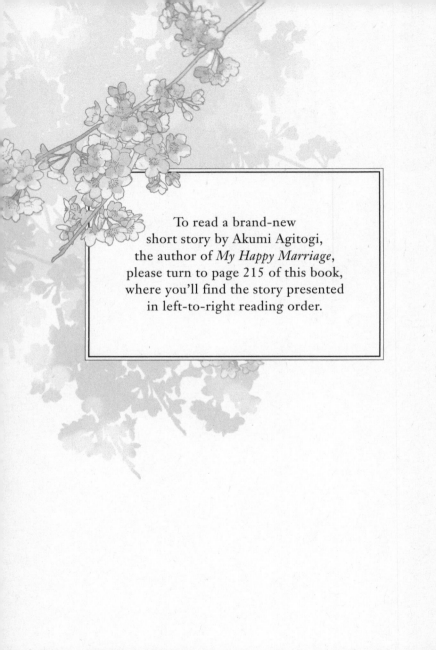

To read a brand-new
short story by Akumi Agitogi,
the author of *My Happy Marriage*,
please turn to page 215 of this book,
where you'll find the story presented
in left-to-right reading order.

This was a surprise. She had honestly thought that Kiyoka, being the man of the house that he was, never stepped foot into the kitchen.

Her thoughts must have been written all over her face. The corners of his mouth turned downward in a pout.

"I know how to make *tea*."

Miyo took the teacup he stiffly pushed at her.

The warmth coming from her fingertips seemed to be the embodiment of his consideration for her, and a smile naturally bloomed across her lips.

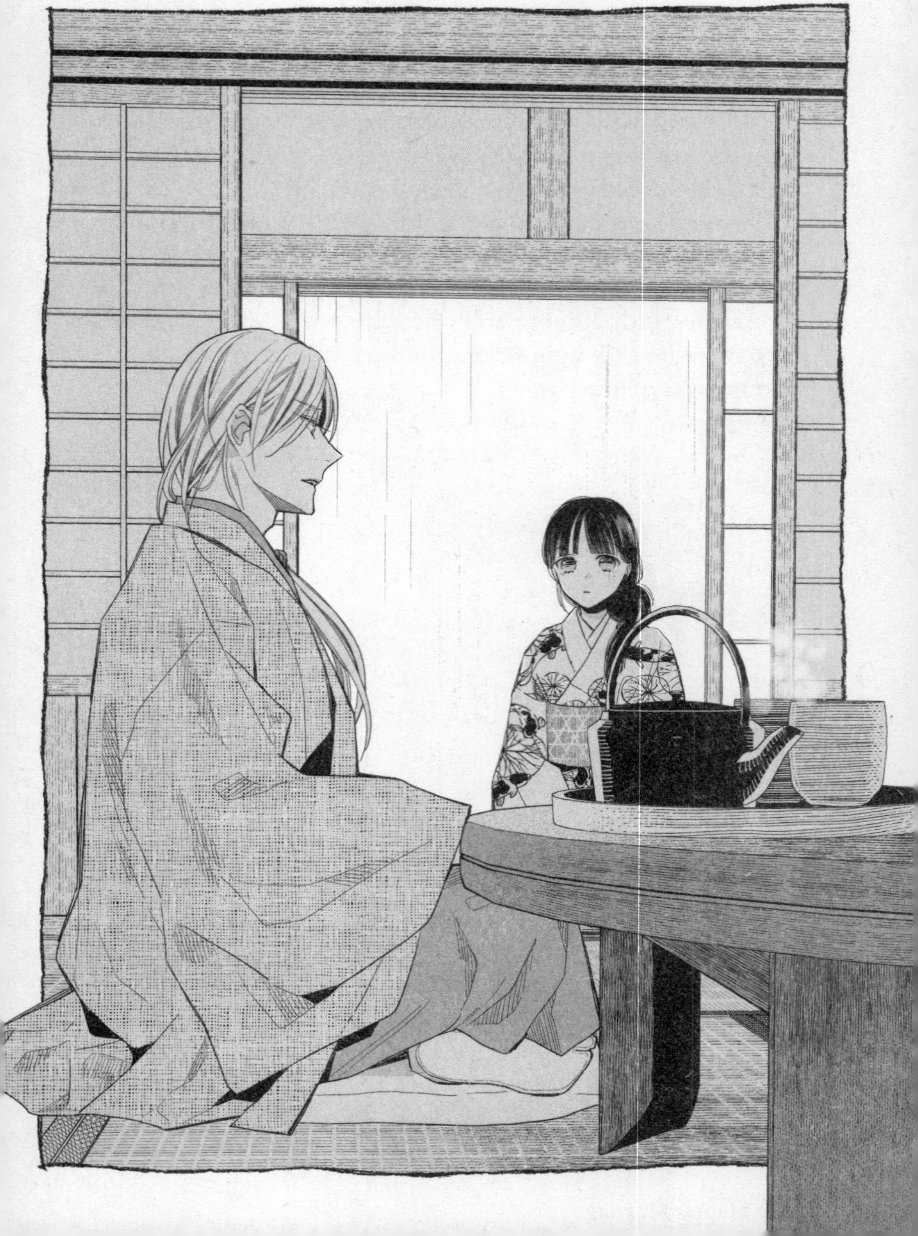

The drying tear tracks on her face chilled in the air.

"Did you have another bad dream?"

A *bad* dream? Something caught at her mind when she heard the word *bad*.

It was bad, yes. Shinichi had always brushed away Miyo's desperate pleas with a single word, and his indifferent attitude toward her had robbed her of her home, of her right to live among the Saimoris as part of the family.

But she remembered the final moment of the dream.

I felt empty.

Frowning, she gazed into Kiyoka's worried eyes.

She was sure that one day, if she could live out a peaceful life with him, she would stop thinking about the Saimori family, with its father, stepmother, and half sister.

And when that happened, everything from back then would grow hazy in her mind, much like how Shinichi's face blurred in her tear-stained vision, until only fuzzy memories remained.

"I...don't know."

Would there ever come a day when a feeling of nostalgia for the past would blot out the pain and suffering still fresh, even now, in her heart? Would she ever become capable of hoping that such a day would arrive?

"Miyo."

"Yes?"

With a small sigh, Kiyoka glanced over at the table.

Sitting atop it was a tray loaded with teacups, much like the one she gave her father in her dream. Beside it was a teapot she had grown accustomed to seeing and using every day since coming to this house.

"I made tea. Do you want some?"

"Oh, you...made tea?"

The sound of pouring rain echoed in her ears.

Miyo blinked open heavy eyelids and gazed past the veranda, into the garden, to find it getting drenched in a downpour.

For a moment, she thought she had never awoken from her dream, and fear seized her. She felt the blood drain from her face, overcome with the distinct sense that she had still been living in the Saimori house this entire time.

"You're awake."

There came a voice. She whipped her head around to find her fiancé, worry written across his beautiful face.

"My lord...?"

"Hmm? You're still half-asleep, aren't you?"

There was bafflement and exasperation in his tone. The question prompted her to think back on everything that happened before she fell into her dream.

Once the chores were finished, Yurie went home and Miyo sat down to rest. And as she did so, she leaned her head against the wooden post beside her and drifted off to sleep.

"Oh—my apologies!"

As clarity came back to her, the more embarrassed she became.

Kiyoka was scheduled to come home early that day, so he must have returned while Miyo was asleep. She was a failure of a fiancée for dozing off without realizing.

As her apology reached his ears, Kiyoka gave a sigh of displeasure. "Enough apologies. Do you know, you were crying out in your sleep?"

"Oh...!"

One remaining tear rolled down Miyo's cheek.

She had assumed that was only in the dream, but it seemed she had shed actual tears in her sleep.

She was not sad because of what Shinichi said to her. She was sad for her past self, a girl who could not even cry when her own father spoke heartless words to her.

Crying out of self-pity is the height of shame.

She desperately tried to keep the tears at bay, but they spilled forth regardless.

For the very first time, she pitied her past self. Until that point, she had been too focused on surviving each day to have the time or energy to look back objectively at herself.

But now she knew—at last someone had told her that she's allowed to care for herself, that she's allowed to express hopes and dreams.

She should have gotten angry with her father. She should have cried.

Perhaps something would have changed if she had. But the Miyo of the past had found it unbelievably difficult to do something so simple.

Enduring and repressing pain and sadness was so much easier than giving any sort of emotional reaction.

I want to go home.

She wanted to go home to a place where she could breathe, where she could *live*. And that was not this house at all.

Shinichi returned his gaze to his desk. His crying daughter was not even a thought in his mind, though perhaps that was because this was only a memory of the past.

The light and the sounds slowly faded and receded.

As relief washed over her, knowing that she could go home to a place where she could relax, she also felt the strangest twinge of emptiness.

❖ ❖ ❖

Shinichi sat at his low desk. He must have noticed that it was his daughter who had come in, but he did not turn around, much less respond.

Miyo knelt beside him and gently set the teacup down within his reach. When she stood to leave, Shinichi at last focused his gaze on her.

"You're still here?" he muttered, an offhand remark.

Yet within this dream Miyo froze. All around her fell silent. *Still.*

She knew the question that came next was, "How long are you going to be here?"

How long…in this study? No—in the house.

It did not matter that Shinichi himself had quashed every opportunity Miyo may have had to become independent. He had stomped all over everything so blithely, so easily, as if presented with nothing more than a bothersome insect.

Now I…remember.

He had said those very words to her in this exact situation. This was a dream of something that really happened.

Ah, but how had she reacted at the time to her father's hurtful words, uttered so quietly? Had they made her angry? Sad? No—neither.

As she looked at her father's face, she found his image blurring.

Lukewarm tears fell onto her roughened, scraped-up, bony hands as she gripped the tray.

At the time, she had felt nothing. Her heart was so firmly closed off that her father's emotionless words had inspired no emotion in her.

But now she felt a clear and keen sadness.

a women's academy to continue her education. Of course he would allow her to go if she asked.

"You? Go to a women's academy? We don't have that sort of money to waste."

What she received in response was a cold dismissal and an even colder stare.

Every time he gave her a look like she wasn't even his own daughter, every time her wishes were shattered, she had the vague sense that something inside of her was breaking. She stopped hoping.

When she wanted to attend a women's academy...

When she was going to be forced to quit her lessons...

When Kanoko and Kaya came and stole or threw out her belongings and she asked that he furnish her with new ones...

When she begged to at least receive a set of basic necessities for herself...

When she requested to at least be allowed to leave the house and work on her own...

Each and every time, she would come to him and ask. She would grovel so low she could feel her forehead scrape along the tatami floor.

But...

The answer was always no.

We don't have that sort of money or time to waste on you. A daughter working outside would ruin our reputation. I'm the one who would have to take the blame should someone uneducated like you end up bringing dishonor to us.

With every rejection, her heart froze over a little more. Her body would grow paralyzed. Asking for anything was wrong. It became ingrained in her mind that all hope was pointless.

"Excuse me," she called, entering her father's study.

How realistic this dream was.

One of the Saimori servants called Miyo over, and she took from her a tray with a teacup on it.

She couldn't refuse. All of the servants were always overly conscientious of her to begin with. They even took care to station her where she would not have any run-ins with the other family members. It was as if they were wholly unsure of what to do with someone like Miyo, who was a daughter of the family and yet treated like a servant.

The family did not have that many servants; it was obvious that the house truly was short-staffed. How could she say no?

Going along with the dream, she obediently took the tray and headed down the hall.

When she lived in this house, she almost never entered her father's study. Rarer still was it for Miyo and her father to speak to one another at all; she had very few memories of that ever happening.

"Father, I'd like to attend a women's academy."

One exception, however, was the memory of a time she made that desire known. She was in elementary school then.

At that young age, she could have never imagined that she would still be working at home like a servant at nineteen.

Her father, Shinichi, had always been indifferent to her.

It did not matter what her stepmother, Kanoko, or her half sister, Kaya, did or said to her. He would watch in silence, refusing to even lift a finger to help her. He acted like she did not even exist.

At the time, however, she had underestimated her father's willingness to grant her requests. After all, she was a daughter of the Saimori family; it was only natural for her to go on to

Rain

by Akumi Agitogi

Rain drizzled gently outside.

The next thing Miyo knew, she was in the Saimori manor. The house was enveloped in the soft sounds of rain.

I must be dreaming.

She had been having so many nightmares of late. It was like the dreams themselves had a will of their own—as though their only purpose was to cause her pain, to remind her that she could never know happiness. The nightmares were constant since the day she came to Kiyoka. This one, she thought, will be much the same.

Suppressing a sigh, she glanced out at the eaves of the house.

It must be the rainy season, I suppose.

She didn't dislike rain. As she watched the droplets fall to the earth and as she concentrated on the quiet sounds of them bursting, she could feel her consciousness meld into the water.

Oh, how pleasant would it be if her whole body and soul would evaporate away and vanish from existence. The thought rolled around in her mind, over and over.

But no matter how she may enjoy the rain, the rainy season itself was a dreary one for her. When it rained, those in the house were shut up inside—Miyo as well as everyone else.

"I'm sorry, Miss Miyo, but could you take this to Lord Saimori?"

"All...right."

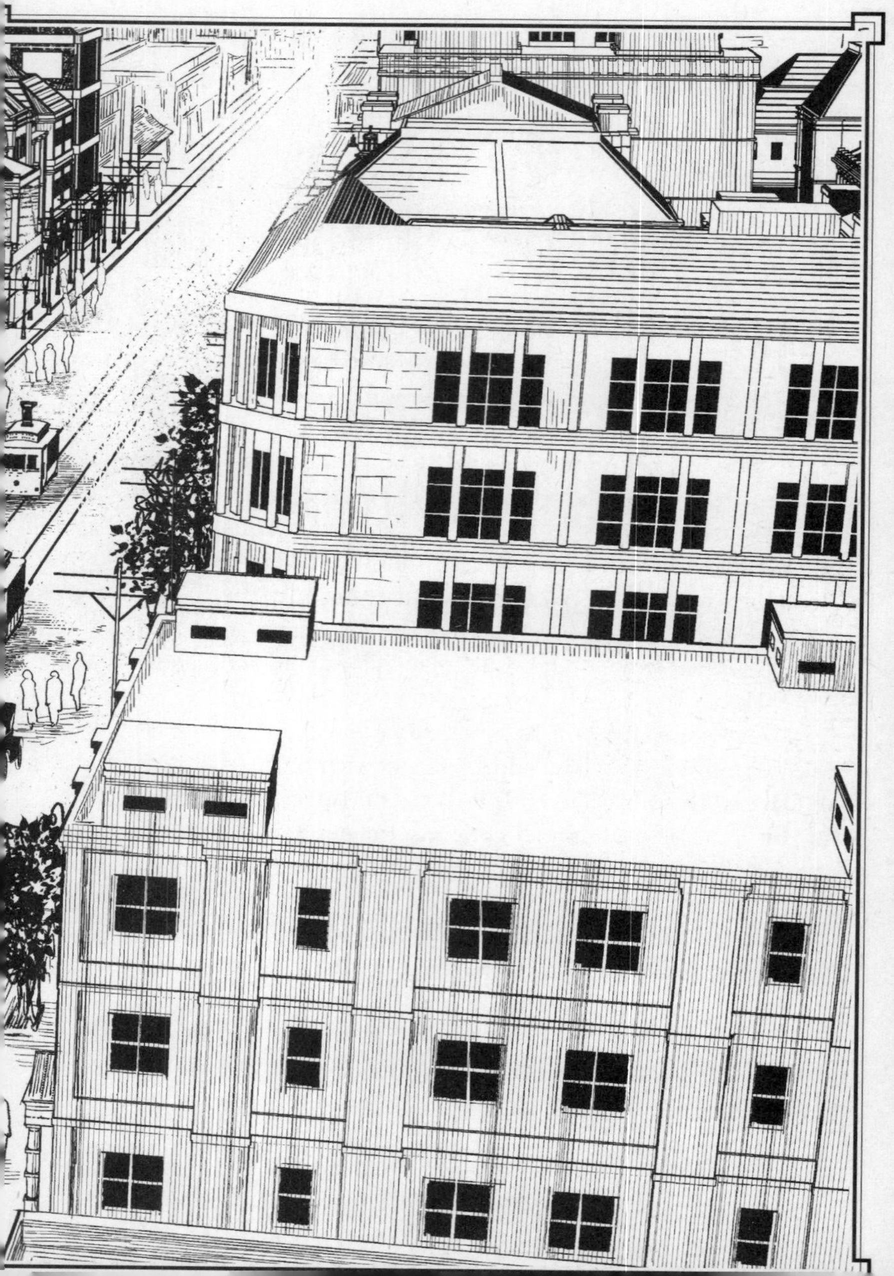

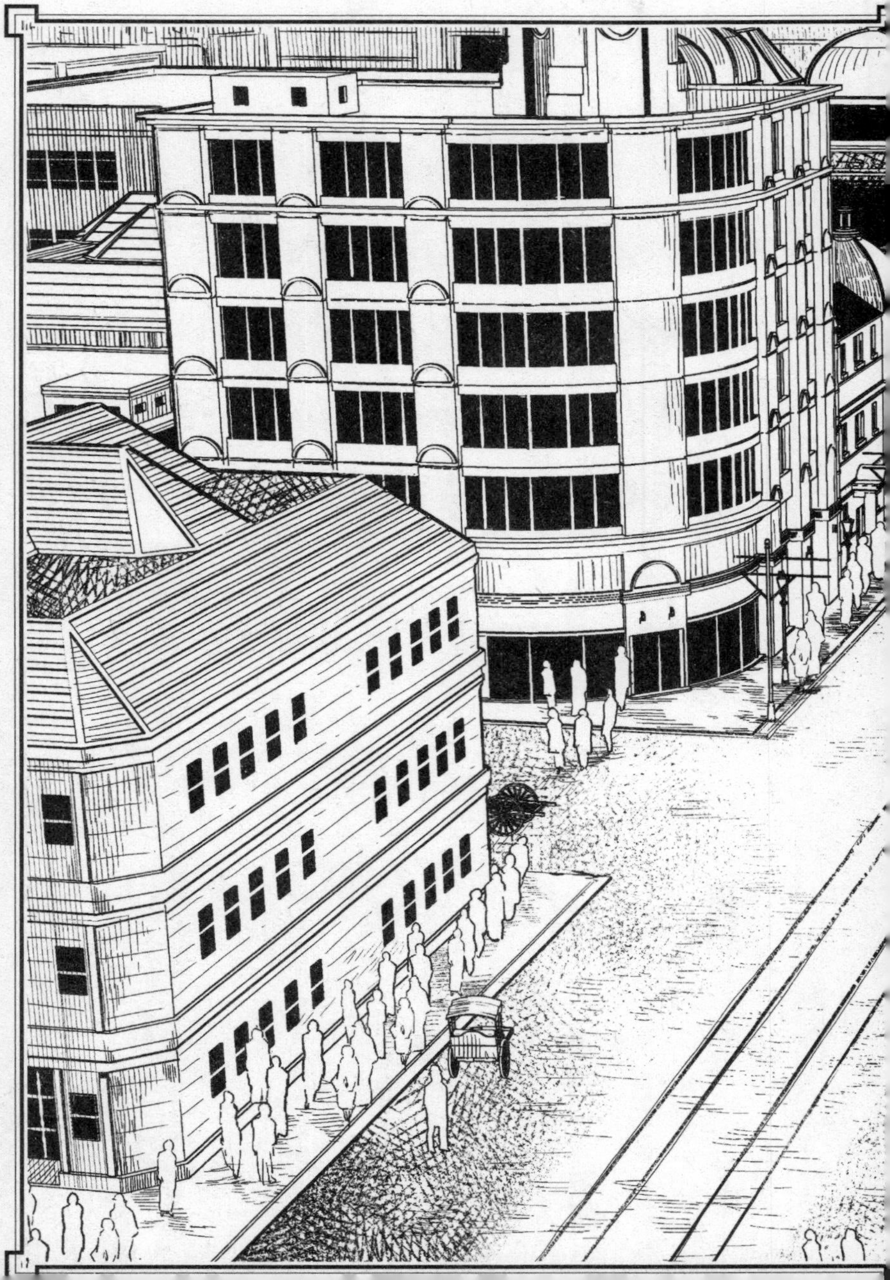

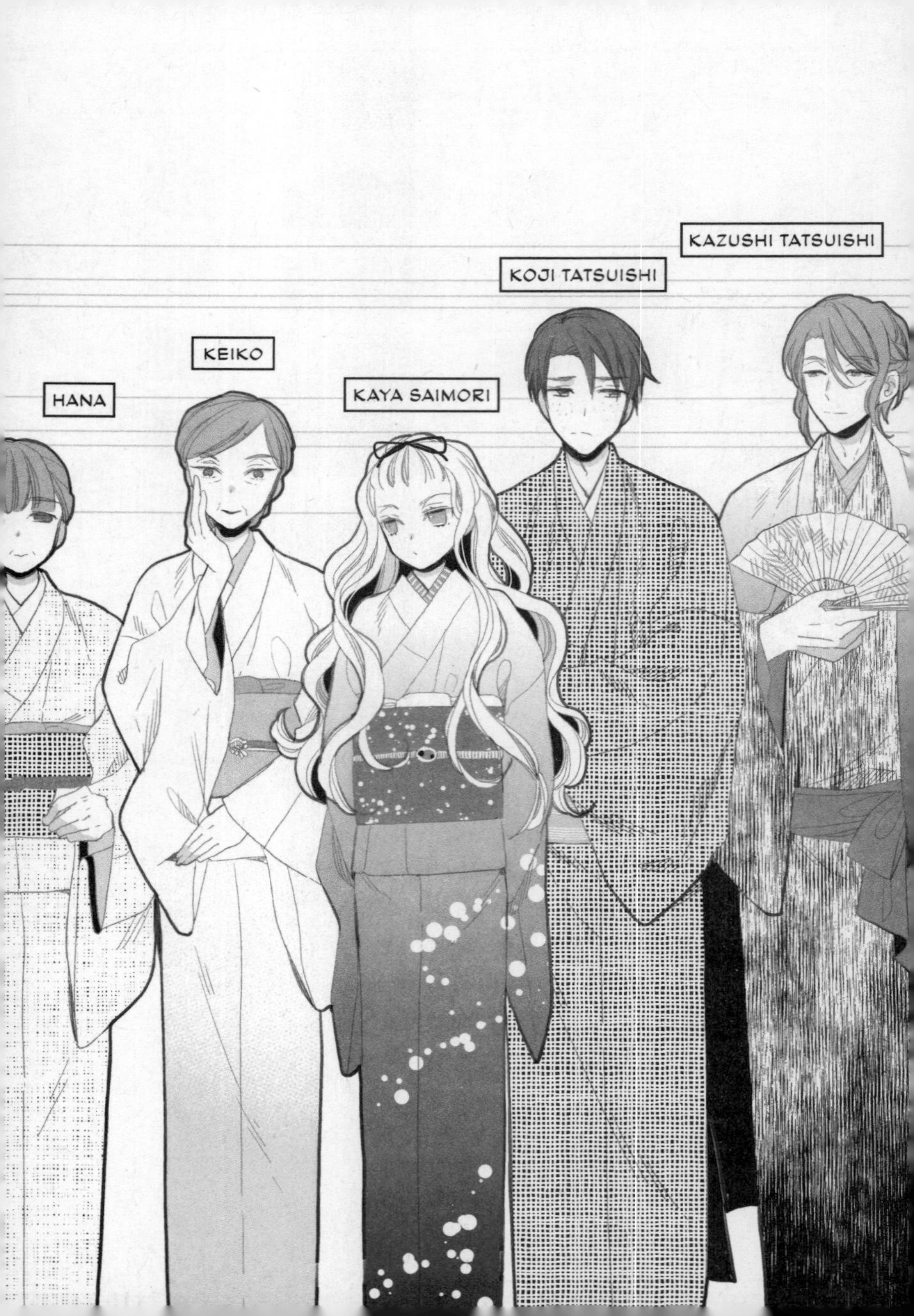
KAZUSHI TATSUISHI
KOJI TATSUISHI
KAYA SAIMORI
KEIKO
HANA

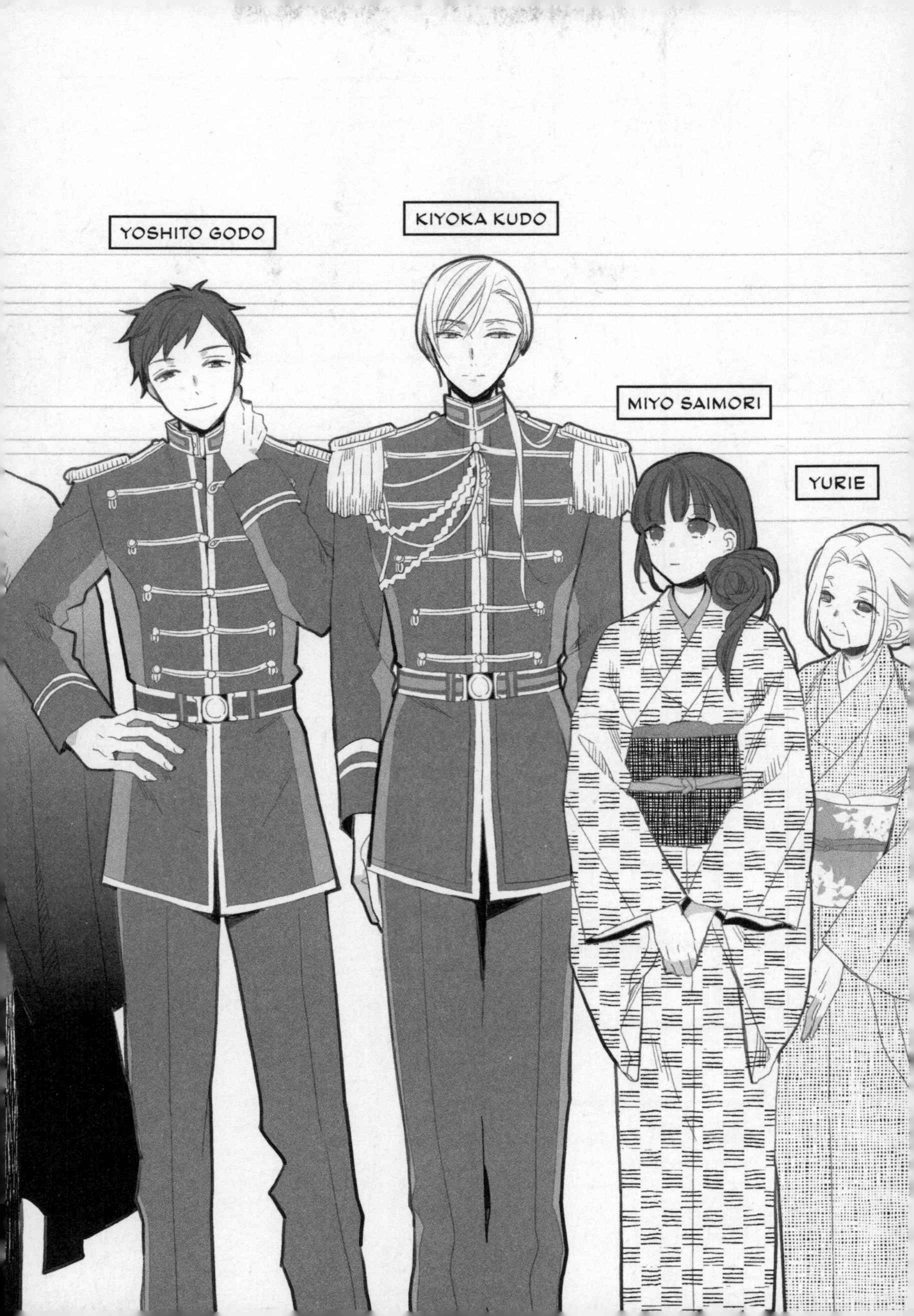
YOSHITO GODO
KIYOKA KUDO
MIYO SAIMORI
YURIE

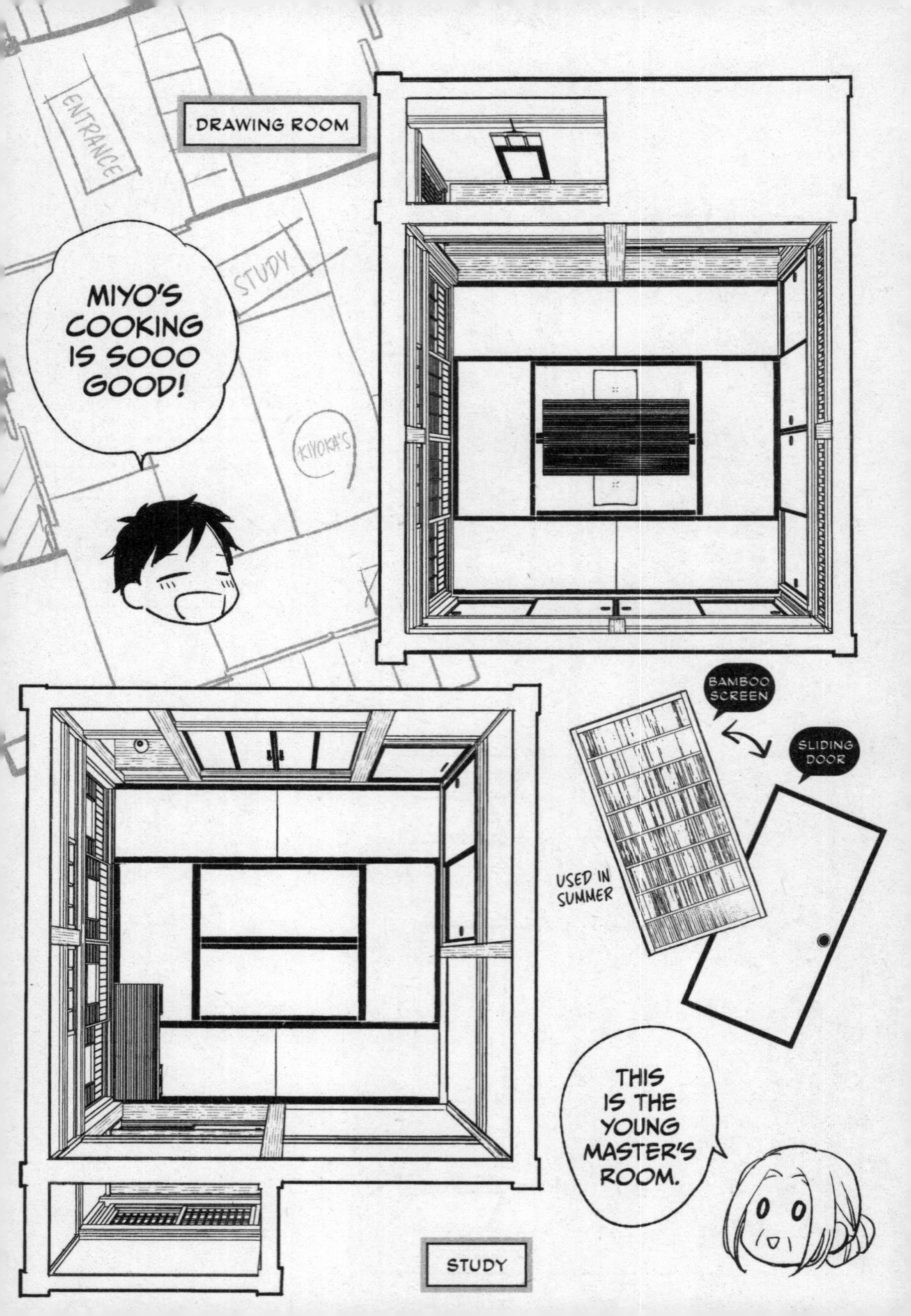
DRAWING ROOM
ENTRANCE
STUDY
KIYOKA'S
MIYO'S COOKING IS SOOO GOOD!
BAMBOO SCREEN
SLIDING DOOR
USED IN SUMMER
THIS IS THE YOUNG MASTER'S ROOM.
STUDY

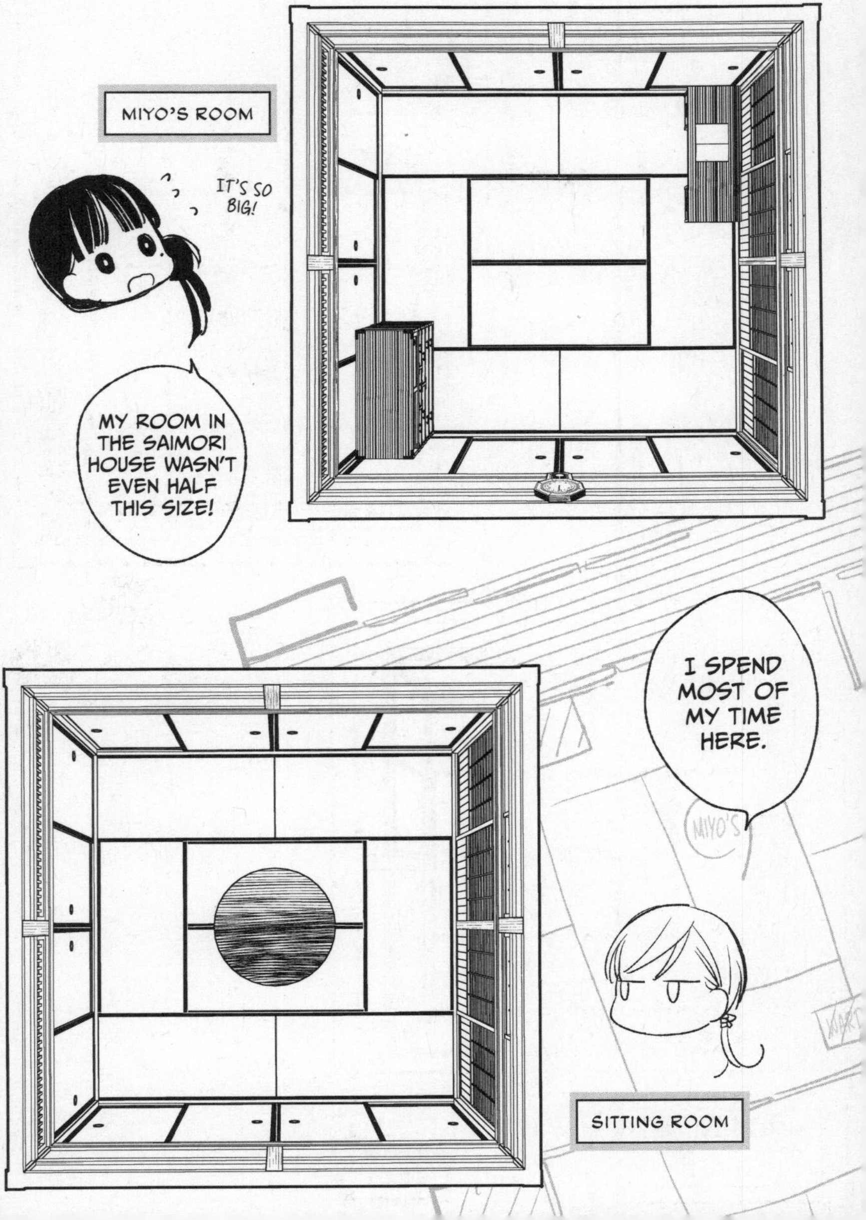
MIYO'S ROOM
IT'S SO BIG!
MY ROOM IN THE SAIMORI HOUSE WASN'T EVEN HALF THIS SIZE!
I SPEND MOST OF MY TIME HERE.
MIYO'S
SITTING ROOM

MY HAPPY MARRIAGE

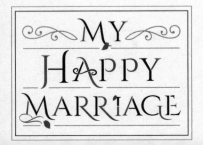

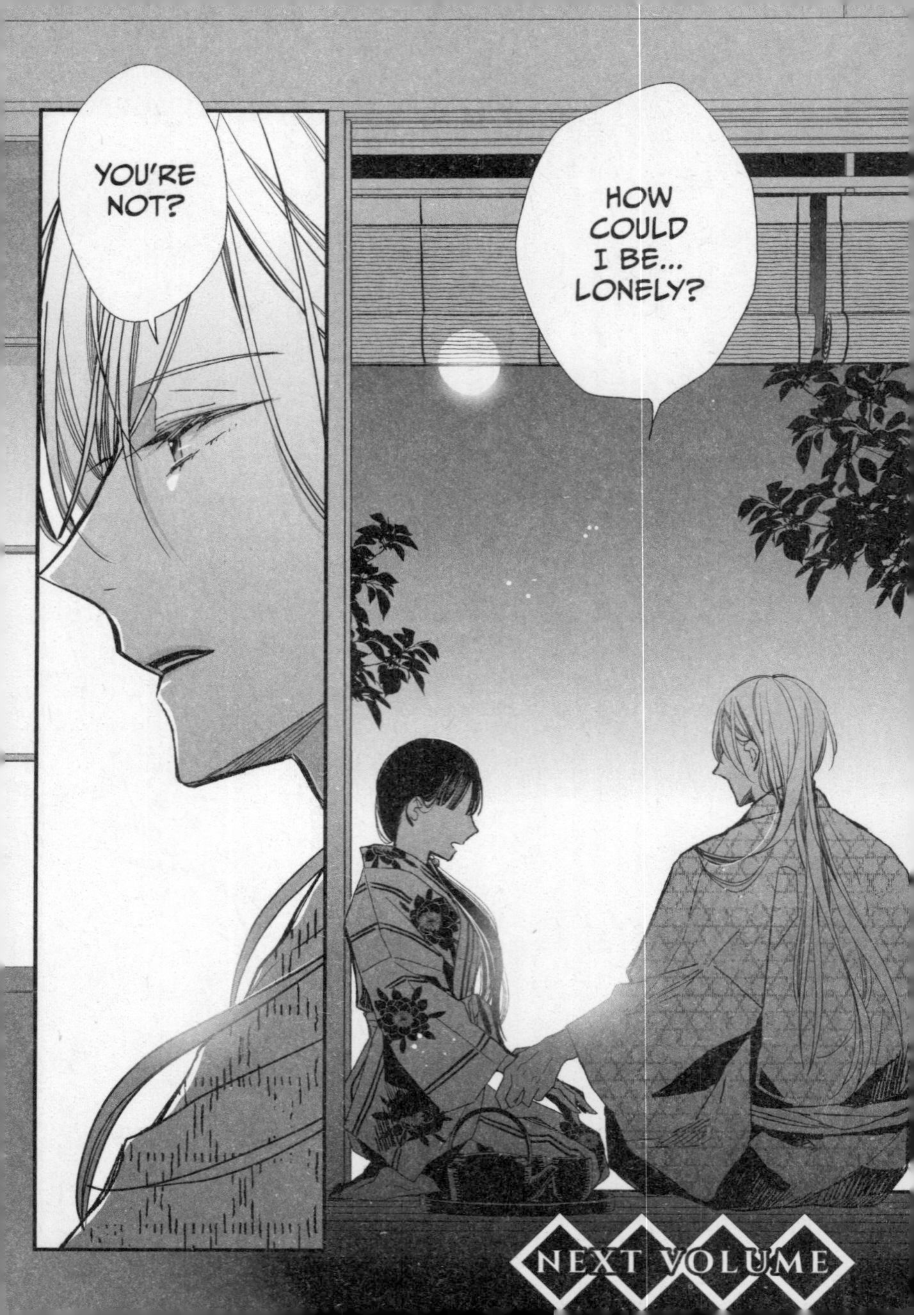
HOW COULD I BE... LONELY?
YOU'RE NOT?
NEXT VOLUME

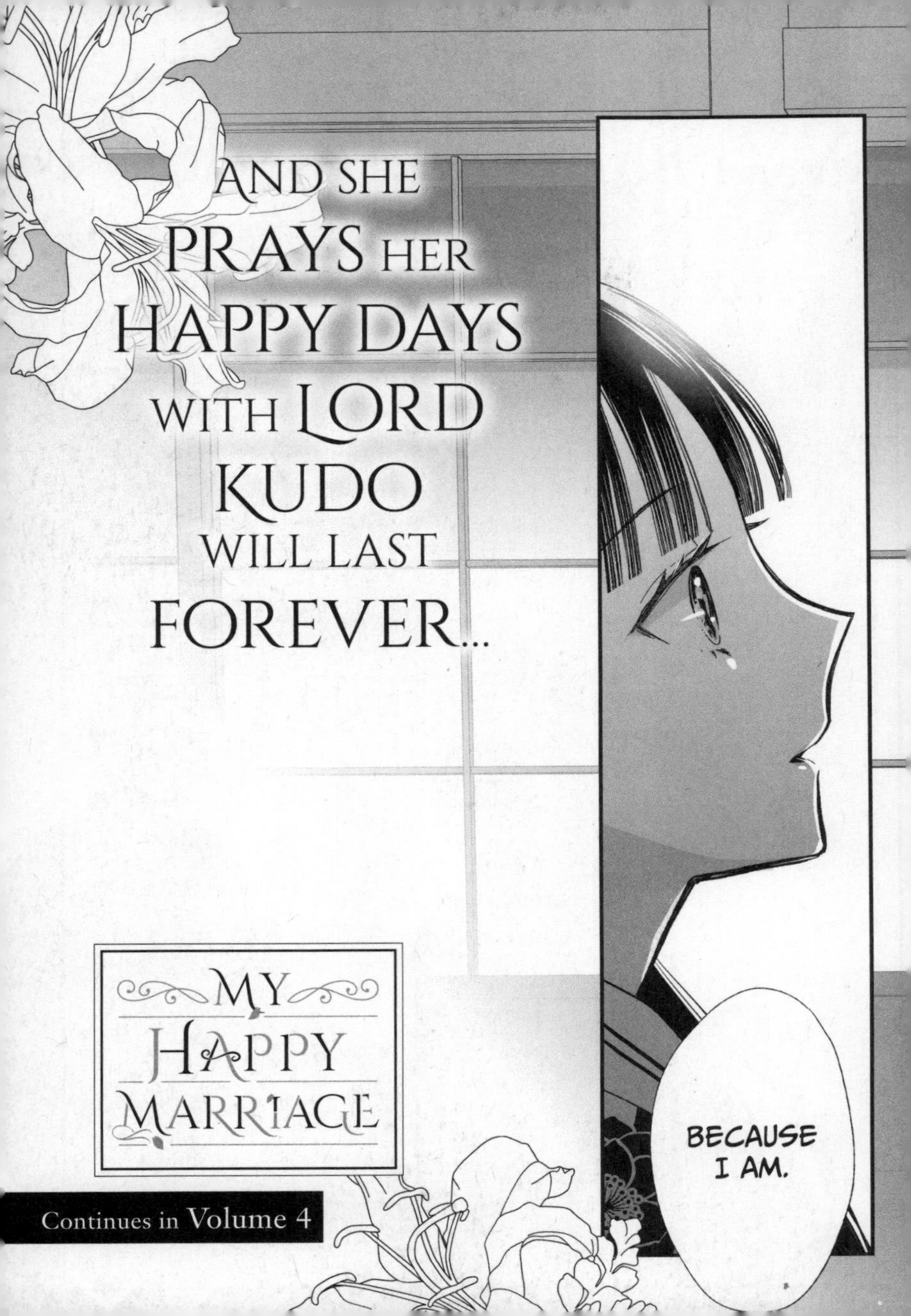
BECAUSE I AM.
AND SHE PRAYS HER HAPPY DAYS WITH LORD KUDO WILL LAST FOREVER...
MY HAPPY MARRIAGE
Continues in Volume 4

MY HAPPY MARRIAGE

3

ORIGINAL CONCEPT
AKUMI AGITOGI
(Fujimi L Bunko/KADOKAWA)

ART
RITO KOHSAKA

CHARACTER DESIGN
TSUKIHO TSUKIOKA

Translator: Jasmine Bernhardt ◆ Letterer: Lys Blakeslee
Logo Designer: Wendy Chan (Yen Press)
Cover Designer: Abigail Blackman ◆ Editor: Sarah Tangney

My Happy Marriage Volume 3
© Akumi Agitogi Licensed by KADOKAWA CORPORATION
© 2021 Rito Kohsaka/SQUARE ENIX CO., LTD.
All rights reserved.
First published in Japan as *Watashi no Shiawase na Kekkon* in 2021 by SQUARE ENIX CO., LTD.
English translation rights arranged with SQUARE ENIX CO., LTD. and SQUARE ENIX INC.
English translation © 2023 by SQUARE ENIX CO., LTD.

ISBN (print): 978-1-64609-156-0
ISBN (ebook): 978-1-64609-635-0

Library of Congress Cataloging-in-Publication Data is available upon request.

Library of Congress Control Number: 2022916028

Manufactured in the United States of America
First Edition: May 2023
1st Printing

Published by Square Enix Manga & Books, a division of SQUARE ENIX, INC.
999 N. Pacific Coast Highway, 3rd Floor
El Segundo, CA 90245, USA

SQUARE ENIX
MANGA & BOOKS

square-enix-books.com